# DATE DUE

| | | | |
|---|---|---|---|
| AP 16'01 | | | |
| MY 5'01 | | | |
| MY 31'01 | | | |
| | | | |
| AP 6'02 | | | |
| | | | |
| OC 28'03 | | | |
| | | | |
| | | | |
| | | | |
| | | | |
| | | | |
| | | | |
| | | | |
| | | | |
| | | | |
| | | | |
| | | | |
| | | | |

DEMCO 38-296

# MUSSOLINI

By the same author

R

# MUSSOLINI

———— ◆ ————

## Jasper Ridley

ST. MARTIN'S PRESS ❧ NEW YORK

Library of Congress Cataloging-in-Publication Data

Ridley, Jasper Godwin.
    Mussolini / Jasper Ridley.
        p.   cm.
    Includes bibliographical references and index.
    ISBN 0-312-19303-3
    1. Mussolini, Benito, 1883–1945.   2. Heads of
state—Italy—Biography.   3. Fascism—Italy—History.
4. Italy—Politics and government—1922–1945.
I. Title.
DG575.M8R48   1998
945.091'092—dc21                                    98-37813
[B]                                                 CIP

First published in Great Britain by Constable
and Company Limited

First U.S. Edition: November 1998

10  9  8  7  6  5  4  3  2  1

TO CHRISTOPHER SMALL

# Contents

# Illustrations

[ ix ]

# Acknowledgements

I wish to thank those people who have helped me with this book, none of whom, of course, have any responsibility for the statements which I have made or the opinions which I have expressed;

Mrs Biancamaria Parkin for reading my typescript, for her information about her youth in Fascist Italy, and for all the other help she has given me;

Anita Garibaldi for information about her father Ezio's relationship with Mussolini, for placing me in contact with valuable informants, and for her constant assistance;

Signora Linda Magagnoli for her reminiscences of the Giornata da Fede on 18 December 1935, the Fascist Youth Movement, and her life in wartime Rome;

The Onorevole Giancarlo Matteotti for his information about the murder of his father in 1924 as he saw it at the age of six;

Romano Mussolini for information about his childhood recollections of his father and their life at Gargnano under the Italian Social Republic in 1944–5;

Signor Pancrazi for information about his experiences as a member of the Fascist Youth and as a soldier in the Italian army in the Second World War;

Professor Salvatore Spinello for his information about his experiences in the weeks before the overthrow of Mussolini in 1943 and on other matters;

Isabel Quigly for her advice on the more subtle problems of translation;

The Lady Soames, D.B.E., for permission to read and to quote extracts from private correspondence between her father and mother,

Winston and Clementine Churchill, which are not yet available to the public;

Ann Hoffmann for her constant help with problems of research;

My wife Vera Ridley for her most useful advice on my typescript;

The Onorevole Giulio Caradonna, Susan Chitty, Lenore Denny, Dr Bill Felton, Alan Hooton, Patricia Neild, the Onorevole Presidente Luigi Preti, Ingrid Price-Gschlössl, my daughter Barbara Ridley, Inge Roberts, Ambasciatore Marchese Rossi Longhi, Denise Sells, Dr Michael Smith and Nicole Swatek for assistance with research, for gifts or loans of books, for hospitality, and other assistance;

Lieselotte Clark and my son John Ridley for assistance with the proofreading;

The staff of the Biblioteca Nazionale in Rome, the British Library, the British Newspaper Library at Colindale, the Churchill Archives at Churchill College, Cambridge, the Kent County Library in Tunbridge Wells, the London Library, the Public Record Office, and the Royal Institute of International Affairs (Chatham House)

The passages from the letters of Clementine and Sir Winston Churchill quoted on Page 179 are reproduced with permission of the Master, Fellows and Scholars of Churchill College in the University of Cambridge, Copyright The Master, Fellows and Scholars of Churchill College in the University of Cambridge.

The passage from Sir Winston Churchill's speech quoted on Page 230 is reproduced with permission of Curtis Brown Ltd, London, on behalf of C & T Publications, Copyright C & T Publications.

All the other passages quoted from Sir Winston Churchill's writings and speeches are reproduced with permission of Curtis Brown Ltd, London, on behalf of The Estate of Sir Winston S. Churchill, Copyright Winston S. Churchill.

Jasper Ridley
Tunbridge Wells
2 June 1997

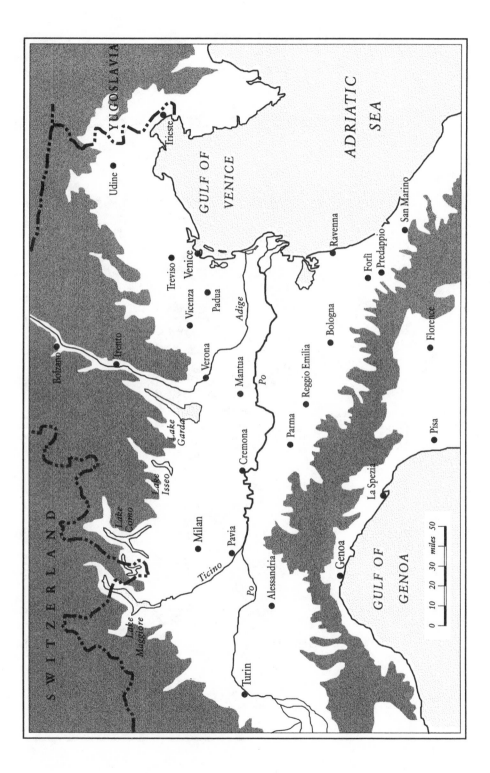

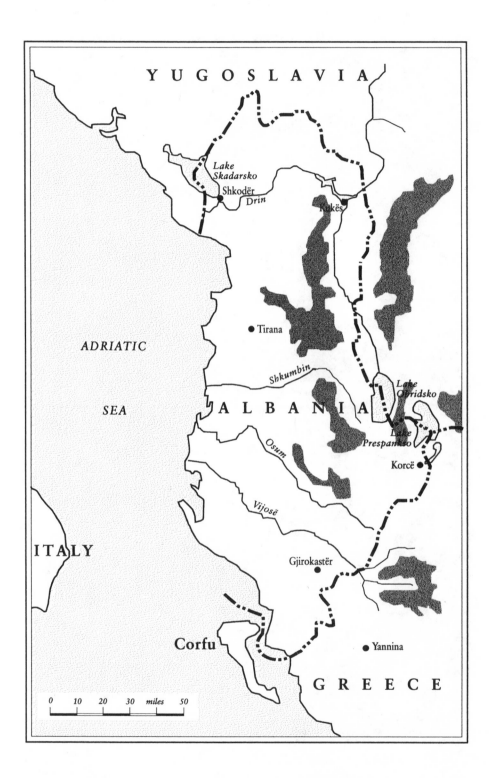

YUGOSLAVIA

*Lake
Skadarsko*

Shkodër

*Drin*

Kukës

*ADRIATIC*

Tirana

*SEA*

*Shkumbin*

A L B A N I A

*Lake
Ohridsko*

*Osum*

*Lake
Prespansko*

Korcë

*Vijosë*

I T A L Y

Gjirokastër

Corfu

Yannina

G R E E C E

0   10   20   30   *miles*   50

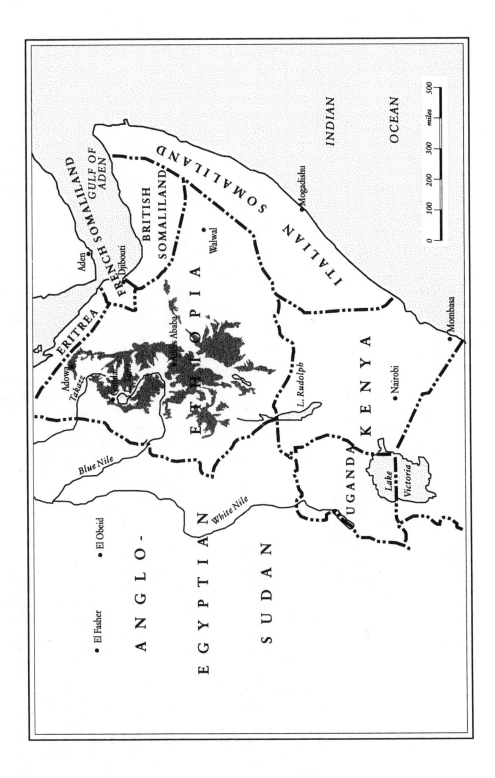

# CHAPTER 1

## ◆

# The Red Romagna

WHEN the eighteenth-century English historian, Edward Gibbon, was writing his *History of the Decline and Fall of the Roman Empire*, he referred to the Emperor Antoninus Pius, who reigned in Rome from AD 138 to 161. Gibbon wrote that it was to Antoninus's credit that nothing of historical interest occurred during his twenty-three-year reign, history being a register of the crimes, follies and misfortunes of mankind.[1] No one can truthfully say this about the man who, 1,750 years later, succeeded Antoninus as the ruler of Rome. The twenty-three-year reign of Benito Mussolini was filled with events of the greatest historical interest, and most of them illustrate the crimes, follies and misfortunes of mankind.

Benito Mussolini, the son of Alessandro Mussolini and Rosa Maltoni, was born in Verano di Costa at 2.45 p.m. on Sunday, 29 July 1883,[2] fourteen months after the death of Giuseppe Garibaldi and four months after the death of Karl Marx. Mussolini greatly admired these two men at some stages of his life, though both of them would have repudiated him for what he eventually became.

Verano di Costa is a little hamlet above the village of Dovia in the parish of Predappio near Forlì in the Romagna, not far from the Adriatic coast of Italy. It was a land of violence and revolution. The violence was older than the revolution, dating back for many centuries before Italy existed as a nation. The Italian peninsula was the most civilized part of medieval and Renaissance Europe, and its leading cultural centre; but the inhabitants practised and admired violence. Italians, in their separate kingdoms, dukedoms and republics, joined societies and killed members of other societies. Bandits robbed travellers on the roads. Men enlisted as mercenaries and killed each other fighting for various dukes and lords and city states. Husbands killed their unfaithful wives. In the Vatican the cardinals poisoned each other; on more than one occasion they almost certainly poisoned the Pope.

There was violence in all the countries of Europe; but in Italy, like in the Balkans and Scotland, there was a cult of private violence which was different from the organized or semi-organized violence of England during her civil wars, of France during the Wars of Religion, and of Germany during the Thirty Years' War. Men were brought up from childhood to believe that if they suffered wrong they should not complain to the authorities but should themselves inflict vendetta – vengeance. The husbands who murdered their wives' lovers did not always do so in jealous rage; they did it coolly, deliberately, because it was their duty to avenge the affront to their honour and to the honour of their family.

When the French Revolution broke out in 1789 and Napoleon's armies invaded the countries of Europe to liberate them from their despots for the benefit of France, Italian violence took a new form. In Germany, Austria, Holland and Spain nationalist revolts broke out against the French; but in Italy they welcomed Napoleon. After his downfall and the re-establishment of the *ancien régime* throughout Europe, the emperors and kings of the Holy Alliance found that it had been easier to defeat Napoleon's army at Waterloo than to deal with the revolutionary secret societies in Italy. The revolutionary struggle of the French Jacobins was carried on by the Carbonari, and afterwards by Giuseppe Mazzini's Young Italy. Mazzini linked revolution with nationalism. He wished to liberate the Italian states from the Habsburg and Bourbon rulers who were oppressing them and unite them in one democratic republic. But events took a different course, and Italy was united under the King of Piedmont, Victor Emmanuel of the House of Savoy.

Although Mazzini was an Italian nationalist he was not hostile to nationalists in other countries. His Young Italy united with Young Germany, Young Poland, Young France, Young Austria and Young Switzerland to form an international organization, Young Europe. Mazzini thought that wars were caused not by popular nationalist movements but by cosmopolitan kings and emperors who spoke French together and who had married each others' sisters and daughters. From time to time these sovereigns went to war with each other, and called on their subjects to fight and die, to decide which of them would rule some province; but after the war had been won and lost, victor and vanquished resumed their friendly relations without very much resentment until the next war broke out. Mazzini and his republican followers wished to see another kind of war, a revolutionary war for democracy which would sweep away the autocratic monarchies everywhere in Europe.

They hoped that their moment had come during the Crimean War in 1854, when Britain and France went to war with Tsarist Russia. They hoped that Austria would be drawn into the war and go down to defeat with Russia; but the British Prime Minister, Lord Palmerston, was determined to prevent it from developing into a war for democracy, and after the Allied victory the Russian and Austrian empires were preserved.

The hopes of the revolutionary republicans rose again during the war between France and Austria in 1859, when Napoleon III led his army into Italy to fight in alliance with Piedmont against Austria for Italian unity and freedom. But after his victory at Solferino he met the Emperor Franz Joseph of Austria at Villafranca and made peace. One of the reasons that he gave for doing this was that he did not want the war to develop into Mazzini's revolutionary democratic war. The European war for democracy remained a Mazzinian dream for fifty-six years until Benito Mussolini and his colleagues launched it in 1915.

Socialism grew out of the French Revolution. If all men were equal, why should some work for long hours and low wages for the profit of a few? The only economic system compatible with Liberty, Equality and Fraternity was one in which the means of production were owned by the Socialist state for the benefit of all the toilers. But socialism took a different form in different countries. In Britain the most eminent of the early Socialist leaders was Robert Owen, a capitalist factory owner who thought that it was wrong that children should work in factories for sixteen hours a day. He went to see the Prince Regent and the Tsar of Russia and tried to convert them to his point of view. They listened to him very sympathetically, but said that they could do nothing about it. In Italy the most eminent Socialist was Filippo Buonarroti. He told his followers to form secret societies, to assassinate rulers, and make a violent revolution.

In 1847 Karl Marx and Friedrich Engels wrote the *Communist Manifesto*, in which they proclaimed that the workers had no fatherland and called on the working men of all countries to unite and make the international Socialist revolution. In 1864 they formed in London the International Association of Working Men, which became known as 'the International' and later as the First International. Some of Mazzini's supporters in London joined the leadership of the International; but Mazzini did not believe in socialism, and in any case he and Marx always split any organization that they could not dominate. The Mazzinians left the International, and in Italy a bitter quarrel broke out between them and the 'Internationalists', as the Socialist supporters of the International were called. Sometimes Mazzinians murdered Internationalists at night in the dark streets of the cities.

The Russian revolutionary leader, Mikhail Bakunin, came to London when he escaped from exile in Siberia, and joined the leadership of the International. He went to Italy to see Garibaldi, whom he greatly admired, and stayed to organize the Italian section of the International. But, like Mazzini, he quarrelled with Marx, and the International split. It was largely a question of personalities, but there were ideological differences. As Marx and Engels grew older, they became more moderate, and came under the influence of those German Socialists who believed that socialism could be achieved by legal, constitutional means, or at least that this form of activity could usefully be carried on in the interests of the Socialist movement. Bakunin and his followers believed not only in revolutionary violence, but also in terrorist assassinations of kings and rulers. The Internationalists not only fought bitterly with the Mazzinian republicans, but also fought equally bitterly among themselves.

In Germany the Marxists triumphed over the Bakuninists. They formed the German Social Democratic Party, which contested parliamentary elections and eventually became the largest single party in the Reichstag. But in Spain and Italy the anarchist followers of Bakunin gained control of their sections of the International. Garibaldi supported them, and the Italian Socialists responded to their policy of revolutionary violence. They made headway in many parts of Italy, particularly in the Romagna, and their most important centre was Bologna.

Benito Mussolini's father Alessandro, the son of a poor peasant, was born in Montemaggiore in the Romagna in 1854, six years before the Kingdom of Italy was formed, when the Romagna was part of the Papal States. All the higher civil servants and government officials were priests; only 26 per cent of the population could read and write;

and the Pope prohibited the building of railways, for fear that they might carry new revolutionary doctrines into the isolated villages. When Alessandro was a young man, he became a blacksmith. Finding no work in Montemaggiore, he moved to Dovia, where he opened a blacksmith's forge. He became an ardent Socialist, and when he was eighteen he joined his local branch of the Bakuninist section of the International. Whenever the villagers in Dovia brought a horse to the blacksmith to be shod, Alessandro expounded the doctrines of socialism to them as he carried out the work. Even those customers who disagreed with him thought that he was a nice fellow and listened to his Socialist propaganda in a friendly spirit.[3]

In the summer of 1874 disorders broke out in many towns and villages of the Romagna. The leaders of the Internationalists, who had formed the Italian Committee for the Social Revolution, decided to launch the revolution in Bologna on the night of 7 August; from there it would spread to Florence, Rome and other cities. Three thousand men, armed with rifles and knives, were to assemble at Imola and march on Bologna; Alessandro Mussolini was to go to Bologna from Predappio with forty-nine of his comrades. That morning the Committee for the Social Revolution issued an appeal to the workers to rise and to the soldiers in the army not to fire on them. 'The first duty of the slave is to revolt; the first duty of the soldier is to desert. Proletarians, revolt! Soldiers, desert! Turn your rifles against the masters who put them in your hands!'[4] Bakunin himself came secretly from Switzerland to take personal command of the revolution.

But things went wrong. Only two hundred, not three thousand, turned up at Imola. Alessandro Mussolini and his forty-nine colleagues duly set out from Predappio, but on the way to Bologna they ran into a force of police who were expecting them. Thirty-two of the Internationalists were arrested. Alessandro Mussolini was one of the eighteen who escaped. Like many other inhabitants of the Romagna, he became one of the *latitanti* – the men who were on the run from the police.[5]

The Internationalist leaders were kept in prison for nearly a year before being brought to trial in Florence on 30 June 1875. The trial lasted for two months. There was much sympathy for them in the Romagna and elsewhere in Italy. On 31 August the jury returned a verdict of not guilty in favour of all except three of the defendants amid an outburst of cheering in the courtroom. At the same time other Internationalists were put on trial at Trani, but they too were acquitted. There was an even more important and longer trial seven months later when seventy Internationalists were tried in Bologna; but the jury found them all not guilty. Only in Rome did the government succeed in obtaining a conviction of the Internationalists, and this verdict was reversed in the Court of Appeal on technical grounds.[6]

In view of the difficulty of persuading juries to convict, the government adopted other methods. A left-wing government had recently come to power. The Prime Minister was Agostino Depretis, who had been Garibaldi's Deputy Dictator in Sicily during the expedition of the Thousand in 1860. The Minister of the Interior was Giovanni Nicotera. He had fought under the revolutionary Socialist Carlo Pisacane in the unsuccessful rising against the King of Naples in 1857. Sentenced to death, he was reprieved, and later joined Garibaldi, commanding one wing of his army in the invasion of the Papal States which was defeated at Mentana in 1867. This old Socialist revolutionary was determined to crush the new Socialist revolutionaries. He said that the so-called Internationalists were nothing but common criminals, like the Camorra in Naples and the Mafia in Sicily.

Nicotera introduced the system of *ammonizione*, which was afterwards used by the government of Benito Mussolini. The Minister of the Interior could serve an order of *ammonizione* on anyone suspected of revolutionary activities. The man on whom the order was served was required to report to his local police station every Sunday morning; he must notify the police of any change of address; he was not allowed to leave the town or parish where he lived, to attend any meeting, to frequent any café or place of public entertainment; and he was subject to a curfew which confined him to his house from one hour after sunset until dawn. If he broke these conditions, he could be sentenced to three months' imprisonment for the first offence, and for the third offence to confinement in a penal settlement for five years.[7]

Alessandro Mussolini, realizing that the authorities would not prosecute him for his part in the abortive rising of 1874, had returned to his home in Predappio; but in October 1878 he was served with an order of *ammonizione*, after the police had reported that he was 'a danger to society and to public security'. The order remained in force for four years. In February 1882 he applied to be released from the order. The authorities were in no hurry to grant his application, but after the local council at Predappio had interceded on his behalf, and had vouched for his good behaviour, the *ammonizione* was revoked in October 1882.

He had meanwhile fallen in love with Rosa Maltoni, who was born near Forlì in the Romagna in 1858. She was the village schoolmistress in Predappio, a kind, intelligent and public-spirited woman who thought it her duty to educate the local children. Like most of the population of the Romagna, she was a devout Catholic. Alessandro Mussolini was one of a substantial minority who were violently anti-Catholic and aggressively atheist; but although feelings between the conservative Catholics and the Socialist atheists ran high, Alessandro and Rosa were sufficiently in love to compromise on their disagreements about religion. Rosa's father had at first been unhappy about his daughter marrying a revolutionary who was subject to an *ammonizione*; but Rosa was so determined that he gave way. Alessandro, to please Rosa, agreed to be married in church, and the marriage took place in Predappio on 25 January 1882.[8]

Their first child, a boy, was born on 29 July 1883. Alessandro again compromised his atheist principles, and allowed the boy to be baptized in church; but he insisted on naming him Benito Amilcare Andrea after three of his revolutionary heroes. Benito Juárez, the President of Mexico, had led the revolutionary liberal forces to victory in a savage civil war against the Catholic conservatives, and had then inspired the Mexican resistance to the French armies sent by Napoleon III to place the Archduke Maximilian of Austria on the throne as Emperor of Mexico. After his victory over the French, Juárez captured Maximilian, who was tried for treason and shot. The royal families and the conservatives in Europe were horrified; the revolutionaries rejoiced, particularly the Italian revolutionaries, for Maximilian was the brother of the Emperor Franz Joseph of Austria, who until recently had oppressed the Italian population in Lombardy and Venetia and was still oppressing the Italians in Trieste and the Trentino.

Amilcare Cipriani had fought with Garibaldi in the unsuccessful attempt to liberate Rome in 1862 which ended in the defeat at Aspromonte. He then went to Paris to fight for the Commune in 1871. He survived the massacre of the Communards by General Gaston de Galliffet's troops after the defeat of the Commune, but was one of the captured rebels sent to the penal settlement in the Pacific island of New Caledonia, and endured the dreadful conditions there for nine years until the Communards were finally granted an amnesty in 1880. Cipriani returned to Italy and joined the Internationalists, who revered him as a hero and martyr for the cause.

Andrea Costa was another Italian revolutionary. By 1874 he had become the most prominent leader of the Internationalists and was the chief organizer of the Bologna rising. He was well known in the Romagna, for he often travelled through the district with his glamorous mistress, the blonde Russian Jewess Anna Rosenstein, who was known as Anna Kulisciov. She was as determined and intelligent a Socialist as Costa. When she was put on trial as an Internationalist and terrorist in Florence in November 1879, she defended herself brilliantly, and was acquitted by the jury.[9]

Costa had just been released from his last prison sentence in France when he surprised his Italian followers by announcing that he had changed his mind and now believed that the Italian Socialists should achieve their aims not by revolutionary violence but by legal constitutional means and by standing as candidates in national and local government elections. Many of his supporters were shocked, and accused him of betraying the cause. Cipriani was especially critical; he persuaded the anarchist section of the Italian Internationalists, meeting in exile at Chiasso in Switzerland, to pass a resolution that the only hope of the Italian proletariat was to prepare for armed insurrection. He was supported by a young revolutionary, Errico Malatesta, who for the next fifty years was the most prominent leader of the Italian anarchists.

But Alessandro Mussolini went along with Costa, and decided to stand as a Socialist candidate for the Predappio district council. He could not stand as long as the *ammonizione* was in force against him, but soon after it was lifted he stood unsuccessfully as a Socialist. He was elected to the council in 1889, and held his seat for eighteen years till he retired in 1907.[10]

His second child, another boy, was born on 11 January 1885, when Benito was eighteen months old. Alessandro had him baptized Arnaldo, after Arnold of Brescia, the revolutionary monk in the twelfth century who had denounced the wealth and luxurious living of the clergy and had been executed at the orders of the English Pope, Adrian IV, in 1155. Alessandro's last child, a daughter, Edvige, was born on 10 November 1888.[11]

CHAPTER 2

━━━━━ ◆ ━━━━━

# The Difficult Child

THE Mussolini children were brought up together in their father's house in Verano di Costa. It was a simple, four-roomed building, sparsely furnished with a few wooden tables and chairs and plain iron bedsteads which Alessandro had made himself in his forge. There were two pictures on the walls – one of the Madonna of Pompeii, whom Rosa particularly worshipped, and the other of Alessandro's great hero, Garibaldi.

Benito and Arnaldo were very close as children, and they remained very close till Arnaldo died at the early age of forty-seven. They slept together in one of Alessandro's large iron beds. From the window at the foot of the bed they could look out at the Rabbi, the river that ran through Predappio. There was an iron chest in the corner of the room which contained family papers. One day the children, rummaging in the chest, found a love letter that their father had written to their mother before their marriage. Benito and Arnaldo found the letter very moving.[1]

Many stories have been told about Benito Mussolini's childhood, but how far can we believe them? Apart from Mussolini's own account, there are stories told by his Fascist admirers when he was dictator and those told by his Socialist and other opponents after his downfall and death. We can probably disregard the tales told by some of his critics of how he tore live chickens in pieces and put out their eyes;[2] but even if we accept only the stories of his supporters, a contradictory picture emerges of little Benito. We are told that he spent many hours alone somewhere in his father's house reading books while his schoolmates were playing games;[3] and we are also told that he became involved in savage fights with the other boys, attacking them with knives. These conflicting pictures are not necessarily incompatible. It is perfectly possible that he engaged both in solitary reading and in fighting with knives; and this fits in well with the two sides of his character which he displayed throughout his life. Sometimes he was a pensive intellectual and philosopher, and sometimes he acted like a brutal gang leader.

Some of the stories were told by Mussolini's Jewish mistress, Margherita Sarfatti, a successful novelist and the wife of a wealthy lawyer in Milan; according to the Socialists, he engaged in tax evasion and black market transactions. In 1925, when Mussolini was the Fascist ruler of Italy, she wrote a biography of him which was published in Italian under the title *Dvx*, though the English version had the less enthusiastic title *The Life of Benito Mussolini*.

She wrote that when he was a child of five he went to the school in Dovia where his mother was the schoolmistress, and terrified the other children, crawling under their desks during lessons and pinching their legs. He particularly singled out for persecution a little girl of seven, the prettiest girl in the class; he would jump out at her from behind a bush as she walked in the fields, or waylay her on her way to school, and force his kisses on her, pull her hair, ride on her as if she were his horse, before brusquely ordering her to go home, as he had finished with her. Margherita Sarfatti wrote at a time when it was fashionable for emancipated women in western Europe, and particularly women writers, to propagate the idea that women enjoyed being raped; and she was sure that Mussolini's victim, although terrified, was already at the age of seven 'woman enough to enjoy being terrorised over by this young man of five'.[4]

This story probably tells us more about the image of Mussolini that his Fascist admirers wished to present to the world in 1925 than about what Benito did in 1888. According to Mussolini's wife Rachele, although he wrote a preface to *Dvx*, he did not like the book; but then Rachele did not like 'la Sarfatti' or any of her husband's mistresses. Mussolini's sister Edvige, who was perhaps less prejudiced than Rachele, confirms that he did not like *Dvx*.[5]

He was involved in fights from his very first day at school, when the other boys threw stones at him and he threw stones at them. He wrote in his so-called autobiography of 1928, which was probably written by his brother Arnaldo, that although he was often beaten at school, he enjoyed his fights and learned that it is through battle that men make friendships and learn to respect their opponents. He tried to conceal from his mother the cuts and bruises that he received at school. At their evening meal he hesitated to stretch out his arm to reach for the bread in case she noticed the wounds on his wrist, though as she was the teacher at the school she ought to have noticed what was going on there.[6]

Sarfatti tells about one of his exploits when he was aged seven. Another boy stole his wheelbarrow and struck him with a stone, cutting his face. Benito complained to his father, who scolded him for coming whining to him like a woman instead of getting his own back on the boy who hit him. 'Don't let me see you again', he told his son, 'until you have had a go at him.' In Alessandro Mussolini's philosophy, a man who suffered an injury should not complain to the authorities, but should inflict his own revenge on his enemy. So Benito found a large stone, sharpened it to make it more jagged, and before supper found the boy who had struck him. He hit the boy three times in the face with the stone, cutting open his face.[7] His father was proud of Benito, and so were his Fascist followers who read about it thirty-five years later in *Dux*.

Sarfatti describes how on one occasion Benito and Arnaldo were digging beside the River Rabbi when a man who had been out shooting came by with some decoy birds in a bag. He put down the bag on the river bank near where Benito and Arnaldo were digging. Taking advantage of a moment when the man's attention was diverted, Benito and Arnaldo stole the birds. The man saw them and gave chase, but the boys forded the river and escaped with their booty.[8]

Although his father sometimes beat him when he was naughty, Benito was happy at home, and loved his parents, his brother and his sister. Alessandro brought him up to be very conscious of the injustices of society, and to hate the bourgeoisie, the oppressors of the proletariat, and the priests who lied to the proletariat in order to make them contented with their lot. Alessandro taught him to resist authority and to rebel. On Christmas Day 1892, when Benito was nine, his mother took him to his first communion; but though he went to Mass to please her, he adopted his father's views on religion.[9]

When he was nine he was sent to a boarding school in Faenza; like many centres of higher education, it was run by priests of the Salesian Order. The discipline was strict, and life for the boys was tough. They rose at 5 a.m. in summer and 6 a.m. in winter, were not allowed to speak during meals, and daily attendance at Mass was compulsory. Benito objected to going to Mass; sometimes he refused to go, and was punished. He soon became convinced that the teachers were singling him out for punishment and that he was being victimized because his father was a Socialist. His clashes with his teachers, his defiance of authority, and his conviction that he was being persecuted have often been cited by hostile biographers as an example of his uncontrollable temper and his persecution mania; but it is hardly surprising that Alessandro Mussolini's son, who had been brought up from infancy in an Italian Socialist atmosphere, rebelled against the priests and believed that they were persecuting him; for were not Socialists always persecuted by priests?

Matters came to a head on the Feast of St John the Baptist, 24 June 1894, a month before Benito's eleventh birthday. He became involved in a fight with an older boy at the school and stabbed him in the hand with a knife. As a punishment, he was locked up alone for hours in a dark room and forced to spend the night in the courtyard with the fierce guard-dogs; he was very frightened of the dogs, and when he eventually succeeded in climbing into the school and reached his bedroom, he was exhausted and feverish. One of the priests told him that he had a conscience that was as black as coal. He was expelled from the school. His mother took him to the house in Ravenna of the boy whom he had stabbed, and made him apologize to the boy and his parents. He noticed that there was a copy in the house of Dante Alighieri's *Divine Comedy* illustrated by Gustave Doré. This was a young thug who appreciated literature and art.[10]

His father arranged for him to go to another school, the Collegio Giosuè Carducci in Forlimpopoli. It was run by lay teachers, not by priests. He stayed there for seven years till he was eighteen. He did brilliantly academically, especially in history, geography and Italian literature. But there was more trouble. On 14 January 1898, when he was fourteen, a boy sitting beside him in the classroom made a smudge on the sheet of paper on which Mussolini was writing out his answer to a mathematical problem. Mussolini took out his pocket knife and was using it to erase the smudge when the boy punched his head. Mussolini drove the penknife into the boy's buttocks.

The teachers threatened to expel Mussolini. His mother came from Dovia to Forlimpopoli to intercede for him with the school governors, and one of the teachers, who was impressed by his academic ability, also spoke on his behalf. The governors decided merely to suspend him from school till the end of term. Next term, in June, he was suspended again for being impertinent to a teacher, but was again allowed to return to the school.[11]

Mussolini's school record, with two knife attacks on his schoolmates, as well as stealing the birds from the hunter, entitles us to say that, in contrast to all the other twentieth-century dictators– Lenin, Stalin, Hitler, Franco, Tito, Mao Tse-Tung and Castro–Mussolini had the unique distinction of having been a juvenile delinquent. Two things may be said in extenuation of his conduct: according to all the versions of the incidents that have been reported, the victims of his knife attacks had always been the aggressors in their fights with him; and his teachers, though they condemned and punished his conduct, did not regard stabbing with knives in the classroom to be as unpardonable an offence as teachers in other countries in other times would have done. He was allowed to remain in the school at Forlimpopoli, and in 1901, when he was eighteen, he passed his examinations with distinction.

During his last two years at school he became interested in sex. He pursued the pretty girls he met in the street, and frequented the brothels in Forlimpopoli.[12]

In January 1901 Giuseppe Verdi died at the age of eighty-seven. He was given a state funeral, and all over Italy meetings were held at which tributes were paid to him. The schoolmasters at Forlimpopoli chose the seventeen-year-old Mussolini to make the speech at the Verdi memorial meeting. He referred to Verdi's operas and to his sympathy with the revolutionary struggles of the Risorgimento. Mussolini's speech was praised by the schoolmasters and by his audience.[13] He loved the music of Verdi and of the other Italian composers. He learned to play the violin, and all his life this remained his favourite relaxation. He had grown up in a world of music, sex and violence, the world of *Pagliacci* (1892), *Cavalleria Rusticana* (1899) and *Tosca* (1900), in which the story culminates, to the accompaniment of beautiful music, in the fatal knife thrust.

When Mussolini was eighteen he finished his education and looked for a job. He became an elementary schoolmaster in the town of Gualtieri in Emilia, near Parma, some hundred miles from Predappio. The job was not well paid, but it conferred a certain status, and entitled him to be addressed as 'Professor Mussolini'. He became friendly at Gualtieri with another Socialist schoolteacher, Nicola Bombacci, a rather weird-looking intellectual with a large shaggy beard. Mussolini had a love affair at Gualtieri with Giulia F., the wife of a soldier who was serving in the army. They went for walks together along the banks of the Po, and had what he called a 'violent and jealous' relationship which was ended when her husband returned home.[14]

Mussolini had followed his successful speech at the Verdi memorial meeting by speaking at various Socialist rallies. On 2 June 1902 the twentieth anniversary of Garibaldi's death was celebrated all over Italy. A speaker had been expected to address a meeting at Gualtieri, but failed to turn up. The chairman of the meeting thought of Mussolini. They found him playing cards in an inn, and asked him if he would take the speaker's place. Mussolini agreed to do so. He spoke about Garibaldi as a revolutionary hero, and urged his audience to play their part in the forthcoming Socialist revolution.[15]

The bourgeoisie certainly believed that the Socialist revolution might be imminent. When Costa persuaded the Italian Socialists to fight parliamentary and local government elections, they did not abandon their ultimate goal of revolution and their willingness to achieve it by the political general strike and riots. Before the end of the 1880s they had begun to sing their song, *Bandiera Rossa* (the Red Flag), which was often called the 'revolutionary hymn', or the 'workers' hymn'. It is perhaps the most rousing of all the songs of the international Socialist movement. Like that other stirring radical anthem, *John Brown's Body*, no one knows who wrote the words or the music. In later years many Socialists believed that their veteran leader, Filippo Turati, had written the words when he was a young man, but he always denied it.[16]

At about the same time the British Socialists began to sing their song, another and different *Red Flag*, with the words written by James Connell to the tune of *Maryland*, the song of the Southern slaveowners in the American Civil War, who had taken the tune of the old German carol, O *Tannenbaum*. The British Socialists sang: 'Let cowards flinch and traitors sneer, We'll keep the Red Flag flying here!' But keeping the red flag flying was not good enough for the Italian Socialists. 'Onward the people to insurrection! The Red Flag will triumph! Long live Socialism and liberty. Onward the people amid the cannon's roar! We want to make a revolution!'

In 1889 a new Socialist International was formed at a meeting in Paris to replace the First International which had collapsed after the split between Marx and Bakunin. The Second International proclaimed 1 May, May Day, as a holiday for the workers, which was to be celebrated every year by a twenty-four-hour general strike. On May Day 1898 rioting broke out in southern Italy and spread to Florence and Milan. In Milan the government called out the army and the soldiers opened fire on the workers, killing five of the demonstrators. The Socialists were indignant, and young Benito Mussolini was as angry as any of them.

Meanwhile the Italian anarchists were pursuing their tactic of achieving the revolution by terrorist acts, announcing that they would destroy 'the oppressors of Humanity, all Kings, Emperors, Presidents of Republics, priests of all religions'. In 1894 the President of the French Republic, Sadi Carnot, was assassinated at Lyons. In 1897 the Spanish Prime Minister, Antonio Canovas del Castillo, was assassinated. In 1898 the Empress Elizabeth of Austria was stabbed and killed as she was getting on to a steamer on the Lake of Geneva. On 29 July 1900 – Benito Mussolini's seventeenth birthday – King Umberto of Italy, who had survived two attempts on his life, was shot dead after distributing the prizes at an athletic meeting at Monza, which was then a small town near Milan. In all these cases the assassins were Italian Anarchists.

Mussolini did not stay long at Gualtieri. He decided to go to Switzerland. He wanted to travel, and he wanted to meet the Swiss and foreign Socialists and anarchists. Ever since the days of Bakunin there had been flourishing anarchist groups among the watchmakers of the Jura; and many Socialists from France, Italy, and especially from Russia, who had got into trouble with the police in their own countries, had turned Switzerland into a haven for revolutionary refugees. Mussolini also wished to avoid doing his military service in Italy, for he knew that he would receive his call-up papers soon after his twentieth birthday.

When he was on the point of leaving for Switzerland, his father was involved in the local elections in Predappio. Alessandro and a group of Socialist comrades gathered outside the polling station, and as they watched the arrival of the voters it became clear that their candidates would be defeated by the Conservative Clerical Party. They became more and more angry, and thought of entering the polling station and destroying the ballot papers. Then they saw some Conservative Clerical supporters arrive with an old cripple pauper, whom the Conservatives were helping to enter the polling station. The Socialists' anger boiled over at the sight of this victim of capitalist oppression and of the injustice of nature being tricked into voting for his oppressors by the Clericals, who falsely told him that his sufferings had been imposed on him by God in order to test his patience and that he would be compensated for them by rewards in the next world.

The Socialists, led by Alessandro Mussolini, broke into the polling station, singing what the police report called 'the workers' hymn' – it was the *Bandiera Rossa*. They tried to seize the ballot box. The polling clerk picked up the ballot box and held it tightly in his arms; but when some of the Socialists began punching him on the head, he raised his hands to ward off the blows, and dropped the box. Other Socialists then seized it, ran out of the polling station with it, broke it open, and scattered the ballot papers in the street.

The authorities declared the election void, and a new election was held in which the Conservative Clericals were victorious. Alessandro Mussolini and other leaders of the Socialists were prosecuted for causing a riot and violating the electoral laws. They claimed that they had acted under intolerable provocation when they saw the Conservatives bringing the crippled pauper to vote. In his speech in court, Alessandro said that Socialists were entitled to resort to violence, because for the proletariat the struggle for socialism could decide the question of life or death. The jury returned a verdict of not guilty.[17]

♦

# CHAPTER 3

# Switzerland

MUSSOLINI waited till the end of the summer term at Gualtieri, and on the last day of term waved goodbye to the friend who had come to see him off at the nearby railway station of Guastalla, and travelled by Parma and Milan to the Swiss frontier town of Chiasso. On 9 July 1902 he took the night train from Chiasso to Yverdon on the Lake of Neuchâtel. He had a little money in his pocket, but no other means of support; he was intending to live by getting odd jobs in Switzerland, and by the charity of any friends he might make there.

He immediately found work in Yverdon as a bricklayer. The builder was doing a repair job on some premises at the top of a high building, and on his first day at work Mussolini had to carry a heavy load of bricks up two flights of stairs 121 times – he obviously kept a careful note of the number. He was required to work for eleven hours a day and was paid thirty-two centimes per hour. He thought that he was being exploited by his petty bourgeois employer, and told him that he would leave the job at the end of the week, preferring to starve than to allow capitalists to exploit him. When he went for his wages on the Saturday evening, the builder paid him only the equivalent of twenty lire and few centimes.[1] 'What should I have done?' wrote Mussolini. 'Kill him. What did I do? Nothing.'[2]

He spent some of the little money that he had in his pocket buying a railway ticket to Lausanne, and spent the next two years travelling, sometimes by train but more often walking and hitch-hiking, between Lausanne, Geneva and Berne, to Zurich, Fribourg, Basle, and La Chaux-de-Fonds in Neuchâtel, and visiting the Italian-speaking canton of Ticino. He sometimes obtained short-term employment as a bricklayer, a carpenter's assistant, or picking fruit; but he soon threw up the jobs and continued on his travels. In the evenings he attended local Socialist Party meetings, or study circles. He immediately attracted attention by his intervention in the discussion that followed the lectures, by his extreme left-wing views, and by the vigour with which he expressed them. After the meeting he usually managed to find some comrade who invited him to come home with him and spend the night in his bedsitter, and he sometimes stayed there for a few days before travelling on to some other Swiss town. During his stay in Switzerland he learned to speak fluent French.

Cipriani in Paris had heard about the young revolutionary from the Romagna who had been named Amilcare after him, and he invited Mussolini to visit him in Paris. Mussolini could not afford the train fare, but in February 1903 he set off to walk to Paris. On the road in France he met a young Russian anarchist who was also walking to Paris, and they continued on their journey together. But the Russian, with his black beard and flaming eyes, looked like a caricature of an anarchist terrorist. He was noticed as they walked through the villages, and the police were informed. In no time he and his companion Mussolini were arrested. When they were released Mussolini gave up his plan to go to Paris, and went to Milan before returning to Switzerland; but he may have succeeded in getting to Paris eighteen months later.[3]

Mussolini wrote articles for various Socialist newspapers – in *L'Avvenire del Lavoratore* of Lausanne and other journals published for Italian refugees in Switzerland, in *L'Avanguardia Socialista* of Milan, and *Il Proletario*, the organ of the Italian Socialists in New York. He wrote several poems which were published in these newspapers, including a sonnet on the French revolutionary Gracchus Babeuf, who was guillotined in 1796 during the Thermidorian reaction and was generally regarded as the first modern revolutionary Socialist.[4]

An article in prose, 'The Sport of the Crowned Heads', which was published in *Il Proletario* in June 1903, was prompted by the forthcoming state visits to London and Paris of Victor Emmanuel III, who had become King of Italy at the age of thirty after the assassination of his father Umberto I in 1900. Mussolini wrote that Victor Emmanuel, after visiting King Edward VII in London, would be welcomed in Paris by the French republican government, the unworthy successors of the men of 1793 who had thrown the head of Louis XVI at the feet of horrified Europe.[5] Mussolini had already developed the style of oratory and journalism that he kept all his life – the short, lucid sentence, coming straight to the point and striking home with savage force. The English historian A.J.P. Taylor once wrote, in connection with Trotsky, that in every forceful writer there lurks a potential dictator.[6] The potential dictator was already lurking in the twenty-year-old contributor to *Il Proletario*.

Sometimes he got into trouble with the police. The Swiss police were tolerant in comparison with the Okhrana in Tsarist Russia; but though the meetings and activities of Swiss and foreign Socialists were permitted as long as they were legal, the Swiss authorities were on their guard against terrorists and anarchists who were planning to assassinate foreign sovereigns or to endanger the capitalist stability of bourgeois Switzerland by general strikes or riots in the streets.

Once in Lausanne, the police found Mussolini sleeping under a bridge and arrested him under the vagrancy laws; but he was released after a night in the cells.[7] He only slept under bridges as a last resort. He usually saved up enough money to buy a drink in a cheap café and made it last all night while he stayed and slept there.

On one bitterly cold night during the winter of 1902–3 he was turned out of a café in Berne at midnight. He went to the house of a Russian anarchist girl whom he knew, but found that she had gone away for a few days; so he broke into the house. The neighbours heard a noise and came to investigate, and found Mussolini sleeping fully dressed on the sofa. He persuaded them not to call the police. They believed his story; after all, he was just the kind of friend whom the Russian girl *would* have.[8]

But in the summer of 1903 he got into more serious trouble with the police. The carpenters in Berne had gone on strike, and were disrupting the building trade. Mussolini spoke at a May Day rally and called for a general strike in support of the carpenters. The authorities took no immediate action, but there was already a note in the Swiss police files about 'the revolutionary Socialist Benito Mussolini'. On 18 June he was arrested, interrogated, and held for twelve days in the prison in Berne before being served with an order of deportation from the canton. He was escorted across the Italian frontier at Chiasso, but promptly took the train to Lugano and proceeded to Lausanne, where the deportation order from Berne was not in force.[9]

He had several love affairs while he was in Switzerland. The most serious was with Eleanora H., a Polish girl who had married a Russian with whom she lived in Geneva. Her affair with Mussolini continued until she and her husband returned to Russia in 1904. She continued for some years to write to Mussolini, but he heard nothing more from her after 1908.[10]

In October 1903 his mother fell ill, and he returned to Dovia to see her; but she recovered, and after spending two months with her, he went back to Switzerland on 27 December, as he knew that he would soon be called up for military service. The Italian Socialist lawyer, Salvatore Donatini had decided to start a magazine, to be called *I tempi nuovi*, and he asked Mussolini to join him in Berne and work on the paper; but when Mussolini reached Berne he found that Donatini had been deported from Berne and had gone to Annemasse in the department of Haute-Savoie in France. In January 1904 Mussolini followed him to Annemasse and spent two months with him there, but the project of starting the newspaper fell through. While Mussolini was in Annemasse he had an affair with an Italian Socialist girl named Emilia.[11]

In 1945, three months after Mussolini's death, the Italian anarchist and feminist Maria Rygier made a sensational revelation about Mussolini's activities in Annemasse in 1904. She revealed that in 1928 she had been told by the Grand Master of the French freemasons, Maurice Monier, that he had seen a document from the French police archives which proved that Mussolini had acted as a police informer in Annemasse, spying on the French and Italian Socialists.[12] In view of the fact that Maria Rygier, who by 1945 had become a liberal supporter of the pro-Allied government in Italy, was bitterly opposed to Mussolini, that her information came at second hand from Monier, and that he, as a freemason, would also have been an enemy of Mussolini, the story is very unreliable, though it is perfectly possible that the French police invited Mussolini to become their spy, and not impossible that he pretended to agree to do so, and then fed them with false information.

By the beginning of 1904 Mussolini had become a well-known figure in the Swiss Socialist movement. On 18 March he attended a meeting held in Lausanne to commemorate the thirty-third anniversary of the establishment of the Paris Commune. The chief speaker was the prominent Russian Socialist, Angelica Balabanoff. She noticed Mussolini the moment she saw him in the audience, and became even more interested in him when he spoke in the discussion after her speech. She was struck by three things about him: his keen intelligence, his piercing, almost hypnotic, eyes, and his dirty appearance.[13] She worked together with Mussolini for several years, first in Switzerland and later in Italy, until he was expelled from the Italian Socialist Party and in due course became the Fascist dictator of Italy. After that she became his bitter enemy.

No two people were more unlike in background and character than Mussolini and Balabanoff, but they both represented important strains in the international Socialist movement. He, the son of a blacksmith in the Romagna, bred in the revolutionary tradition of his father and neighbours, expressed the burning sense of injustice, the resentment and hatred – which cannot merely be described as envy – of the poor against the rich. She, the daughter of a wealthy landowner in the Ukraine, was typical of the aristocratic and middle-class Socialist with a guilty conscience and the desire to help the suffering mass of humanity. As a child, Angelica had felt a deep sense of shame when she saw the peasants kiss the hem of her father's coat when he returned to the estate after a prolonged absence. She was equally upset when her pious mother took Angelica with her on one of her visits to distribute charitable gifts to the poor on the estate, who gratefully thanked her ladyship for her kind condescension. Angelica wanted to shout out to them that they had no reason to be grateful because the wife of their oppressor was giving them a few crumbs from the rich man's table.

Angelica decided to go abroad and studied in Brussels and London before graduating at Leipzig University. She joined the Russian Socialist refugees in Switzerland, living on the small allowance that she accepted from her family and on her earnings as a journalist.[14] She came into contact with the Italian Socialist leaders, and settled in Rome, becoming one of the most prominent members of the Italian Socialist Party before returning to Russia and working for the Bolsheviks in the very hard conditions of the first years after the October Revolution of 1917. She did not know that the result of all her idealism and self-sacrifice would be to place the peasants, who had kissed the hem of her father's coat, under the rule of Stalin.

She wrote four books in which she dealt at some length with Mussolini: the German, English and Italian versions of her memoirs, which are three different books published in 1928, 1938 and 1946, and her book *Il traditore Mussolini* (Mussolini the traitor) in 1945. The first two books were published when Mussolini was ruling Italy, and the last two soon after his downfall and death. She was a woman of the highest moral principles – Mussolini himself called her in 1913 a noble-hearted and generous woman – and by 1928 she had broken with the Bolsheviks because she disapproved of the immoral means that they used to attain their praiseworthy ends. But this does not mean that everything she wrote about Mussolini was true. By 1928 she hated Mussolini with an intensity that people feel only for their former comrades who have deserted to the enemy. Some of her criticisms of Mussolini are convincing, because they fit in with what we know of his character from other reliable sources, and especially from his own writings; but it is very difficult to believe some of her other stories.

She wrote that when she first met Mussolini she was struck by how dirty he was, because though many other young Socialists among the refugees in Switzerland were shabbily dressed, not many of them were dirty and unshaven. We can well believe that Mussolini was unkempt, because a person dresses to express his personality and to suit the image that he wishes to present to the world; to impress his friends and the members of his circle; to show the social class and the age group to which he belongs; to comply with the accepted conventions or ostentatiously to defy these conventions. Mussolini, all his life, dressed to fit the part that he was playing. Sometimes he wore the austere black shirt of his Fascist followers; sometimes the starched wing collar and bowler hat, or the white tie and tails, of the King of Italy's Prime Minister; sometimes the well-tailored and bemedalled uniforms of the Commander-in-Chief of the Italian Army, Navy and Air Force.

In Switzerland in 1904 he wore the tattered jacket and the ragged trousers of the oppressed and defiant revolutionary tramp, the heir to the *sans-culottes* of the French Revolution of 1789. He may sometimes have been unshaven, though the photographs that were taken at the time show that on other occasions he had a neatly trimmed moustache and also sometimes a dark beard, like so many Socialists, and indeed many conservative bourgeois too, in the first decade of the twentieth century. In the photographs his clothes look reasonably tidy, if informal and of poor quality.

In *Il traditore Mussolini*, Angelica Balabanoff wrote that Mussolini told her that he had syphilis. She did not repeat this allegation next year in the Italian edition of her memoirs, but wrote that he had told her that his father was a syphilitic drunkard. A postmortem analysis of Benito Mussolini's brain indicates that he did not have syphilis.[15] If he said that his father was a drunkard and had syphilis, we may be sure that he was not criticizing his father, whom he always admired, but was boasting of Alessandro's splendid defiance of bourgeois conventions in his drinking and sexual habits.

It is not impossible that Benito may likewise have boasted falsely about his own syphilis in order to shock his respectable acquaintances and to impress the anarchists and the down-and-outs who had rejected the bourgeois lifestyle. But so many prominent historical and twentieth-century characters have been falsely accused by their political opponents of having syphilis that the whole syphilis story must be regarded with considerable suspicion. When authors like Angelica Balabanoff write about people whom they hate and describe what they said and did fifteen or forty years earlier, they may exaggerate, misinterpret, and even actually invent discreditable episodes, sincerely believing that these really occurred.

The day after he first met Angelica Balabanoff at the Commune anniversary meeting, he went to Zurich to attend a conference of the Union of Italian Socialists in Switzerland.[16] The Russian Socialist Vladimir Ilyich Ulyanov, who had adopted the pseudonym 'Lenin', was living in Zurich at this time, and there has been much discussion as to whether Mussolini and Lenin met there on 19 or 20 March 1904. Mussolini told the German writer Emil Ludwig, in 1932, and also apparently his sister Edvige, that he did not remember meeting Lenin; but his wife Rachele thought that he had met him. The German doctor Georg Zachariae, who cared for Mussolini during the last year of his life when he was head of the republican Fascist government on Lake Garda, and E.F. Moellhausen, who also met Mussolini at the same time, have both given full accounts of what Mussolini told them about long discussions that he had with Lenin; but the statement that Mussolini is supposed to have made to Zachariae that he was 'for some time a member of Lenin's circle' is certainly untrue, and Moellhausen's account of what Lenin said to Mussolini seems very improbable.[17] If Mussolini did meet Lenin, it must have been a very brief meeting, because it could only have occurred on 19 or 20 March 1904, and on both these days Mussolini was busy attending the conference in Zurich which Lenin did not attend.

A few days later Mussolini took part in a debate in Lausanne with an Italian champion of Christian Socialism, Alfredo Taglialatela.*

* The name is often written 'Tagliatela'.

Mussolini, like all the Socialists of the Romagna, had adopted the militant atheism of the Italian Socialist movement. Ever since Pope Pius VI issued his encyclical against the French Revolution in 1791 the Catholic Church had been in conflict with revolutionary movements and the revolutionaries had been enemies of the Catholic Church. This had led to great antagonism in Italy and to exceptionally cruel civil wars in Spain and Mexico. When the Socialists took over the leadership of the revolutionary movement from the Jacobins, the hostility to the Church continued, although Pope Leo XIII's famous encyclical *De Rerum novarum* in 1891 was softer towards socialism than his predecessors had been towards the nineteenth-century revolutionary radicals. Leo admitted that the working class in modern society suffered hardship and oppression and were justified in seeking to improve their lot; but he strongly condemned the violent methods and the godless doctrine of the revolutionary Socialists and anarchists. *De Rerum novarum* increased the hostility between the Catholic Church and socialism.

Britain was the only country where Christian socialism made any real headway. Many British Socialists, particularly in the nonconformist working-class areas, believed that a true Christian must be a Socialist, and that British socialism owed more to Methodism than to Marxism. In Germany and Austria the Christian Socialist movement which developed in the 1880s took a more objectionable form. It became anti-Semitic, condemning the Jews for having murdered Christ in ancient times and for being the leading capitalist exploiters in the modern world.

The atheist Socialists, though denying the divine nature of Christ and the existence of any God, were prepared to praise Jesus the man as a champion of the poor and the oppressed, who as a result was condemned to a cruel death by the ruling class of his time. In 1792 the French revolutionary leader Camille Desmoulins declared that he was a follower of the 'sans-culotte Jesus'. Mussolini was at first less sympathetic than many Socialists towards Jesus. During his stay in Switzerland he attended a lecture by the Belgian Socialist leader Emile Vandervelde on the *sans-culotte* Jesus. Mussolini intervened as usual in the discussion that followed the lecture, and said that if any of the ancient religious leaders had contributed anything of value to modern Socialists, it was Buddha rather than Jesus, because Buddha was a scholar who had expounded his philosophy in forty volumes. Vandervelde raised a laugh among the audience by pointing out that Caiaphas and Pontius Pilate had cut short Jesus's career before he had had time to write forty volumes.[18]

Taglialatela was having very little success in his attempts to persuade Italian Socialists to be Christians; but in September 1903 he gave a lecture in Lausanne. Mussolini attended the lecture and denounced Taglialatela's views. Taglialatela challenged Mussolini to a debate, and it took place before an audience of five hundred in Lausanne on 25 March 1904.[19] Mussolini moved the motion that 'God does not exist, and for science to include religion is an absurdity'. He argued that the laws of physics that governed heat, electricity, light and sound 'respond neither to the lamentations nor to the prayers of men'.

Mussolini's supporters were so favourably impressed by his speech that they told him he should publish it in book form, and an enlarged version was published in Lugano later in 1904 under the title *L'uomo e la divinità* (Man and divinity). The opening sentence was 'God does not exist'.[20] It was a topical subject, because in July 1904 Professor Giulio Carrora was prosecuted at La Chaux-de-Fonds, at the instigation of the Catholics of Neuchâtel, on a charge of talking blasphemy in his lectures; but he was acquitted.[21]

Mussolini was extending his knowledge of Socialist literature. He read the works of Peter Kropotkin, the Russian prince who had made a sensational escape from the Peter and Paul prison in St Petersburg, had come to western Europe, and had several times been arrested, imprisoned and deported as a terrorist in France and Switzerland for propagating anarchist doctrines. In August 1904 *L'Avanguardia Socialista* of Milan published a summary by Mussolini of Kropotkin's memoirs, *Les paroles d'un révolté*, which Mussolini had translated into Italian from the French original.[22]

Mussolini had also learned German, which he eventually spoke as fluently as he did French. He had already read the *Communist Manifesto* and Marx's *Das Kapital* in an Italian translation, but he now read Marx's other works in German. He also read Engels, and the works of Karl Kautsky, who since Engels's death and the 'revisionist' defection of Eduard Bernstein was considered to be the most eminent German Marxist theoretician. At this time Lenin was one of his great admirers, though later, when Kautsky had criticized the actions of the Bolsheviks in Russia after the October Revolution, Lenin denounced him as 'the renegade Kautsky'.

In 1904 the Socialists were reading with great interest Kautsky's latest book, *The Day after the Social Revolution*, in which he described the society that he hoped and believed would be established after the Socialists had come to power. This was a subject that had been almost entirely neglected by Socialist theoreticians, and Marx had touched on it only briefly in his *Critique of the Gotha Programme*. Mussolini decided to translate Kautsky's book into Italian. According to Angelica Balabanoff, he told her that he wished to translate the book, but that he did not know the German language, and she gave him lessons in German; but this must be wrong, because Mussolini already knew enough German to have read and admired *The Day after the Social Revolution*, though Balabanoff may have helped him with the translation.[23]

In April 1904 he was again in trouble with the police. When he first came to Yverdon, his Swiss visa allowed him to stay in Switzerland for eighteen months till 31 December 1903; but as this date approached, he began to fear that he would have to return to Italy just at the time when he would be receiving his call-up papers for the army. It occurred to him that it would be quite easy to alter the '3' in his visa to a '5', and he did this, making it appear that he had been granted permission to stay in Switzerland till 31 December 1905. But in April 1904 the police in Geneva discovered the forgery. Mussolini was arrested, and after he had been held for a few days in prison in Geneva he was ordered to be deported from the canton.

The Socialists in Geneva had succeeded in getting one of their leaders, the advocate Adrien Wyss, elected to the Great Council of the canton. Wyss protested in the council against the order to deport Mussolini, and the Socialists held protest demonstrations in the streets in Geneva. Several local party branches passed resolutions calling for a twenty-four-hour general strike. Meanwhile the police were taking Mussolini to the frontier, but in view of the protests they broke their journey and handed him over to the authorities in Luzern, and he spent Easter in the jail there.

The Socialists and Radicals in the Ticino, knowing that Mussolini would be brought into the canton on his way to the Italian frontier, joined in the protests against his deportation. The Radical member, Antonio Fusoni, protested in the Great Council of the Ticino. The protests were successful, and Mussolini, who was being taken to the frontier at Chiasso, was released at Bellinzona and allowed to stay in the Ticino. The authorities in Geneva revoked the deportation order, and Mussolini stayed in Geneva, Lausanne and other parts of Switzerland during the summer and autumn of 1904.[24]

In April 1904 Mussolini was tried in his absence by a court martial at Forlì and sentenced to one year's imprisonment for failing to report for military service. But a few months later the Italian government granted an amnesty to army deserters. Mussolini had been contemplating going to New York; but he wished to see his father and mother, who were very anxious that he should return to Italy, and he realized that unless he answered the call-up for the army he would have to remain in exile for the rest of his life. He left Switzerland in November 1904. He immediately reported for military service at Forlì, and in January 1905 joined the tenth Bersaglieri regiment at Verona.[25]

His secretary, Yvon De Begnac, told a different story about Mussolini's call-up for military service, in the book on Mussolini's youth which he wrote in 1936. When Mussolini was the Fascist ruler of Italy, neither he nor his supporters ever tried to conceal his Socialist past. His wife, his sister, his son Vittorio, Margherita Sarfatti and De Begnac wrote proudly about his father Alessandro's and his own revolutionary activities, his life as a tramp in Switzerland, his arrests and prison sentences there and in Italy, and even his opposition to the Libyan war in 1911, though De Begnac wrote about this in a way that underestimated the extent of his opposition to the war. But there was one exception: his admirers never admitted that he went to Switzerland to evade military service.

De Begnac wrote in 1936 that while Mussolini was in Switzerland he went to the Italian consulate in Bellinzona on 10 July 1903 and told them that he expected to receive his call-up papers and wished to do his military service. Owing to a slip-up at the consulate the military authorities at Forlì were not informed about this, but 'the amnesty cancelled the administrative error'.[26] There seems no doubt that De Begnac invented this story in order to hide the fact that Mussolini, in the first place, evaded military service. Mussolini himself, in the autobiography that he wrote in 1911 when he was still a Socialist, did not mention that he had made any approach to the consulate at Bellinzona, but wrote: 'In the spring of 1904 I should have become a soldier. I decided instead to return to Switzerland.'[27]

A month after he joined the army, he heard that his mother, who was only forty-six, was dying of meningitis. He was given compassionate leave and hurried to Dovia, arriving in time before her death on 19 February 1905. Among the letters of condolence he received was one from his commanding officer at Verona, Captain Achille Simonotti. In his reply to Simonotti on 26 February he wrote that he had burned most of the letters of condolence, as he could not keep them all, but he would always keep and treasure the captain's letter. He would honour his mother's memory by doing his duty as a soldier and a citizen, not with tears and lamentations but by performing deeds worthy of the heroes who had cemented with their blood the unity of the motherland, if the barbarians of the north should once again try to reduce Italy to a 'geographical expression'[28] – a phrase that the Austrian statesman, Prince Clemens von Metternich had contemptuously used before 1848 to deny that the separate Italian states could be regarded as a nation.

This letter was first published in Mussolini's newspaper *Il Popolo d'Italia* on 18 November 1922, three weeks after the March on Rome had made him Prime Minister. It was well calculated to show his Fascist blackshirts the great patriotism of their leader; but it was a strange letter for a Socialist to write in 1905, and Mussolini's critics have accused him of betraying his Socialist principles in order to curry favour with his commanding officer. There was in fact nothing in the letter which directly conflicted with Mussolini's Socialist views, for although the Italian Socialists condemned the army as an instrument used by the bourgeois state to suppress the proletarian revolution, they had always admired Garibaldi and the heroes of the Risorgimento, and would have opposed any attempt by the Austrian government to restore Italy to the conditions that she had endured in Metternich's time. But it was not quite the party line in 1905, and certainly shows that Mussolini at the age of twenty-one was already capable of combining political extremism with tactical manoeuvring and personal flattery, as he was to do so successfully in later years.

CHAPTER 4

## The Trentino

M USSOLINI served in the army for twenty-one months, devoting himself entirely to his military duties and writing only one political article. In later years he said that he enjoyed his period of military service, realizing that a man must learn to obey before he can know how to command; and certainly for nearly two years Mussolini the disruptive schoolboy and Mussolini the revolutionary tramp and journalist were replaced by Mussolini the obedient and efficient soldier.[1]

When he was discharged from the army in September 1906, he obtained a position as a schoolmaster at Tolmezzo near Venice. He had a love affair at Tolmezzo with the wife of the owner of the lodging house where he stayed; he described her in his autobiography of 1911 as 'a woman of about 30 and still beautiful and charming despite her adventurous past'.[2] Her husband found out about their relationship, but contented himself with punching Mussolini.

He resumed his Socialist and journalistic activities. On 17 February 1907 he was one of the speakers at a meeting in Tolmezzo on the anniversary of the martyrdom of Giordano Bruno, who had been condemned by the Roman Inquisition for asserting, among other heresies, that the earth moved round the sun and not the sun round the earth, and after being imprisoned for seven years was burned alive in Rome on 17 February 1600. Mussolini used the occasion to make a violent attack on the Catholic Church. On 2 June he again attacked the Church in his speech on the twenty-fifth anniversary of C .ribaldi's death.[3]

In August 1907 he left Tolmezzo, and in February 1908 became a teacher at Oneglia on the Riviera.[4] He spent the school holidays with his father, who had moved from Dovia to Forlì. Here he resumed his acquaintance with Rachele Guidi. They had first met at his mother's school in Predappio in 1900, when Rachele, who was nearly nine years younger than Benito, was attending the school at the age of eight and he was helping his mother as an unpaid part-time teacher. They met again in Forlì in 1908, when he was twenty-five and she was sixteen, and they fell in love. Rachele's father had died when she was seven, and she was now working as a domestic servant in the house of a middle-class gentleman in Forlì. Benito would sometimes walk with her, and escort her home to her employer's house; but she always refused his invitation to have a cup of coffee with him in a café, which would have compromised her reputation.[5]

After Alessandro Mussolini moved to Forlì, he invited Rachele's mother, Anna, to live in his house as his housekeeper. This seems to be the only basis for the story, which was afterwards told by Benito's opponents, that Anna had been Alessandro's mistress, that Rachele was his illegitimate daughter and Benito's half-sister, and that her marriage to Benito was incestuous.

Rachele had beautiful blond hair, which at this time she tied in plaits. Many years later her sister-in-law Edvige wrote that long before the Hollywood film star Jean Harlow was acclaimed as the world's first 'platinum blonde', Rachele Guidi was a natural platinum blonde.[6] She has often been described as a homely peasant woman, but she was attractive and not unintelligent, though her prejudices often prevented her from forming a balanced judgment of a situation. She had a powerful personality. As a little girl at school, when the boys threw stones at her she threw stones at them, and on one occasion threw a stone which cut open the cheek of a boy with whom she later became good friends.[7]

She never allowed herself to be dominated by Mussolini, with whom she lived for thirty-five years. Their marriage was a very happy one, though he was often unfaithful to her, and she was not prepared to turn a blind eye to his love affairs. She raised the roof whenever she discovered that he had another mistress, but their relationship survived all their matrimonial tiffs.

Rachele's employer did his best to discourage her from marrying a notorious Socialist agitator like Benito Mussolini,[8] and his objection to the marriage was increased by the events of the summer of 1908. There were strikes in the towns, and agricultural riots in the countryside, of the Romagna. The Socialists in Predappio supported a strike of workers in a factory where threshing machines were made, and protested against the employment of outside blacklegs in the factory. On 13 July they held a demonstration in Predappio; according to Mussolini, some seven thousand demonstrators came out into the streets and took possession of the town, which they occupied all day. The authorities called out the troops, but it was nightfall before they had cleared the town of the demonstrators.

Five days later, on the afternoon of 18 July, Mussolini was standing in the street in Predappio when the manager of the factory, Emilio Rolli, came riding by on his bicycle. Mussolini was carrying a cudgel in his hand, and called out to Rolli: 'I'll give you a good belting' ('*ti svirgolo*'). Rolli hurriedly cycled on, but later that afternoon the police arrived. Rolli had made a complaint that Mussolini had threatened to assault him. Mussolini was arrested and taken to the prison in Forlì.

On 22 July Mussolini was brought before the court in Forlì and charged with threatening to assault Rolli. He was found guilty, and sentenced to three months' imprisonment. He appealed to the district Court of Appeal in Bologna, and on 30 July was released pending the hearing of his appeal. In November the Court of Appeal upheld his conviction, but reduced the sentence from three months' to twelve days' imprisonment; and as he had been in prison from 18 to 30 July, he was allowed to go free.[9]

A few weeks later, Mussolini was approached by the Socialists of Trent. The Trentino, with the towns of Trent, Bolzano and Merano, was the only Italian territory, apart from Trieste and Istria, which had not been liberated from the rule of Austria after the war of 1866. There was an active Socialist movement in the Trentino, under the leadership of a young lawyer, Cesare Battisti. He was the editor of the Socialist daily newspaper in Trent, *Il Popolo*. The Socialists also had a weekly newspaper in Trent, *L'Avvenire del Lavoratore*, and they invited Mussolini to become its editor. He accepted, and arrived in Trent on 6 February 1909.[10]

The Italians in the Trentino considered themselves to be victims of national oppression by Austrian imperialism, and longed for the day when they would be united with their brothers in the other parts of Italy. The German-speaking population in the Trentino considered themselves to be Tyroleans. Their organization, the Volksbund, revered the memory of the Tyrolean patriot Andreas Hofer, who had led the Tyrolean national resistance against Napoleon and had been executed by a French firing squad in 1810. The Catholic organization, the People's Party, favoured unity with Catholic Austria, and still distrusted the movement for Italian unification, as they had done throughout the Risorgimento. Their newspaper, *Il Trentino*, was edited by a young journalist, Alcide De Gasperi, who forty years later, after Mussolini's death, became Prime Minister of Italy. Battisti in *Il Popolo* carried on a polemical struggle against both the Volksbund and De Gasperi, and when Mussolini became editor of *L'Avvenire del Lavoratore* he joined in on Battisti's side.

The Socialists in the Trentino had to work out the correct Socialist policy in this situation. The Austrian Social Democrats had won 87 of the 510 seats in the Imperial Parliament in Vienna, and from time to time they protested in Parliament when the authorities in the Trentino committed a particularly oppressive act against the local Italian population; but they were reluctant to alienate the electorate in Austria by becoming too closely identified with Italian nationalism. This made the Italian nationalists in the Trentino distrust the Italian Socialists, who were linked to their Austrian Socialist comrades in the Second International.

The traditional Socialist policy was to support movements for national liberation from foreign imperialist oppression even when these movements were under the leadership of the national bour-geoisie, but to point out to the people that only the Socialists could lead the struggle to victory because in the last resort the bourgeoisie, fearing the revolutionary action of the proletariat, would hesitate to launch a national revolution. This line was challenged by the Polish Jewess Rosa Luxemburg, who had emigrated to Germany and became one of the leaders of the left wing of the German Social Democrat Party. Reacting perhaps against the nationalists in her native Poland, she argued that progressive movements of national liberation could no longer develop in Europe but only in Asia and Africa and the under-developed world; in Europe nationalist move-ments would always be a cloak for the imperialist ambitions of the national bourgeoisie or of the imperialist nations which used them for their own ends. Rosa Luxemburg's views were opposed by Lenin, who urged Socialists to support the movements for national indepen-dence in Ireland, Poland and other European countries oppressed by a foreign imperialist power.

In 1909 Mussolini, like Lenin, supported the traditional Socialist policy. He supported the movement for national liberation of the Trentino from the Emperor Franz Joseph's Austria, but insisted that Italian Socialists would never be tricked by talk of national liberation into supporting the Italian bourgeoisie in a war against Austria. This has made it possible for Mussolini's Fascist admirers to claim that in 1909 he was a champion of the national struggle for Italian independence in the Trentino, and for his anti-Fascist critics to accuse him of having pursued a Socialist and anti-nationalist policy in contrast to the nationalist policy which he advocated after he became a Fascist.

As editor of *L'Avvenire del Lavoratore*, Mussolini directed his fire chiefly at the Catholics. On 17 February 1909, soon after he arrived in Trent, he denounced the Catholic Church on the anniversary of the martyrdom of Giordano Bruno.[11] At Easter he wrote an article in *Il Popolo* about the crucifixion entitled 'The Human Easter'.[12] No God had come to the assistance of Jesus as he endured the agony of death on the cross, and he himself had cried out: 'Father, father, why have you abandoned me?' He described how Jesus, whom he saluted as the 'sweet vagabond of Palestine', with his fine Galilean head and his exquisite Semitic profile, had gazed lovingly on the grieving Magdalene with those eyes which had seen the sufferings of the poor slaves oppressed by pagan Rome, the champion of the rich. In another article he wrote that Christ did not repulse the amorous advances of Pontius Pilate's wife, and could not resist the passionate kisses and the insidious caresses of Mary Magdalene.[13]

The polemics in the Socialist and Catholic journals were carried on with much personal bitterness. After an article in *Il Trentino* had made slanderous innuendoes about Battisti's wife, Mussolini made allegations in *L'Avvenire del Lavoratore* about the morals of a priest who was active in the Catholic party. On 29 May Mussolini was prosecuted in the court at Trent for libelling the priest, and was sentenced to a fine of thirty crowns or three days' imprisonment. Almost as soon as he had paid the fine he was prosecuted again after he had written an article in *Il Popolo* accusing three Catholic priests of sexual misconduct and embezzling money from the church funds. On 5 June Battisti, as editor of the paper, was sentenced to seven days', and Mussolini to three days', imprisonment, this time without the option of a fine; but Mussolini appealed against the sentence, and on 9 June the Court of Appeal quashed the conviction.[14]

During his stay in Trent Mussolini fell in love with a married woman, Fernanda Oss Facchinelli, who worked at the trade union headquarters. She gave birth to his son, who died when he was a few months old, and Fernanda herself died of tuberculosis soon afterwards. Mussolini kept up contact with her mother, and when he was Dictator he helped the old lady financially. His other mistress at Trent was Ida Irene Dalser, the daughter of an innkeeper in Sardinia. Like Mussolini, she was aged twenty-six. She was attractive, lively, enterprising, and neurotic.[15]

In June he spoke at public meetings in several towns in the Trentino. He visited Innsbruck, the capital of the Tyrol, where he gave a talk about Bruno, in which he again attacked the Church, and another on the Paris Commune.[16] In a speech in Trent on 25 June he attacked bourgeois nationalism, and dissociated the proletariat and the Socialists from it. The bourgeoisie were not truly patriotic; both in their commerce and their culture, they crossed national frontiers and were internationalist in their approach. But the bourgeoisie had invented two words, parliament and patriotism, in order to bamboozle the workers. 'The proletariat is anti-patriotic by definition and necessity.' If there was a war, the Socialists would have only one duty: war on the frontier must be the signal for a general strike, for insurrection, and for civil war within the country.[17]

The police in Trent wanted to get rid of Mussolini, and in June asked Baron Haerdti, the Minister of the Interior in Vienna, for an order expelling him from the territory of the Austro-Hungarian Empire. Haerdti rejected their request; but as Mussolini continued to cause trouble, they made another request to the minister for a deportation order on 10 July. This time Haerdti agreed to deport Mussolini as soon as he had given the government a suitable pretext.

The authorities did not have to wait long. The Socialists were exasperated at the repeated prosecutions of Battisti and Mussolini, and they organized a protest demonstration in the street in front of the house of the public prosecutor in Trent. Battisti, Mussolini, and Augusto Avancini, a Socialist member of the Parliament in Vienna, were prosecuted for organizing the demonstration, and on 3 August they were all sentenced to a fine of thirty crowns or three days' imprisonment.[18] A few days later Mussolini wrote an article attacking a Catholic priest, whom he called 'a dog with hydrophobia'.[19] On 13 August he was sentenced to seven days' imprisonment without the option of a fine. When the magistrate imposed the sentence, Mussolini thanked him for giving him the opportunity to have a rest in prison.

Meanwhile the police in three countries were collaborating to frustrate Mussolini's activities. On 5 August the Berlin police wrote to

the police in Vienna that they had been notified by the police in
Berne that the former schoolmaster, Benito Mussolini, now living in
Trent as editor of *L'Avvenire del Lavoratore*, a newspaper of anarchist tendencies, had been arrested on several occasions in Switzerland
in 1903 and 1904 as a social-revolutionary agitator. The information
was passed on to the police in Trent. The Italian police in Forlì had
got their own file on Mussolini: born on 29 July 1883 at Predappio;
a member of the Dovia Socialist fraction; height, 1.67 metres (5 feet
5½ inches); build, robust; hair, light chestnut brown; face, pallid;
forehead, high; eyes, dark; nose, aquiline; beard, dark chestnut
brown; mouth, large; expression, agreeable.[20]

On 31 August Mussolini was arrested by the police in Trent and
charged with violating the laws regulating the freedom of the press
by his articles in *L'Avvenire del Lavoratore* and *Il Popolo*. He was
twice interrogated in prison about his anarchist activities in Switzerland, and was then ordered to be deported from Austrian territory.
The Socialist deputies in the Parliament in Vienna protested against
the deportation order, and the Socialists in Trent organized protest
demonstrations; but the authorities stood firm. On 26 September
Mussolini was taken in a carriage to Mori, perhaps to avoid any
possible Socialist demonstrations at the railway station in Trent. At
Mori he was placed on a train to the frontier post at Ala, where he
was handed over to the Italian authorities.

Next day the Socialist trades unions in Trent called for a twenty-
four-hour general strike in protest. But the Catholic organizations
instructed their supporters not to support the strike, and it was only
a partial success.[21]

When he got home to Forlì he wrote a novel, *Claudia Particella,
the Cardinal's Mistress*. It has often been said that he wrote it in
imitation of Garibaldi, who towards the end of his life had written
a novel, *Clelia*, about a young girl who is lured into the Vatican by
a cardinal before being eventually rescued and protected by a kindly
Jew. But Garibaldi's Clelia and Mussolini's Claudia are two very
different characters. Clelia is an innocent young virgin in the contemporary Rome of 1869. Claudia is a sophisticated courtesan –
'capricious and thoughtful, cruel and kind' – who enslaves the cardinal, and several other aristocrats whom she encounters in Trent in
1619, with her 'diabolical black eyes', until she is eventually poisoned
by the cardinal's secretary, Father Benicio, because she has repulsed
his amorous advances.[22] Garibaldi was indignant at the outrage

committed on Clelia; was Mussolini fascinated by the driving ambition of Claudia?

At the same time Mussolini wrote another, very different, book. His *Il Trentino veduto da un socialista* (The Trentino as seen by a Socialist) was an unemotional and detached examination of the political, economic and demographical situation in the Trentino. He wrote that the district that the bureaucrats of the Austrian Empire called South Tyrol was divided into two parts, the Trentino properly so called and the Alto Adige. In the Trentino over 70 per cent of the inhabitants were Italian, though only a very few of them spoke literary Italian and not their own local dialect. In the Alto Adige the population was mixed Italian and German, and both languages were spoken. There were two parts of the same province, two parts that were not only different but formed an irreconcilable antithesis to each other.

He wrote about the tyranny of the petty Austrian bureaucrats in the Trentino, but when he came to consider possible solutions to the problem, he rejected the policy put forward by the Italian nationalists of going to war with Austria to liberate the Trentino and the Alto Adige. Apart from all other considerations, Italy was not militarily powerful enough to win a war against the Austro-Hungarian Empire; and if the Austrians won the war, they might once again annex Venetia and the Italian provinces that had been liberated in 1866.[23]

In Forlì, Mussolini wished to live as man and wife with Rachele Guidi, who was now seventeen. She had waited for Mussolini. She had been disappointed that he had not once written to her from Trent, except to add a postscript addressed to her at the end of the only postcard that he sent to his father. But she had assumed that this was because he had been too busy with his journalism and politics.[24] No one had told her about Fernanda Facchinelli and Ida Dalser.

Rachele's mother was not eager for her to marry Benito, for she thought that life would be hard for the wife of a revolutionary Socialist agitator. Alessandro Mussolini agreed with her, for he felt guilty about the hardships that he had inflicted on Rosa through his own revolutionary activity. But Benito and Rachele were determined to live together. According to Rachele, Benito eventually persuaded Alessandro and her mother to consent to their union by going to their house with a revolver in his hand and threatening to kill her and then commit suicide unless they agreed to allow her to live with him.[25] If Rachele's story is true – and not all the stories that she tells in her memoirs are strictly accurate – Mussolini almost certainly did not seriously intend to carry out his threat, but was merely indulging in a dramatic gesture in which Rachele willingly participated.

Their parents abandoned their opposition, and on 17 January 1910 Benito and Rachele began living together. There was neither a civil nor a religious marriage ceremony, for this would have been against Mussolini's principles. Rachele happily agreed to live with him without being lawfully married, because she was in general sympathy with his political and religious views. She was probably already pregnant, because her first child and Benito's was born seven and a half months later at 3 a.m. on 1 September 1910. It was a little girl. They called her Edda.[26]

On 27 January, ten days after Benito began living with Rachele, his father fell seriously ill. He was rushed to hospital; but although he was sent home on 9 February he was a shadow of his former self. He survived for another nine months, but then had a relapse. Benito sent telegrams to his brother Arnaldo and to his sister Edvige, who had married Francesco Mancini in 1907, summoning them to their father's bedside. They arrived in time, but Alessandro Mussolini died at 4 a.m. on 17 November 1910 at the age of fifty-six.[27]

Shortly before he began living with Rachele, the Socialists of Forlì decided to start their own local newspaper, and appointed Mussolini as the editor. He named the newspaper *La Lotta di Classe* (The Class Struggle). In the first issue on 9 January 1910 he denounced parliamentarianism and called for 'the struggle of class against class – a struggle which culminates in a total revolution'.[28] Throughout 1910 he put forward extreme Socialist doctrines in the paper, especially attacking militarism, and the nationalism of the Mazzinian republicans. 'The Republicans want a national alliance,' he wrote on 2 July, 'we want an international alliance. The proletariat must no longer shed its precious blood in a holocaust for the patriotic Moloch. The national flag is for us a rag to be planted on a dunghill.'[29]

In August he spoke at a conference of the Socialist Youth at Cesenatico. He called on them to work for a disruption of military discipline, as a first step to abolishing the army, for the army and the bureaucracy were the two props of the bourgeois state.

On 5 November he announced that his newspaper would continue, doggedly and violently, its anti-militarist and anti-patriotic propaganda; he said 'anti-patriotic', because he renounced a patriotic policy that weakened the class struggle. He knew that this propaganda was dangerous, and could lead to his newspaper being prosecuted before a military tribunal, but he was willing to suffer for his cause. 'We will not defend our country because we have no country to defend.'[30] On 5 August 1911 he wrote in *La Lotta di Classe*: 'If the Motherland – a lying fiction which has had its day – should call for more sacrifices of money and blood, the proletariat who follow the directions of the Socialists will reply with a general strike. The war between the nations will then become a war between the classes.'[31]

Mussolini had been studying and reading – in Switzerland, the Trentino, Predappio and Forlì. Apart from Marx and Engels, he had read the works of the German Marxist writers Kautsky and August Bebel; but he preferred the Russian anarchists, Bakunin and Kropotkin, the French anarcho-syndicalist Georges Sorel, and Gustave Hervé, who had called on the young conscripts to refuse military service: '*Their* France, young worker, is in no way your country.' But Mussolini also read the works of famous authors, ancient and modern – Plato, Aristotle, Dante, Nicolò Machiavelli, Vilfredo Pareto and Friedrich Nietzsche.

When he first became politically active, his hero was Marx. In 1932 he told Emil Ludwig that he acquired a medallion with Marx's head on it, which he always carried with him.[32] But by 1910 he was turning more towards Sorel and the French syndicalists and away from Marx and the German Marxists. Sorel believed that the Socialist revolution could not be achieved by the proletarian masses unless they were led by an élite. Mussolini, like Sorel, had read Gustave Le Bon's book *La Foule*, which since its publication in 1888 had been translated into many languages. The English edition was published under the title *The Crowd*, though perhaps 'The Mob' would have been a better translation.

Le Bon was in no sense a Socialist, but a cynical French bourgeois who viewed the Paris mob of 1789 as it was seen by Charles Dickens in *A Tale of Two Cities* and by Baroness Orczy in *The Scarlet Pimpernel*, not as the great democratic and liberating force which was admired by the European radicals and Socialists. Le Bon thought that the mob was a dangerous force which would always be influenced by emotion, not reason, even if the mob consisted of no more than a few hundred intellectuals and politicians assembled in a parliament. 'The mob', wrote Le Bon, 'is always ready to revolt against a weak ruler and to bow down slavishly before a strong one.' But he recognized that the mob could be stirred to do brave actions which none of the individual members of the mob would do if left to themselves. The mob was particularly likely to be inspired by patriotism; the mob in France in 1793 had not only lynched aristocrats but had also bravely defended their country against the foreign invader.[33]

Mussolini was fascinated by Sorel's idea of the élite. He called them the *gerarchia* (hierarchy). He often used the term. A few years later he started a journal which he called *Gerarchia*, and after he had founded the Fascist Party he called the party leadership – the national and regional secretaries and officers – the *gerarchia*, and made it plain that all his hopes for the salvation of Italy rested on the *gerarchia*.

Mussolini was also impressed by the ideas of Giuseppe Prezzolini, a young Socialist syndicalist who was only a year older than Mussolini himself. Prezzolini was one of the intellectuals associated with the literary and philosophical periodical *La Voce*, which was started in December 1908. He stated that his aim was that foreigners should no longer think of Italy as a land of cheap hotels, easy women, beggars and brigandage, but of inventions and exhibitions, with a stock exchange that could compete in importance with the London Stock Exchange and the Paris Bourse.

In the summer of 1908 Prezzolini's book *Old and New Nationalism* was published. 'History has demonstrated', wrote Prezzolini, 'that throughout time and space, ranging from the most primitive and least populated to the most developed and populated societies, from the Papuans to the Yankees of North America, there have always been two classes of persons . . . one dominating and the other dominated.' When the book appeared, Mussolini was in Trent, and he wrote a very favourable review in *L'Avvenire del Lavoratore*. Four days after he was expelled from the Trentino, on 1 October 1909, he wrote to Prezzolini and congratulated him. He told Prezzolini that his 'superb mission' was to 'create the Italian soul', to create the greater Third Italy.[34]

In 1902 Lenin had formulated his views on the leadership of a revolutionary party in his book *What is to be done?* He wrote that a mass political party, with its roots in the trade union movement, could develop only a 'trade union consciousness'. It could disrupt and weaken the bourgeois state by strikes, but not even a political general strike could overthrow the bourgeoisie. To capture the state power and establish the dictatorship of the proletariat, there must be an organization of 'professional revolutionaries'.[35] Under his leadership the Bolshevik Party became an organization of professional revolutionaries who captured the state power in Russia in 1917.

Mussolini's *gerarchia* has often been compared to Lenin's professional revolutionaries, but there were two important differences. Lenin's party was organized on the principle of 'democratic centralism'. At least in theory, and for some years in practice, the party leadership was democratically elected by the party members, and the leadership, after free discussion, reached its decisions which then had to be followed and obeyed by all party members. Lenin himself always had to persuade a majority on the Central Committee and the Politburo to support his proposals, and on several important occasions he was defeated on a majority vote. It was only at the end of his life, and afterwards under Stalin, that these elections and voting became a formality and a sham.

Mussolini never believed or pretended that his *gerarchia* would be elected by the party members. The *gerarchia* would simply take over the leadership of the movement because of their consciousness that they were born leaders and that it was their function and duty to lead; and the rank and file would accept them as leaders because they were impressed by the self-confidence and leadership qualities of the *gerarchia*.

The other difference between Lenin and Mussolini was that Lenin always accepted Marx's materialist conception of history, the belief that history was governed by inevitable historical laws, and that revolutionaries were mere pawns in carrying out this inevitable historical process. 'The conscious element', wrote Lenin, 'plays so subordinate a part in the history of civilisation.' History was 'a process of natural history governed by laws.' He believed in the 'necessity of another society which must inevitably grow out of the preceding one, regardless of whether men believe in it or not, whether they are conscious of it or not'.[36]

Mussolini, while he admired Marx for his vigour and his belief in violence, was never impressed by his historical determinism. By 1910 Mussolini was openly, though mildly, criticizing this aspect of Marxism and praising the French syndicalists who rejected it. 'Men make their own history, but not just as they please,' wrote Marx.[37] Mussolini intended to make history exactly as he pleased. It was only in 1943 that he began to realize that this was not always possible.

# CHAPTER 5

# The Libyan War

THE year 1911 was a fiery one. All Europe had a very hot summer. In England, where King George V was crowned in June, the temperature in London at the beginning of September rose to 92 Fahrenheit. In Bradford in the West Riding of Yorkshire the drought caused the local municipal water board to cut off the supply of water to houses from 6 p.m. to 9 a.m. The summer was also fiery in the political sense, for it is only subsequent generations who believe in retrospect that the years before 1914 were a time of complacent security. It was a period of fear. There was fear of the outbreak of a European war, with the terrible new weapons that had been developed in the last thirty years, when a German gunboat was sent to Agadir in Morocco to counter the French occupation of Fez. There was fear of a civil war in Ireland, fear of the suffragettes in England, fear of revolution in every country in Europe, and fear that kings, presidents and prime ministers everywhere would be assassinated by anarchists.

At the end of August and the beginning of September the danger of war over Agadir increased with an exchange of sharp notes between France and Germany. In Italy a local government official was killed in Verbicaro in Calabria by rioting peasants who believed that the new sewage system would infect them with some terrible disease. In northern France there were serious 'food riots', with twenty thousand workers on strike, an attack on the prison at St Quentin, and the troops called out. In Spain a miners' strike in Bilbao and the Asturias led to the proclamation of martial law. In Vienna a Socialist demonstration against the high cost of living turned to violence; the cavalry charged the rioters, and four demonstrators were killed and ninety injured. News was arriving of riots and murders in India and China and a revolution in Mexico;

and England experienced a series of schoolboy strikes in London, Nottingham and Birkenhead.

On 14 September Tsar Nicholas II attended a gala performance at the theatre in Kiev accompanied by his Prime Minister, Peter Arkadievich Stolypin. The revolutionaries hated Stolypin because he had ruthlessly suppressed their activities, and they had made several attempts to assassinate him, but had succeeded only in seriously wounding his daughter. During the performance in Kiev, Stolypin was shot in the back of the head by a middle-class gentleman, Mordka Bogrov, who was nearly lynched by the members of the audience. The Russian press hastened to point out that Bogrov was a Jew who had pretended to convert to orthodox Christianity. Stolypin died of his wounds four days later.[1]

The murder of Stolypin was condemned in the Establishment newspapers all over Europe; but Mussolini applauded it in *La Lotta di Classe*. He wrote that Stolypin had been sentenced to death by the nemesis of justice. 'Stolypin, grim, sinister, bloody, has well deserved his fate. The Russia of the proletariat is celebrating and is awaiting the scattering of the bones of the Little Father [the Tsar] whose hands are red with blood . . . Glory to the man who carried out this sacred act of vengeance.'[2]

At the height of all this trouble, a new and unexpected crisis arose in the last week of September. The Italian government informed the Turkish government that in view of the failure of the Turkish authorities to maintain order in their North African province of Libya, the 'general exigencies of civilisation' made it necessary for Italy to undertake the military occupation of Libya; and almost before the Turks had had time to reply, an Italian expeditionary force had captured Tripoli, the capital of Libya, the Italian Navy had attacked the Turkish torpedo fleet off the Libyan coast, and Italy had declared war on Turkey.[3]

In nineteenth-century Italy, as in several other countries in the twentieth century, a nation that had won its independence from a foreign oppressor proceeded to oppress and destroy the independence of other nations. Between 1870 and 1905 Italy acquired territories in East Africa that had not already been annexed by Britain and France, and established the colonies of Eritrea to the north, and Italian Somaliland to the south, of Abyssinia. Italy's conflicts with Abyssinia were less successful. At the battles of Dogali in 1887 and Adowa in 1896 the white and black Italian troops were routed by the greatly superior Abyssinian forces. Dogali and Adowa were regarded as humiliations by that generation of Italians, who were told that the black Abyssinian savages had tortured their Italian prisoners and mutilated the corpses of the Italian dead. The clamour for revenge supplemented the feeling that Italy, having become a nation, should proceed to become an empire, and that the Risorgimento must be completed by the acquisition of colonies in East Africa.

The Italians were also interested in North Africa, where they had been trading and settling ever since the days when the whole of North Africa from the Red Sea to the Atlantic was part of the Ottoman Empire, though as the government of the Sultan in Constantinople grew weaker, his viceroys in North Africa became increasingly independent. In 1829 France invaded and annexed Algeria. The French attempt to gain control of Egypt in 1840 through an alliance with the Sultan's viceroy, Mehemet Ali, was defeated by the British Foreign Secretary, Lord Palmerston; but in 1881 France annexed Tunisia. This angered the Italians, who had hoped to make some agreement with France for establishing a joint zone of influence there. It angered them so much that they made a fundamental switch in their foreign policy and entered into the Triple Alliance with Germany and their old enemy, the Emperor Franz Joseph of Austria-Hungary. The Italian desire to join in the carve-up of the Turkish Empire increased when France occupied Morocco in 1907 and Austria annexed Bosnia-Herzegovina in 1908. The Italians complained, a little hysterically perhaps, that they were being encircled by France and Austria. If France could seize Morocco and Austria could seize Bosnia, why should not Italy seize Libya?

The Italian Socialist Party condemned the imperialist designs of the Italian bourgeoisie and their republican allies; but a growing minority among the Socialists supported imperialist expansion. They could find quotations from the sacred Socialist texts to justify their policy. Engels had written that the French annexation of Algeria was historically progressive because France was economically more advanced than Algeria; and for the same reason he had even supported the war of the United States against Mexico in 1846, which had been opposed by liberals in the United States as a war instigated by the Southern slaveowners to introduce slavery into Texas and the other territories acquired from Mexico. In 1864 he supported the annexation of Schleswig-Holstein by the Prussian statesman, Otto von Bismarck, and the Austrians on the grounds that the Danes were only 'semi-civilised'.[4]

After Engels's death his friend Eduard Bernstein, who had been his closest collaborator in the last years of his life, developed ideas about socialism which were roundly condemned as 'revisionism' by Lenin, Rosa Luxemburg and the revolutionary leftists in the Second International. One of Bernstein's revisionist doctrines was that in wars between countries at different stages of economic development, 'the higher civilisation can claim a higher right', and that 'savages have only a conditional right to the land occupied by them'.[5]

Marx had a sentimental humanitarian streak in his nature which made him rather more inclined than Engels to support oppressed groups that were being eliminated by advanced and progressive historical forces. He condemned the Highland clearances in Scotland and the eviction of 'the brave Gaels' from their homes by the Duchess of Sutherland;[6] and he denounced British imperialist policy in India and China during the Indian Mutiny and the Opium and Arrow Wars. This led him on one or two occasions to make off-the-cuff remarks to the effect that anyone who frustrated British imperialist domination was doing a good job of work. The imperialists in the Italian Socialist Party seized on these quotations. They claimed that Italy was a 'proletarian' nation,[7] oppressed by the wealthy capitalist nations of Britain and France, who denied the Italians their share of African colonies. By seizing Libya before the British or French seized it, Italy would be liberating North Africa and the Mediterranean from British and French imperialism.

But the editor of *La Lotta di Classe*, who had so violently attacked nationalism and patriotism in his paper during the last two years, stood firm with the majority of the Socialist Party in their opposition to the Libyan war. This was embarrassing for his Fascist supporters in later years. Margherita Sarfatti wrote that while she and many Socialists opposed the war 'on principle as an act of violence', being 'victims . . . of a misguided idealism', Mussolini 'felt no superstitious horror of warfare in general. It was only on grounds of political strategy that he disapproved of the Libyan adventure.' De Begnac made the same point less forcibly.[8] But this completely misrepresents Mussolini's attitude in 1911.

The Socialist Party leadership, a little half-heartedly, called for a general strike against the war, especially for a railway strike to prevent the troops from reaching the embarkation ports from where they were to sail to Libya. In most parts of the country the strike was not very effective; too many Italian proletarians patriotically supported the war. But in the Red Romagna it was much more successful.

When the Socialist leaders in the Romagna met in Forlì to discuss their course of action, Mussolini wished to go further. He proposed that they should call on the workers to blow up the railway track with bombs, which would be the only really effective way of stopping the troop transports. The party rejected this proposal; but Mussolini addressed a meeting in the town square at Forlì on 24 September. He spoke for an hour, calling on the workers to blow up the railway line. He was applauded by his supporters in the crowd, who cried: 'Long live the general strike! Down with the war!' Two other revolutionaries who were prominent in the Romagna also spoke at the meeting. One of them was Pietro Nenni, who thirty-five years later led the Socialist Party into a united front with the Communists in the general election of 1948, and as a result caused a crisis in the British Parliamentary Labour Party.* The other was the trade union leader, Aurelio Lolli.[9]

The French and British press condemned the Italian invasion of Libya. So did the press in Germany, Italy's ally in the Triple Alliance; in Austria, her other ally, the ministers in Parliament and the press maintained an ominous silence. But the foreign protests were low-key, and the Italian government drew the correct conclusion that the Great Powers would remain neutral and not intervene. Only the international Socialist movement unreservedly condemned Italian aggression; but the Italian proletariat did not respond. The correspondent in Rome of the London *Times* wrote that though there had at first been little enthusiasm in Italy for the war, once it had begun public opinion had changed. 'The cry of protest raised by the Socialists meant little or nothing,' he wrote on 3 October, 'the failure of their anti-war demonstrations served only to show that patriotism is still alive in Italy.'[10]

Mussolini informed the readers of *La Lotta di Classe* that to understand the reason for their failure to stop the war they would have to study Marx's writings. The people had been gulled by the patriotic

---

* Thirty-seven left-wing British Labour MPs sent Nenni a telegram wishing him success in the election. This angered the British Labour government, who were pursuing an anti-Communist and pro-American policy. The signatories of the 'Nenni telegram' were either expelled from the Parliamentary Labour Party or forced to retract their message to Nenni.

propaganda of the journalists and the Church, for the priests who yesterday had opposed Italian unification were today the most ferocious patriots. There had been a reconciliation between the Quirinal (the King's palace) and the Vatican, because they were both at the service of the Bank of Italy.[11]

For three weeks the authorities took no action against Mussolini; but on 14 October, while he was having lunch in the Café Garibaldi in Forlì, the police entered the café and arrested him. Nenni and Lolli had been arrested two hours earlier. On 18 November they were all tried in the court at Forlì. Mussolini was charged with having incited the people to commit violence in his speech on 24 September.

After his lawyer had pleaded on his behalf, he was asked if he wished to say anything more to the court. He said: 'If you find me not guilty, I will be pleased; if you find me guilty, I will be honoured.'[12] They found him and his colleagues guilty. On 23 November Nenni was sentenced to one year and fifteen days in prison and a fine of five hundred lire, Mussolini to one year in prison, and Lolli to six months and a fine of three hundred lire.

They all appealed, and their appeal was heard in the Court of Appeal in Bologna on 19 February 1912. The Court of Appeal upheld their convictions, but reduced Nenni's sentence to six and a half months in prison, Mussolini's to five and a half months, and Lolli's to four and a half months. As the period they had spent in prison, before their trial and appeal, was taken into account, Mussolini was released on 12 March 1912.[13]

Like many other political prisoners of the period, he spent his time in prison writing. At the age of twenty-eight he wrote his autobiography, *My Life from 29 July 1883 to 23 November 1911*. It was written for the benefit of his Socialist supporters. He presented himself as the violent, uncompromising revolutionary leader at war with society. He described his resentment at the way the priests had treated him at school, his expulsion for attacking another boy with a knife, his wanderings as a tramp in Switzerland, his clashes with the police, and his terms spent in prison. He wrote about his many love affairs, in Forlimpopoli at the age of sixteen, in Switzerland four years later, and at Tolmezzo in 1907. He referred to his many mistresses by their Christian names and the initial of their surnames – to Vittorina F. in Forlimpopoli, to Giulia F. in Gualtieri, to Eleanora H. in Geneva, to Luigia P. at Tolmezzo; but it would have been easy to identify the various ladies from his descriptions of them.

He certainly gave the impression that nearly all the women whom he pursued fell deeply in love with him, but he mentioned his failures as well as his successes. Throughout his life Mussolini hardly ever attempted to suppress information about his defeats, but explained them away with plausible arguments. He wrote in his autobiography in 1911 that he once saw a pretty girl in the street and followed her, but she repulsed him. He found out who she was and wrote love letters to her, but she did not reply. Eventually he had to accept defeat, but the experience did not shake his self-confidence. He was pleased when he heard that she had kept his love letters, and he soon fell in love with another girl. In the winter of 1899–1900 he visited a brothel in Forlimpopoli. He wrote that a prostitute sat on his knee and kissed him, and he paid fifty cents to lose his virginity.[14]

In a passage in his autobiography which has often been quoted, he wrote that he was attracted to a girl, Virginia B., who lived next door to him in the hamlet of Verano. One day in the summer of 1901, when nearly all the inhabitants of Verano had gone to hear a wandering friar who was preaching in the church, he entered Virginia's house where he found her alone. He pushed her into a corner behind a door and had sex with her. She burst into tears, and insulted him, saying that he had robbed her of her honour. 'Perhaps I had,' wrote Mussolini, 'but what honour was she talking about?' He added that his relationship with Virginia B. lasted for three months before he broke it off and began an affair with another girl, Venezia P. This passage has often been quoted to show Mussolini's callousness; but he did not mean to imply that Virginia was a woman without honour, for he called her 'prudent' and 'generous'.[15] He was writing as a Socialist revolutionary and free-thinker to expose the cant of the priests and the conventional bourgeois who believed that a woman lost her honour if she had sex with a man outside marriage.

It was all very different from that middle-class German Socialist intellectual, Dr Karl Marx, living in Victorian London, a revolutionary in doctrine but a conventional bourgeois, though an impoverished one, in his lifestyle, going for picnics on Primrose Hill with his aristocratic wife Jenny von Westphalen and their children, with the maidservant Helene Demuth carrying the picnic basket. When they got home in the evening Marx had sex with Helene, but managed the affair so discreetly that for many years only his great friend Engels knew that Marx was the father of Helene's illegitimate son.[16] But Mussolini was not a middle-class German Victorian gentleman;

he was an Angry Young Man from the Romagna at the dawn of the twentieth century.

He ended his account of his love affairs by stating that after sowing his wild oats he had fallen in love with Rachele and loved her as he had never loved a woman before.[17] So while he wrote at such length about the love affairs in which he had been involved before he became engaged to Rachele, he did not mention Fernanda Facchinelli and Ida Dalser in his account of his seven months' stay in Trent. He did not want Rachele to read about the mistresses he had had after he had asked her to live with him.

One beautiful woman was not impressed by Mussolini. 'He is nothing of a Marxist,' wrote Costa's mistress, Anna Kulisciov, 'nor is he really a Socialist at all. He has not the mentality of a scientific Socialist. Nor is he really a politician. He is a sentimental poetaster who has read Nietzsche.' She did not realize that the sentimental poetaster was turning into a skilful and ruthless politician.[18]

The picture of himself which Mussolini presented in his autobiography was calculated to impress his Socialist readers, but it was only half true. It showed him as he had been a few years before. He gave a true picture of the nineteen-year-old revolutionary from the Romagna, the anarchist tramp in Switzerland; but he did not reveal that this anarchist tramp, at twenty-eight, had become a rising and ambitious left-wing politician who was undoubtedly conscious that it would help his political career if his readers and followers believed that he was still an anarchist tramp.

Two days after he was released from prison, an anarchist tried to assassinate King Victor Emmanuel III. A deputation of all parties in the Chamber of Deputies, including the Socialist leaders Leonida Bissolati, Angelo Cabrini, and Ivanhoe Bonomi, went to the Quirinal to congratulate the King on his escape. Mussolini, in *La Lotta di Classe*, denounced the three Socialists, who obviously thought of themselves as future members of the King's government. He wrote that it was true that the Socialist Party had renounced assassination as a political weapon; but this was no reason why their parliamentary leaders should join in a monarchist Te Deum.[19] On 20 April he gave notice in *La Lotta di Classe* that he intended to move a resolution at the annual national congress of the Socialist Party in July expelling the right-wing parliamentary leaders from the party because of their 'reformist' policy of class collaboration and their renunciation of the revolutionary struggle.

The congress opened on 7 July 1912 at the Ariosto Theatre in Reggio Emilia, and Mussolini moved his resolution on the afternoon of the second day. After the usual long-winded and evasive speeches of the party leaders, his speech, in the same style as his newspaper articles, electrified the delegates. He spoke in short, forceful sentences, driving the point home with striking gestures with his right hand. He said that the grant of universal suffrage was not enough to ensure the victory of the proletariat; revolutionary action was still necessary. He ended by declaring that Bissolati, Cabrini and Bonomi could go to the Quirinal if they wished, and also to the Vatican, but the Socialist Party did not want them, not today, not tomorrow, never. His resolution expelling them was carried by 12,566 votes against 5,633, with 2,027 abstentions.[20]

The congress proceeded to elect a new National Executive Committee composed of prominent leftists. It included Mussolini and Angelica Balabanoff, who had settled in Italy and had become active in the Italian Socialist Party. Bissolati and Bonomi formed a new, independent Socialist Party, which pursued moderate 'reformist' policies, advocating political reforms, not violent revolution.

Mussolini's speech and the victory of the Left at the congress caused a stir not only in Italy but also in the international Socialist movement. Lenin, who was living in Vienna, wrote about it in his newspaper *Pravda*, which he had launched four months earlier. In the issue of 28 July he expressed his delight that the Italian Socialist Party had taken the revolutionary road at the congress.[21] Mussolini particularly appreciated the tribute that he received from Cipriani in Paris. In an interview in the French Socialist paper *L'Humanité*, Cipriani stated that the triumph of the Left at Reggio Emilia was due to one man – Mussolini. 'I like that man very much. His revolutionary doctrines are the same as mine.' Mussolini reprinted Cipriani's comments in *La Lotta di Classe*.[22]

## CHAPTER 6

———— ◆ ————

# Red Week

THE national daily newspaper of the Socialist Party, *Avanti!* had been founded in 1896 by Turati and his comrades. In 1912 the editor was the Jewish lawyer, Claudio Treves, who had advocated a moderate line in the paper. But in October the new National Executive Committee decided to get rid of Treves and appoint Mussolini as editor of *Avanti!* Treves made difficulties about going, claiming that he had a contract of employment with the newspaper; but it was eventually agreed that he should leave at the end of November, when Mussolini would replace him. Treves had been paid one thousand lire per month, and the party offered the same salary to Mussolini; but Mussolini said that he did not want so much, and accepted only five hundred lire per month.[1]

In the meantime he continued to edit *La Lotta di Classe*, concentrating particularly, in his articles, on the struggle against nationalism and war. The war between Italy and Turkey was ended in October 1912 by the Treaty of Ouchy; Turkey ceded Libya to Italy, and the Italians remained in occupation of Rhodes and the Dodecanese Islands, which they had seized during the war, until the terms of the peace treaty had been fulfilled. But the day before the Treaty of Ouchy was signed, Serbia, Bulgaria, Montenegro and Greece declared war on Turkey. When war broke out in the Balkans there was always a risk that it might escalate into a European war. In November 1912 a congress of the Second International was held at Basle, at which the Socialists went further than they had gone at Stuttgart in 1907 in their opposition to war. All the Socialist parties in Basle agreed that if war broke out they would organize a general strike in all their countries to stop the war.

Mussolini acclaimed the decisions of the Basle congress in *La Lotta di Classe*. On 30 November he wrote that a great event had occurred the previous Sunday in Basle: the Socialist world had told the cruel governments of the bourgeoisie that the glorious red spectre of the International would prevent the slaughter of their brothers by calling a general strike in Italy and France, in Austria and Germany, in England and Russia. 'Long live the Socialist International!'[2] It was the last number of *La Lotta di Classe*. Next day he began work as editor of *Avanti!*

As the editorial office of *Avanti!* was in Milan, Mussolini had to move there from Forlì. Rachele and Edda, who had just celebrated her second birthday, remained in Forlì. Mussolini had not been long in Milan before Ida Dalser arrived. She had left Trent and opened a beauty parlour in Milan. He did not cohabit with Ida, but often visited her and had sex with her. He would have found it hard to get rid of her even if he had wanted to do so; but he did not want to, as he still found her very attractive, though he realized that there would be trouble if Rachele found out. His problem was temporarily solved when Ida left for Paris and opened a beauty parlour there.[3]

It was now that he met Leda Rafanelli. She was born in 1880 in Alexandria in Egypt; her father, a small trader, was a member of the Italian colony there. She converted to Islam and became an anarchist. When she was twenty she came to Italy, probably because the British authorities in Egypt had threatened to deport her as an anarchist trouble-maker. In Italy she wore Arab dress, and took every occasion to proclaim that she was a Muslim; and she also joined the Italian Socialist Party. She wrote *The Prince's Bastard Daughter* and other daring novels which were published by an enterprising young publisher, Arnoldo Mondadori. In 1913 she was living in Milan. She was thirty-three and Mussolini was thirty.[4]

They formed a close friendship which lasted for eighteen months till it was broken because of political disagreements. She never became his mistress, though he was always asking her to do so. He wrote her forty-one letters which she kept and published more than thirty years later, after Mussolini's death. Many of them were written in the middle of the night. All of them were short, and some consisted of only two or three lines. In his love letters, as in his other writings, Mussolini was brief and came straight to the point.

When she said that she was sure that he had no need of her, as he must have other mistresses, he said that there were only two women whom he saw regularly. One of them was ugly but had a generous and noble nature; the other was beautiful, but was mean-minded and scheming, and was a Jewess. Leda told him that it was unworthy of him to refer to this woman's Jewish origin.[5] The ugly and noble-hearted woman was Angelica Balabanoff; the beautiful scheming Jewess was Margherita Sarfatti. Mussolini did not tell Leda anything about Rachele or Ida Dalser, and when she found out about them she was annoyed. But neither Rachele nor Ida were in Milan at this time, and both Balabanoff and Sarfatti lived and worked with Mussolini at the *Avanti!* office.

When Balabanoff turned against Mussolini after he became a Fascist, she made many accusations about his conduct when she worked with him on *Avanti!* Her worst accusation was that he was a coward, afraid to address hostile political meetings, afraid to visit the doctor, afraid of dogs, afraid to go anywhere near a cemetery, and afraid to walk alone in the streets at night.[6]

She gave as an example of his cowardice his behaviour on May Day 1913, when the Socialists planned to hold a public meeting in the town square at Forlì in commemoration of the Paris Commune. Mazzini had condemned the Commune in 1871, and forty-two years later his republican supporters in the Romagna announced that they would prevent the Socialists from commemorating the Commune in Forlì, if necessary by violence. Mussolini, who had gone to Forlì for the meeting, telegraphed to Balabanoff in Milan to come and speak at Forlì: 'Only you can instil such enthusiasm. You must come. Please don't refuse.' In her memoirs she wrote that Mussolini wanted her to speak at the meeting so that she, and not he, would be the target of republican violence.

Balabanoff spoke first at the meeting, though she had difficulty in making herself heard above the clamour of the republicans in the square. Then there was an explosion, and Mussolini and Balabanoff were told that the republicans had thrown a bomb in a nearby street and that a Socialist had been killed. Mussolini then suggested abandoning the meeting, but Balabanoff insisted on finishing her speech. Mussolini did not attempt to speak.

The police had been informed that the republicans were planning to kill Mussolini and Balabanoff when they went to the station to catch their train back to Milan, and they were driven to the station in two coaches under police escort. On their way, someone fired a shot at the first coach, and one of the policemen was wounded; but Mussolini and Balabanoff, who were in the second coach, reached the station unhurt and returned safely to Milan. Balabanoff wrote that on their journey to the station Mussolini 'shrank down in his seat, trembling and cursing. Long after we were clear of the crowd he was still shaking.'[7]

It is impossible to believe Balabanoff's stories about Mussolini's physical cowardice, because we know of too many occasions on which he displayed his courage. But she may have been on stronger ground when she criticized him for lacking the moral courage to 'swim against the tide' – an expression often used by Socialists before and during the First World War to mean resisting the pressure of public opinion whipped up by the bourgeoisie and their journalists. Balabanoff, who herself often swam against the tide, wrote that Mussolini was never prepared to do so. She believed that he only became a Socialist because so many other people in the Romagna were Socialists; and she cited several examples of how, when he was editor of *Avanti!*, he published, or refused to publish, articles in the paper in order to please influential leaders of the Socialist Party. Her stories show that by 1913 Mussolini was a shrewd political tactician as well as a revolutionary extremist, who was not prepared to fight a battle in circumstances when he knew that he would be defeated. He wished, like a good general, to fight the enemy on ground of his own choosing, where he could bring his superior force to bear at the decisive point and win the battle and the war.

The trouble at the meeting in Forlì was typical of the situation in the Romagna. Balabanoff wrote that in the Romagna, apart from a few large landowners and the priests, everyone was either a republican, a Socialist or an anarchist, and that, although the Socialists and the anarchists hated each other, they sometimes united against the republicans. These quarrels between the three left-wing parties often led to violence. The pointlessness of these constant conflicts was duly noted by the ambitious young man from the Romagna who had been named after the republican Benito Juárez, the anarchist Amilcare Cipriani, and the Socialist Andrea Costa.

Mussolini was winning praise on all sides for his work as editor of *Avanti!* When he took over from Treves in December 1912 the daily circulation was 34,000; in little more than a year, by the summer of 1914, he had increased the sales to 60,000 a day with an occasional circulation of 100,000 when he featured some special article.[8] He had meanwhile launched another journal of his own in November

1913, which he called *Utopia* after Sir Thomas More's famous book. It was a theoretical organ in which he could discuss more academic themes than in *Avanti!*, and without being forced to follow the party line. In *Utopia* he reviewed the recent philosophical publications, and Rosa Luxemburg's heavy and complex book *The Accumulation of Capital*, which caused her Socialist comrades to say that she was the only person who really understood the second of the three volumes of Marx's *Das Kapital*. He also wrote a book, *Jan Hus the Truthful*, a short biography of the Czech Protestant martyr who was burned as a heretic in 1415. Mussolini denounced the persecution of Hus by the Catholic Church.[9]

A month after Mussolini became editor of *Avanti!*, in January 1913, the farm workers at Roccagorge near Frosinone in central Italy rioted in protest at the failure of the authorities to provide a sanitation system. The troops were called out: they opened fire, killing seven farmers and wounding at least twelve. This was followed by riots, with the army firing on the demonstrators, in several places in central Italy and in Sicily. Mussolini denounced this 'State assassination' at the 'orders of Savoy'[10] (King Victor Emmanuel's family name), and called on the proletariat to resist the violence of the state with their own defensive violence, while awaiting the day when they would capture the state power from the bourgeoisie by revolutionary action. He and *Avanti!* were prosecuted for this article on a charge of sedition and incitement to violence, but they were acquitted. While Mussolini castigated the government of the Liberal Prime Minister, Giovanni Giolitti, and his corrupt freemason friends, many Conservatives and right-wing groups criticized Giolitti for his weakness when confronted with the Red menace.

A young anarchist worker, Augusto Massetti, was so indignant at the shooting of the rioters and demonstrators by the army that he fired a shot at an army officer; the officer had played no part in the shooting of the demonstrators, but Massetti was taking revenge on the officer class as a whole. He was tried on a charge of attempted murder, but was certified as insane and confined in a lunatic asylum. The syndicalist trades unions called for a twenty-four-hour general strike on 7 June 1914 to show the labour movement's solidarity with Massetti. The date was deliberately chosen as a provocation to the Conservatives and royalists who always held demonstrations on 7 June to celebrate the anniversary of the promulgation of the Liberal constitution of the Kingdom of Piedmont in 1848. The National

Executive of the Socialist Party officially supported the twenty-four-hour general strike, and Mussolini in *Avanti!* called on all workers to join it.

The strike was almost complete, and passed off without violence in most parts of Italy; but in Ancona the army was called out to help the police to separate the strikers from the Conservatives demonstrating on Constitution Day. The strikers attacked the troops, who opened fire, killing three of them and wounding at least ten. Next day the Ancona branch of the General Confederation of Labour (the official Socialist trades unions) called an indefinite general strike in protest against the action of the army; but in Milan the strike had already begun the previous evening at the call of the local trades unions.

Mussolini was in Milan, and his conduct on that evening is alone enough to rebut Angelica Balabanoff's accusation of cowardice; for he was at the head of the demonstrators in the Piazza del Duomo when the police charged. By his side was his Socialist comrade, Filippo Corridoni. Mussolini was struck by a policeman's baton, and Corridoni was arrested.

The events in Italy, which became known as 'Red Week', alarmed the bourgeoisie throughout Europe. *The Times* of London, which for the previous weeks had been chiefly concerned with the escalation of arson, assaults on magistrates, and other acts of violence by the suffragettes in England, had become alarmed by 10 June at what it called 'Terrorism by a Labour Minority' in Italy; but its Rome correspondent admitted that the strike was virtually 100 per cent effective in Rome and in all the major cities of Italy except Venice, where it obtained very little support; and the trams continued to run in Milan and Genoa. In Turin two strikers were killed, a trooper who fell from his horse was trampled to death by the crowd, and twenty rioters and twenty policemen were injured. The worst trouble was again in Ancona, where the strikers attacked the police and the army with stones and bottles. Several strikers received wounds from baton blows, and one soldier and one policeman were wounded by revolver fire. On 9 June the state of siege was proclaimed in Ancona, and the town was handed over to the control of the army.

The Liberal Prime Minister, Antonio Salandra, who had replaced Giolitti, issued orders to the prefects to enforce law and order, but to exercise the greatest possible restraint when dealing with strikers and demonstrators. This did not please the right-wing parties. In

Parma and Milan the Conservatives held counter-demonstrations, and organized armed groups of young Conservatives who attacked and beat up the strikers.

But on the morning of 9 June the National Executive of the Socialist Party had still not officially supported the unlimited general strike; and next day the General Confederation of Labour called for an end to the strike, ordering all workers to return to work by midnight on 10 June.[11] The anarchist leader Errico Malatesta could scarcely believe the news. He promptly issued his own appeal to the workers: 'It is now not a question of a strike but of revolution. Down with the indifferent! Down with the traitors! Long live the Revolution!'[12]

But Mussolini loyally followed the official party line. On 11 June he addressed a rally in the Arena in Milan, and called on the strikers to return to work at once; he had only just received news that the strike had been called off, because the authorities had cut off all telegraphic communication with the General Confederation of Labour headquarters in Rome. Next day he wrote in *Avanti!* that the strike had been an unprecedented success which had taught the proletariat how to perfect a new form of struggle; but his real opinion was very different. He thought that Red Week was 'not revolution' but 'chaos'.[13]

There is no doubt that the fiasco of Red Week shook Mussolini's faith in the Socialist Party and was the first event that led him to his break with socialism. A party that mouthed revolutionary slogans and which called on the workers to strike and demonstrate against the bourgeois state, but then drew back from the brink when confronted with the enemy; a party that engaged in endless violent conflicts with republicans and anarchists, but never won a decisive victory over them; a party whose members from time to time killed a policeman or army officer but did not break the power of the police and the army – such a party did not appeal to Mussolini.

If only he could forget what he had read in Marx and Kropotkin, and remember only the lessons he had learned from Machiavelli, Nietzsche, Sorel, Pareto, Le Bon and Prezzolini. He wanted to prove to himself and to the world that he was one of the hierarchy who dominated, not one of the majority who allowed themselves to be dominated; one of Le Bon's strong rulers whom the mob slavishly obeyed, and not a weak one against whom they revolted; an orator who could inspire the crowd to heroic deeds by appealing to its nobler motives, especially to its patriotism; a leader who swam not against the tide but with the tide, leading his admiring followers to victory.

The temptation was great; but it would mean betraying the Socialist internationalism in which he had been brought up since early childhood by his father and his comrades in the Socialist movement. He could not support an imperialist war fought to acquire a colonial empire in Africa. It might have been different if it had been a war that could plausibly be regarded as a just and revolutionary war to liberate Italian soil from Austrian oppression; but this was a hypothetical situation which was most unlikely to arise, as the Emperors of Austria and Germany were Italy's allies in the Triple Alliance.

Mussolini had to deal not with a hypothetical situation but with the actual situation that existed in the spring of 1914, when he was editor of *Avanti!* and had to put over the party line in the paper. So he continued to apply his journalistic brilliance in denouncing militarism and the patriotism of the bourgeoisie and the republican nationalists. He trumpeted the slogan that had often been used by Socialists in several countries of the world since it was first proclaimed by the Italian Socialists at the time of the war in Abyssinia in 1896: 'Not one man, not one penny, for imperialist war!'[14]

# CHAPTER 7

———— ◆ ————

# The Break with Socialism

ON 28 June 1914 the Archduke Franz Ferdinand, the heir to the Austrian throne, was assassinated with his wife in Sarajevo by Serbian nationalists. He was paying the first visit by a member of the Austrian imperial family to the province of Bosnia-Herzegovina which Austria had annexed in 1908. Mussolini's editorial comment in *Avanti!* next day was more restrained than his jubilation at the assassination of Stolypin in 1911. He described the deaths of the Archduke and his wife as a 'tragic event', but nevertheless rejoiced that a blow had been struck against the Habsburg monarchy, which, not content with oppressing Hungarians and Croats, was now aiming to extend the territories of the Empire by annexing Serbia.[1]

The Austrian government was indeed intending to use the assassination at Sarajevo as an excuse to conquer Serbia. They accused the Serbian government of conniving at the assassination, and sent a forty-eight-hour ultimatum to Serbia in terms so humiliating as to be almost unacceptable, for some of the demands infringed Serbian sovereignty. The Serbian government nevertheless decided to accept it, but was then persuaded by the Tsar of Russia to send a reply that courteously rejected some of the Austrian demands. On 28 July Austria declared war on Serbia, and two days later Russia ordered general mobilization. The German Emperor, after initially trying to restrain Austria from starting a European war, decided to support his Austrian ally and on 1 August declared war on Russia.

He also decided to put into operation the plan that had been drawn up by Field Marshal Count Alfred von Schlieffen, the former Chief of the German General Staff, though Schlieffen himself had died in 1913. The Schlieffen Plan was that if Germany became involved in war with Russia she should immediately launch a preventive strike against Russia's ally, France. As it would facilitate the invasion of France if German troops could pass through Belgium, the German government asked Belgium to allow this; and when Belgium refused, Germany declared war on Belgium. Britain was bound by the treaty of 1839 to defend Belgian neutrality, and from even earlier times it had been a principle of British foreign policy not to allow a great European power to control the Belgian coast. On 4 August Britain declared war on Germany, and the Allies – France, Britain, Russia, Belgium and Serbia – were at war with the Central Powers, Germany and Austria.

As the crisis developed at the end of July, Mussolini continued his anti-war propaganda in *Avanti!* 'One cry alone,' he wrote on 26 July, 'will arise from the proletariat in the piazzas and streets of Italy: "Down with the war!" The time has come for the Italian proletariat to hold fast to their old slogan of "Not one man, not one penny!" at whatever cost.'[2]

The Executive Committee of the Socialist International hurriedly met in Brussels on 29 July, with Angelica Balabanoff representing the Italian Socialist Party. Now was the time for all Socialist parties to implement the policy on which they had decided at Stuttgart in 1907 and at Basle in 1912 and call a general strike in every belligerent country to stop the war. They expected the powerful Austrian Social Democrat Party to take the lead, since undoubtedly Austria had started the war. But the Austrian Socialist delegates told their colleagues in Brussels that they proposed to do nothing of the kind. The workers in the Socialist stronghold of Red Vienna were clamouring for revenge against the Serbs who had murdered their Archduke. They were shouting *'Alle Serben müssen sterben!'*[3] (all Serbs must die) and were eagerly supporting the war. The Austrian Socialist leader, Viktor Adler, said that it was better to be wrong with the working class than right against the working class.[4]

The French and Belgian Socialists then decided to support their governments. The French Socialist leader, René Viviani, had become Prime Minister in June, and he and Vandervelde in Belgium, who joined the government in August, called on the French and Belgian workers to defend their country against the German invaders. Even the veteran French Socialist Jean Jaurès, who had been more closely associated than any other Socialist leader with the struggle against the impending war, said at a meeting in Brussels on 29 July that the French government could in no way be blamed for starting the war.

This did not prevent Jaurès from being assassinated two days later, after he had returned to Paris, by a young French nationalist student who thought that he was a pacifist and a traitor to his country in the pay of the German government.

The minority of Socialists who opposed the war regarded Jaurès as a martyr for Socialist internationalism. On 4 August Mussolini spoke at a memorial meeting in Milan in honour of Jaurès. He said that Jaurès had been murdered by right-wing nationalists who wrongly accused him of being in German pay, and had died as a martyr for peace. But Viviani said that Jaurès had decided to support the war, and he called on the French proletariat to honour the memory of Jaurès by fighting bravely for their country.[5]

The German Social Democrat Party, the strongest in Europe, held out for a day or two longer than most of the other Socialist parties against the popular clamour for war; but then they too gave in. The German Socialist deputy Wilhelm Dittmann, returning by train to Berlin for the meeting of the Reichstag, met Socialists who had been called up for the army singing Socialist songs on their way to the front. They called on Dittmann not to let them down but to support them while they were fighting for the Fatherland. On 3 August the German Social Democrat deputies in the Reichstag decided by 78 votes against 14 to vote in favour of the war credits. The Austrian Socialist newspaper, the *Arbeiterzeitung*, in an article called 'The Day of the German Nation', praised the German Social Democrat Party for patriotically deciding to support the war.[6]

Only a handful of German Socialists opposed the war. They were led by Karl Liebknecht and Rosa Luxemburg, who were imprisoned. In the Russian Socialist party, Lenin and the Bolsheviks opposed the war, and called on the proletariat to transform the imperialist war into civil war.

The Italian Socialists were in a different position from the other Socialist parties. Under the treaty of 1882 Italy, as a member of the Triple Alliance, was pledged to enter the war on the side of Germany and Austria; but public opinion in Italy was strongly opposed to Austria, the oppressor of the Italians in the Trentino, and was against supporting Austria and Germany in the war. Even the Italian bourgeoisie and the government preferred to remain neutral, at least for the time being, and to see how the war developed before joining in. So it was not difficult for the Italian Socialist Party to adhere to its anti-war attitude.

But the republicans hoped that Italy would enter the war on the side of the Allies. They thought that this was Mazzini's war for democracy against the autocratic emperors. When Mussolini was in the Trentino in 1909 he had opposed going to war with Austria to liberate the Trentino because Austria would win and seize more Italian territory; but Austria would not win if France and Britain were fighting on Italy's side. The republicans called on the Italian people to support gallant little Serbia and gallant little Belgium against the Austrian and German bullies, to stand with republican France and constitutional Britain against German and Austrian imperial militarism. All the democratic forces were on the side of the Allies. The Czech liberal leader, Tomaš Garrigue Masaryk, who was a deputy in the imperial Austrian Parliament in Vienna, supported the Allies. Soon after the war broke out he escaped from Vienna to Rome, and then went on to London, where he called on the Czech troops in the Austrian army to desert to the enemy and fight for the Allies.

The Garibaldi family supported the Allies. The great Garibaldi's son, Ricciotti, had carried on his father's tradition of being a '*condottiere* of freedom', travelling to far-distant countries to help oppressed nations who were fighting for their independence. Ricciotti had led a band of Garibaldini volunteers to fight for Greece against Turkey in 1897 and for the liberal revolutionaries in Mexico in 1911. He was now too old at sixty-seven and too crippled by rheumatism to fight himself, but his son Peppino led a band of volunteers, including five of Peppino's brothers, to fight for France in the First World War. One of the brothers, Ezio Garibaldi, was a friend of Mussolini's. Ezio had wished to become a journalist, and at his request Mussolini had given him a job as a reporter on *Avanti!*[7]

Peppino Garibaldi's volunteers served on the Argonne front in France. They distinguished themselves by their outstanding courage, suffering heavy losses as they captured the enemy positions, in traditional Garibaldini fashion, at the bayonet point in the face of intensive rifle and machine-gun fire.

There was one fly in this democratic ointment – Tsarist Russia; and the German Social Democrats had hastened to unearth old quotations from Marx and Engels about the duty of Socialists in any war to support the nations who were fighting against the Tsar. The republicans and Socialists who supported the Allies said that the presence of Russia alone did not altar the fact that basically the allies were fighting for democracy; and in any case, the situation had changed since Marx and Engels had called on the workers to fight against Nicholas I, the gendarme of Europe. Nicholas II had granted some liberal reforms after the revolution of 1905, including a legislative assembly, the Duma. The development in Russia towards constitutional government would be hastened, and the position of the Russian liberals strengthened, if Russia took her place at the side of the Western Allies in defence of democracy. The leading Russian Marxist, G. V. Plekhanov, and the leading Russian anarchist, Kropotkin, called on the Russian workers to support the war.

Throughout August Mussolini continued to advocate the party line in *Avanti!*, but he had been profoundly shaken by the inability of the other parties in the Second International to stop the war, and particularly by the failure of the German and Austrian parties to denounce the aggressive policy of the German and Austrian Emperors. He told a friend: 'The Second International is dead.' Lenin made exactly the same remark on the same occasion; but Lenin drew the conclusion that it would be necessary to form a new, third International. Mussolini drew a very different conclusion. In 1932 he told Emil Ludwig that it was the betrayal of the internationalist cause by the German Social Democrats in 1914 that had led him to repudiate international socialism and in due course to form the Fascist Party.[8]

On 9 September 1914 he addressed a rally in the Teatro del Popolo in Milan, demanding that Italy stay neutral. He denounced the campaign for intervention on the Allied side. He said that he had some sympathy with republican France, but that Italians should not forget that France had sent her troops to crush Mazzini's Roman Republic in 1849, had betrayed Italy by making the peace of Villafranca with Austria in 1859, and had shot down Garibaldi's volunteers at Mentana in 1867. Someone in the audience shouted out: 'That was bourgeois France!' Mussolini replied: 'When I say France I mean bourgeois France; but proletarian France did not protest.'[9] He was now using nationalist arguments to justify his Socialist internationalist policy.

On 12 September he published in *Avanti!* an article by the Socialist dissident Sergio Panunzio, who supported the republican policy of intervention on the side of the Allies. Panunzio put forward the usual republican arguments for supporting the war of democracy against German and Austrian militarism, quoting Marx's and Engels's statements in 1848 and 1870 to show that they were not pacifists and supported progressive wars by Germany; it was therefore justifiable for Italian Socialists to support progressive wars against Germany.

Next day Mussolini published a much longer article signed in his own name, rebutting Panunzio's arguments. Throughout his life Mussolini occasionally, though not often, distorted the facts and misquoted historical sources in order to prove his point. He did so on this occasion, confusing – and it must have been a deliberate confusion – the declaration of the First International in July 1870 supporting Germany at the outbreak of war, and the International's second declaration two months later condemning Bismarck for continuing the war against republican France after the overthrow of Napoleon III's Second Empire. Mussolini put forward a vigorous defence of Socialist internationalism and the anti-war policy of the Italian Socialist Party, but his arguments were not very convincing.[10]

That same night, at 2 a.m., he wrote a letter to Leda Rafanelli, telling her that though he thought that he had crushed Panunzio in his article in next day's *Avanti!*, he was sad and depressed at the number of his Socialist friends who had become intoxicated by the clamour for war. 'In a few days I shall no longer trust you or even myself ... It is terrible; Ciardi, Corridoni, *la* Rygier, apologists for war! It is a contagion that spares no one. But I wish to hold the rampart till the end.' When he spoke to Leda a few days later, he told her that he had met two old friends, students from the Romagna, on their way to enrol as volunteers in the army. 'They were full of enthusiasm to give their lives ... It shook me.'[11]

He held the rampart for another month, while more of his Socialist friends joined the republicans in demanding intervention on the side of the Allies. The interventionists formed an organization that they called the Fasci d'azione rivoluzionaria intervenista, after the fasces, the bundle of sticks carried by the lictors in ancient Rome; one stick could be broken, but fastened together they were unbreakable.

One of the most ardent supporters of intervention was Massimo Rocca, the editor of the Bologna newspaper *Il Resto del Carlino*, where he wrote under the name of Libero Tancredi. Leda Rafanelli met Rocca towards the end of September, and he told her that he had talked to Mussolini, and believed that Mussolini would shortly come out in favour of intervention on the Allied side. Leda could not believe it, but Rocca said that he was sure of it. He added that he thought that Mussolini was not very intelligent.[12] Other people who met Mussolini in later years formed the opinion that he was not very intelligent, including several British diplomats in the 1920s and 1930s, and Mussolini was able to exploit their underestimation of his intelligence to his own advantage.

Rocca decided to force the issue. On 7 October he published in *Il Resto del Carlino* an article entitled 'The editor of *Avanti!* is a man of straw: Open Letter to Benito Mussolini'. He accused Mussolini of writing one thing when he believed another, of having no national discipline or moral courage. *Il Resto del Carlino* would not meddle with Mussolini's conscience, which was his private business; but they were concerned when he worked on behalf of traitors to the Motherland, and allowed himself to be influenced by people like the staunch internationalist, Costantino Lazzari, and Balabanoff, 'that Russian champion of German Socialism'. Mussolini was not acting in good faith, but was helping the government to betray the future of the country.[13]

Leda read the article in *Il Resto del Carlino* when she was on the point of leaving Milan for the winter; but before going to catch her train she went to Mussolini's house. She said to him that he would of course have to reply in *Avanti!* without delay to Rocca's open letter. He said that he certainly intended to do so, and commented that Rocca's reference to Angelica Balabanoff showed his petty bourgeois mentality. He then walked with Leda along the street till they came to a point where they separated, she going one way and he another. She said to him: 'Goodbye; keep calm,' and he said: 'Goodbye, and thank you.' It was the last time she ever spoke to Mussolini.[14]

Next day both *Avanti!* and *Il Resto del Carlino* published Mussolini's reply to Rocca. 'In the face of the storm which is agitating Europe today,' he wrote, 'all those who, instead of making history, are only observing it, are men of straw, even if they are called Tancredi.' He ended his article: 'We will see who is the man of straw, I or Libero Tancredi, or rather Massimo Rocca.'[15]

It was his last stand for Socialist internationalism. On 18 October he published an article in *Avanti!* under the heading: 'From absolute neutrality to an active and working neutrality'. He wrote that absolute neutrality meant supporting the Triple Alliance of the monarchies of Italy, Austria and Germany. Socialists did not always advocate neutrality and oppose war; when they had made the Socialist revolution they would have to wage a revolutionary war against foreign sovereigns who would intervene to crush the revolution. He also pointed out that famous Socialists like Cipriani, Vaillant in France, Hyndman in England and the Russian Kropotkin were now supporting the Allies in the war. The Italian Socialist Party must not allow the letter of socialism to destroy the spirit of socialism.[16]

Mussolini's article alarmed the Socialist leaders. Next day fourteen members of the National Executive of the Italian Socialist Party met in Bologna to discuss it; they included Lazzari, Pagnacca Serrati, Angelica Balabanoff and Mussolini himself. They argued all day on 19 October till late into the evening, with Lazzari, Serrati and Balabanoff speaking with especial bitterness against Mussolini's attitude. When the discussion was resumed on the morning of 20 October, Mussolini moved a resolution: that while the party reaffirmed its opposition in principle to all wars, it believed that the line hitherto pursued in *Avanti!* of absolute neutrality in all circumstances was too dogmatic; the party should substitute a policy of flexible neutrality to meet a changing international situation. Only Mussolini voted in favour of the resolution, which was defeated by thirteen votes to one.

The leaders decided instead to pass a resolution which declared that they believed in absolute neutrality, not the ambiguous neutrality of the government, and opposed the slaughter that was now devastating Europe and inflicting suffering on the workers of Belgium, France, Germany, Russia, England, Austria and Serbia. The resolution denounced the betrayal of socialism by the German and other Socialist parties. 'We will be faithful to our flag; and on this flag is written: Proletarians of all the world, unite!' The resolution was carried by twelve votes to one, with only Mussolini voting against, and Adolfo Zerbini abstaining.[17]

Mussolini demanded that the National Executive should convene an extraordinary party congress to discuss the party's attitude to the war; but his request was rejected. He resigned as editor of *Avanti!*, and on 15 November he published the first number of his own newspaper, which he called *Il Popolo d'Italia*. Writing with all his usual passion and brilliance, he launched a campaign supporting the republicans and calling for Italian intervention in the war on the side of the Allies. The Socialist leaders condemned him as a traitor. They accused him of having been bribed by the French intelligence service to change his attitude, pointing out that for nearly three months after the outbreak of war he had strongly supported the party's policy of opposition to the war, and had then suddenly made what we would now call a 100 per cent U-turn and advocated the intervention-ist policy that he had hitherto so roundly condemned.

French gold is much too simplistic an explanation, but Mussolini's change of policy in October 1914 certainly needs to be explained. It is not enough to say that to advocate neutrality in August 1914 could be interpreted as opposing the intervention of Italy on the side of the Central Powers under the terms of the Triple Alliance, and that Mussolini, as editor of *Avanti!*, had to express official party policy in the newspaper; for we know from his private letter to Leda Rafanelli how opposed he was in September to intervention on the side of the Allies, how shaken by the adherence of so many of his Socialist comrades to an interventionist policy, and how determined that he at least would continue to hold the rampart till the end.

The explanation of Mussolini's change in October lies surely in Angelica Balabanoff's analysis of his character. Whatever other vir-tues he may have had, and for all the courage that he showed when facing police baton charges, and would soon show facing the enemy fire in the trenches, Mussolini did not have the courage to swim against the tide of public opinion. The friends whom he most admired in the Socialist Party, the most vigorous and determined elements, were in favour of war, and he felt that they would soon succeed in winning the support of the majority of the people. He wanted to be with them, to be popular with the masses, to gain the applause of the crowd. All his life he wanted to be on the winning side, though he got it badly wrong in 1940.

On 24 November, at a meeting of the Milanese branch of the Socialist Party in the Teatro del Popolo in Milan, Mussolini was expelled from the party after a bitter debate in which he had defended his conduct, and his policy of intervention in the war, in the face of interruption and booing. He said that they were expelling him because they loved him, though they did not realize it; that he was being loyal to the spirit, if not to the letter, of socialism; and that whatever resolutions they might pass, he would remain a Socialist all his life and would never abandon the principles of socialism.[18] He was to move a long way from this position during the next thirty years.

The First World War split the Socialist movement is every country in Europe, but nowhere as bitterly and with such far-reaching consequences as in Italy. The Socialist attitude to war is complex. While the officer class, and the majority of the population, patriotically support every war in which their country is engaged, and while pacifists oppose all wars and endure persecution rather than support a war, Socialists oppose reactionary, unjust imperialist wars but support progressive, just, revolutionary wars. They have to analyse every war that breaks out and decide in which of the two categories it falls.

If it is an unjust imperialist war, they must oppose it, swimming against the patriotic tide, whatever the consequences may be to themselves, and denouncing as a traitor any Socialist who supports the war and urges the workers to die and murder their foreign brothers for the sake of increasing the profits of their bourgeoisie. If it is a just, revolutionary war, then Socialists must ardently support it and denounce as a traitor and counter-revolutionary any Socialist who opposes and sabotages the war effort. This dilemma was vividly illustrated by the policy of the Communist parties in every country during the Second World War, when they characterized the war as an imperialist war until the Soviet Union joined the Allies; they then proclaimed it to be a just war, and called for the ruthless suppression of those 'Trotskyists' who continued to pursue the same policy as the Communists themselves had adopted before 22 June 1941.

In October 1914 Mussolini decided that the First World War was a just, democratic war, while his former Socialist comrades continued to believe that it was an unjust, imperialist war. This caused an irreparable split between them, and they drifted further and further apart. The Socialists denounced Mussolini as a traitor in the pay of the French bourgeoisie, and Mussolini denounced the Socialists as traitors to their country and in the pay of the German ambassador, Prince Bernhard von Bülow. By 1918 he was demanding that the Socialist Party be suppressed. The difference between Mussolini and the Socialists in their analysis of the nature of the First World War led almost inevitably to the castor oil and beatings, the arson and the killings, of 1921, to the murder of Matteotti in 1924, and to the execution at Giulino di Mezzegra on 28 April 1945.

◆

# CHAPTER 8

# The Interventionist

As soon as Mussolini launched his campaign in *Il Popolo d'Italia* in favour of Italian intervention in the war, his opponents began to ask where he had obtained the money to finance the paper. On 18 November 1914, three days after the first issue of the paper was published, the Zurich newspaper, the *Neue Zürcher Zeitung*, published a statement which had been issued by the German news agency, that the French government was financing *Il Popolo d'Italia*.[1] Mussolini denied this two days later, just as Lenin in 1917 denied that he had received money from the German government. In fact, the French and Belgian governments financed Mussolini in 1914 for the same reason that the German government financed Lenin in 1917 – because they thought that it was in their interest to do so; and Mussolini and Lenin happily accepted the money, not intending to become agents of France and Germany, but in order to further the policy in which they believed. They denied it because they thought it would discredit them and their cause if the truth were known.

In both cases the money was paid indirectly. The funds to launch *Il Popolo d'Italia* came in the first place from Filippo Naldi, the proprietor of *Il Resto del Carlino*, which had welcomed Mussolini with open arms when he came over to their side. In November 1914 Mussolini wrote to his sister Edvige from Switzerland – he did not reveal that he was in Geneva – telling her that he had gone to Switzerland for a few days to make arrangements for financing *Il Popolo d'Italia*.[2] Some of the money sent to Mussolini by Naldi came from the French and Belgian governments. A few years later, Mussolini was being subsidized by wealthy industrialists in Milan and Turin.

The republicans led the agitation for intervention. The British ambassador, Sir Rennell Rodd, informed the Foreign Office in London that the Italian industrialists were opposed to entering the war on the Allied side because of their links with Germany. The majority of the Socialists opposed all wars. Most of the aristocracy were opposed to intervention, because they regarded central Europe as the mainstay of aristocratic privilege. The Church was against the war. It was 'the intelligent bourgeoisie and the people who followed them' who brought Italy into the war, with the republicans enthusiastically supporting the idea of the war for democracy.[3] Mussolini played an active, though not outstandingly prominent, part in the interventionist campaign. A popular history of the agitation leading to Italy's entry into the war, which was published in 1916, referred to Mussolini on only thirteen of the four hundred pages of the book; but his role was not unimportant, particularly in Milan.[4]

Mussolini's split with the Socialists affected his private life. It ended his friendship with Leda Rafanelli; but soon afterwards Ida Dalser returned to Milan, and Mussolini resumed his affair with her, for he continued to live in Milan while Rachele and the four-year-old Edda stayed in Forlì. He was worried about Ida, because he knew that Rachele would raise Cain if she found out about her, which was very likely, as Forlì was in closer contact with Milan than with Trent, and the editor of *Il Popolo d'Italia* in 1915 was more in the public eye than the editor of *L'Avvenire del Lavoratore* in 1909.

By the middle of December 1914 the Serbs had launched an offensive that drove the Austrian army back across the Hungarian frontier. Mussolini praised them in *Il Popolo d'Italia* in an article entitled 'Long live Serbia!' on 12 December. Once again the old Austrian eagle had driven its claws into the body of the Serbs; but the Serbs had fought gloriously and had driven out the eagle, while Italy, a great power with forty million inhabitants, Italy the mother of heroes, had remained neutral – neutral from commercial calculation, neutral to her shame.[5]

At Christmas news arrived that Bruno and Costante Garibaldi had been killed fighting in the French Army in the Argonne. Their bodies were sent to Italy, and their funeral in Rome was attended by 300,000 people. In an article in *Il Popolo d'Italia* on 8 January 1915, Mussolini wrote that it was the largest number of people who had ever assembled in the streets of Rome. He praised the Garibaldi brothers for carrying on the republican tradition of their family in fighting for the cause of democracy and revolution, for the France of Blanqui, while the King of Italy and the Pope remained neutral and Italian Socialists were acting as the secret army of the Austrians.[6]

He emphasized this theme day after day in his paper: France, Britain and Russia were fighting for the oppressed little nations of Serbia and Belgium with the support of Socialists of the eminence of Vandervelde, H.M. Hyndman, Plekhanov and Kropotkin; but the Italian Socialists were adopting a cowardly neutrality, lining up with the Quirinal and the Vatican in opposing the democratic revolutionary war against the Habsburg monarchy.

In the spring, the interventionist campaign became more widespread and strident, taking increasingly unconstitutional and violent forms. All over Italy the republicans filled the town squares and occupied the town halls, shouting 'Long live Italy! Long live war!' In Milan they broke into the law courts, and the judicial business was suspended until they were induced to leave.[7]

The Milanese Fasci d'azione called for a great demonstration in the Piazza del Duomo in Milan on the evening of Sunday, 11 April. Their appeal to 'Milanese proletarians' was published in *Il Popolo d'Italia* on 10 April under the headline: 'Fascists of Italy, occupy the piazza tomorrow at whatever cost!' They denied that the revolutionary Fascists were warmongers or nationalists, but claimed that neutrality was supported only by the monarchy, the Vatican, the bourgeoisie, and by the German-loving Socialists bought by Bülow's gold. 'Proletarians, come into the streets and the piazzas with us and cry: "Down with the corrupt mercantile policy of the Italian bourgeoisie" and demand war against the Empires responsible for the European conflagration. Long live the war of liberation of the peoples!'[8]

Mussolini repeated the call in *Il Popolo d'Italia* on the Sunday morning. He reminded his readers that on 18 October 1914 he had written that it was necessary to kill the letter, in order to preserve the spirit, of the Italian Socialist Party. 'Today we say: It is necessary to assassinate the Party in order to save Socialism.'[9]

Mussolini himself had gone to Rome to take part in another interventionist demonstration there on 11 April. As he began to speak, the police charged. He was struck by a police baton, and arrested, but he was released a few hours later.[10]

The interventionist campaign intensified in May. On 5 May, the fifty-fifth anniversary of the expedition of Garibaldi and the Thousand from Quarto near Genoa to liberate Sicily, a monument to the Thousand was to be unveiled at Quarto. The interventionists turned it into a great demonstration for war. The survivors of the Thousand came, with Ricciotti Garibaldi hobbling on two sticks, and his son Peppino, who had returned from the front in France to help the interventionist campaign. The principal speaker at Quarto was the poet and novelist Gabriele D'Annunzio, who had placed his reputation and his fiery oratory at the disposal of the interventionists.[11]

The Socialists and Giolitti's Liberals, who opposed intervention, could not swim successfully against this tide. On May Day the Socialist deputy, Nino Mazzoni, came to Milan to address a meeting, and spoke about his solidarity with the German and Austrian Socialists. In an article in *Il Popolo d'Italia* on 3 May entitled 'A Disciple of Radetzky' – the Austrian Commander-in-Chief in Italy in 1848 – Mussolini wrote that Mazzoni, speaking in Milan, the 'city of the Five Days' (a reference to the rising in Milan on 19–23 March 1848), had 'dared to make an impudent and brazen apology for Austria and Germany'.[12]

On 11 May Mussolini addressed a great interventionist demonstration in Milan. Speaking from the window of the *Popolo d'Italia* office, he said that if Italy did not wage war on her frontiers, there would be civil war inside the country, and that meant revolution. Three days later the interventionists in Rome, after listening to an inspiring speech by D'Annunzio, tried to storm the Chamber of Deputies at the Palazzo di Montecitorio, but were driven back by police reinforcements after a violent confrontation.[13]

The interventionists did not know that their efforts were unnecessary. Salandra's government had been negotiating with both the Allies and the Austrians. Too late the Austrian government followed the Germans' advice and offered to cede the Trentino to Italy; but Salandra could get a much better offer from the Allies, and on 26 April 1915 signed the secret Treaty of London. Britain and France agreed that if Italy came into the war on their side, they would give Italy, after they had won the war, not only the Trentino but also Trieste, Fiume and the neighbouring districts with a population of 100,000 Slavs; Rhodes and the Dodecanese Islands, which belonged to Turkey but whose population was almost entirely Greek; and Jubaland in British East Africa (later called Kenya) which would be added to Italian Somaliland. At the special request of the Italian government, the terms of the treaty were kept secret from their gallant Serbian allies, who had been encouraged to hope that they would be given the territories in the Austrian Empire which had Slav populations. The problems involved in promising the same territory to two different allies were exacerbated when Greece came into the war on the Allied side, and hoped that she would be granted the Greek-speaking Dodecanese. Later in the war the British government implicitly promised to give the Turkish province of Palestine to both the Arabs and the Jews.

On 23 May 1915 the Italian government ordered general mobilization, and declared war on Austria next day. War with Germany, Turkey and Bulgaria followed in due course. On 23 May Mussolini wrote in *Il Popolo d'Italia*: 'From today there are only Italians . . . All Italians are united in a bloc of steel . . . General Cadorna has unsheathed the sword and will advance to Vienna. *Viva l'Italia!*'[14]

◆

# CHAPTER 9

# Corporal Mussolini

ENERAL Count Luigi Cadorna, who had first joined the army in 1866, was Commander-in-Chief of the Italian forces. He decided to remain on the defensive in the mountainous country of the Trentino, but to launch an immediate offensive on the front on the River Isonzo in the territory to the north of Trieste, for he knew that the Austrians had few troops there, having sent most of their manpower to fight the Russians on the Eastern Front. Fierce fighting took place in very bad weather in June 1915, and the Italians advanced through the pouring rain and captured a number of strong-points; but they suffered heavy casualties. In August Cadorna launched a second offensive on the Isonzo front; but though he outnumbered the Austrians, he advanced very slowly, and again with high casualties.

The Socialists continued to oppose the war. Some of their right-wing leaders did so a little half-heartedly; but the zealous internationalists, like Angelica Balabanoff, redoubled their attacks on the imperialist war and re-emphasized their solidarity with their Socialist comrades in enemy countries. They denounced Mussolini as a hypocrite for not immediately volunteering for the army, and for sitting in the *Popolo d'Italia* offices in Milan while thousands of Italian soldiers were dying on the Isonzo front. He said that he had volunteered at once, but had been told by the military authorities to wait until his class was called up. This is very likely, for the army would have found it difficult to absorb immediately all the nation's manpower. His friend Filippo Corridoni had already joined the army, and had taken part in the fighting on the Isonzo in the summer campaign.

Mussolini did not have long to wait, for he was told to report to the army barracks in Milan on 31 August 1915. He joined the 11th

Regiment of the Bersaglieri, leaving his assistants at the *Popolo d'Italia* to carry on the paper in his absence. Two days later he left for Brescia, and reached the front line at Udine on 17 September. The captain of his battalion, who was a reader of *Il Popolo d'Italia*, offered to appoint him as editor of the regimental newspaper at Udine; but Mussolini wished to fight the Austrians in the front line.[1]

He was almost immediately promoted to the rank of corporal, and carried out the ordinary duties of an NCO on active service. He was popular with his comrades in the army. In 1945 a man in Milan told the British historian Christopher Hibbert that he too had been a corporal in Mussolini's battalion, and that although Mussolini was a show-off and talked too much, he was 'a nice chap'.[2]

He occasionally wrote an article for *Il Popolo d'Italia*, and kept a war diary which was obviously written for publication and was serialized in fifteen instalments in *Il Popolo d'Italia* between 28 December 1915 and 15 February 1917. It did not contain many references to military operations, perhaps in order to satisfy the censor, and avoided political controversy; but there was a great deal about the hardships endured by the soldiers in the front line during the cold winters and the fighting in the snow on the plateau of the Carso behind the town of Gorizia. He also wrote letters from the front to his sister Edvige, who published many of them more than forty years later.[3]

In the middle of October 1915 Cadorna launched another offensive, and the third and fourth battles of the Isonzo continued, with a few days' respite, for seven weeks. But the Austrians, though still outnumbered, had consolidated their position, and the Italians had failed to reach any of their objectives when the attack was finally called off on 5 December. The casualties, like those on the Western and Russian fronts, were very high, far heavier than had been known in earlier wars. In 1859 all Europe had been shocked at the number of killed and wounded at the Battle of Solferino, where the combined French, Italian and Austrian casualties had been as high as 40,000. In the Battles of the Isonzo from October to December 1915 the Italians lost 113,000 men and the Austrians 90,000.

On 23 October Corridoni was killed in action on the Isonzo front. Margherita Sarfatti told a story about this which became part of Fascist mythology. She wrote that one day a Socialist soldier, who had been unwillingly conscripted into the army, came up to Mussolini and asked him: 'Are you Mussolini?' When Mussolini said that he was, the Socialist soldier said: 'Well, I have a nice piece of news for you. Corridoni has been killed, and serves him right.' The soldier then proceeded to curse Corridoni as one of the men responsible for dragging Italy into the war. Sarfatti then described how Mussolini had leapt to his feet and pointed his rifle at 'this brute', when a sergeant came up and asked: 'What are you doing, Corporal?' Mussolini, 'sadly, with death in his heart, dropping his rifle, went on his way'.[4]

Like so many of Sarfatti's other stories, this is probably untrue, though Mussolini did not wish to deny it when she published it in 1925. It is difficult to reconcile it with Mussolini's *War Diary*, where he did not mention the incident, but wrote that on 1 November 1915 'Lieutenant-Colonel Cassola told me in passing a sad piece of news, the death of Corridoni'. Next day he added in his diary for 2 November: 'Corridoni has been killed on the battlefield. Honour, honour to him!'[5]

During the last weeks of the offensive, Mussolini received a letter from Ida Dalser telling him that on 11 November, in the maternity hospital in Milan, she had given birth to his son, whom she had named Benito Albino. Soon afterwards Mussolini fell ill with paratyphoid, and on 24 November he was sent to the military hospital at Cividale. While he was there, the King visited the hospital, and met Mussolini for the first time. When Mussolini was better, he was sent for convalescence to Treviglio near Milan, and then given a month's leave.

The news of the birth of Ida's baby seems to have had the effect of increasing his attachment to Rachele. Although his relationship with Ida must have been more than a passing affair, he had never intended that she should supplant Rachele; and it was probably in order to safeguard Rachele's position against Ida that he now decided to marry her. As soon as he was granted leave, he went to Forlì, and he and Rachele were married in a civil ceremony on 16 December. Nine months later, on 21 September 1916, their second child was born. This time it was a boy, whom they called Vittorio.

From Forlì Mussolini went to Milan to see Ida and her baby. He was delighted to see his son. He arranged for Ida to stay in the Hotel Gran Bretagna in Milan, and wrote in the hotel register that she was his wife.[6]

During his stay in Milan he wrote a number of articles for *Il Popolo d'Italia* denouncing defeatism. He quoted with approval the phrase that was being used to bolster morale in France: '*Gémir c'est trahir*' (to groan is treason).[7]

He made financial provision for Ida to enable her to maintain herself and the baby, and then rejoined his unit. In the spring of 1916 the fighting started again when Cadorna launched another offensive on the Isonzo front which was designed to prevent the Austrians from sending reinforcements to the Germans at Verdun on the Western Front. In May the Austrians launched a counter-offensive in the Trentino, and on the Isonzo the fighting continued throughout the summer. Mussolini was a member of a reconnaissance party that was sent to skirmish with the Austrians on 15–17 July, and he was slightly wounded by shrapnel; but he wrote to Edvige not to worry, as he was not seriously hurt. He warned her not to have any illusions that the war would soon be over, for if it was to end in victory it was certain to continue throughout the winter and for the whole of 1917.[8]

He received some worrying news from Milan. Ida Dalser had begun proceedings against him in the courts for alimony, claiming that the financial settlement that he had made in her favour was insufficient. She stated that she was his wife, and to prove it referred to the entry that he had written in the register of the Hotel Gran Bretagna, though she could not produce any marriage certificate. This greatly disturbed Mussolini. The court made no ruling as to whether Ida was Mussolini's lawful wife, but ordered him to pay an additional sum for her maintenance. His love for her turned sour, and he ended his relationship with her. She would not accept this. She went to Rachele's house and made a scene, insisting that she, and not Rachele, was Mussolini's lawful wife.[9]

He received other disturbing news in July. His friend Cesare Battisti, with whom he had collaborated in Trent in 1909, had escaped from Austrian territory before the outbreak of war, and had volunteered for the Italian Army. Mussolini now heard that Battisti had been taken prisoner by the Austrians, who had adopted the attitude that, as a native of the Trentino, he was an Austrian subject who had deserted to the enemy. He was convicted of high treason, and hanged. Mussolini wrote an article in *Il Popolo d'Italia* expressing the universal execration aroused against 'the great criminal of Vienna' (Franz Joseph) and promising that those responsible would be forced by harsh punishment to expiate their crime. The army must be given guns, more guns, because victory was the best way to honour this most virtuous martyr for the Italian cause.[10]

On 4 August 1916 the army on the Isonzo front, which had been placed by Cadorna under the command of the King's cousin, the Duke of Aosta, launched another offensive aimed at capturing Gorizia. After fierce fighting, the Italians entered Gorizia on 9 August. It was hailed throughout Italy as a great victory; but after this initial success the offensive petered out, though fighting on the Carso plateau continued till the middle of November. Again the casualties were very heavy. In all the campaigns of 1916 the Italians lost 405,000 men killed and wounded, and 78,000 taken prisoner. The Austrians lost 200,000 killed and wounded, and 60,000 taken prisoner.

After the sixth Battle of the Isonzo Mussolini was promoted to the rank of *caporalmaggiore*. The equivalent rank in the British Army is lance-sergeant. This explains the confusion that has arisen in the minds of British biographers and their readers as to whether the highest rank that Mussolini attained during the First World War was corporal or sergeant.

It was during the cold, damp weather and the military inactivity of the winter that on 22 February 1917 Mussolini and some soldiers in his unit were testing out a gun on the Isonzo front. At about 1 p.m., after a number of rounds had been fired, Mussolini warned the lieutenant in charge that the gun was getting overheated. The lieutenant said that as there was only one more shell to be fired, the gun would stand one more round; but when it was fired the gun exploded. Mussolini wrote in his *War Diary* that two men were killed and five wounded, though his biographers put the casualties higher, and say that five were killed and many wounded.[11] Mussolini was severely wounded; several shell splinters were lodged in his body, his left thigh suffering the most serious injuries, with a broken bone.

He was carried, in great pain, to the field dressing station and taken from there in an armoured car to Camp Hospital No. 46 at Ronchi, where he was operated on to remove the shell splinters.[12] His biographers have stated that he refused to accept an anaesthetic, and he himself confirmed this to Emil Ludwig in 1932. When Ludwig asked him why he had refused the chloroform, he said it was because he wanted to keep an eye on the doctors; but it is more likely to have been because he wished to demonstrate his heroism to himself and to those who watched him. The story may well be true, though it is a little surprising that the medical officer did not order Corporal Mussolini to submit to the chloroform.

After two days, though he was not well enough to write himself, he was able to dictate a letter to Rachele telling her that he had been wounded but that she was not to worry. She went at once to Ronchi, and was allowed to see him. According to a story in a newspaper article that was published in later years, the King visited the hospital on 7 March. 'How are you?' asked the King. 'Not too well, Your Majesty,' replied Mussolini.[13] If there is any truth in this story, Mussolini took good care not to mention it in his *War Diary* – not surprisingly, in view of his attitude to the monarchy and to 'Victor Savoy' in 1917.

He made a good recovery, but was still seriously ill on 18 March, when the Austrian artillery shelled the hospital. Mussolini and the Italians believed that the Austrians were deliberately targeting the hospital, which was a flagrant breach of the laws of war, as the hospital was clearly marked with a red cross. The hospital authorities, believing that the shelling was deliberate and would shortly be resumed, evacuated all the patients to another hospital; but Mussolini was too ill to be moved. He wrote in his *War Diary* that he remained alone with two doctors, the chaplain, and the nurses in the hospital at Ronchi; he told Emil Ludwig that he was one of only three patients who stayed there. It seems strange that if it had been possible to bring him to Ronchi in an armoured car immediately after he had been wounded, he could not be moved twenty-four days later when his condition had certainly begun to improve; but perhaps there was no suitable transport available, and there is no reason to doubt the truth of his statement in the last entry in his *War Diary*.

Mussolini was still walking on crutches when he hobbled into the office of *Il Popolo d'Italia* in Milan on 15 June 1917, having been discharged from the army;[14] but he was soon able to dispense with the crutches and resume his normal physical and mental activity. He was now an ex-serviceman who had shed his blood for his country, a war hero whom no one could accuse of hypocritically evading military service as he settled down in civilian life and launched a press campaign for a continuation of the war till victory had been won, for more sacrifices, and for the elimination of defeatism and pacifism.

CHAPTER 10

———— ◆ ————

# The Fascio di Combattimento

W HILE Mussolini was in hospital the Russian Revolution of March 1917 overthrew Tsarism and converted Russia into a constitutional and democratic republic. The liberals in the Allied countries were pleased that they no longer had to bear the moral burden of an alliance with Tsarist Russia. Mussolini's sister Edvige expressed a widespread feeling when she wrote of her joy that in their progressive war 'Liberal England, Jacobin France, and Risorgimento Italy' were no longer allied to the Tsar's Cossacks and the regime of the deportations to Siberia.[1] Within a month of the Russian Revolution, the United States of America had entered the war on the side of the Allies, thus completing the democratization of the Allied cause.

The German Kaiser had already realized that he was losing the war, chiefly because of the effectiveness of the Allied blockade, and in December 1916 he made overtures to the Allies for a negotiated peace. The Allied governments refused to negotiate; with the support of liberal opinion from David Lloyd George and Georges Clemenceau to Masaryk and President Woodrow Wilson in the United States, they proclaimed that this must not be just another nineteenth-century war, to be ended by a peace that was followed by another war a few years later. It must be a 'war to end war', a war 'to make the world safe for democracy', a war to grant the right of self-determination to oppressed subject peoples in central Europe.

On 3 August 1917 Mussolini published an article in *Il Popolo d'Italia* with the title '*Delenda Austria*', in imitation of the slogan issued more than two thousand years before in ancient Rome by Cato, '*Delenda est Cartago*' (Carthage must be destroyed). He demanded that when the war had been won, the Austrian Empire must be broken up, and freedom and independence granted to the peoples of Bohemia, Transylvania, Italy and Bosnia.[2] He repeated the slogan 'Delanda Austria' on several occasions during the next year.

Meanwhile the German government was giving every encouragement to the anti-war Socialist internationalists everywhere except in Germany. They gave facilities to Lenin to return from Switzerland to Russia through Germany on the so-called 'sealed train', accompanied by a small party of anti-war Socialists which included Angelica Balabanoff. When he reached Petrograd, Lenin launched a propaganda campaign against the new liberal government, offering the people bread for the hungry workers in the towns, land to the peasants on the estates of the great landowners, and peace to the soldiers at the front. It was the offer of peace which was most effective. The Russian Army had suffered heavy losses, and the soldiers deserted in large numbers and walked home to their villages, in some cases after shooting their officers. In June 1917 the Socialist government of Alexander Kerensky ordered an offensive against the Germans at the request of their Western allies; but it was a costly failure, and the desertions from the army increased.

On the Isonzo front Cadorna launched another offensive in June. Again, after an initial success, it petered out, the Italians losing 24,000 men killed and wounded and 2,000 prisoners. The Italian Socialists intensified their opposition to the war, though their propaganda in *Avanti!* and their other newspapers was restricted by the censorship. In the Chamber of Deputies Treves issued the call 'No one in the trenches next winter!' which was taken up as a slogan by the Socialists.

Pope Benedict XV, from the outbreak of war, had emphasized that it was the duty of the Catholic Church to pursue a strict neutrality between the two belligerent blocs. In August 1917 he issued an appeal to both sides to make peace, hinting that Austria might well agree to cede Italian territory to Italy, and stating that Catholics in the armies of both the Allies and the Central Powers could not be blamed for doing their duty.

In *Il Popolo d'Italia*, Mussolini campaigned against a premature negotiated peace and for a continuation of the war until complete victory had been won. He demanded a more vigorous prosecution of the war, as the brave soldiers at the front were being let down by the weak and inefficient government. He denounced the attitude of Treves and the Pope. He demanded the internment of all enemy aliens and the confiscation of their property, which should be used to increase the pensions of the disabled war veterans and the widows and orphans of the fallen. He demanded that the government take firm action to suppress bureaucratic inefficiency, war profiteering, and the treasonable activities of the Socialists and the elements in the Vatican who opposed the war. A similar campaign was being waged in the popular press by Clemenceau in France and in Britain, in a cruder and more vulgar manner, by Horatio Bottomley and by Lord Northcliffe's journalists in the *Daily Mail* and his other newspapers.

Under pressure from Mussolini and his supporters the government ordered the internment of all enemy aliens. This had one advantageous result from Mussolini's point of view: Ida Dalser, as an inhabitant of the Trentino, was an Austrian subject, and she was arrested and interned at Caserta,[3] which temporarily put an end to her harassment of Mussolini. But there is no evidence to support the allegation, which was made by Mussolini's enemies, that he himself arranged for the authorities to intern Ida, or that he had this ulterior motive in mind when he demanded in *Il Popolo d'Italia* that enemy aliens should be interned.

Mussolini was now involved in a love affair with Margherita Sarfatti, who worked with him at *Il Popolo d'Italia*. Roberto Sarfatti, her son by her husband, had joined the army, and was killed in action in February 1918. Mussolini wrote a glowing tribute to him in *Il Popolo d'Italia*.[4]

In April 1917 the Socialists in the neutral countries of Sweden and Holland invited the Socialist parties in all the belligerent countries to send delegates to an international Socialist conference in Stockholm. The German and Austrian governments granted exit permits for their Socialists to attend; the Allied governments refused exit permits, but then the British government, under pressure from Kerensky's government in Russia, agreed to issue the exit permits. When Ramsay MacDonald, the leader of the anti-war section of the British Labour Party, attempted to sail from Aberdeen to Sweden, the secretary of the seamen's trade union, Havelock Wilson, who strongly supported the war, called on the seamen to refuse to sail if MacDonald was on board. The idea of a Socialist leader being thwarted in his political objective by a strike of trade unionists delighted the Conservatives, and the satirical journal *Punch* published its famous cartoon of a disconsolate MacDonald sitting forlornly on his baggage on the dockside, under the caption 'Hoist with his own petard'.[5] Mussolini, in *Il Popolo d'Italia*, denounced the Socialist traitors who wished to fraternize with enemy subjects in Stockholm. He was particularly delighted with the action of Havelock Wilson and the British seamen, and warmly praised it as a splendid example of the patriotism of the proletariat.[6]

In June 1917 mutinies broke out in the French Army, when the troops on the Western Front were called upon to take part in what they considered to be another pointless and costly offensive. General Robert Nivelle was replaced as Commander-in-Chief by General Philippe Pétain, who suppressed the mutinies; but with mutinies in Russia and in France, and the Pope's peace appeal, the Italian government were fearful about the morale and loyalty of their soldiers when Cadorna launched yet another offensive on the Isonzo in August. With the Russian Army disintegrating, the Austrians had transferred many troops from the Eastern to the Isonzo front. Cadorna's offensive failed again, and at the end of September the Austrians launched their counter-attack.

On 24 October, in misty autumn weather, they attacked at Caporetto, and after two days' fighting they routed the Italians. Cadorna ordered a retreat to the line of the River Piave, sixty miles to the south-west. On 28 October the Austrians entered Udine, and the Italian retreat continued; but by 9 November the Italians had safely crossed the Piave, and held the line of the river. Their losses were very heavy: 40,000 men killed and wounded and 3,500 cannons captured, with 1,700 bombards and 3,000 machine-guns. But the most serious aspect was that 280,000 men had allowed themselves to be taken prisoner, and another 350,000 had deserted and gone home. Altogether the Italians had lost nearly half their total army.[7] This was disaster and desertion on the Russian scale.

The government resigned, and Vittorio Emanuele Orlando became Prime Minister. Cadorna was dismissed, and was replaced as Commander-in-Chief by General Armando Diaz, whose subordinate commanders were General Gaetano Giardino and General Pietro Badoglio. A number of deserters, who were caught, were shot. Six French and five British divisions were sent to Italy to help stem the Austrian advance, and the Italian line held on the Piave. Repeated Austrian attacks throughout November and December failed, and the fighting ended on Christmas Day.

Throughout the Caporetto retreat, Mussolini tried to stiffen the

Italian resistance by his articles in *Il Popolo d'Italia*. On 20 November 1917 he was one of the speakers at a meeting in the Scala Theatre in Milan to welcome the French and British troops who had been sent to the Italian front. He said that when the Germans were advancing on Paris in September 1914, the people of Paris had cried out: 'No, Kaiser, you will not reach Paris!', and he would never reach it. The people of Milan would give the same warning to the German and Austrian Kaisers. They would emulate their ancestors in the twelfth century who had defied and defeated the German Emperor Frederick Barbarossa. They were prepared to die, but were not prepared to be slaves.[8]

Mussolini continued his propaganda line in his speeches at public meetings and every day in *Il Popolo d'Italia*. He condemned the shooting of the deserters. It was not the soldiers who had cracked under the strain who should be blamed for the disaster of Caporetto, but the government, the general staff, the corrupt war profiteers, and the Socialist traitors who were tolerated by the government.[9]

Among the British troops who had been sent to the Italian front was an officer on the staff of Military Intelligence, Lieutenant-Colonel Samuel Hoare, who seventeen years later became British Foreign Secretary. He was informed by one of his junior officers that it might be worth while contacting and financing a Milanese journalist named Benito Mussolini. Hoare telegraphed to Sir George Macdonagh, the Director of Military Intelligence in London, who authorized him to subsidize Mussolini's activities. In 1954 Hoare (now Lord Templewood) wrote about it in his autobiography. '"Leave it to me" was the answer that Mussolini sent back through my intermediary. "I will mobilise the *mutilati* in Milan, and they will break the heads of any pacifists who try to hold anti-war meetings in the streets." He was true to his word, the Fasci . . . made short work of the Milanese pacifists.'[10]

At the most critical moment of the retreat to the Piave, the Bolsheviks seized power in Russia on 7 November. Next day Leon Trotsky, whom Lenin had appointed as his Commissar for Foreign Affairs, broadcast an appeal to all the belligerent governments to enter into peace negotiations. The German and Austrian governments accepted, but the Allied governments indignantly rejected his invitation. In the eyes of the Allies, Lenin and Trotsky now joined the Pope and the other supporters of a negotiated peace, and were their enemies and German agents.

From the very beginning the politicians and journalists in the Allied countries noticed that a high proportion of the Bolshevik leaders were Jews, and they began referring to the 'Bolshevik Jews' who were agents of the German Kaiser and of Field Marshal Paul von Hindenburg, the Commander-in-Chief of the German Army. Mussolini joined in this denunciation of the Bolsheviks as Jewish agents of the Germans. On 11 November 1917, four days after the Bolsheviks seized power, he wrote in *Il Popolo d'Italia* that 'Jewish-German Bolshevism' had carried through the revolution as a result of an unholy alliance between the German High Command and the synagogue. There was no need for Hindenburg to march on Petrograd because he had already captured it by means of the Bolshevik leaders, whose true names betrayed their racial origin – Ceorbaum (Lenin), Apfelbaum (Zinoviev), Rosenfeld (Kamenev) and Bronstein (Trotsky).[11] He was wrong about Ceorbaum and Apfelbaum, and never repeated the mistake; after this one lapse, he always referred to Lenin, correctly, as 'Uljanov'. But he was right about Rosenfeld and Bronstein, and in his belief that Grigorii Zinoviev, Lev Kamenev, Trotsky and a large proportion of the Bolshevik leaders were Jews.

But he did not allow this reference to the Jewish origin of the Bolshevik leaders to deflect him from his main line of attack, that the Bolsheviks were German agents. Three weeks later he wrote an article, 'The Peace of Infamy', denouncing the idea of a negotiated peace and Trotsky's call for an end to the war. 'Lenin's government is German. We must always remember that Ulyanov returned to Russia through Germany . . . The government of Petrograd is a creation of Germany.'[12] His criticisms increased when Lenin's government signed the Treaty of Brest-Litovsk with Germany and withdrew from the war. He called it the triumph of 'Hindenburg and Lenin'.[13]

During the eventful days of early November 1917, Georges Clemenceau came to power in France. His political career, like Mussolini's, had consisted in moving from the extreme Left to the extreme Right; and after campaigning in his censored newspaper for three years for a more vigorous prosecution of the war and against the weakness and incompetence of successive French governments, he himself became Prime Minister at the age of seventy-six. Mussolini welcomed his appointment; he wrote that Clemenceau had many faults, but, despite his age, he was full of vigour and would vigorously wage war; he would not pursue a democratic or aristocratic policy, not a *sans-culotte* war or a clerical war, but simply war – 'war *tout court*'.[14]

In January 1918 Clemenceau ordered the arrest of Louis Malvy, who had recently been Minister of the Interior, and of Joseph Caillaux, a former Prime Minister, on charges of high treason. Malvy was accused of having failed to suppress the activities of a German spy ring that had formed around the anarchist newspaper *Le Bonnet Rouge*, and Caillaux of having plotted with German agents abroad to conclude a negotiated peace. The German spies connected with *Le Bonnet Rouge* were tried by court martial, and shot. Malvy was convicted on a lesser charge and banished from France, and Caillaux was held in prison without trial for more than two years till he was tried and convicted, but released, in 1920.

Mussolini, in *Il Popolo d'Italia*, applauded Clemenceau's actions in an article entitled '*Exécuté!*',[15] and urged the Italian government to follow his example in dealing with traitors and those who favoured a negotiated peace. His agitation, and Clemenceau's example, had some effect. At the end of January Lazzari and Bombacci, the secretary and vice-secretary of the Socialist Party, were arrested and charged with defeatist activity, and in May Serrati was arrested. In October 1914 Rocca had accused Mussolini of being under Lazzari's influence, and Bombacci had been Mussolini's friend when they were both schoolmasters at Gualtieri in 1902; but in 1918 Mussolini warmly welcomed their arrest.[16]

But Mussolini was not satisfied with the actions of the government, and called for the appointment of a dictator. War could not be waged effectively, and won, democratically; if democracy should be the rule, war was the great exception. Democracy in wartime, taken to its logical conclusion, had led to the establishment of soviets in the Russian Army and the complete collapse of discipline, the disintegration of the army, and the shameful peace. The ancient Romans had defended their democracy in times of danger by appointing a dictator to rule during the emergency; and were not Clemenceau in France, Lloyd George in England, and Wilson in the United States in effect democratic dictators? Dictatorship was the means to achieve the democratic end.[17]

In January 1918 Wilson issued his Fourteen Points which should serve as conditions of peace. They included the formation of a League of Nations and the self-determination of peoples, who were to choose by a free vote in a plebiscite the country to which they wished to belong. Mussolini denounced the idea of a plebiscite. No plebiscite was necessary to show that the Trentino, Trieste, Istria and Dalmatia should belong to Italy; the Italian people had already voted for this with their blood. The martyrdom of Cesare Battisti in the Trentino, of Guglielmo Oberdan in Trieste, of Nazario Sauro in Istria, and of Francesco Rismondi in Dalmatia were a sufficient plebiscite.[18]

The chief targets of Mussolini's attacks were the pacifists – in France the supporters of the international Socialist anti-war conference at Kienthal; in Britain the Labour Party leader, Ramsay MacDonald, the anti-war Liberal MP, Joseph King, and Lord Lansdowne,[19] who had written a letter to *The Times* in favour of a negotiated peace; in Russia Trotsky, with his appeal over the radio to all governments to attend a peace conference; in Italy Lazzari and the other Socialist leaders, and Pope Benedict XV. In January 1918 Mussolini received a letter from a soldier at the front who told him that he and his comrades felt that the Pope was against Italy. In *Il Popolo d'Italia* of 15 March Mussolini ended his article with the same words: 'The Pope is against Italy'; but the censor cut out this sentence.[20]

On 3 March 1918 Mussolini addressed a meeting in Parma of the Association of Disabled and Wounded Ex-Servicemen and War Widows. He said that no one in his senses wished to continue the war for a day longer than was necessary; but it must continue until it could be ended by a victorious peace, not by a shameful negotiated peace. No one believed this more strongly than the soldiers at the front and the widows of the fallen, for they knew that if there was a premature negotiated peace their sufferings, and the deaths of their loved ones, would have been in vain.

He said that there were four kinds of pacifists. First, those misguided humanitarians who wished at all costs to avoid bloodshed today, without realizing that this would lead to far greater bloodshed tomorrow; secondly, those who were cowards; thirdly, the capitalists, who were against war because it interfered with the profits they made in international trade; and fourthly, the traitors and German agents. He believed that the Socialists were in this fourth category.[21] On 24 November 1914, when he was expelled from the Socialist Party, he had declared that, though they expelled him, he would never abandon socialism; on 2 March 1918 he wrote in *Il Popolo d'Italia*: 'International Socialism is a German weapon.'[22]

In June 1918 the Austrians launched an offensive against the Italian forces on the Piave. The Italian line held, and after a week's fierce fighting the Austrians abandoned the attack. They had lost 96,000 men killed and wounded; the Italians lost over 40,000.

On 7 August Mussolini wrote that he thought that the war was certain to continue throughout the next winter;[23] but next day the Allies began their final victorious offensive on the Western Front; and on 24 October Diaz launched an attack along the Piave. After initially meeting stiff Austrian resistance, the Italians captured the town of Vittorio Veneto on 29 October, and the next day the Austrian morale broke. The Austrian retreat turned into a headlong rout; nearly 500,000 Austrian soldiers surrendered to the Italians; and on 3 November the Austrians asked for an armistice, which was signed next day. On 9 November revolution broke out in Germany, and the Kaiser fled to Holland; and on 11 November the war ended on the Western Front with the complete surrender of the Germans. In the three and a half years of war the Italians had lost more than 600,000 killed and over 1,000,000 seriously wounded, including 220,000 permanently disabled.

Mussolini and all the patriotic Italians who had supported the war hailed the glorious victory of Vittorio Veneto. Mussolini called it the greatest of all the victories of all the armies that had fought in the war.[24] But the peace conference that opened in January 1919 at Versailles was less satisfactory for Italy. The Allies, departing from all previous precedents, informed the Germans that they would not be allowed to attend the peace conference but that when the Allies at the conference had decided on the peace terms the Germans would be notified and would be required to accept them without discussion. The smaller Allied nations, though they nominally attended the conference, found themselves largely excluded from the decision-making process, which was delegated to the four leading Allied powers – France, Britain, the United States and Italy. The Italian Prime Minister, Orlando, was soon informed that he was very much the junior member of the Big Four, and was expected to agree with everything laid down by Clemenceau, Lloyd George and Wilson.

The peace treaty that was signed at Versailles on 28 June 1919 was labelled a 'Diktat' by the Germans; and it was almost as much a Diktat from the Italian point of view. The Italians were given the Trentino and the city of Trieste, but not Fiume, not the rest of Istria, not Dalmatia, not the international recognition of their zone of influence in Albania, not the Dodecanese Islands; and the British were in no hurry to fulfil the terms of the Treaty of London of 1915 and cede them Jubaland in East Africa. The 600,000 Italian dead had given their lives only to gain Trieste and the Trentino, which Austria had been prepared to cede to Italy in 1915 if Italy remained neutral.

While the Socialists pointed out that 600,000 Italian lives had been lost in vain in the war that they had always opposed, Mussolini denounced Orlando for betraying Italy. He also denounced the Socialists and their internationalism, for he had now reached the point where he regarded any form of Socialist international solidarity as a crime against Italy. During the war, great suffering and food shortages had been caused in Germany, Austria and Hungary as a result of the blockade that was so effectively enforced by the British Navy; and the Allies continued to enforce the blockade after the armistice was signed in November 1918, not intending to lift it until the Germans had finally accepted the peace terms that were being discussed at Versailles. The continuation of the blockade was strongly criticized by the Socialists and by the humanitarian organizations in the Allied countries, and the volume of protest persuaded the Allied governments to lift the blockade in March 1919.[25]

Humanitarian relief organizations rushed food to the populations of Germany, Austria and Hungary. The Italian Socialists invited the hungry children of Vienna to come to Italy, where they would be cared for and fed by Italian families. Mussolini strongly criticized the Italian Socialists for this 'sickly internationalism', this 'provoking sentimentality'.[26] Why did they not raise money and offer food and other help, not to the children of enemy Austrians, but to Italian children, to the orphans of the Italian soldiers who had fallen during the war, killed by the Austrians whose children were now being fed by the Socialists?

As it became clear that in post-war Italy the hostility between the republican nationalists and the Socialist internationalists would continue and increase, Mussolini decided to form the various Fascist groups, which had been operating since the interventionist campaign of 1914–15, into a national organization. The inaugural meeting of the Fasci di Combattimento was held in the offices of the Circolo dell'Alleanza Industriale e Commerciale in the Piazza San Sepolcro in Milan on 23 March 1919. Ferruccio Vecchi presided at the meeting. It was not very well attended, but those present cheered the speeches of Mussolini and Michele Bianchi, and adopted the programme that Mussolini had drawn up for the new organization.[27]

The programme demanded votes for all Italians over the age of eighteen without any property qualification, including women. In Britain, the vote had been granted in 1918 to women at the age of thirty – men were entitled to vote at twenty-one – but in most countries of Europe and the world women were not entitled to vote. The programme demanded a system of election by proportional representation. The qualifying age for deputies in the Chamber, which had hitherto been thirty-one, should be lowered to twenty-five. The Senate (the upper house) was to be abolished. The deputies who were elected at the next general election were to form a National Assembly that was to remain in session for three years and promulgate a new constitution for Italy. There must be a maximum eight-hour working day for all Italian workers. Fiume and Dalmatia should be given to Italy.

The meeting passed a resolution that declared their admiration for the sons of Italy who had fallen in the fight for the greatness of Italy and the freedom of the world, and their support for the League of Nations.[28] A few years later, Mussolini was expressing his contempt for the League of Nations; but the statement in support of the League was probably inserted because of the great popularity in Italy of President Wilson, the originator of the idea of a League of Nations.

The first Fascio, or local branch of the organization, was immediately formed in Milan, and the second in Genoa. During the next eight days, before the end of March, branches had been formed in six other cities, and by the end of August the Fascists had sixty-seven branches, one in nearly all the major Italian towns. But by 31 December 1919 many of these branches had been wound up, and there were only thirty-one Fascist branches with a total membership of 870.[29] How could this new Fascist organization hope to compete against the established political parties – the Conservative and Liberal parties of Salandra, Orlando and Giolitti, the Catholic People's Party, and the Socialist Party, which was growing in strength as the people became disillusioned with the war and resentful about the high cost of living, and as news came in of the growth of Bolshevik power and influence in Russia and in central Europe?

# CHAPTER 11

◆

# The Bolshevik Menace

THE Italian Socialists were winning support in 1919 and their
trade unions were growing in strength and influence; but they
were hated by the Mazzinian republicans who had supported
the war and by many ex-servicemen. The Socialists pointed out that
Italy had gained practically nothing from the war that they could
not have obtained from Austria by remaining neutral. They told the
ex-servicemen that they had been dupes of the capitalists who had
sent them to risk their lives in the trenches, and 600,000 of their
comrades to their deaths, in an unjust imperialist war which had
been fought, not for Italy, but solely in the interests of the Italian
bourgeoisie. Mussolini and the Fascists and the republicans told the
ex-servicemen that they were heroes who had fought and shed their
blood for Italy and had won the glorious victory of Vittorio Veneto
and the war, despite the defeatist agitation of the Socialist traitors,
the agents of Germany and Austria. The Fascist message went down
better than the Socialist message with the ex-servicemen. Men do
not like to be told that they have been duped; they prefer to be
praised as heroes.

As the ex-servicemen hated and vilified the Socialists, the Socialists
began to hate and vilify the ex-servicemen. Socialist workers attacked
ex-servicemen in the streets, and occasionally murdered them.
There was particular trouble on the railways, for the railway men's
trade unions were strong and militant. Railway drivers and
crews sometimes refused to run trains if army officers or Catholic
priests were among the passengers; they would stop the train and
refuse to go any further till the army officer and the priest left the
train.

There were many strikes. The Socialist trade unions repeatedly
called strikes – railway strikes, tram strikes, postal strikes, strikes

in the public services, strikes in industry. The strikes were usually accompanied by violence. The Socialists beat up workers who refused to join the strike and who crossed the picket lines to work as black-legs. Sometimes they killed them.

The ex-servicemen formed themselves into bands to fight the Socialists. They became known as the *arditi* and the *squadristi*. They claimed to be defending themselves against Socialist violence, and attacking the Socialists in retaliation for the Socialist attacks on blacklegs and ex-servicemen; but the *arditi* and Mussolini's Fascist squads gave back more than they had received, and their violence usually exceeded the Socialist violence. In April 1919, in retaliation for the Socialist violence, the *arditi* burned down the offices of *Avanti!* in Milan. The action had not been officially authorized by the Fascist organization, but Ferruccio Vecchi and other Fascists took part in it.[1]

The Italian dissatisfaction with the Treaty of Versailles and the policy of Britain and France flared up when the Allies awarded the town of Fiume and the surrounding country to the newly created state of Yugoslavia and not to Italy. D'Annunzio raised a band of volunteers and seized Fiume, ignoring the orders of the Italian government, and the demands of Britain and France, to evacuate the town and hand it over to the Yugoslavs. Mussolini, in *Il Popolo d'Italia*, applauded D'Annunzio's patriotic enterprise in seizing Fiume, and raised money to finance D'Annunzio.[2]

Many of Mussolini's supporters went to Fiume to join D'Annunzio; but Mussolini himself thought that he could do more for the Italian cause by remaining in the *Popolo d'Italia* office in Milan. He worked there every day with Margherita Sarfatti and his other assistants. He practised fencing in the courtyard of the office. This was not only good exercise, but also made him able to fight duels with politicians whom he had insulted in *Il Popolo d'Italia*. He took flying lessons, and obtained his air pilot's certificate after he had been involved in an accident in his aircraft which put him on crutches for a few weeks.

He stored arms, including bombs, in the *Popolo d'Italia* office, so that they could be used by the Fascist *squadristi* in their encounters with the Socialists. The bombs were hidden in bookcases, but were sometimes left lying on the tables in the room where the sub-editors worked. Margherita Sarfatti became alarmed on one occasion when Mussolini, who still occasionally smoked, absent-mindedly put his lighted cigarette on top of a bomb. When she pointed out to him what he had done, they both laughed.[3]


A general election took place in Italy on 16 November 1919. Mussolini was one of the Fascist candidates in Milan. Another was the famous conductor Arturo Toscanini, who had been persuaded by Mussolini to stand as a Fascist. Mussolini declared in his election manifesto that a vote for the Fascist candidates would be a vote for national syndicalism, for a transformation of parliamentary institutions, for the creation of economic councils that would regulate the national economy, and for 'the expansion and affirmation of Italy in the world'. There were several violent incidents during the election campaign. Mussolini in *Il Popolo d'Italia* called for 'Violence against violence'.[4]

The Fascists were decisively defeated in the election. Mussolini received 4,637 votes, while the Socialist candidates received 160,000 votes. The Socialists became the largest party in the new Chamber of Deputies, with 156 seats. The Catholic People's Party won 101 seats, and the remaining seats were divided between various right-wing parties. The Fascists did not win any seats.

The Socialists celebrated their electoral victory, and were particularly pleased at the complete defeat of the Fascists. They marched through the streets of Milan that night with torches, carrying a coffin. They stopped in front of Mussolini's house and shouted out that it contained Mussolini's corpse. Mussolini was not at home. Rachele, who was in the house with the children, hid them in an upstairs room with no window, and seized a hand grenade that Mussolini kept in the house, ready to use it if the Socialists attacked. But they went away.[5]

The Socialists believed that Mussolini was politically dead. 'There is a corpse in a state of putrefaction,' wrote the editor of *Avanti!*, 'which has been fished out of the canal. We are talking about Benito Mussolini.'[6]

Two days after the general election, on 18 November, Mussolini, Ferruccio Vecchi and a number of other Fascists were arrested on the order of the Prefect of Milan; he had received a complaint from Turati, Treves and other Socialist leaders that Mussolini and the Fascists were storing arms, intending to use them either to help D'Annunzio in Fiume or to overthrow the government. The Prefect sent a telegram to the Prime Minister, Francesco Nitti, informing him that he had arrested the Fascists. Just over an hour later he received a telegram from Nitti stating that it was a very serious matter to arrest so prominent a political figure as Mussolini, and that, unless the Prefect was certain that the arrest was justified, Mussolini should be released at once. On the afternoon of 19 November Mussolini was released, having been in custody for less than twenty-four hours. Ferruccio Vecchi and the other Fascists were held for three weeks, but were released on 9 December, and no criminal proceedings were brought against any of them.[7]

Mussolini and the nationalists who supported D'Annunzio criticized the Italian government for its attitude about Fiume and for other aspects of its Balkan policy. They wanted Italy to have not only Fiume but also Dalmatia, with its Italian minority, which they thought had been promised to Italy by Britain and France during the war. They had designs on Albania. In 1916 an Italian expeditionary force had landed in Albania to fight the Austrian invaders, and they remained in occupation of the country after the war. The Albanians expected them to leave; but though the Italians withdrew from the rest of Albania, they continued to hold the port of Valona. They successfully repulsed an Albanian attack on Valona; but the Socialists in Italy condemned the Italian presence in Albania as imperialist aggression, and in June 1920 Giolitti, who had just become Prime Minister, agreed to evacuate Valona. Mussolini denounced this in *Il Popolo d'Italia* as an act of cowardice and betrayal.[8]

There was trouble at Split in Dalmatia in the summer of 1920 when the native Croatian population made several attacks on Italian settlers, culminating in the murder of an Italian naval officer. On 13 July the Fascists in Trieste burned down the Balkan Hotel, the Slav cultural centre in the city, in reprisal for the murder of the Italians in Split. The Fascists were also continuing their action against the Socialists, and eight days later burned the Rome office of *Avanti!*

In *Il Popolo d'Italia* of 23 July Mussolini justified the burning of the office of the newspaper of which he had once been editor on the grounds that the Socialist deputies in the Chamber advocated violent revolution and shouted down their political opponents. 'The burning of the Roman *Avanti!* is considered by us to be a logical and legitimate reprisal against those who preach violence every day ... What is the difference between a mob who burn a newspaper office and Socialist deputies who deprive deputies of other parties of freedom of speech?' He described the burning of the Balkan Hotel in Trieste as 'the masterpiece of Trieste Fascism'.[9]

The government and the police did not approve of these acts of violence, but made only half-hearted and ineffectual efforts to stop them. The Socialists accused the authorities of pro-Fascist bias, of taking no action against the Fascist arsonists and killers, and arresting only Socialists who killed or wounded Fascists in self-defence. The statistics bear out their allegations of police partiality to the Fascists, for more Socialists than Fascists were arrested.[10]

The Allied governments had become seriously alarmed at the spread of Bolshevism. They sent arms and small detachments of troops to help the anti-Bolshevik forces in the Russian Civil War, and imposed a blockade of Bolshevik territory in Russia which caused great hardship to the population and difficulties for Lenin's government; but the Bolsheviks survived, and defeated all the anti-Bolshevik armies in the civil war. On 4 March 1919 the Third International (the Communist International, or Comintern) was founded in Moscow. On 21 March, two days before the inaugural meeting of Mussolini's Fascist organization, the Communists seized power in Hungary. Lenin hailed the establishment of communism in Hungary as more important than the Bolshevik revolution in Russia. The Italian bourgeoisie and anti-Communists were worried, for they were conscious that Hungary was not very far from Italy.

The Allied governments overthrew the Communist regime in Hungary, encouraging Czechoslovakia and Romania to send troops to invade Hungary. The Hungarian Communists drove back the Czechs, but the Roumanians entered Budapest. The Communist leaders fled to Russia, and a right-wing dictatorship was established under Admiral Niklos Horthy, who had been Commander-in-Chief of the imperial Austrian Navy during the First World War. His government pursued a strongly anti-Semitic policy, due largely to the fact that so many of the Hungarian Communist leaders were Jews.

Angelica Balabanoff had stayed in Russia after the Bolshevik revolution, and Lenin appointed her to be one of the assistants to Zinoviev, the first secretary-general of the Comintern. Angelica did not like Zinoviev, and was shocked at the way in which he worked to discredit and ruin other Communists and Socialists with whose policies he disagreed or whom he personally disliked. She afterwards wrote that, with the exception of Mussolini, Zinoviev was the most despicable person she had ever met.[11] She was particularly indignant as she watched Zinoviev and the Comintern split the Italian Socialist Party; it divided into a pro-Bolshevik section, which became the Italian Communist Party, and the official Socialist Party of Turati and Treves.

Mussolini, in *Il Popolo d'Italia*, called on the Italian people to resist Bolshevism and its centralized tyranny. He told a meeting at Cremona on 5 September 1920 that the Fascists were not opposed to socialism except when it was used as a mask for Bolshevism, which had turned Russia into an enormous prison. A fortnight later he wrote in *Il Popolo d'Italia* that if the Socialist Party came to power in Italy, the Italians would be ruled from the Kremlin in Moscow and forced to obey the *ukase* of His Majesty Lenin I.[12]

The growth of Bolshevism had led the anti-Bolshevik politicians and journalists to revise a little their evaluation of it. It was difficult to portray the Bolsheviks simply as wartime agents of Germany when they were continuing their activities after the defeat of Germany in the war, and were concentrating on promoting revolution in Germany. The right-wing propagandists decided that the Bolsheviks were agents, not of the German High Command, but of international Jewry, and intensified their denunciations of the 'Bolshevik Jews' in every country of Europe and in America.

In Britain Winston Churchill, the Secretary of State for War, analysed the part played by Jews in the international Communist movement in an article, 'Zionism versus Bolshevism', which he wrote in February 1920. He had been impressed by the theories of Mrs Nesta Webster, who had traced the origins of the French Revolution of 1789 to the conspiracies fomented by the Illuminati,[13] a group formed in 1776 by the German Jew Adam Weishaupt. Churchill believed that there were three kinds of political conceptions among Jews. There was the 'national' Jew, who was a patriotic citizen of the country where he lived, and the Zionist Jew, who wished to create a national home for the Jews in Palestine; but as well as these two admirable kinds of Jew, there was also a third kind who was 'absolutely disruptive'. This was the 'international Jew', who from Weishaupt in the eighteenth century and Karl Marx in the nineteenth century to the international Jew of the present day – Trotsky in

Russia, Bela Kun in Hungary, Rosa Luxemburg in Germany, and Emma Goldman in the United States – were 'leaders of a world wide conspiracy for the overthrow of civilisation'. Churchill thought that when a Gentile like Chicherin was nominally the Russian Foreign Minister, it was his subordinate, the Jew Maxim Litvinov, who really controlled Bolshevik foreign policy.[14]

Mussolini, too, examined the connection between the Jews and Bolshevism, but his approach was different from Churchill's. On 4 June 1919, when the Communists were still in power in Hungary, he wrote an article on Bolshevism in *Il Popolo d'Italia*. He asked what was the nature of the Bolshevik revolution in Russia. He rejected the Communists' claim that it was the proletarian Socialist revolution, because Marx had said that the proletarian revolution, which would introduce socialism, was the next historic stage after the bourgeois revolution which had established capitalism, and a bourgeois revolution had not yet taken place in Russia.

But if the Bolshevik revolution was not the proletarian Socialist revolution, what was it? Mussolini thought that it would be incorrect to call it a German-Jewish revolution led by Jewish agents of Germany; it was a revolution instigated by international Jewry, an act of 'Jewish vengeance against Christianity'. Eighty per cent of the Russian Communist leaders were Jews, and in Budapest seventeen of the twenty-two rulers of Communist Hungary were Jews. Bolshevism was financed by the banking houses of Rothschild, Warburg, Schiss and Gugenheim, who were of the same blood as those who ruled from Petrograd to Budapest. 'Race does not betray race … Bolshevism is being defended by international plutocracy.' It was Jewish finance, not the Russian, French or Italian proletariat, who maintained Bolshevism in power. There was a danger that the Gentiles might reply to this Jewish revolution with 'a pogrom of catastrophic proportions'.[15]

Mussolini did not maintain this anti-Jewish line for long. Several wealthy Jewish businessmen were financing the Fascist Party, and they, and perhaps Margherita Sarfatti, may have urged Mussolini to abandon anti-Semitism. He may also have realized that anti-Semitism was unlikely to attract much support in Italy. There were few countries in Europe where there was so little anti-Semitism. In 1911 there were 32,825 Jews among Italy's population of 34,600,000.[16] They were nearly all Sephardic Jews, descended from the Jews who, at the end of the fifteenth century, fled from the Spanish kingdom of Naples, where the persecution of the Spanish Inquisition was much fiercer than in Rome or the other Italian states.

The Italian Jews were subjected to penal legislation until well into the nineteenth century, but it was religious, not racial, persecution. In real life, as well as in Shakespeare's *Merchant of Venice*, the Italians who spat on Shylock's Jewish gaberdine warmly welcomed his Jewish daughter Jessica when she converted from Judaism to Catholic Christianity. In the nineteenth century religious anti-Semitism was ended by the liberal Risorgimento, which swept away all the anti-Jewish laws. After 1860 only a few Jesuit and other extremists were anti-Semitic, for religious persecution of the Jews was associated with the elements who had opposed the Risorgimento, the unification of Italy, and the principles on which the new Kingdom of Italy was based.

The acquisition of Trieste after 1918 added another six thousand Ashkenazic Jews to the number of Jews in Italy; but the Jews in Trieste had become as prosperous, as assimilated and as accepted under the Austrian Empire as the Sephardic Jews in Italy, and their position did not change under Italian rule. Italy was not affected by the influx of low-class Ashkenazic Jews from Russia, Poland and eastern Europe at the end of the nineteenth, and the beginning of the twentieth, century, which fuelled racial anti-Semitism in Germany, Austria and France, and to a lesser extent in Britain.

On 19 October 1920 Mussolini wrote an article in *Il Popolo d'Italia* in which he clearly repudiated the idea that Bolshevism was a Jewish phenomenon. His article was prompted by the legislation in Hungary which deprived Jews of the right to vote in parliamentary elections, to attend high school, and to partake in the liberal professions. Mussolini wrote that this legislation was explained by the fact that in the Communist government that had governed Hungary a year before, Bela Kun was a Jew and so were five of the six leading commissars; but this anti-Semitism was unjustified, because Bolshevism was not financed or instigated by Jewish financiers. On the contrary, it had had disastrous consequences for the Jews in Russia.[17]

Mussolini sometimes wrote in *Il Popolo d'Italia* about events in other countries. He championed the cause of Sinn Fein in Ireland and the struggle for Irish independence. When the Lord Mayor of Cork,

Terence MacSwiney, went on a hunger strike in an English prison as a protest against the British government's policy of repression in Ireland, Mussolini joined in the indignant demand that MacSwiney should be released from prison which was voiced in Ireland and in many countries throughout the world. He wrote that the Italians knew very little about the movement for Irish independence, but it was a question of fundamental justice for the Irish people. 'Mac-Swiney is at death's door. Long live the Irish Republic!'[18] The British government refused to give way and the Lord Mayor of Cork remained on hunger strike till he died.

Mussolini also wrote about events in Germany, where right-wing groups, composed largely of ex-servicemen, fought alongside the regular army and the police against Communists who had tried to seize power in Berlin, Munich and other German cities. These ex-servicemen's organizations, which were usually anti-Semitic, often murdered Communists and Socialists when they took them prisoner. They murdered Karl Liebknecht, Rosa Luxemburg, Leo Jogiches and Eugen Leviné, as well as the Social Democrat Minister of Finance, Matthias Erzberger. Their attitude and actions were not very different from those of the *arditi* and Mussolini's Fascist squads in Italy; but Mussolini felt no sympathy for the German anti-Bolshevik killers. He strongly condemned them in *Il Popolo d'Italia*[19] as barbaric Germans typifying the cruel nation that had tried to enslave Europe during the war, and must never be allowed to rise again to threaten Italy and the other victorious Allies for a second time.

Another great wave of strikes began in the summer of 1920. In July the tram drivers in Rome insisted on flying the red flag with the sickle and hammer at the front of the trams. The tram company refused to permit this, so the drivers took the trams back to their depots and came out on strike. The *arditi* and the Fascists attacked the tram drivers, and the Socialist Party complained that the police were not protecting the strikers against the Fascists. The tram drivers all over Italy then went on strike in protest. In Ancona, which was once again a centre of revolutionary activity, there was an armed battle between strikers and the army. *Avanti!* praised the courage of a 'small handful of thirty young workers armed with rifles and two machine-guns, who had held out for a day and a half against the entire garrison of Ancona'.[20]

Meanwhile the Poles, who had invaded the Ukraine, had been defeated by the Bolsheviks, and the Red Army was advancing on Warsaw. This caused great alarm among the anti-Communists in western Europe. The French sent military aid to the Poles; and in London, *The Times* serialized a new book, *The Last Days of the Romanovs*. The last chapter described the murder of the Tsar and his family, and how the murderers 'accomplished the task for which their Jewish employers had detailed them'.[21]

While the Poles drove back the Red Army from Warsaw, the strikes spread in Italy. The agricultural labourers went on strike throughout the Po valley; they beat up blacklegs and thoroughly alarmed the landowners. In Turin and Milan, the metalworkers' trade unions demanded higher wages and control of the management of the factories. The employers imposed a lock-out and closed the factories. The trade unions called on the metalworkers to seize the factories, to run them themselves, and to sell the metal products well below the market price. The factory owners warned the public that anyone who bought them would be receiving stolen goods, but many people took the opportunity to buy them cheaply.

The workers flew the red flag over the factories, and appointed 'Red Guards' to protect them against an attempt by the owners to recover them. In Turin the Red Guards became suspicious of a prison officer and a nationalist student who walked past the factory, and killed them. Was this the revolution? Or would it turn out to be a damp squib, like Red Week in 1914?

The workers remained in occupation of the factories for nearly the whole of September. The factory owners called on the Prime Minister, Giolitti, to send troops to evict them; but Giolitti took no action. Mussolini was as reluctant as Giolitti to challenge the workers to a battle that he knew he would lose. During the five weeks in which the workers occupied the factories, he wrote about other things in *Il Popolo d'Italia*.

After nearly a month, Giolitti invited representatives of the factory owners and the trade unions to meet him in Rome. He told the employers to agree to the higher wages demanded by the unions, to pay the workers for all the days that they had been in occupation of the factories, to discuss with the unions ways in which the workers could share in the management of the factories, and not to victimize any of the strikers. The owners agreed after making a public protest against being forced to accept these terms.[22]

It was victory for the Socialist trade unions. As shares slumped on the stock exchange and the Italian lira fell on the world markets, people spoke about the imminent Bolshevik revolution in Italy. In Moscow, Angelica Balabanoff went to see Lenin, and told him the wonderful news from Italy. Lenin did not share her enthusiasm. He thought that the British and French imperialists would never allow the Socialist revolution to take place in Italy, but would crush it as they had crushed the revolution in Hungary. She reminded him that the British and French imperialists had failed to destroy the Bolshevik revolution in Russia. He said that Russia was different. The Bolsheviks had been able to survive because of the great spaces in Russia, and because the Russian people were 'so patient, so accustomed to privation' that they had been prepared to bear the hardships of the Allied blockade which the proletariat in the Western countries would not have endured.[23]

The veteran anarchist leader Malatesta, who had returned to Italy, was as pessimistic as Lenin. 'If we let this favourable moment pass,' he said when the workers occupied the factories, 'we shall later pay with tears of blood for the fear we have instilled in the bourgeoisie.'[24] When the time came for the Reds to pay, Mussolini would be there.

# CHAPTER 12

♦

# Castor Oil and Arson

THE occupation of the factories by the metalworkers, and Giolitti's failure to use force to eject them, shook the Italian upper and middle classes. Within six weeks of the metalworkers' return to work, the middle classes had begun to join the Fascists. At Fascist meetings the speakers denounced the Bolsheviks, the Senate, the Papacy and the King. Many middle-class conservatives did not approve of these denunciations of the Senate and the Papacy, and were shocked by the Fascists' criticism of the King. The country landowners, especially those among them who joined the officer corps in the regular army, had been devoted to the royal house of Savoy ever since the days of Victor Emmanuel II and the Risorgimento. Many of them felt a personal loyalty to Victor Emmanuel III. The little King, only 5 feet 3 inches in height, had great dignity and a likeable personality, and had done what was expected of him during the First World War. But these ardent royalists would be prepared to forgive the Fascists a great deal, even their opposition to the monarchy, if the Fascist squads fought the Socialists and destroyed the Bolshevik menace.

In Bologna and Ferrara, the Socialists had won a large majority at the elections in November 1919. The Socialist city councils removed the national tricolour flag from the city halls and hoisted the red flag in its place. In Ferrara they changed the weekly rest day from Sunday to Monday. They encouraged families not to have their children baptized with the traditional Christian names of the Catholic saints, but to give them suitable Socialist first names, like Ateo, Spartaco, Lenin and Ribellione.[1]

A local Fascist branch opened in Ferrara in October 1920; its members met every day in the Café Mozzi behind the Piazza del Duomo. Within a month three hundred members had joined the

[ 103 ]

branch.[2] One of the young men of Ferrara who joined was Italo
Balbo. He was born in a village near Ferrara in 1896. As a young
teenager he became a great admirer of Mazzini's works and joined
the Republican Party, supporting the interventionist campaign in
1914–15 and joining the army when Italy entered the war. He served
with distinction at the front, and was indignant when he heard that
while he was fighting for his country the Socialists were holding
anti-war demonstrations in Ferrara. He wrote home in disgust about
'these scoundrels of local neutralism' who were a disgrace to Ferrara,
and suggested that they be given a good whipping; he told his friends
that after the war, when he had finished fighting the Austrians, he
would return to Ferrara and deal with the 'other Austrians' there.[3]

In the last week of the war he won a military decoration in the
victory of Vittorio Veneto, and on his discharge from the army
studied at Florence University before returning to Ferrara in November 1920. He immediately went to the Café Mozzi and joined the
local Fascio; their republicanism was no drawback in his eyes. He
was eager to fight against 'the traitors and the denigrators of the
victory'.[4]

Balbo and his Fascist friends began by tearing down the red flag
from the city hall and other public buildings in Ferrara and replacing
it with the national tricolour. They also beat up Socialists and Communists. A group of Communists waited for some Fascists as they
went to the Café Mozzi and killed three of them. A crowd of fourteen
thousand turned up at the funeral on 20 December. The middle class
in Ferrara were joining the Fascists in large numbers. The branch
membership rose in a month from three hundred in November to
nearly three thousand in December.[5]

The same thing was happening, though not on quite the same
scale, in the Red strongholds of Bologna and Milan. There, too, the
Fascists repeatedly hauled down the red flag from the public buildings. In Lucca, where the Catholic People's Party – the Popolari –
had gained control of the council, the party's white flag was flown
from the town hall. The Fascists tore it down and raised the national
tricolour.

In the countryside, throughout the Po Valley, the large landowners
were having trouble with the Socialists, who demanded that the large
estates should be taken from the landowners and farmed by peasant
collectives. The Socialist collectives were particularly active and
threatening in the province of Ferrara, where 60 per cent of the

agricultural land was owned by some twenty large landowners, who were known as the agrarians. The wealthiest of them, like Giovanni Grosoli, Giuseppe Vicentini and Vico Mantovani, were also directors and large shareholders in banks.[6] Some of the smaller landowners, and the tenants of Mantovani and the other agrarians, preferred to farm their own land and did not wish to join collectives; but they were afraid of the Socialist leaders of the collectives as well as of the large landowners. They joined the collectives, but privately told the agrarians that they had been forced to do so against their will.

By Christmas 1920 the agrarians had turned to the Fascists for help, and Mantovani had become a personal friend of Mussolini's. The agrarians asked the Fascists to send their squads to protect the peasants from the Socialists in the collectives. The most active of the Fascist squad leaders who were sent into the countryside was Count Dino Grandi, of Mordano in Emilia. After reading law at Ferrara University, he had served in the army during the war, and at the age of twenty-five had joined the Fascists.

The Fascists resorted to propaganda as well as to force. They explained to the agrarians that it was not enough to denounce the collectives; they must try to win the support of the peasants. The Fascists proclaimed that the fundamental principle of their agricultural policy was that the land should belong to those who farmed it; but it would not be in anyone's interest, and least of all in the interests of the national economy, if the large estates were broken up. They therefore believed that the agrarians should grant tenancies to the peasants at reasonable rents. The Fascists persuaded the agrarians that this was the best they could hope for, and the agrarians were not at all dissatisfied with the arrangement.

Grandi's squads beat up the Socialists in the collectives. Just as the Socialists had forced many unwilling peasants to join the collectives for fear of violence, so Grandi's Fascists forced many of the peasants to leave the collectives for fear of even greater violence. It did not take Grandi long to make the peasants more frightened of the Fascists than of the Socialists. By the spring of 1921 the collectives had been destroyed.

Grandi and Balbo's *squadristi* were united by a feeling of comradeship – in most cases by the comradeship of the trenches. They chose their own squad leaders, not by any formal election but by universal acclaim. They sang songs with stirring tunes – 'To arms, to arms, Fascists!', in which they sang of how they were fighting the Bol-

sheviks, and their principal song, 'Giovinezza' (Youth). It had originally been sung before the First World War by youth groups on
rambling expeditions, and during the war by the soldiers at the
front. The Fascists adapted the words, declaring that 'Fascism is the
salvation of our liberty'.

On 23 January 1921 Balbo for the first time led the Fascists in
the city of Ferrara on a raid into the countryside, and followed it
up with many similar raids in February and March. They marched
into villages within a twenty-mile radius of Ferrara, beating-up
Socialists, occasionally killing them, and burning Socialist newspaper
offices, meeting places, and local party headquarters. Sometimes they
merely harassed the Socialists, shouting obscenities at them in the
street and driving close to them on their motor-cycles.[7]

Sometimes they forced Socialists and Communists to drink castor
oil, causing them to have diarrhoea. The ex-servicemen knew about
castor oil from the army, where it had been used during the war by
medical officers. It was widely believed that the castor oil was Balbo's
idea, but there is no evidence of this. The castor oil has attracted
much attention because of its originality and coarseness, and it has
also been used as a kind of excuse by apologists for the Fascists,
from Margherita Sarfatti in 1925 to commentators in Italy and in
Britain in 1997. The castor oil is contrasted with far more terrible
methods employed by the Bolsheviks in Russia and the Nazis in
Germany. This overlooks the fact that the castor oil was only a
minor sideline. The Fascists' chief weapon was arson. They made
fifty-seven raids between January and March 1921 and burned down
twenty-five buildings. They killed twelve Socialists, and several Fascists were killed.[8] The authorities did very little to stop the Fascists.
Many policemen sympathized with them because of their hatred of
the Bolsheviks.

The question of police partiality to the Fascists was raised by the
Socialists and Communists in the Chamber of Deputies in February
1921, when the Socialists moved a resolution regretting that the
government and the local authorities were doing nothing to stop the
organized violence in Emilia which was leading to civil war, and
were even preventing the victims of violence from defending themselves. The resolution was moved by the Socialist deputy, Giacomo
Matteotti, who always enraged his opponents by the provocative
vigour of his language. Several Conservative deputies spoke in favour
of the Fascists. One speaker admitted that a few of them might have

gone too far, but said that the Fascists were patriots who had fought for their country and were 'determined to defend the fruits of their victory against Bolshevism'; they had been obliged to act because of the failure of the Prime Minister, Giolitti, to prevent Socialist violence and the seizure of the factories in September 1920.

Giolitti intervened in the debate. He argued that if he had resorted to force during the occupation of the factories it would have led to heavy loss of life; but he said nothing about the Fascist violence in Emilia beyond giving a vague assurance that all crimes committed there would be dealt with by the judicial authorities. All the parties except the Socialists and the Communists voted against the Socialist motion, which was defeated by a majority of 159.[9]

Mussolini, in an article headed 'Lies' in *Il Popolo d'Italia*, defended the action of the Fascist squads and criticized Matteotti's speech, referring to him not as the '*Onorevole Matteotti* ('the Honourable', the title by which members of the Chamber of Deputies are always addressed) but as the '*disonorevole Matteotti*', though after making his point he duly called him '*Onorevole Matteotti*' in all subsequent references to him. Mussolini wrote that four Fascists had been killed in Ferrara, two in Bologna and one in Modena, and many others had been wounded in other parts of Italy.[10]

Three weeks later he explained the Fascist attitude to violence. For the Fascists, violence was not a caprice but a surgical necessity, a sad necessity. Violence was a fact of life, but like all other aspects of life it must be kept within limits. It must be the exception, not the rule; a chivalrous, not a provocative, violence, not the cowardly violence of the Socialists when thousands attacked one man alone; an intelligent, not a brutish, violence; the violence of warriors, not of hooligans. The Fascists resorted to violence not for personal revenge, but for national defence.[11]

Malatesta and other anarchist leaders had been arrested for having instigated violence during the occupation of the factories. Some anarchist groups decided to retaliate against the Fascists and the bourgeoisie for the arrest of their leaders and the attacks by the Fascists on the proletariat. On 21 March 1921 a young anarchist, Biagio Masi, called at Mussolini's house in the Foro Buonaparte in Milan intending to shoot him. Mussolini was out, so Masi called again next day, and spoke to Mussolini; but as Mussolini was surrounded by a group of friends, Masi thought that this was not a good moment to assassinate him. He left Milan and went to Trieste, where he told a friend about his unsuccessful attempt to kill Mussolini. The friend told the Trieste police, and Masi was arrested.[12]

But by the time that the story of Masi's botched attempt had been revealed in *Il Popolo d'Italia*, other more determined anarchists had been at work. A small group acting independently of Malatesta placed bombs in various buildings in Milan, including a power station and the Diana Theatre. The bomb in the Diana Theatre exploded during a performance, killing eighteen members of the audience and wounding many others. There was great indignation in Milan, and Mussolini voiced and exploited it in *Il Popolo d'Italia*. 'The blood that was spilt last night, blood of people who had nothing to do with political struggles, little people's blood, proletarian blood, the blood of women and children, cries out for vengeance. We send our heartfelt sympathy to the dead and the wounded, and are waiting for popular justice to express itself.' The Fascist squads attacked and wrecked the offices of Malatesta's newspaper, *Umanità Nuova*, and by threats of violence to the printers prevented the further publication of the paper.[13]

The outrage at the Diana Theatre was condemned in nearly all the Italian press; but the Communist paper, the *Ordine Nuovo* of Turin, condemned the hypocrisy of those who became indignant about the deaths in the Diana Theatre but expressed no regrets at the killing of peasants by Fascist squads near Bologna, Ferrara and elsewhere. Mussolini wrote that there was no comparison between the battles around Ferrara and Bologna, where Fascists and Socialists killed each other in fair fight, and the murders in the Diana Theatre. He would not blame the father of the little girl of five who was killed by the bomb in the theatre if he went to Turin to take vengeance on the apologists for the murder of his daughter. When the Socialist deputy Cagnoni adopted the same line as the Communist newspaper about the bomb in the Diana Theatre, Mussolini wrote that Cagnoni's face should become the national spittoon. He accused the Italian Communist Party of sympathizing with the bombers. The Fascists would reply to this Communist provocation with lead and fire, and the eighteen innocent dead of the Diana would be fighting at their side.[14]

In April 1921 Giolitti, who had been harassed by the constant criticism and political manoeuvring of the other parties in the Chamber, decided to ask the King to dissolve Parliament and to hold a general election. His supporters and political commentators afterwards considered that this was an error of judgment on his part which had disastrous long-term consequences for Italy. Mussolini put up Fascist candidates all over the country. He himself stood again in Milan, and the great landowner and banker Mantovani also stood as a Fascist candidate.

Mussolini opened the Fascist election campaign at a rally in the Grand Theatre in Bologna on 3 April. He referred in his speech to the Communist deputy Francesco Misiano, who had been a deserter from the army during the war because he did not wish to fight in an imperialist war, but had nevertheless been elected top of the poll in both Turin and Naples in November 1919. When he mentioned the deserter Misiano, the audience shouted 'Death to Misiano!'[15]

During the six weeks' election campaign he addressed meetings nearly every day all over northern Italy. His appeal was to the fear of Bolshevism of the middle class and to the nationalism of the working class. He spoke about Dante, Galileo, Verdi, Mazzini, Garibaldi, D'Annunzio and the nation of Vittorio Veneto. He did not believe that proletarians of the noble Italian race would support those who cried 'Welcome to the Germans!' and 'Long live Austria!' And what kind of internationalism were they offered? The Amsterdam, the Moscow, or the Vienna version?* He proudly gave figures for the number of army and naval officers who were standing as Fascist candidates, and said that Italian Fascism believed in a national socialism. He clearly stated that he was a republican. During the terrible first ten months after the war, many people had cried 'Long live Lenin! Down with the King!'; but the Fascists had cried 'Long live Italy!' Today the Fascists would again cry, not 'Long live the King!', but 'Long live Italy!'[16]

There was even more violence than usual during the election campaign. Mussolini said that forty Fascists had been killed, and referred to several of these cases, including the young man who was murdered in front of his mother in Novara.[17] The Socialists, on their side, complained of the Fascist violence, and said that many workers had been afraid to vote Socialist because of Fascist threats.

The election result was a triumph for the Fascists. The popular

---

* The Second International in Amsterdam, the Third International in Moscow, or Austrian socialism (the 'two and a half') in Vienna.

vote for the Socialists fell by 30 per cent, but under the electoral system this setback was not fully reflected in the Chamber. The Socialists lost 34 of the 156 seats they had won in 1919 before their split with the Communists. In 1921 they held 122 seats and the Communists 16. The Popolari gained 6 seats, increasing their strength from 101 to 107. The Republicans, Conservatives, Nationalists and Liberals and a few other small parties between them had 252 seats. The Fascists, who had had no deputies in the previous Chamber, won 38 seats in 1921. Mussolini himself was one of the new Fascist deputies; the others included Mantovani, Grandi, Cesare De Vecchi of Turin and Roberto Farinacci of Cremona. After some thought, Mussolini decided that the Fascist deputies should sit on the extreme right of the Chamber, to the right of the Conservative deputies.

The deserter Misiano had again been elected for both Turin and Naples. On 15 June, the day the new Chamber first met, the Fascist deputies forcibly ejected him from Montecitorio (the Parliament building in Rome). Some years later De Vecchi proudly described how it was done. De Vecchi and Silvio Gay found Misiano sitting on a settee in the lobby. Gay ordered him to leave Montecitorio. Misiano said that he had a right to be there because he had been duly elected by his constituents. At this Gay hesitated, because he knew that in law Misiano was correct; but De Vecchi seized Misiano by his coat collar and pulled him to his feet. He told him that he had no right to disgust everyone by his filthy presence. 'I began dragging him along the passage,' wrote De Vecchi, 'having covered his face with spittle.'

Five or six more Fascist deputies then arrived, led by Alfredo Misuri and Francesco Giunta. They took over from De Vecchi, and dragged Misiano by the coat collar towards the entrance to the building. Giunta gave Misiano a hefty kick which sent him reeling down the stairs into the street, where the members of the Royal Guard were on duty. They helped Misiano to his feet, and protected him from further molestation. By now the other Communist deputies were loudly protesting in the Chamber at the way in which their colleague had been treated. According to De Vecchi, no one protested louder than Bombacci, who at this time was acting as the leader of the Communist Party parliamentary group.[18] Bombacci said that Misiano was justified in deserting during an imperialist war.

The Communist deputies demanded that the Fascists who had

assaulted Misiano should be found guilty of contempt and expelled from the Chamber. The Catholic Popolari deputies, including the newly elected Alcide De Gasperi, and all the right-wing parties opposed this demand, and passed a motion that Misiano should not be readmitted to the Chamber until a tribunal at Palermo, which was sitting to consider his case, had decided whether he was eligible to sit as a deputy. This view was supported in a passionate speech by the Nationalist deputy Raffaele Paolucci, much-decorated war hero. He said that the soldiers who had fought for three years for their country had returned home after the war, not marching under triumphal arches as they had expected, but furtively by night, for fear they would be assaulted and murdered by Socialist traitors and deserters.[19] All the deputies except the Communists and the Socialists voted to exclude Misiano.

Mussolini himself had taken no part in the assault on Misiano. It was part of his leadership technique to remain apart and aloof from his followers. He did not fraternize with the other deputies, and only came to Montecitorio on the comparatively few occasions when he wished to speak in a debate. But he wrote an article in *Il Popolo d'Italia* justifying the ejection of Misiano. He explained that the Fascist deputies had resorted to violence against Misiano because neither they nor the Italian people could allow a deserter to sit in the Chamber; but having taken this justifiable and necessary action, the Fascist deputies would not again resort to violence and would henceforth observe all the accepted rules of good conduct in the Chamber; for he was sure that Misiano, after the treatment that he had undergone, would not venture to reappear at Montecitorio.[20]

# CHAPTER 13

◆

# The Treaty of Pacification

THE Red and Fascist violence continued after the general election. There was a difference between the violence of the two sides in the conflict. The Socialist violence was what it had always been in Italy – the spasmodic and unorganized violence of individuals; from time to time three or four Socialists would waylay a Fascist in the street and murder him. The Fascist violence was organized and disciplined. The members of the Fascist squads showed the same discipline and military efficiency that most of them had learned in the army. They would march through the streets in perfect step like trained soldiers, and would not lift a finger, or throw a stone at a Socialist onlooker or a Communist newspaper office, until their squad leader gave the order to burn or kill. Then they burned and killed far more thoroughly than the Socialists or Communists did.

In some districts the Communists and Socialists formed Red Guards, which became known as the Arditi del Popolo. But the Communist Party was numerically weak, as the majority of Socialists had remained in the Socialist Party after the Communists split it in January 1921. The National Executive of the Socialist Party instructed their members not to retaliate against the Fascists, and most of their party branches obeyed these instructions. Balbo despised the Socialists for this. He wrote contemptuously in his diary of the Socialists, those self-styled revolutionaries; when the Fascists attacked them, they did not have the courage to retaliate, but went whining to the authorities to ask for protection from the police whom they had always vilified as agents of the bourgeoisie.[1]

In the few areas where the local Socialists formed Arditi del Popolo, they were under the disadvantages of their military inexperience, the disapproval of their party leaders, and the hostility of the police, of the local army units, and of the prefects (the agents of the national government in the provinces). Some policemen and prefects were impartial between the Fascists and the Socialists. The prefect of Bologna, Cesare Mori, was a career policeman. He was incorruptible, and had no political ambitions. He was a loyal monarchist, nationalist and Conservative, who thought that the Socialists constituted the greatest threat to the state; but he was determined to uphold the law impartially, and to arrest anyone, whether Socialist or Fascist, who broke the law. He was a thorn in the flesh of the Fascists, who hated him for his impartiality between patriots and Bolsheviks.[2] But there were not very many prefects and policemen like Mori.

The prefect of Ferrara, Samuele Pugliese, hardly bothered to hide his sympathies for the Fascists. In May 1921 a local policeman in Ferrara arrested Balbo for having a revolver without a licence. Hundreds of Fascists from the neighbouring villages came into Ferrara to join their comrades in the town and demand the release of Balbo. Pugliese immediately gave orders that Balbo was to be set free, and no proceedings were brought against him. In the province of Ferrara in 1921, there were forty-nine reported incidents of violent clashes between Fascists and Socialists. The police arrested thirty-three Fascists and 110 Socialists.[3]

In some districts the prefects and police actually helped the Fascists, providing them with motorized transport and occasionally with revolvers. In many areas the local army officers were Fascist sympathizers. The Army High Command and the generals had not yet come over to the Fascists; but many of the junior officers supported them. Some of these officers had been comrades of the local Fascist leaders in the trenches during the war.

Even those prefects and policemen who were not positively pro-Fascist usually preferred them to the Bolsheviks. Throughout the whole of Italy, in the first six months of 1921, the Fascists made 2,039 complaints to the authorities about Socialist violence; the police arrested 1,422 Socialists and took no action in 617 cases. The Socialists made 1,274 complaints to the police about Fascist violence; the police arrested 396 Fascists and took no action in 878 cases.[4]

But many Italians were worried about the continuing violence, including many middle-class Conservatives who might otherwise have been sympathetic to the Fascists. Some of these Conservatives believed that all means were justified in the fight against Bolshevism. The younger men joined the Fascists and were exhilarated by the danger, the comradeship, and perhaps by the brutality of the squads.

But others, particularly the older middle-class Conservatives, were shocked by the squads' activities. They were not altogether convinced by Mussolini's argument that the Fascist violence was the violence of warriors, not the violence of hooligans. When they saw the photographs, so proudly published by the Fascists, of the local headquarters of a Communist Party branch after the squads had wrecked it, with the floor covered with shattered furniture, torn-up documents and photographs, and the glass of the broken windows and mirrors,[5] they thought that this looked very much like the work of hooligans.

This was almost certainly the reason why Mussolini was prepared to agree to call off his squads' violent action against the Socialists and Communists. At Easter 1921 the Church authorities in Milan had called on Fascists and Socialists to agree to a truce during Holy Week. It was a few days after the bomb in the Diana Theatre, and Mussolini was able to reject the proposal on the grounds that no truce was possible with the Communist apologists for the bombers.[6] But in July, soon after the general election, Giolitti resigned, and Bonomi became Prime Minister. He had been one of the leaders of the right-wing Reformist Socialist Party since he had been expelled from the Socialist Party after Mussolini's speech at the congress of Reggio Emilia in 1912. Bonomi invited representatives of all the political parties and the trade unions to attend a meeting with the President of the Chamber, Enrico De Nicola, to discuss the possibility of a permanent truce.

The Communists refused to attend. The Popolari and the republicans sent their best wishes for the success of the talks, but also refused to attend, on the grounds that the participation of neutrals who had played no part in the fighting would not help to persuade the combatants to agree to a truce. The Fascists, the Socialists, and the Socialist trade union confederation accepted the invitation, and met on 28 July in the President of the Chamber's office at Montecitorio. Mussolini, De Vecchi, Cesare Rossi and four others represented the Fascists.

They signed the Treaty of Pacification on 3 August. It declared that in order to enable Italy to return to a normal political life and economic development, the Fascists agreed to cease all hostilities against supporters of the Socialist Party and the Communist Party, and the Socialist Party declared that they had no connection with the Arditi del Popolo. The parties would respect each other's emblems, though the President of the Chamber pointed out that only the government, and not the political parties, could decide which flag flew over public buildings. In every province the observance of the treaty would be supervised by a committee of two Fascists and two Socialists and an independent chairman appointed by the Fascists and Socialists, or, if they could not agree, by the President of the Chamber. Any breach of the treaty would be reported to the judicial authorities. The parties would ensure that their followers observed the treaty, and declared that they would adhere to it and support it in their newspapers.[7]

On the same day Mussolini warmly supported the Treaty of Pacification in *Il Popolo d'Italia*. He wrote that it was a victory for Fascism. It would restore peace to Italy, and enable the Fascists to devote all their energies to political activity; and it would also have favourable repercussions abroad, as it would show foreign nations that Italy was a united country which must be respected. He was sure that all Fascists would observe the treaty, because they were a military aristocracy, and would therefore know how to obey.[8]

But his followers did not like the treaty, and almost immediately important Fascist leaders began to express their opposition to it. Three days later, Grandi criticized the treaty in the local Bologna Fascist newspaper, *L'Assalto*. He wrote that the Fascists were not cannibals who wanted war at all costs; they believed that there must be peace. But peace could only be achieved by negotiations between two parties who wanted peace; it could not be achieved when one party, the Socialists, were acting in bad faith. The treaty was not a victory for the Fascists, as Mussolini claimed, but a victory for the 'bourgeois Socialists', by which he meant Bonomi and his moderate Socialist Party.[9]

This was open rebellion. Mussolini replied to Grandi next day in *Il Popolo d'Italia*: the great Fascist family must not tear itself apart by internal disputes. But Grandi continued his criticism in *L'Assalto*. On 14 August a meeting in Bologna of representatives of 144 local Fascist branches passed a resolution declaring that the Treaty of Pacification had no value, and demanding the convening of a national congress of the Fascist organizations.[10]

Balbo was as much opposed as Grandi to the treaty, but he replied to it by action instead of words. He proposed to organize a march on Ravenna, where the town council was controlled by a coalition of republicans and Socialists, and pay homage to Dante at his tomb on the six hundredth anniversary of his death. He submitted the proposal to Mussolini; the Fascist squads would occupy Ravenna for twenty-four hours and then withdraw, and perfect discipline would of course be preserved. Although it was technically not a breach of the treaty, Mussolini did not like the plan, which was at best a provocation and at worst could lead to violence; but in view of the dissatisfaction in the organization, he felt obliged to agree.

On 9 September 1921, three thousand Fascists from all parts of Emilia began marching on Ravenna. As they marched through Bagnara di Romagna, one of the Fascists was shot dead by a sniper, and the Fascists took what Farinacci called 'reprisal action' to avenge his death. On 12 September they marched into Ravenna, singing patriotic songs from the First World War, and paid homage at Dante's tomb. Some snipers fired on the *squadristi* in Ravenna. The Fascists retaliated by setting fire to the Socialist Party offices in the city.[11] As Mussolini had feared, the treaty was broken.

Some of the *squadristi* were not as disciplined as Mussolini and Balbo hoped and made out. At the end of September some Fascists in Bologna forced their way into the house of the Socialist member of the Chamber of Deputies, Edoardo Bogiankino, although two policemen were on guard at the door. The Fascists spat on Bogiankino's wife, gashed a portrait of Karl Marx, and chalked on the wall: 'Death to Bogiankino and Lenin!'[12]

Mussolini was facing a formidable revolt of his Fascists. Balbo believed that it would be necessary to get rid of him, and went to see D'Annunzio, who had finally been forced to leave Fiume in January 1921 by the blockade imposed by the Italian government to appease the indignation of Britain and France. Balbo sounded D'Annunzio on the possibility of his replacing Mussolini as leader of the Fascists; but D'Annunzio, who was not really interested in internal Italian politics, did not want the job.[13]

Mussolini was in serious trouble; but he was now, at the age of thirty-eight, a different Mussolini from the naughty schoolboy, the anarchist tramp in Switzerland, the Socialist journalist, the front-line soldier, and even from the interventionist editor of *Il Popolo d'Italia*. The Mussolini of 1921 was a skilful politician, who possessed all the skills that would be needed to extricate himself from the very difficult position in which he was placed. He was trying to ride two horses at the same time, to reassure the Conservatives that he was a responsible statesman who was against disorder and the violence of the squads, but also to retain the loyalty of the squads by allowing them a free hand to resort to illegal violence. He managed to ride these two horses successfully for many years. It was a brilliant political feat.

He had hoped to win the support of the respectable bourgeoisie by signing the treaty with the Socialists; but he was forced to retain the support of the Fascists by ending the treaty. Angelica Balabanoff accused him of being afraid to swim against the tide; but it was impossible for him to swim against this Fascist tide. There was no point making a good impression on the Conservatives if the Fascists threw him over, for without the support of his Fascists he had nothing to offer the Conservatives. He, the Duce, the great leader, was compelled to say, with the French radical of 1848, Alexandre Ledru-Rollin and the British Conservative Edwardian Prime Minister, Arthur Balfour: 'I am their leader, I must follow them.' But he must not allow his followers to realize that he was following them. With their devotion to the leadership principle, to the doctrine of hierarchy, they would never follow a leader who surrendered to his rank and file.

He was helped by the fact that, in theory if not in practice, the Fascists believed in obedience to the leader. They were not Girondin, Jacobin, Socialist or anarchist revolutionaries, with an innate urge to rebel and split. They considered themselves to be revolutionaries, but were really disciplined soldiers, ex-servicemen who had been trained to obey and who wanted to obey, provided only that they were given the orders that they wanted to receive.

Mussolini began to pave the way for his retreat by accusing the Socialists of breaking the treaty, and publishing in *Il Popolo d'Italia* of 9 September[14] the names of fifteen Fascists who had been killed by Communists between 5 August and 4 September, while the treaty was in force – in Bologna, Piacenza, Florence, Rovigo, Bari and Cremona. Most of them were under the age of twenty-four, and the majority had been killed in Bologna. He claimed, truthfully, that during this period the Fascists had observed the treaty and had not resorted to any reprisals; but the reprisals began the very next day, while Balbo's squads were marching to Ravenna.

Mussolini agreed that the national congress, which the Fascists in Bologna had demanded, should be held on 7 November in Rome. He decided that before the congress was held he would transform the Fasci di Combattimento into a political party which would be called the National Fascist Party.[15] In the provinces the head of the party would be the *ras*, with absolute powers over the party members in his district. The *ras* was to be appointed by the leader. It was essential to emphasize the supreme power of the leader when he was on the point of capitulating to his followers.

The Fascist gains in the general election had made the international press take an interest in Mussolini, and articles about him were beginning to appear in the French and English newspapers. He attracted more international publicity when he was challenged to a duel by the Socialist deputy Ettore Ciccotti, after Mussolini had described him in *Il Popolo d'Italia* as the 'most despicable of the men who infect Italian public life'. Duels were illegal in Italy, but were often fought; Mussolini had already fought several duels, including one with Treves, in which he had slightly wounded Treves.

He now saw to it that his intention of breaking the law and fighting a duel with Ciccotti received the widest publicity in *Il Popolo d'Italia* and in all other Italian newspapers; and reports about it appeared on several days in the London *Times*. Readers were told that Mussolini had chosen swords, that the duel would be fought somewhere near Leghorn, and that the police were following Mussolini wherever he went in order to prevent it.

It was then reported that the duel had been about to take place in a garden in Leghorn on 27 October 1921, when the police rushed into the garden and stopped it. Mussolini and Ciccotti ran into the house and locked the doors, and the police made no further attempts to stop the duel. The two adversaries then fought with their swords in one of the rooms in the house for an hour and a half. In the fourteenth round Mussolini slightly wounded Ciccotti; but Ciccotti was so exhausted that he nearly had a heart attack and was unable to continue. It was announced that the fight would be resumed next day, but nothing more about the duel appeared in the newspapers.[16]

The press reports were probably inaccurate, at least in some of the details; but it was good publicity for Mussolini on the eve of the party congress. It proved that although he had made a treaty with the Socialists, he was not afraid to meet a Socialist in a duel.

On the first day of the congress the Communist and Socialist trade unions called a twenty-four-hour general strike as a protest against the holding of the congress in Rome; but as the Fascists had already arrived in Rome, it did not seriously inconvenience them. Mussolini spoke on the second day. He devoted his speech almost entirely to attacking the Socialists and stressing the patriotism of the Fascists. He praised Francesco Crispi, the Prime Minister in the 1890s, who had had imperial aims beyond the Mediterranean. It was necessary to ensure the welfare of the Italian race, which was a greater concept than the Italian nation. He emphasized that the Fascists rejected all forms of internationalism, because the dream of a united human race was Utopian, and not based on reality; there was nothing to indicate that the millennium of universal brotherhood was imminent. For the first time in his life, he repudiated national as well as international socialism: 'In economic matters we are decidedly anti-Socialist.' He ended by declaring that the Fascists were animated by their love for their mother, whose name was Italy.

When he finished his speech he was received in absolute silence, which lasted for several seconds. During those seconds of silence he must have feared the worst; but it was only that the audience had not realized that this stirring peroration was the end of his speech. As he moved to descend from the rostrum, the cheering began and turned into a great ovation. He had said nothing about ending the treaty; if he had announced it at the congress, it could have been interpreted as a surrender to the pressure of the rank and file. But the rumour had gone round that he was about to repudiate it, and the Fascists were determined to make a great show of unity. Balbo, in his speech, said that he accepted the treaty because as a soldier he knew that it was his duty to obey the leader. The loudest applause of the congress came when Mussolini and Grandi embraced on the platform.[17]

A week later Mussolini officially notified the President of the Chamber of Deputies that he was ending the Treaty of Pacification. On 1 December he explained it in a speech in the Chamber which was constantly interrupted by the Socialist deputies, especially by Matteotti. They accused him of surrendering to the pressure of the rank and file and allowing them to resume their murderous attacks on their political opponents.

Mussolini said that the treaty had been a praiseworthy attempt to end the state of war that was raging in the country, and he thanked the President of the Chamber for his part in achieving it; but unfortunately the 'Social-Leninists' had used the treaty to intensify their attacks on the Fascists. He apologized for the fact that the Fascists in Trieste had killed an innocent young man in the mistaken belief that he was a Communist who had murdered a Fascist; but he compared this one tragic error with all the murders of Fascists by the Communists and Socialists since 3 August. He blamed the Bonomi government for its failure to preserve law and order. If the government had suppressed the Bolsheviks, it would not have been necessary for the Fascist squads to perform this duty.[18]

The year was ending happily for the Fascists. In December the Chamber, after hearing the report from the tribunal at Palermo, decided that Misiano, as a deserter, was ineligible to take his seat, and his election for Turin and Naples was annulled.[19] In the country, the Fascists were going from strength to strength. On 31 December 1920 there were 88 Fasci di Combattimento in Italy, with 20,615 members; on 31 December 1921 the National Fascist Party had 834 branches with 249,036 members.[20] They had severely weakened the Socialists and Communists in northern Italy; and with the end of the treaty, they could look forward to greater successes in 1922 and to burning more Socialist and Communist offices.

—— ◆ ——

# CHAPTER 14

# The General Strike

WHILE Mussolini was first restraining and then unleashing his *squadristi*, he was also launching a new intellectual journal like the *Utopia* which he had edited before the war. He called it *Gerarchia*, and appointed Margherita Sarfatti to be the editor. In the second number, which appeared in the autumn of 1921, he wrote an article in which he went further in repudiating democracy than he had gone in 1918 when he demanded the appointment of a dictator in wartime as a means to establish democracy as an end. Now, in *Gerarchia*, he wrote that the most important contribution of Fascism was to repudiate the 'principles of 1789'. The French Revolution had introduced the reign of democracy and capitalism. Democracy had perhaps been necessary in the nineteenth century to offset the evils of capitalism; but in the twentieth century Fascism would introduce a state-controlled economy in which democracy would be a hindrance to efficient administration.[1]

Soon afterwards he made another shift of emphasis, if not a change of line, when he wrote an article in *Il Popolo d'Italia* on 2 November 1921 on the commercial treaty that Bonomi's government had signed with Bolshevik Russia. Mussolini approved of the treaty, which he thought would be to Italy's economic advantage, and would accelerate the transformation of Russia into a capitalist economy; because really, despite all their fine words, Lenin's government was a bourgeois government. Another advantage, from Italy's point of view, would be to strengthen Russia as a counterweight to Anglo-Saxon imperialism. Clemenceau had dreamed of overthrowing Bolshevism in Russia by means of the blockade, and Trotsky of exporting Bolshevism throughout the world; but Clemenceau's dream had been shattered by the defeat of the White General Peter Wrangel and Trotsky's by the rout of the Red Army before Warsaw; so it should now be possible for the Western powers and Bolshevik Russia to live together in peace.[2]

Mussolini developed this theme in an article in *Gerarchia* in September 1922. He wrote that while the Russia of the Romanovs had been based on Byzantine cruelty, the Russia of Ulyanov would be based on Western capitalism.[3]

Mussolini's opinion about relations with Bolshevik Russia was shared by the British and French Prime Ministers, David Lloyd George and Aristide Briand; and at the meeting of the Supreme Council of the Allies at Cannes early in January 1922, which Bonomi also attended, they decided to invite the Bolshevik government, as well as the United States, to a conference of heads of government to be held in Genoa in April. Mussolini went to Cannes as the diplomatic correspondent of *Il Popolo d'Italia*. On 7 January Briand granted him an interview in the Hotel Carillon, in which he expressed conciliatory views about the treatment of Germany which Mussolini reported without comment in *Il Popolo d'Italia*. Mussolini asked Briand what he thought about the growth of Fascism in Italy, but Briand refused to comment on Italian internal politics. Mussolini himself was interviewed at Cannes by the Paris newspaper *L'Excelsior*. He was responsible and moderate, and said that he was in favour of trade relations with Bolshevik Russia.[4]

The decision to invite the Bolsheviks to the Genoa conference caused great indignation in conservative and right-wing circles in France, Italy and Britain, particularly because, as it was to be a conference of Prime Ministers, Lenin himself would be invited. Both Briand and Bonomi were forced to resign, and were replaced as Prime Ministers by Raymond Poincaré and Luigi Facta. Lloyd George survived the storm, despite strong criticism from the Conservatives in Parliament and the press and from Winston Churchill in his own Cabinet. The Conservative journalist Lovat Fraser, writing in the *Sunday Pictorial* and *The Times*, called on the women of Britain to prevent Lloyd George from sitting down and shaking hands with Lenin, whose Bolsheviks had been responsible for the 'enforced degradation of Russian womanhood'. He reminded his readers that the British Prime Minister, William Pitt, would not have agreed to meet Robespierre and Marat.[5]

The press in Italy and France wondered what Mussolini would do if Lenin came to Genoa; would the Fascist squads try to assassinate him? Mussolini reassured them. He wrote that he was sure that Lenin would not leave the Kremlin; he would send his Commissar for Trade and Industry, Leonid Borisovich Krassin, or his diplomat V.V. Vorovsky to represent him. If Lenin came, the Fascists would treat him with the respect due to the head of a foreign government, and would give another proof of their perfect discipline; but if the Italian Communists took advantage of Lenin's presence to attempt to introduce Bolshevism into Italy, the Fascists would be the most ardent leaders of the popular resistance.[6] Mussolini was right; Lenin did not go to Genoa, but sent his Commissar for Foreign Affairs, Georgi Vassilievich Chicherin, who took the opportunity to meet the German Foreign Minister, Walther Rathenau, at Rapallo and sign a German-Soviet treaty of friendship and economic co-operation.

In March 1922 Mussolini went to Berlin. Although the purpose of his visit was to interview the leading German statesmen on behalf of *Il Popolo d'Italia*, he was again interviewed himself by German journalists who were conscious that he was a rising man in Italian politics. He interviewed the German Chancellor, Karl Joseph Wirth, and Rathenau. Before Rathenau became Foreign Minister, this Jewish industrialist had been in charge of German finances and had so far prevented Germany from going bankrupt; and he had made a favourable impression on the Allied leaders. In *Il Popolo d'Italia*, Mussolini expressed his admiration for Rathenau and his achievement. When Rathenau was assassinated three months later by a group of young German anti-Semitic nationalists, Mussolini strongly condemned the murder as another proof of the folly of trusting the German nationalist barbarians.[7]

While Mussolini was exhibiting his moderation to foreign journalists, his *squadristi* were being far from moderate. In January 1922 Mussolini ordered Balbo to draft regulations for the organization of the squads; this would keep Balbo busy and prevent him from plotting with D'Annunzio to oust Mussolini. Balbo directed that the *squadristi* were to wear black shirts with black sashes and leather belts, breeches and puttees, and preferably also a black fez. The officers were to wear Roman eagles, and the units were given the names of the army groups of ancient Rome. A squad was to consist of between twenty and fifty men; four squads were to form a *centuria*; four *centuriae* a cohort; and between three and nine cohorts a legion, which would be commanded by a consul, who would be subject to the inspector-generals. The officers would no longer be elected by the squads, but nominated by Mussolini; and every member of the squads, like all members of the Fascist Party, would be under the supreme authority of the Duce.[8] Mussolini issued an order that all party members were automatically to be members of their local squad. He probably did so because the Socialists were demanding that the squads should be suppressed. It would now be impossible to suppress the squads without also suppressing the Fascist Party, and Mussolini was confident that Facta's government would not dare to do this.

Balbo and the squads became more daring in 1922. They did not merely burn Communist and Socialist Party offices, but marched in great strength into towns and cities where the Socialists and Communists had a majority on the council. The squad leaders entered the town halls and suggested to the Socialist councillors that they should resign and leave the town. The councillors, seeing the Fascists standing there with their cudgels and revolvers, did not wait to be asked twice.

In May 1922 Balbo carried out his greatest operation so far. It was in his own stronghold of Ferrara, which was controlled by a coalition of Socialists and Popolari. Once again Mussolini was worried about Balbo's daring plan; he did not wish to drive the Popolari into a coalition with the Socialists. But again he allowed Balbo to proceed. On 12 May Balbo led 63,000 Fascists into Ferrara. They occupied the city for forty-eight hours, taking over the administration and preserving perfect discipline; Balbo had forbidden them to drink any alcohol, or to visit brothels, during their stay in Ferrara.[9] Mussolini hailed Balbo's exploit as a great victory.

A fortnight later, twenty thousand Fascists occupied Bologna. They were angry that the prefect, Mori, was trying to enforce the law impartially. They entered Mori's office at the city hall and demanded that he resign. He refused, and barricaded the city hall against hundreds of Fascists who besieged it. Balbo ordered his men to piss against the wall of the building outside Mori's office, but hesitated to use violence against a government official. Facta removed Mori from Bologna and appointed him prefect of Bari in the South, where there was far less Fascist activity.[10] It was a triumph for the Bologna *squadristi*.

A Fascist was killed in the little Adriatic port of Cesenatico near Rimini. Balbo was determined to show the Reds that 'a Fascist cannot be killed with impunity'. He had a good target – the Hotel Byron in

Ravenna, an old palazzo that was the headquarters of the Socialist co-operatives in the district. For twenty years it had been the pride of the Socialist movement in the Romagna. Balbo's squads burned it to the ground; it burned better because of the water shortage in Ravenna. The secretary of the co-operative stood watching, holding his head in his hands in despair, with the tears rolling down his cheeks. Balbo almost felt sorry for him, but then reflected that unfortunately there can be no half-measures in a civil war.[11]

On 28 July Balbo and his squads occupied Ravenna. This time they were not visiting Dante's tomb, but had come to destroy the power of the Reds in the city. When they tried to enter the working-class districts, the Communists fired on them and killed nine Fascists. Balbo burned the headquarters of the Socialists, the Communists and the anarchists in Ravenna. He went to the chief of police and told him that he wanted motorized trucks to remove his men from the town; unless he obtained them within half an hour he would burn the house of every Communist and Socialist. The chief of police gave him the trucks, hoping to get rid of the Fascists; but this was a trick on Balbo's part. Having obtained the trucks, he used them to carry his squads on the most extensive campaign in which the Fascists had ever engaged.

For twenty-four hours on 29 July 1922, and on what Balbo called the 'terrible night' that followed, his squads burned the headquarters of every Communist and Socialist organization in the provinces of Ravenna and Forlì. He wrote in his diary that huge columns of fire and smoke covered the whole plain of the Romagna, for the Fascists 'had decided to end the Red terror once and for all'; and they encountered very little resistance from the 'Bolshevik rabble', who had fled. The Italian Army watched, but did nothing.[12]

In the Chamber, the Republican Democrats, the Popolari, the Socialists and the Communists united to condemn Facta's failure to act against the Fascists, and they brought down his government. The King summoned the opposition leaders, including the Socialist Turati, to the Quirinal and discussed the possibility of their forming a ministry; but they could not agree among themselves, so the King recalled Facta. The Communists then proposed to the Socialists that they should call a general strike as a protest against the government's failure to suppress the Fascist violence. The Socialists agreed, and on 30 July, the day after Balbo's devastation in the Romagna, the Socialist trade unions called a general strike to begin at midnight on

31 July. Turati declared that it was a general strike in support of law and order, to maintain the authority of the state.[13]

The Fascists were ready. On 31 July the national party secretary, Michele Bianchi, sent out a circular to all party branches telling them to prepare to break the general strike. He drafted a statement, which Mussolini published in *Il Popolo d'Italia* on 1 August, the first day of the strike. It announced that unless the government broke the strike within forty-eight hours, the Fascists would do the job for them and would 'supplant the State, which will once again have shown its impotence'.[14] If it became necessary for the Fascists to intervene at the expiry of the forty-eight hours, they expected all civil servants to repudiate the authority of the political leaders who had betrayed them and to continue to carry out their duties under the direction of the Fascists.

The Fascists did not wait for forty-eight hours before acting as strike-breakers. They broke the transport strike, dragging the striking tram drivers and conductors out of the trams, beating them with cudgels, and driving the trams themselves. The most violent incidents were in Genoa, La Spezia and, as usual, in Ancona. In Genoa a Communist sniper fired at a tram that was being driven by Fascist strike-breakers; the army then appeared on the streets in armoured cars, and opened fire with machine-guns on the Communists, while the police made house-to-house searches in the working-class districts, looking for arms and snipers. The acting British consul-general in Genoa wrote that 'the Fascisti, who were organised on military lines, assisted the police in quelling disturbances, and as a matter of fact did most of the fighting themselves'. Three people were killed and about fifty wounded. In Ancona the Fascists burned the offices of several Socialist trade unions and clubs.

The crunch came in Milan, where Mussolini had lived and worked in the *Popolo d'Italia* office for the past three years while the red flag flew over the city hall. He himself was in Rome on 3 August 1922, when the Fascist squads, after breaking the tram strike, marched into the city hall and ordered the Socialist councillors to leave the building. The councillors complied under protest, and hastened to leave not only the building but also the city. The Fascists hauled down the red flag and raised the national tricolour for the first time since 1919. In the evening D'Annunzio appeared and made a speech from the steps of the city hall, in which he appealed for calm and an end to the hatreds that were dividing Italy.

In the absence of the city councillors, the prefect took over the administration of the city. The Fascists claimed that in Milan, as in other places where they had driven out the Socialist councillors, they found evidence of corruption and maladministration. There is no doubt that in Milan the city had incurred a very large debt on account of Socialist spending.

The Fascists had broken the general strike throughout Italy in less than a day, and on the evening of 3 August the Socialist trade unions called on the workers to return to work.[15] The British acting consul-general in Genoa was very pleased. 'It is to be hoped therefore that the action of the fascisti will have a beneficial effect,' he wrote on 7 August.[16]

It was a victory for the Fascists everywhere except in Parma. When the squads tried to enter Parma to break the strike there, the local army commander erected road blocks and stopped the Fascists. Bianchi sent a hurried message to Balbo ordering him to avoid a confrontation with the army; but Balbo believed that the army commander was bluffing, and tried to force his way past the road block. The officer was not bluffing. He opened fire on the Fascists. Balbo tried again next day, but on 5 August abandoned his attempt to enter Parma, after fourteen of his Fascists had been killed.[17] He was determined to make another attempt to capture Parma at some time in the future.

A debate on the strike and its failure took place in the Chamber of Deputies on 11 August. After Facta and several nationalist and Fascist speakers had condemned the strike, the Communist deputy Raposti said that it had been fully justified, and that he regretted that the workers had not responded by violence to the violence used against them by the Fascists. The Fascist deputies howled him down, and he was unable to make himself heard above the uproar. The Fascists rushed at him, but the Communist and Socialist deputies gathered round him to shield him from the Fascists. The Fascist deputy Giunta, who had kicked the deserter Misiano down the steps of the Parliament building, shouted out that he would shoot Raposti, and put his hand in his hip pocket; but some of his friends seized him and prevented him from drawing his revolver.

Facta and his ministers, realizing that they were in the line of fire between the Fascists and the Communists, hastily left the Chamber, and the President of the Chamber announced that the debate would be suspended. During the adjournment, another Fascist deputy drew his revolver and pointed it at Raposti; but one of Facta's junior ministers intervened and persuaded him to hand over the revolver. When the session was resumed, the President called on Raposti to continue his speech; but again the Fascist deputies shouted him down, and after the uproar had continued unabated for ten minutes, he eventually abandoned his attempt to speak.[18]

The British ambassador, Sir Ronald Graham, watched the scene from the visitors' gallery; but he was not particularly shocked, and felt a good deal of sympathy for the Fascists in their campaign against the Bolsheviks. He reported to the British Foreign Secretary, the Marquess Curzon, that 'irritation was growing' among the respectable classes in Italy over the Fascists' 'excesses and pranks, which varied in degree from clubbing Socialist leaders to death to forcing a whole Communist council to imbibe large doses of castor oil – probably a case for a mental rather than a physical purge'. But he did not regret that 'Fascism has emerged triumphant from the recent crisis'.[19]

CHAPTER 15

# The March on Rome

THE Fascists had successfully marched on Ferrara, Bologna, Ravenna and Milan; after their victories of 29 July and 3 August, they began to ask each other why should they not march on Rome. The idea of a March on Rome spread among the Fascist rank and file. Mussolini was not so sure. The army had stopped the Fascists from marching on Parma; might they not also stop a march on Rome? When the Fascists marched on the other cities, they were marching against the Socialist city councils; but if they were to march on Rome they would be marching against the central government – perhaps even marching against the King.

It was important for Mussolini to reassure the Conservatives, and especially the army leadership, that he was not against the King; but he would have to be careful here. The Mazzinian republicans who had played such a leading part in the interventionist campaign and in the *arditi* were an important element in the Fascist squads. They would not be favourably impressed if they believed that Mussolini was repudiating republicanism in order to curry favour with the Conservative monarchists.

On 22 August Mussolini published in *Il Popolo d'Italia* a letter from some army officers. It expressed their admiration for the Fascists who were fighting against the Bolsheviks, but emphasized their devotion to the Crown. 'If the Fascists go against the Crown, we will give the order "Open fire!"', Mussolini replied in *Il Popolo d'Italia* next day. The Crown was not in jeopardy because the Crown had not placed itself in jeopardy. The Fascists were not against the Crown, but for a greater Italy.[1]

He went further in a speech at Udine on 20 September. He said that Fascism in its inception had been a republican movement, but political forms were not unalterable. The Fascists stood for national

[ 129 ]

unity; if the monarchy was the symbol of national unity, it would not come into conflict with the Fascists. During the Risorgimento the two forces of monarchy and revolution had worked together to make Italy great.[2]

Mussolini was still skilfully riding his two horses – the respectable conservative horse and the revolutionary Fascist horse. While his *squadristi* were talking about a march on Rome, he was in Rome taking part in back-stage talks with political leaders of all parties – with the Prime Minister Facta, with Nitti, with Giolitti – about the possibility of making some political deal that would enable him and other Fascists to take office under them in a coalition government.[3] But his influence as the leader of a party with thirty-eight seats in the Chamber was not as strong as his influence as the leader of a party whose members were marching on Rome. He must at all costs retain the loyalty of the Fascist *squadristi*.

On 24 September he addressed a rally of thirty thousand Fascists at Cremona. There were shouts in the audience: 'To Rome, to Rome!' Mussolini said that the Italians who had stood firm on the Piave and had marched forward from the Piave to victory at Vittorio Veneto should march on from there to Rome.[4]

The Fascists were making preparations to hold their national party congress at Naples on 24 October. Balbo was planning another march on Parma, the only city in northern Italy where the Socialists still controlled the council and had not been driven out by the Fascists. He went to Parma in disguise and walked around the working-class districts to see if the Socialists had made defence preparations. But on 11 October Mussolini sent Balbo a message to forget about a march on Parma and meet him in Milan on 16 October to discuss a march on Rome.[5]

Mussolini appointed four 'Quadrumvirs' to organize the March on Rome – Bianchi, Balbo, De Vecchi, and General Emilio De Bono, a fifty-six-year-old regular army officer, tall, slim, with a pointed white beard, who had had a distinguished record in the war against Turkey of 1911 and in the First World War, when he had commanded a brigade on the Isonzo front. He had recently joined the Fascist Party. Both De Bono and De Vecchi were personal friends of Queen Margherita the Queen Mother, the widow of the murdered King Umberto. She had told them that she admired the Fascists.[6]

Mussolini explained to the Quadrumvirs that he thought it necessary to organize a march on Rome because a purely parliamentary solution to the crisis that had developed in Italy would be 'contrary to the spirit and interests of Fascism'. But when should the march take place? Balbo thought that they should act at once. 'If we do not attempt the coup d'état now,' he said, 'in the spring it may be too late.' De Vecchi and De Bono wished to postpone it for a month to allow proper preparations to be made; but Bianchi agreed with Balbo. The decision rested with Mussolini. He decided that preparations should begin at once, but that the actual date of the march should not be decided until the party congress in Naples on 24 October. Balbo was not happy about the eight days' delay.[7]

The party congress in Naples was the first important Fascist rally to be held in the South, where the party had been gaining in strength in recent months. Many of these new party members were Conservatives who were devoted to the monarchy, and they came to the congress with a penny coin bearing the King's head in their coat lapels as a demonstration of loyalty to the King.[8]

When the congress opened, Mussolini addressed a party rally in the San Carlo Theatre in Naples on 24 October. He went further than ever before in his declaration of support for the monarchy. He said that the Italian monarchy, the monarchy of the House of Savoy, would never oppose the will of the nation. He then addressed an open-air rally in the Piazza del Plebiscito. He said that he had offered to serve in any government if the Fascists were given five ministries, including the Ministry of Foreign Affairs, but that the politicians would offer the Fascists only under-secretaryships. The time had come when the Fascists would undertake the government of Italy; 'the government will either be handed to us or we shall seize it by marching on Rome'.[9]

That evening Mussolini and the Quadrumvirs and a number of other leading Fascists met at the Hotel Vesuvio in Naples and fixed the final details of the March on Rome. The operation would start at midnight on the night of 26–27 October. The Fascists would seize the strong points in the cities of northern Italy. On Saturday, 28 October the Blackshirts would assemble at three points to the north of Rome – at Santa Marinella near Civitavecchia, at Monterotondo, and at Tivoli – and the three columns would march on Rome. They were to avoid any confrontation with the army, but otherwise nothing was to prevent them from reaching the capital. Balbo said that he would send a group of *squadristi* secretly into Rome to operate as terrorists and place bombs in various places in the city if the government used force to resist the Fascists' march. The meeting ended without ceremony with a few curt words from Mussolini, and the members present left after giving each other the Roman salute.[10]

Next day Balbo met Grandi in the Hotel Excelsior in Naples, and told him about the plans for the March on Rome. Grandi was taken aback; he said that it would be madness to try it. Balbo laughed, and said that since Grandi had become a deputy in the Chamber he had lost all his nerve.[11]

With just over forty-eight hours to go before the action was due to begin, Mussolini returned from Naples to Milan. Everyone there was expecting a Fascist rising, as Rachele Mussolini noted in her diary on 26 October. 'People stop me in the street and ask whether it is true that there is going to be a revolution. I reply that I know nothing, but I don't think I sound very convincing.'[12]

In the North, the Fascists began to occupy the municipal buildings and the strong-points and take over the government of the towns. When they occupied the city hall in Florence they found that General Armando Diaz, the commander-in-chief who had led the army to victory at Vittorio Veneto, was being entertained there at a banquet. They treated him with the greatest respect.[13] Meanwhile the Black-shirts were converging on the three assembly points, and the Quadrumvirs were heading for Perugia, from where they were to direct operations. When they reached Perugia they issued their proclamation to the Italian people, which had been drafted by Mussolini. It stated that Fascism had decided to use its sword to cut the Gordian knot that was throttling the life of Italy.[14]

On Friday, 27 October – much too late – Facta's government acted against the Fascists. Facta had done nothing while the Fascists were burning the Socialist and Communist headquarters throughout the Romagna and forcibly taking over the town halls from the elected Socialist councillors; but now it was Facta's own government which was threatened. He therefore proclaimed that the government and the country were confronted with an insurrection, and that the army would act to maintain law and order.

In Rome, General Emanuele Pugliese had twelve thousand troops under his command. He closed the theatres, commandeered the trams, erected barbed-wire defences around important public buildings, and occupied the Fascist Party headquarters. In Turin, Genoa,

Bologna and Milan the army took control of the situation. Armoured cars patrolled the streets. The office of *Il Popolo d'Italia* was guarded by troops, and Mussolini could not leave the building without passing through an army checkpoint.[15]

Mussolini was determined to avoid a clash with the army. The Fascists in Milan suggested that they should take over the offices of the prestigious newspaper *Il Corriere della Sera*, which had criticized the Fascists for planning an insurrection. Mussolini forbade it. He told Rachele that if anyone telephoned him at his house when he was out and asked if the Fascists could seize the *Corriere della Sera* building, she was to reply firmly: 'No.'[16]

In Cremona there was a clash between Farinacci's Fascists and the army, who resisted the attempt by the Fascists to seize control. The army opened fire, and the Fascists were driven back, leaving eight Blackshirts killed and thirteen wounded. But in Pisa and Bologna the army adopted a friendly attitude towards the Fascists, though they prevented them from seizing the prefect's office. In Perugia and Mantua the troops watched passively while the prefect surrendered the town to the Fascists. The army allowed the Fascists to seize nine thousand rifles and ten machine-guns from the military stores in Spoleto and seven thousand rifles and thirty machine-guns in Foligno. In Siena the army commander, on his own initiative, delivered arms to the Fascists.[17]

Facta sent orders to the prefect of Milan to arrest Mussolini. The prefect refused to obey the order. Afterwards some Fascists claimed that they had persuaded the prefect to disobey the government by promising him promotion after the Fascists came to power.[18] They need not have troubled to offer the prefect this inducement, for he knew that the Fascist bandwagon was rolling, that most of his colleagues believed that the Fascists would win and wanted them to win. The Fascists in Milan were fraternizing with the troops and shouting 'Long live the army, long live Mussolini!'[19]

Mussolini still wished to pretend that he was not involved in any unusual activity. On the evening of 27 October he took Rachele and their daughter Edda, who was aged twelve, to their box at the Manzoni Theatre to see a performance of the comedy *The Swan* by the Hungarian dramatist Ferenc Molnár, whose farces were very popular in Italy, though he had been a propagandist for Austria during the war. As they sat in the box waiting for the performance to begin, all eyes in the theatre were turned on Mussolini, with people looking at him through their opera glasses. He whispered to Rachele: 'We must pretend we know nothing about anything.'

When the performance began and the lights in the auditorium were extinguished, Mussolini's secretaries several times knocked on the door of the box, and Mussolini slipped out to hear the messages and deal with the matters that they had reported to him; but he was back in his seat in the box when the lights went up during the interval. Halfway through Act II he suddenly said to Rachele: 'Now's the time, let's go.' They quietly left the box and the theatre and returned home. The telephone messages were coming in fast, with news that the Fascists were ready to march from Santa Marinella, Monterotondo and Tivoli.[20]

That evening Facta went to the King and advised him to proclaim the state of siege that under the constitution would have enabled the army to rule by martial law and act without restraint against the Fascists. The King agreed, and told Facta to draft the decree for him to sign. Facta returned to the Quirinal at 6 a.m. on 28 October with the decree for the King's signature. The King refused to sign it; he had changed his mind during the night.

In 1945 Victor Emmanuel gave his explanation of why he refused to proclaim the state of siege on 28 October 1922 and thereby allowed Mussolini to come to power. He said that he had been informed that 100,000 Fascists were marching on Rome and that he thought that the 5,000 to 8,000 troops and police defending the capital would be unable to stop them.[21] The Fascists had been very successful in spreading rumours that greatly exaggerated their strength. Sir Ronald Graham did not accept Victor Emmanuel's figure, but he wrote to Curzon on 29 October that there were 60,000 Fascists marching on Rome from the north.[22]

In fact there were only 26,000 Fascists marching on Rome on 28 October, though they certainly had far larger reserves in the north of Italy. Most of these 26,000 carried rifles or revolvers, but many of them had only cudgels. General Pugliese had 12,000 troops in Rome, with all the weapons of the Italian Army at their disposal, including artillery.[23] There is no doubt that if the army had opened fire they would have scattered the Fascists and put an end to the March on Rome, and perhaps also to Mussolini's political career.

But could the King rely on the loyalty of the army? Would the army have obeyed orders to fire on the Fascists or would they have mutinied and gone over to the Fascists? The reports were coming in of how the army had welcomed the Fascists in many places in the North. If some of the army obeyed the King and others went over to the Fascists, there would be civil war – not merely the occasional killings and the arson of the recent Fascist operations, which both the Fascists and their opponents had described as civil war, but real civil war.

During the night the King consulted as many advisers as he could find. He consulted Salandra, the Liberal Prime Minister in 1915 who had brought Italy into the war. De Vecchi arrived in Rome – the army at the road blocks made no difficulty about admitting the Quadrumvir – and Grandi came too. More importantly, General Diaz arrived secretly from Florence, and he and General Pecori Giraldi came to the King. Giraldi afterwards wrote that the King had asked them what the army would do. 'Majesty,' said Diaz, 'the army will do its duty, but it would be better not to put it to the test.' Giraldi added that he himself gave almost the identical reply to the King's question.[24]

Graham shared the King's doubts about the loyalty of the army. On 28 October he wrote to Curzon that only 20 per cent of the troops would support the government against the Fascists. The police, and to a lesser extent the royal guards, could be relied on, 'but my view is that if the Fascisti refuse a constitutional solution and force matters, opposition to them will be very half-hearted'.[25]

The King's refusal to proclaim the state of siege was approved by nearly everyone in Italy except the Socialists and the Communists. When the King told Salandra a few hours later and asked him to say frankly if he thought he had been right, Salandra said that he thought that the King had been absolutely right, because he did not have sufficient force available to resist the Fascists.[26] Graham agreed; he wrote to Curzon on 31 October that 'everybody knew perfectly well that the troops would refuse to take any forcible action whatever against the Fascisti, with whom they were in sympathy'. He thought this was not surprising, because since the war officers had been insulted when they appeared in the streets and were officially advised to wear civilian dress to avoid provoking incidents, whereas the Fascists had always praised the army. Graham thought that the King's 'wise action' in refusing to sign the decree for the state of siege 'not only saved His Majesty's position, but has created a positive wave of enthusiasm in his favour'.[27]

When the King told Facta of his decision, Facta resigned. The King asked Salandra to form a government, and to offer portfolios in his Cabinet to Mussolini and other Fascists. On 28 October Mussolini received a telephone call in Milan from the King's private secretary asking him if he and four other Fascists would serve in Salandra's government. This was the proposal that Mussolini had made to Salandra a few weeks earlier, and which Salandra had rejected; now it was Mussolini who rejected it. He said that the Fascists had not gone to the trouble of marching on Rome in order to get a few seats in a Salandra government; he would accept nothing less than the office of Prime Minister. Next day the King's secretary telephoned him again, inviting him to form a government and offering to send a special train to bring him at once to Rome.

Mussolini refused the offer of a special train, but took the ordinary night sleeper to Rome. When he arrived at Civitavecchia at 8 a.m. on Monday, 30 October, he was welcomed by three thousand of his Fascists under the command of Carlo Scorza, who had arrived there on the march to Rome. He spoke a few words to them, and continued his journey by train to Rome. He booked in at the Savoia Hotel, and went to the Quirinal for his audience with the King. Thousands of Blackshirts were already entering Rome. The army at the road blocks made no attempt to stop them.[28]

Within a few hours the story was circulating in Rome that Mussolini had gone to see the King wearing his Fascist black shirt, and that his first words on entering the royal presence were: 'Majesty, I bring you the Italy of Vittorio Veneto, reconsecrated by a new victory.' The stories became part of Fascist legend; but they were untrue. Rachele wrote that before leaving Milan, Mussolini had told her that he must remember to pack his morning dress for his audience with the King; and he always denied that he had said to the King that he was bringing him the Italy of Vittorio Veneto.[29]

The King asked him if he would form a government. He agreed, and returned to the Quirinal a few hours later with his list of ministers; in recent years, it had usually taken the Prime Minister several days to form a government. At the age of thirty-nine, he was the youngest Prime Minister in Italian history. The record had previously been held by Cavour, who became Prime Minister of the kingdom of Piedmont in 1852 at the age of forty-two. Most recent Prime Ministers had been over sixty when they first took office.[30]

Mussolini himself became Minister of the Interior and Minister for Foreign Affairs as well as Prime Minister. There were thirteen other members of his Cabinet. Only three of them were Fascists. Three were Democratic Republicans, two were members of the Catholic Popolari Party, one was a Nationalist and one a Liberal. The remaining three were distinguished figures who had never taken part in politics. General Diaz became Minister of War; Admiral Paolo Thaon di Revel Minister of the Navy; and the eminent philosopher Giovanni Gentile Minister of Education. Several Fascists were appointed as under-secretaries. The Quadrumvir General De Bono became Chief of Police.

More Fascists from the North had come into Rome; they now amounted to fifty thousand. They were welcomed by most of the population, especially by the troops guarding the city. Graham repeatedly referred to their discipline and good behaviour. 'Considering that the Italian race is temperamentally undisciplined,' he wrote to Curzon, 'the order and discipline shown by the Fascisti has been remarkable.' He was not unduly perturbed when some of them forced their way into the working-class districts of Trionfale and San Lorenzo, were fired on by Communists, and proceeded to kill two Communists and burn several Communist and Socialist offices. He again praised the Fascists for their splendid display of discipline when they all marched past the Quirinal on 31 October in a display of loyalty to the King, who came out on the balcony with General Diaz to receive their salute.[31]

From there they marched to the railway station. Mussolini was determined to give a final proof of Fascist discipline by getting them to leave Rome before they could cause any irritation among the inhabitants. His government commandeered the necessary trains, and, with the help of an efficient railway administration, sent fifty thousand Fascists home within three days.[32]

Mussolini himself remained in Rome as Prime Minister. He had only three Fascists in his Cabinet and only thirty-eight Fascist deputies in the Chamber; but with the King, the army and a majority of Italians behind him, it was enough. 'Mussolini is completely master of the situation,' wrote Graham to Curzon on 31 October, 'and has an opportunity which no previous Italian minister has enjoyed.'[33]

# CHAPTER 16

◆

# Prime Minister

USSOLINI had won power by combining the roles of a responsible conservative politician and a revolutionary leader. He had kept aloof from the violent actions of his followers without losing their support. When his Blackshirts marched on Ferrara, Bologna and Ravenna, he had remained in Milan; when they marched on Milan, he was in Rome; when they marched on Rome he was in Milan. But in the eyes of all the marching Blackshirts, he was their Duce to whom they were passionately devoted. To Angelica Balabanoff, his absence from the scene of action might be a proof of cowardice; and his Socialist and other critics laughed at him for marching on Rome in a railway carriage. But both his Conservative allies and his Fascist followers preferred it that way.

On 1 November 1922, his second day as Prime Minister, he had a conversation with the British ambassador. Two months before, Graham had called him the 'able but enigmatic leader, Mussolini the ex-Communist'. He was suspicious of Mussolini because some of his articles in *Il Popolo d'Italia* had been critical of British policy, and because of his Napoleonic pose, standing with his hand across his breast and thrust under the lapel of his coat, never smiling, and 'wrapped in fierce gloom'. But Graham formed a very different impression after his talk with Mussolini on 1 November. Mussolini had been friendly, spoke slowly, and had 'a good deal of dignity'. He told Graham that he wished to develop friendly relations with Britain. 'His foreign policy would be nationalist in a good sense; Italian interests would be his one supreme consideration, just as British interests ought to be mine.' Graham was pleasantly surprised by Mussolini's attitude.[1]

Mussolini adhered to this conciliatory line in a series of interviews that he gave, in the first days after he took office, to the Rome correspondents of the London *Sunday Express*, of *Le Temps*, *Le Petit Parisien* and other Paris newspapers, and to representatives of the American press. He said that he would defend Italian interests, but emphasized that he wished to live in friendship with all other nations. He pleased the London *Times* with his telegrams to Poincaré and to Bonar Law, who had just taken office as Prime Minister in the new Conservative government in Britain, greeting them as premiers of the nations whose friendship with Italy was 'consecrated by the blood shed in common to attain victory'. *The Times* thought that the telegrams were 'a profession of faith in the alliance of the three free peoples of the West'.[2]

He adopted a very different pose when he addressed the Chamber of Deputies and the Senate for the first time as Prime Minister on 16 November.[3] He said that for the second time in a decade, as in May 1915, the Italian people had intervened to overthrow a government in defiance of the decision of Parliament. He had become Prime Minister by 'right of revolution', and would use his position to strengthen the power of his Blackshirts. With 300,000 armed young men behind him, who were ready to perform his commands with religious devotion, he could have punished all those who had slandered Fascism. 'I could have made this dingy and gloomy hall into a bivouac for my legions . . . I could have barred up Parliament and formed an exclusively Fascist government. I could have; but at least for the moment I did not wish to do so.' He was not going to use his Fascists as instruments of the capitalists against the proletariat. Lenin was turning for help to the Western capitalists, and had given them many privileges. He would not give privileges to the capitalists, for no one would receive privileges in Fascist Italy.

With only thirty-eight Fascists out of 535 deputies in the Chamber, some of Mussolini's closest colleagues had advised him to ask the King to dissolve Parliament and hold a general election. But first he wished to change the electoral system; so instead of dissolving Parliament, he asked the Chamber and Senate to grant him emergency powers to carry through reforms of the finances, the government bureaucracy, the army and education. He told them that if they did not vote him these emergency powers, he would at once dissolve Parliament.

In other circumstances and in other countries, the threatening tone that Mussolini had adopted might have infuriated the deputies; but it was just the kind of tough talk that his Fascist followers wanted, and the deputies chose to interpret his words as a reassurance that, although he could have sent in his Blackshirt squads to disperse them by force, he had no intention of doing so. Turati, for the Socialists, was the only party leader who said that Mussolini's speech was an insult to Parliament, that Mussolini had declared that he would allow Parliament to go on existing as long as it did not live. The Popolari Catholics, the Republicans, the Independents and Nationalists, and even Bonomi's right-wing Socialists, voted for Mussolini and granted him his special powers, with only the Socialist and Communist deputies voting against. All the other parties were afraid of him, and afraid of antagonizing public opinion if they opposed him; and they all preferred him to the Reds.

It was hatred of the Reds that united the rest of the nation behind Mussolini. The industrialists and landowners hated them because they believed that they would confiscate their property. The Popolari and the Catholics hated them because they were atheists and attacked the Church. Many people hated them because they feared that they would establish a Bolshevik dictatorship directed from Moscow. But most Italians hated them because they hated internationalists who felt solidarity with Socialists of other countries and not with Italian nationalists.

On 18 November Mussolini left for Lausanne to attend another session of the Conference of the Allied Powers which was deciding the terms of the peace treaty with Turkey. Before he arrived, the Swiss government hastily revoked all the deportation orders that had been made against him in the various cantons in 1903 and 1904.[4] At Lausanne he was to meet the British Foreign Secretary, Lord Curzon, and the French Prime Minister and Foreign Minister, Poincaré. He invited Curzon and Poincaré to meet him for preliminary discussions at Territet, a small town in Switzerland near the Italian frontier. When they arrived, Mussolini was surrounded by Fascist Blackshirts as he advanced to greet them, which they did not appreciate. He told them that he would not participate in the conference at Lausanne unless Italy was treated as an equal.[5] This pleased Curzon even less; his acquaintances knew that he never treated anyone as an equal.

They then went to Lausanne for the conference. Mussolini gave interviews to several foreign journalists at the Grand Hôtel des Alpes, and made a favourable impression on the London *Morning Post*. The correspondent of *Le Temps* asked him about his policy towards the Vatican. He was conciliatory but non-committal; he said that the Vatican was a power that no one could ignore, but that politics and religion must not be confused.[6]

He returned to Rome to make another aggressive speech in the Senate on 27 November.[7] He said that he had no intention of suppressing Parliament as his opponents had suggested, but that, in view of the endless discussion in which some deputies engaged, it was necessary for Parliament to adjourn while the government got on with remedying the ills that were afflicting the country. He did not wish to abolish the freedoms that the Liberal revolution had given to Italy; but he would not allow the fanatics and the rabble to ruin the liberty of forty million Italians.

On 7 December he left Rome to attend another international conference, this time in London, to discuss the question of German reparations. It was the first and only time in his life that he visited England. He arrived during one of the famous London fogs which so often occurred before the clean air legislation of the 1950s. He complained that the fog penetrated everywhere, into his clothes, his bedroom, and even into his suitcases; and when he returned to Italy he told Rachele that he wished never to go to England again, and he never did.[8]

When his train arrived at Victoria Station in London at 11 p.m. on Friday, 8 December, he was greeted by thirty Italian Fascists living in London, who were dressed in their black shirts. He went on to Claridge's Hotel, where he stayed during the three days that the conference lasted. He gave a press conference as soon as he arrived at the hotel to a large number of British and Continental journalists who had gathered there at midnight.

He got a good reception from the British press. The popular Conservative newspaper, the *Daily Mail*, was particularly enthusiastic. The *Times* correspondent, like so many men and women who met him, was impressed by his powerful and almost hypnotic eyes. Nearly all the British press wrote that he was a great leader who had saved Italy from chaos. At his press conference the only discordant note came from the correspondent of the Labour Party newspaper, the *Daily Herald*, who asked him about his relationship with the Italian Socialists. He replied that there was no possibility of any agreement, compromise or truce between the Fascists and Socialists in Italy.

The son of the manager of Claridge's Hotel told the press that his father believed that Mussolini was the greatest man in the world. When Mussolini was told about this, he said to a member of his entourage that the English were the most accomplished hypocrites in the world.[9]

*The Times* expressed the view of the British Conservative Establishment. When Mussolini began marching on Rome, they were as unhappy as Facta at his unconstitutional action, and regretted that Fascism, which 'arose to combat Socialism' and 'was formed to restore the authority of the law . . . had trampled the law underfoot'. But they immediately followed this pronouncement with another editorial article on 'The Communist Peril', which dealt with the much greater danger of Communists masquerading as Labour candidates in the municipal elections in London. *The Times* changed its line after Mussolini became Prime Minister. They now wrote that Fascism was 'a healthy reaction against the attempt to spread Bolshevism in Italy'. It had used 'White Terror' as a weapon, but such methods would cease now that it had gained power. *The Times* were only a little pained when Mussolini told the deputies that he might have made the Chamber a bivouac for his Blackshirts. They compared him to Oliver Cromwell; but they always compared Lenin and Trotsky to Marat and Robespierre.[10]

After spending three days at the conference in 10 Downing Street and being received by King George V at Buckingham Palace, Mussolini left London on the morning of 12 December. There was a large crowd of Italian Fascists in black shirts to give him a rousing send-off from Victoria Station.[11]

It is not surprising that the British press admired Mussolini. The British government had always believed that parliamentary democracy was an unsuitable form of government for countries less politically developed than Britain. In India and their colonies they governed by authoritarian methods, either directly or through despotic native princes. In central and South America they had favoured dictators who would maintain law and order and protect the lives and property of British subjects who traded there. They believed that Mussolini had shown that a strong authoritarian ruler was needed in Italy too.

There had been a violent anti-Bolshevik campaign in the British press. They had read about the crimes committed by the Bolsheviks in Russia, of how they had murdered the Tsar and his family and the nobility, and had herded aristocratic and middle-class ladies into the churches where they were raped by the Bolshevik Jews. Mussolini was fighting against the Bolsheviks in Italy, so the British Conservatives were on his side. His methods might seem a little rough by British standards; but, as an Italian, he would know best what methods to adopt with his fellow-countrymen.

But Lord Curzon and the Foreign Office had their anxieties about Mussolini. The Italians had been in occupation of Rhodes and the other Dodecanese Islands since they captured them during the war of 1911–12. By the terms of the peace treaty, they had agreed to return them to Turkey when the Turks had fulfilled all the terms of the treaty; but the treaty had been abrogated when Italy and Turkey entered the First World War on opposite sides. In the secret Treaty of London in 1915 the British and French governments had promised to give the islands to Italy if Italy entered the war on their side; but the majority of the population in the Dodecanese spoke Greek, and after Greece joined the Allies Britain and France wished to give the Dodecanese to Greece. They told the Italians that the terms of the Treaty of London had been overruled if they conflicted with the principle of self-determination of peoples which had been laid down in President Wilson's Fourteen Points and adopted in the Treaty of Versailles. The Italians also hoped to be granted a zone of influence in Albania, and were still waiting for the British government to cede them Jubaland in East Africa; but Curzon took the attitude that the questions of Jubaland and the Dodecanese should be settled together.

When Mussolini met Curzon at Territet, he said – or Curzon thought he said – that unless Italian aspirations in the eastern Mediterranean were granted, Italy would not support Britain and France in the negotiations at Lausanne. Curzon interpreted this as a threat, and resented it; he instructed the Permanent Secretary at the Foreign Office in London to raise it with the Italian ambassador. The ambassador said that Mussolini had been misunderstood, and the matter was cleared up before Mussolini arrived in London.[12] Curzon was not convinced. He had been thoroughly put off by Mussolini's attitude at Territet, by his escort of Blackshirts, and by his theatrical poses. In their private letters and memoranda, he and his staff repeatedly showed their contempt for Mussolini, whom they regarded as a ridiculous buffoon. This did not matter to Mussolini. His Fascist followers in Italy did not think of him as a ridiculous buffoon; and if the British Foreign Office did, and therefore failed to take him seriously, so much the better.

The question confronting the London Conference was Germany's failure to pay the reparations imposed by the Treaty of Versailles. This led to a sharp difference of opinion between France and Britain. Poincaré wished to take drastic action to force Germany to pay; Curzon was more conciliatory, and thought it wiser to help Germany to overcome her financial difficulties. In January 1923 the French Army invaded Germany and occupied the Ruhr; they seized the coal from the mines in part payment of the reparations. The German government called on the population of the Ruhr to engage in passive resistance, and clashes occurred between the local inhabitants and the French troops in which several German civilians were killed. Curzon expressed Britain's disapproval of the French action, but advised the Germans to abandon their resistance.

Mussolini adopted a position midway between France and Britain. The French proposed that all the Allies should contribute troops to a joint military occupation of the Ruhr; but Mussolini refused to send Italian troops, and only Belgium agreed to join in the French action. The British government hoped that Germany would not continue her resistance to the French occupation, but rejected a proposal from Mussolini that Britain and Italy should make a joint recommendation to the German government to submit to the French demands.[13]

Curzon became suspicious of Mussolini when the British embassy in Paris discovered that immediately after the London conference Mussolini had made a secret approach to France suggesting that France and Italy should form an anti-British bloc. When the Marquess of Crewe, the British ambassador, asked Poincaré about it, Poincaré confirmed that Mussolini had made this proposal to France; but when Curzon raised it with the Italian ambassador in London, the ambassador denied it. Crewe was not sure whether Mussolini had been plotting with the French against Britain, or whether Poincaré had invented the story in order to cause ill-will between Britain and Italy; but Graham had no doubt that Mussolini's foreign policy 'will be one of pure opportunism, and Italian friendship is on offer to the highest bidder', though he thought that Mussolini would prefer to work with Britain 'at a price'.[14]

*    *    *

As soon as Mussolini returned from London, he set about dealing with the opposition in Italy. He had obtained his emergency powers to govern without Parliament, but it was essential to hold new elections at which he could obtain a majority in the Chamber of Deputies. He proposed to do this by changing the electoral law, replacing the system of proportional representation by one under which the party obtaining a simple majority of seats would be awarded double the number of its elected candidates, in order to ensure that the government would have a working majority in the Chamber and could govern the country without being hampered by factious opposition there.

On 30 December 1922, acting as Minister of the Interior under the emergency powers, he ordered the arrest of Amadeo Bordiga, Antonio Gramsci and all the members of the Executive Committee of the Communist Party except for two who were deputies in the Chamber and had parliamentary immunity.[15] The Communist Party was not suppressed, but was continually harassed by the police, and began to organize as an underground illegal organization. Mussolini took no steps against the Socialists or any other political party, and they continued to operate openly, and to publish their newspapers which were neither suppressed nor censored; but if they published articles that criticized Mussolini and the government there was a chance that local Fascists would burn down their offices and perhaps murder one or two of their sub-editors.

Mussolini had renamed his Fascist squads the Voluntary Militia for National Security, a subsidiary force to help the police and army to maintain order and defend the state. In November 1922 he appointed a new body, the Fascist Grand Council,* consisting of the most eminent party leaders, to advise the Duce and to be, under him, the highest body in the party. This would reinforce the position of the central party administration and the hierarchy against the party in the provinces and the rank and file. But Mussolini discovered, as he had done when he made the Treaty of Pacification with the Socialists in 1921, that the Fascists would only acclaim him as their leader and follow him unquestioningly as long as he allowed them to do what they wanted to do – to beat up, and occasionally kill, the Reds,

---

* The 'Gran Consiglio' should accurately be translated as the 'Great Council'; but like Napoleon's 'Grand Army' ('Grande Armée') the incorrect translation 'Fascist Grand Council' has become part of the English language, and I have retained it for this reason.

and burn their party premises. Although he had announced that the victory of the Fascist revolution had ended the civil war and that 'normality' was now restored, more Socialist offices were burned, and more Socialists assaulted and killed, in 1923 than in any previous year.

But Mussolini tried to keep on good terms with the trade unions, including the Socialist trade unions, and to win their members, and even their leaders, away from the Socialists and into the Fascist trade unions which had now been formed. This accompanied his propaganda line that in Fascist Italy capitalists and proletarians would work together for the benefit of their country. He had some success, as the trade union members realized that by remaining loyal to the Socialist Party they would risk victimization, and perhaps violence and death; but by joining the Fascist unions they would gain some benefits, which the employers would feel obliged to grant for their own safety, even if these benefits were less than the demands put forward by the Socialist trade unions in 1920, which had often bankrupted the employers.

On 18 March 1923 Mussolini spoke at the opening session of the second congress of the International Chambers of Commerce. He said that it had been possible to hold the congress in Rome, only five months after 'the movement which brought to power the young forces of war and victory', because political and economic life was thriving in Italy. He said that the leading economic principle of his government was that the state must renounce its economic functions, which it was incapable of fulfilling. He would give free play to private enterprise and forgo any measure of state control that might perhaps 'satisfy the demagogy of the Left', but, as experience had shown, would be absolutely fatal to the economic development of any country. The British commercial attaché in Rome, Mr J.H. Henderson, was very impressed. In his annual report to the Foreign Office in London for 1923 he wrote that it was difficult to find a historical parallel for Mussolini's great achievement.[16]

Mussolini's relations with the Catholic Church and its Popolari supporters were more complex. He was eager to gain the votes of the 107 Popolari deputies in the Chamber, and the support of the Church in the country; but though Pope Pius XI and the Vatican hierarchy supported him in his fight against communism, some of the rank and file of the Popolari, including some priests, were shocked by the Fascists' conduct.

One of the most outspoken critics of the Fascists was Father Giuseppe Minzoni, the parish priest of Argenta near Ferrara. One evening early in August 1923 he was set on in the street by some men who began beating him with cudgels; but some passers-by arrived, and the assailants ran off. A fortnight later, on the night of 23 August, Father Minzoni was walking with a friend when they were attacked by two men, who beat them on the head with cudgels. The friend, who was wearing a hat, survived, but Minzoni, who was bare-headed, died from the blows. The murderers were identified as two local Fascists. They were prosecuted for murder, but acquitted for lack of reliable evidence.

Balbo, who was the local Fascist *ras* of Ferrara, expressed his regret at Father Minzoni's death, and the Fascist newspapers paid tribute to Minzoni as a courageous opponent; but in August 1924, on the anniversary of his death, the republican newspaper *La Voce Repubblicana* published an article which alleged that Balbo had used his influence to shield the murderers and to hush up publicity about the murder. Balbo sued the newspaper for libel, but lost the case and was ordered to pay costs. He resigned his position in the militia. Mussolini accepted his resignation with regret, and two years later appointed him Under-Secretary for Air.[17]

As usual, Mussolini had logically thought out his position, and justified it theoretically in *Gerarchia*. He had explained to the readers in March 1923 that government must always be based on force. Consent could never be absolute, for there would always be at least a few dissidents; and they would have to be overcome by force. So the force of the Fascist state must be strengthened.[18] But he probably regretted that the two Fascists had hit Father Minzoni quite so hard. Usually his Blackshirts merely beat up and injured their opponents, which caused less of a scandal than when they killed them.

Several other members and supporters of the Catholic, Liberal, Democratic and Republican parties were assaulted because they had ventured to criticize Mussolini and the Fascists. The remaining Communist activists who had not been arrested were less likely to be attacked, perhaps because the object of the beatings was to intimidate the waverers, and the Fascists realized that it would be impossible to intimidate the Communists. In 1923 it was Catholic activists who were most likely to be beaten up.[19] But the Church and the Popolari

Party did not turn against Mussolini; he was better than the Communists.

The view that Mussolini was better than the Communists was an important factor influencing the decision of the British government that King George V should pay a state visit to Italy in May 1923, which was seen everywhere as a sign of British approval for Mussolini's regime, especially after King George awarded Mussolini the Order of the Bath. But Curzon persuaded the British Cabinet to reject the King's suggestion that a Cabinet minister should accompany him to Rome to negotiate a treaty by which Jubaland was ceded to Italy. Curzon did not want any negotiations about Jubaland to take place during King George's visit.[20]

◆

# CHAPTER 17

# Corfu

MUSSOLINI was not satisfied with the Order of the Bath; he wanted Jubaland, Fiume and the Dodecanese. He wanted to succeed in Fiume where D'Annunzio had failed. He entered into direct negotiations with the Yugoslav government in Rome and Belgrade, but the talks made no progress. He had talks in Rome with the Greek Foreign Minister about the Dodecanese; both sides described the talks as friendly, but here too no progress was made. When he asked the British government about Jubaland, Curzon repeated that it had always been made clear that Jubaland would only be ceded as part of a general settlement with Turkey and Greece of the questions of the eastern Mediterranean.[1]

In the summer of 1923 the Greek government became alarmed at reports that Italy was reinforcing the garrison in the Dodecanese, and feared that Mussolini was preparing to proclaim the annexation of the islands. They informed the British government, to whom Greece had looked for protection in recent years. Curzon raised the matter with the Italian ambassador in London, who assured him that Mussolini had no such intention.[2]

As always when the British became worried about what Mussolini was going to do, they were reassured by Senator Salvatore Contarini, the Permanent Secretary-General at the Italian Foreign Office. This professional diplomat seemed to the British and other foreign governments to be the great restraining influence on Mussolini, a pillar of respectability and moderation. He did not appear in quite the same light to his staff in the Italian Foreign Office, for he had a violent temper. He would sometimes throw his documents on to the floor of his office, and when his secretary bent down to pick them up, he would give the secretary a kick on the buttocks. This was something that his Minister of Foreign Affairs, Mussolini, never did; but the staff did sometimes complain that Mussolini showed no interest in them as individuals. When they returned to the Foreign Office after an absence on holiday or a foreign posting, he never asked them how they had got on while they were away.[3]

Mussolini's difficulties with Greece and Yugoslavia were solved by a chance misfortune that turned out to be a stroke of good fortune for him. When Albania became independent from Turkey in 1912, a dispute arose between Albania and Greece about the exact line of their frontier. The matter remained in abeyance during the First World War, but in 1921 the League of Nations referred it to the Conference of the Ambassadors of the leading Allied powers – Britain, France, Italy and Japan – who in November 1921 sent the Italian General Enrico Tellini to head a joint Greek and Albanian commission to settle the frontier line.

On the morning of 27 August 1923 the members of the commission set out in three cars to drive from Yannina in Greece to Santi Quaranta in Albania. The Albanians travelled in the first car, Tellini and the other Italians in the second car, a few minutes behind, and the Greeks a few minutes behind the Italians in the third car. The Albanians reached Zeti, about four kilometres from the frontier on the Greek side, where the road passed through a forest. The Albanians drove on without hindrance; but when the Italians arrived a few minutes later they found the road blocked by trees and branches that had been thrown across the road after the Albanians had passed. The Italians stopped their car, and some of them got out to remove the obstruction. Then a band of men opened fire on them, and Tellini and the other four Italians were killed. It was nearly an hour before the car carrying the Greek representatives arrived and found the bodies.

When a report on the murder reached the Italian government, they immediately alleged that the murderers had been Greek bandits and that the Greek government officials at Yannina had connived at the murder. Why otherwise did the third car carrying the Greek representatives, which was supposed to be following a few minutes behind the Italian car, take an hour to arrive? They did not believe the Greek story that their car had been delayed through being involved in a collision with another car soon after leaving Yannina, or that footprints showed that the murderers had fled across the Albanian frontier and were therefore Albanians, not Greeks.[4]

At 8 p.m. on 29 August the Italian minister in Athens presented an ultimatum to the Greek government. He demanded that the Greek High Command should publicly apologize for the crime, that all the members of the Greek government should attend a funeral service for the murdered Italians, that the Greek Navy should salute the Italian flag, that the murderers should be arrested within five days and should suffer the death penalty, and that Greece should pay the Italian government an indemnity of fifty million lire. The Italian demands must be accepted within twenty-four hours and the idemnity paid within five days.

An hour before the Italian ultimatum expired, at 7 p.m. on 30 August, the Greek government accepted most of the Italian demands, but explained that under Greek law the judges had discretion in each case whether to apply the death penalty for murder, so they could not guarantee in advance that the murderers of the Italian officers would be sentenced to death. They also considered that the fifty million lire demanded as compensation was excessive, and proposed that the proper amount should be decided by the League of Nations.[5]

Next day, at 3 p.m. on 31 August, an Italian fleet of seventeen warships under the command of Vice-Admiral Emilio Solari arrived off Corfu. Solari informed the Greek prefect on the island that the Italians were occupying Corfu not as an act of war but in order to force the Greek government to comply with their demands for satisfaction for the murder of General Tellini and his team. Solari demanded that the prefect lower the Greek flag over the citadel within two hours, by 5 p.m., or he would bombard Corfu; but by the time that Solari's officer delivered his demand, the prefect had only half an hour in which to comply. At 5 p.m. precisely Solari, seeing that the Greek flag was still flying over the citadel, ordered his gunners to fire three blank rounds, and five minutes later opened fire on the citadel.

There were only 169 Greek soldiers in the barracks in the citadel, which was occupied by a training school for the civilian police, by six thousand refugees who had fled when Mustafa Kemal's Turkish troops captured Smyrna, and by a boys' orphanage organized by the Lord Mayor of London's Fund. A hundred yards away there were barracks occupied by a thousand Armenian orphan children who had been brought there by the Save the Children section of the American Near East Relief. The British consul, after visiting the hospitals in Corfu, reported that four people had been killed and sixteen wounded in the bombardment; but two days later Dr Kennedy of the Save the Children Fund said that at least sixteen had been killed and thirty-two wounded admitted to hospital. In Rome the Italian government officials gave the figures as thirteen killed and eight wounded.[6]

The British Prime Minister, Stanley Baldwin, and his Foreign Secretary Lord Curzon were both on holiday in France, and the British ambassador in Rome, Sir Ronald Graham, was shooting in Scotland.[7] Mr Baldwin saw no reason to interrupt his holiday at Aix-les-Bains; he had never been very interested in foreign affairs. Curzon left Bagnoles-de-l'Orme at once for London, breaking his journey in Paris to discuss the situation with Poincaré. He had already written in a note on the situation: 'The terms demanded by Mussolini seem to me extravagant – much worse than the ultimatum after Sarajevo.'[8] Graham did not return to Rome till Curzon told him to do so in a telephone call on 6 September, complaining that 'whenever a crisis occurs our ambassadors always seem to be shooting or holidaying'.[9]

This left the chargé d'affaires in Rome, H.W. Kennard, to deal with Mussolini, who explained his attitude not only to Kennard but also to Ward Price, the *Daily Mail* correspondent in Rome. He told Price that he was sure that the British government would have acted in the same way as he had done if British officers had been murdered in Greece. Curzon admitted to the Italian ambassador that Great Powers had resorted to gunboat diplomacy in the past, but at that time there was no League of Nations.[10]

Mussolini instructed the Italian delegates in Geneva to argue that the League of Nations had no right to discuss the Greek complaint, because the League had referred the Greek–Albanian boundary question to the Ambassadors' Conference, and because Italy had not committed aggression against Greece, having made it clear that the occupation of Corfu was only temporary until Greece had complied with the Italian demands. The Italian ambassador at the Conference of Ambassadors in Paris adopted the same attitude: Italy would be reasonable, and would listen to any representations made in the Ambassadors' Conference, but not to the League of Nations.

Curzon became increasingly irritated with Mussolini, and aware of the weakness of his position, as he received conflicting advice from Lord Robert Cecil, the British delegate to the League of Nations in Geneva, from Lord Crewe at the Ambassadors' Conference in Paris, from Mr Charles Henry Bentinck in Athens, and from a slightly diffident Mr Kennard in Rome, who was conscious that he was only a first secretary and chargé d'affaires. Cecil wrote that the delegates of the smaller states would insist on discussing the situation in the General Assembly, and that it would be a heavy blow to the prestige of the League, and to the hopes placed in it by mankind, if it failed to deal with this first challenge to its authority. Both Crewe and Kennard assured Curzon that Mussolini would never agree to submit to the authority of the League.[11] It did not really help Curzon that his Prime Minister bestirred himself to send him a telegram from Aix-les-Bains on 5 September: 'I completely support your policy of supporting League of Nations.'[12]

The British press and public were disappointed in Mussolini, and thought that he had behaved badly about Corfu. 'What a swine this Mussolini is,' wrote Winston Churchill to his wife.[13] All the press was critical, except the *Daily Mail*. But the French press supported his action in Corfu, and were encouraged to do so by Poincaré. The British Foreign Office thought that Poincaré was supporting Mussolini in order to win him over to support France against Britain over the French occupation of the Ruhr; but Crewe did not think that this was Poincaré's motive. It was because the French government feared 'that if Signor Mussolini received a check now of a humiliating kind, it might mean his fall and an outbreak of Communism' in Italy.[14]

On the morning of 4 September Mussolini presided at a Cabinet meeting at which it was decided that if the League of Nations declared that it had authority to deal with the Corfu incident, Italy would leave the League. When someone referred to the critical attitude of the British press, Mussolini said that he hoped to teach the British a lesson in political 'realism' and the 'futility of conventional phrases'.[15] That evening Kennard asked for an interview with Mussolini, and urged him not to carry out his threat to leave the League of Nations. Did Mussolini not realize that the situation might develop to a point where it would no longer be a dispute between Italy and Greece but between Italy and fifty other nations, as he was 'practically flinging defiance in the face of the whole world'? Mussolini said that the attitude of the League was prompted by men like Camille Huysmans of Belgium and Karl Branting of Sweden, who were Socialists and hated Fascist Italy.[16]

Kennard wrote to Curzon that Mussolini was 'a mixture of megalomania and extreme patriotism' who believed that if he weakened in his stand against the League of Nations 'the whole Fascist fabric might collapse like a pack of cards', and he might therefore even be prepared to start a European war rather than retreat. He must therefore be regarded as a mad dog, and every effort must be made to humour him. There was of course the alternative of shooting the mad dog, but this would lead to the fall of Fascism; Italy would then succumb to anarchy, to a military dictatorship, or to something worse.[17]

Some British diplomats disagreed. Bentinck in Athens sympathized with Greece, and thought that the fall of Mussolini, and even internal disorder in Italy, would be a lesser evil than if Mussolini were to triumph over Corfu; for this would lead to Italy replacing Britain as the dominant power in the Mediterranean. Lord Robert Cecil in Geneva believed that the fall of Mussolini might lead to chaos in Italy, but that his successful defiance of the League of Nations might lead to chaos in Europe. He was impressed by the opinion held by some of the delegates he had met in Geneva, like Nincic of Yugoslavia and Benes of Czechoslovakia, 'that this is only the first of several troubles that Italy and Mussolini may cause us in the near future'.[18]

But how could they stop Mussolini? Curzon went so far as to consult the Treasury about the possibility of enforcing any financial or economic sanctions that the League of Nations might impose against Italy. The Treasury reported that it would involve setting up an elaborate system of controls which would be greatly resented by British businessmen; and those other nations who did not observe the League's sanctions would capture British markets. Unless other countries, especially the United States, joined in, sanctions would be completely ineffective.[19] The British government had not found any technical difficulties about imposing the blockade against Bolshevik Russia; but they did not wish to disrupt the Italian economy if this might bring about the fall of Mussolini. The Conservative Establishment newspaper, the *Morning Post*, thought that the issue was simple: 'Mussolini versus Lenin'.[20]

The Assembly of the League of Nations decided to ask the Ambassadors' Conference to settle the Corfu incident. The ambassadors informed the Greek government that they supported the Italian demands. Greece paid fifty million lire to Italy; and Mussolini evacuated Corfu.[21]

Lord Robert Cecil was worried. 'A powerful member of the League', he wrote, 'has refused to carry out its treaty obligations under the Covenant and has succeeded in doing so with impunity, some might even say with an increase of prestige . . . The authority of the League has been challenged in a sphere which is precisely that for which it was created.'[22] He was right in thinking that it had increased Mussolini's prestige. It made him very popular in Italy; even the Socialists did not venture to criticize him. *Avanti!* condemned not Mussolini but the hypocrisy of the British imperialists who had so often resorted to gunboat diplomacy, but objected when Italy did the same.[23]

Curzon's son-in-law, Mr Oswald Mosley, was an MP in 1923; he had left the Conservative Party and was about to join the Labour Party. He believed that Britain should take a firm stand against Mussolini. He was disgusted at Baldwin's lack of interest, and did not think that his father-in-law had done enough. He began to admire Mussolini; he thought that he had upheld the interests of his country much more vigorously than Baldwin and Curzon.[24]

The Yugoslav government had seen what Mussolini could do, and that whatever he did the British would not stop him. After the Corfu incident, the negotiations with Yugoslavia about Fiume made much better progress. In January 1924 Mussolini reached an agreement with Yugoslavia: Italy should have the town of Fiume, and Yugoslavia would retain the port of Baros and other outlying areas. Nor did the Greeks argue any more about the Dodecanese, which remained under Italian occupation. In 1925 Mussolini promulgated a law requiring all inhabitants of the Dodecanese to adopt Italian nationality.[25]


In December 1923 a general election was held in Britain. The Labour Party under Ramsay MacDonald fought the election on a programme that included granting diplomatic recognition to the Bolshevik government of Russia, and of making a commercial treaty with Russia, which was now called the USSR (Union of Socialist Soviet Republics). The Conservatives bitterly opposed the recognition of the Soviet government. They were the largest party in the House of Commons, but were outnumbered by the Labour and Liberal MPs The Liberals agreed to support Labour, and in January 1924 MacDonald became Prime Minister and Foreign Secretary in the first Labour government in Britain. He decided to recognize the Soviet Union.

Mussolini had also decided to recognize the Soviet government. He would suppress Bolshevism in Italy, but would abandon all attempts to overthrow it in Russia. Soon after he came to power he had a talk in Rome on 4 December 1922 with Krassin, the Soviet Commissar of Trade and Industry.[26] It was the beginning of negotiations for diplomatic recognition and commercial relations between Italy and the Soviet Union. Progress was slow, because the Soviet government struck a hard bargain; but by January 1924 Mussolini was on the point of recognizing the Soviet Union – the first power in western Europe to do so.

When MacDonald heard what Mussolini was about to do, he was disappointed, because he wished to be the first government to recognize Soviet Russia. He asked Mussolini to defer recognition for a few days until Britain and Italy could recognize the Soviet Union together. Mussolini had criticized MacDonald as a pacifist during the war; but he was eager to be on good terms with a man who was more likely than a Tory imperialist Foreign Secretary to cede Jubaland to Italy. He agreed to defer recognition of the Soviet Union until MacDonald was ready. The British Foreign Office then informed the world press that Britain was going to recognize the Soviet government.

Mussolini was very angry. He thought that MacDonald had double-crossed him by persuading him to delay recognition and then unilaterally announcing Britain's intention. MacDonald apologized; he said that there had been a misunderstanding. He had never intended that there should be a joint Anglo-Italian statement about recognizing the Soviet Union, but had thought that Mussolini would make the announcement in Italy at the same time as MacDonald announced it in London.

MacDonald now made another suggestion to Mussolini. He explained that George V had strongly objected to receiving a Soviet ambassador, the representative of a government that had murdered his cousin the Tsar. But if a Soviet ambassador was accredited to London, the King would have to receive him; so MacDonald proposed instead that Britain and the Soviet Union should be represented in London and Moscow by chargés d'affaires, because chargés d'affaires did not present their credentials to the King. He asked Mussolini to do likewise and exchange chargés d'affaires, not ambassadors, with the Soviet Union.

Mussolini was annoyed with MacDonald. He refused, and threatened to publish the correspondence with MacDonald about recognizing the Soviet Union. This caused real consternation in the British Foreign Office; on no account must the correspondence be published, for it would reveal King George's role in the matter. Mussolini agreed not to publish the correspondence, but unilaterally recognized the Soviet Union and agreed to exchange ambassadors, not chargés d'affaires. So there would be an Italian ambassador, and only a British chargé d'affaires, in Moscow. He appointed Count Alessandro Manzoni as ambassador, and ordered him to leave for Moscow at once to make sure that he was the first Western ambassador to arrive. Manzoni left by the night train that same evening, without having had time to buy a fur coat to keep him warm during the Russian winter.[27]

With these diplomatic successes to his credit, in addition to his consolidation of his power at home, Mussolini was unstoppable. The Chamber voted the new electoral law. At the general election on 6 April 1924, 66.3 per cent of the electors voted for the Fascist and government candidates – some out of fear, but most from patriotic enthusiasm. In the larger towns, where foreign journalists were watching, the opposition parties were able to operate; in the remoter country areas there was a good deal of intimidation. One Socialist candidate was murdered, and Socialist and Communist canvassers risked their lives if they distributed their election literature. The voters went to the polls through streets decorated with Fascist flags, and found Fascist scrutineers in the polling stations.

The Fascists won 225 seats. They had 260 deputies in the new Chamber; the other parties supporting them had 116 deputies, giving Mussolini's government 376 of the 535 seats in the Chamber. The Socialist share of the vote fell from 25.7 per cent in 1921 to 10.1 per cent, though the Communists increased their share from 3.5 per cent to 5.8 per cent. The Socialists and Communists between them lost 72 of their 138 seats. The Popolari share fell from 21.2 per cent in 1921 to 9.1 per cent, and their seats in the Chamber from 107 to 40. They were not helped by the Vatican, who ordered priests to take no part in the elections.

In Sicily, the former Prime Minister, Orlando, had always had strong links with the Mafia, and several of his candidates were returned; but some sections of the Mafia split and formed a 'Young

Mafia' who supported the Fascist candidates. They knew that they now had to deal with a party, and a party boss, who could fight the Mafia with their own weapons and beat them.[28]

# CHAPTER 18

———— ♦ ————

# Matteotti

W HEN the new Parliament met on 30 May 1924 the Socialist deputy Matteotti made a blistering attack on the conduct of the general election.[1] His powerful voice could not be drowned by the indignant shouts of the Fascist deputies as he listed examples of violence and intimidation used by the Fascists throughout the country. He stated that less than a hundred of the five hundred Socialist candidates had been able to move freely in their constituencies; some of them had been afraid to stay in their own homes. He demanded that the result of the elections should be annulled, and hinted that the Socialist deputies might withdraw from the Chamber in protest. This tactic of withdrawing from an assembly in protest followed a well-known Italian tradition, for one of the famous incidents in the history of ancient Rome was when the plebs, in the first years of the republic in about 500 B.C., withdrew to the Aventine Hill in protest against patrician rule, and forced the patricians to grant them a voice in the government of the republic.

Matteotti was saying openly what many Italians were saying in private – that the intimidation, beatings and occasional killings were planned by a group of leading Fascists who were close to Mussolini. People called them 'the Cheka', the name of the secret police of the Communist government in Russia.

Matteotti was expecting that he too would be murdered, like the other Socialist victims of the Fascist *squadristi* and the Cheka. 'You may kill me,' he said, 'but you will never kill my ideas ... My ideas will not die ... My children will be proud of their father ... The workers will bless my corpse ... Long live Socialism!'[2]

His speech enraged the Fascist deputies. Giunta, who three years before had led the group that kicked the deserter Misiano out of the Parliament building, shouted out that Matteotti was a bandit. During the next few days Matteotti was violently denounced in the Fascist press. They wrote that he was a mischief-maker who had slandered the Fascists, and that his refusal to accept the result of the general election and his threat to withdraw to the Aventine was undermining the constitution and law and order. On 1 June Mussolini wrote in *Il Popolo d'Italia* that Matteotti deserved a worse fate than merely to be called a bandit by Giunta. Cesare Rossi, a member of Mussolini's entourage, uttered threats among his friends about what he would do to Matteotti.[3]

But on 7 June Mussolini made a conciliatory speech in the Chamber, deploring political quarrels and appealing for national reconciliation. On the same day the London journal *The Statist* published an article by Matteotti in which he wrote that he had evidence that high officials in the Italian government and the Bank of Italy had accepted bribes from the Sinclair Exploration Company in the United States to grant them facilities to search for oil in Emilia and Sicily.[4]

At 4.30 p.m. on Tuesday, 10 June Matteotti had just left his flat in the Lungo Tevere Arnaldo da Brescia in central Rome on his way to the Chamber of Deputies when five men, who were waiting in a car outside his flat, leaped on him and forced him into the car. He was a tall and powerful man and put up a strong resistance, but they succeeded in getting him into the car and drove off at top speed. The caretaker at the block of flats where Matteotti lived had noticed the car earlier in the afternoon being driven round and round the block. Her suspicions had been aroused, and she had taken the registration number; and the men had got out of the car and threatened her.[5]

Next morning, as Matteotti had not returned home, his wife went to the police and claimed that her husband had been abducted; and the caretaker gave the registration number of the car to the police. The police did nothing. When the Matteotti family lawyer asked them what they were doing and who was the owner of the car, they were embarrassed and at first did not reply; but when the lawyer threatened to inform the press about the police inactivity, they revealed that the car belonged to Filippo Filippelli, the editor of the Fascist newspaper *Corriere Italiano*. The car was found abandoned in a street in Rome. There were bloodstains on the inside and outside of the car.[6]

On 12 June the matter was raised in the Chamber of Deputies, and Mussolini was asked to make a statement. He said that the police under General De Bono were energetically pursuing inquiries in an attempt to trace Matteotti, but that the government had no idea where he was. At this a Republican deputy shouted out that this proved that Mussolini was an accomplice in the murder. Amid uproar in the Chamber, the Socialist and Communist deputies accused Mussolini and the Fascists of having murdered Matteotti. Mussolini was unusually agitated, and one of the officials of the Chamber noticed that he was trembling. At the end of the debate the Socialists announced that their deputies would take no part in the proceedings of the Chamber as a protest against the murder of Matteotti. On 27 June they left the Chamber. In the political jargon of the day, they withdrew to the Aventine Hill; and they became known as 'the Aventines'.[7]

It was not until 16 August that Matteotti's body was found buried on waste land about twenty kilometres north of Rome. He had been beaten with cudgels and had died either from a haemorrhage or from a heart attack while he was being beaten.[8]

Matteotti had two sons aged six and four, who loved him. Signora Matteotti did not tell them what had happened; she said that their father had gone away on a long journey. Whenever the front door-bell rang, the children ran to the door to see if it was he. They noticed that there was always a group of men standing outside the house; they were members of Mussolini's secret police who were keeping the family under observation and making it difficult for their friends to contact them. The Matteotti children wondered why their playmates did not visit them any more. When they were a little older their mother told them the truth.[9]

In the Chamber, Mussolini expressed his horror at the murder of Matteotti. He sent his condolences to Signora Matteotti, and arranged for her to be paid a pension.[10] He promised that the government would see to it that the police found the murderers and brought them to justice, and he gave orders to De Bono to see that this was done. But he strongly denied that he, the government or the Fascist Party had anything to do with the murder, and threatened to punish the Socialists and the opposition press if they propagated the libel and tried to use the murder as an excuse to overthrow the government.

Police inquiries showed that Matteotti had been killed by five Fascists – Amerigo Dumini, from the Florence squad, Albino Volpi, Amieto Poveromo, Giuseppe Viola and Augusto Malacria. They were arrested. The police also arrested Filippelli, the owner of the blood-stained car, and Filippo Naldi, the editor of another Fascist news-paper, and charged them with being accessories to the murder. Under interrogation, Dumini said that they had abducted and killed Matte-otti on the orders of Rossi and Giovanni Marinelli, who was a member of the Fascist Grand Council, and, like Rossi, one of Musso-lini's personal entourage. Rossi and Marinelli were arrested. They told the police that they had given orders for Matteotti to be abducted because they thought that this was what Mussolini wanted. Accord-ing to Rossi, Matteotti's speech in the Chamber on 30 May had infuriated Mussolini, who had said to them: 'What is the Cheka doing? What is Dumini doing? That man, after that speech, should no longer be in circulation.'[11]

There were three judicial inquiries into the Matteotti murder: the Senate inquiry of 1924; the trial of Dumini and his colleagues in 1926; and a further inquiry in 1947, after the fall of Fascism. No conclusive new evidence came to light in 1947. There is no doubt that Dumini and his four associates murdered Matteotti and acted on the orders of Marinelli and Rossi. They had apparently originally intended to kidnap Matteotti to a remote place in a forest in Tuscany, where they would kill him and dispose of his body in a grave where it was unlikely to be found; but Matteotti put up such a fierce resist-ance in the car that they panicked and murdered him just outside Rome, and buried the body there.

There is far less evidence that Mussolini was personally implicated. There are a number of stories told by journalists and other writers; one of them is that Dumini went to Mussolini immediately after the murder and showed him a piece of the bloodstained fabric of the car to prove that he had carried out his orders. But none of these stories are substantiated. Rossi's statement is the only real evidence against Mussolini. Did Mussolini say 'What is the Cheka doing? What is Dumini doing? That man, after that speech, should no longer be in circulation'? Or did Rossi invent it in order to excuse himself, pleading that he was only obeying Mussolini's orders, or to implicate Mussolini out of spite, because Mussolini had not protected him and had allowed him to be arrested? If Mussolini did say it, what did he mean? That he wanted Marinelli and Rossi to get Dumini to kill Matteotti? Or did he not really mean it at all, and was it just an outburst of rage?

His question 'What is the Cheka doing?' is surprising. Mussolini always publicly denied the existence of any Cheka among his entourage, and ridiculed this name given by his opponents to his staff. Would he have used it privately in his conversation with his staff? Or was it in fact a sour joke, meaning: 'I don't see any sign of this imaginary Cheka getting rid of this troublesome opponent'?

After 1945 Rossi wrote about the Matteotti murder in his book *Il delitto Matteotti*. Although he repeated his statement that Mussolini had said that Dumini and the Cheka should prevent Matteotti from circulating, he wrote that the most serious charge against Mussolini was that he allowed a political climate to develop in which it was possible for the murder of Matteotti to take place, along with the fatal attack on Father Minzoni, and all the other killings and beatings by Fascists of their political opponents. This is undeniable. The Fascists, bred in the tradition of violence in Italian politics, their First World War experiences and their hatred of Socialist internationalists, whom they regarded as traitors, had adopted murder as a regular weapon; and as Mussolini relied on the Fascists, and had no alternative but to rely on them, he, implicitly at least, allowed them to murder. The element in Matteotti's murder which particularly shocked many conservatives and moderate Italians was that the murderers were not rank and file Fascist *squadristi* from the provinces, but members of Mussolini's personal entourage in Rome.

When the news of the disappearance of Matteotti first broke on 12 June, it created a storm that shook the government. Afterwards political commentators and historians believed that Mussolini's regime was tottering, but just survived, because his opponents missed their opportunity and he was able to recover and save the situation. In fact, he was never really in danger. He may have given the impression to observers who saw him in the Chamber that he was rattled and nervous, but he remained master of the situation.

He turned at once for support to his Fascists. On 13 June he gave orders to the squads – now called the militia – in all the great provincial centres to be ready to march again on Rome to defeat by force any attempt to overthrow him.[12] No one could have stopped the militia except the army, and the army did not want to get rid of Mussolini; nor did anyone else except the Socialists and Communists. All the others, though they deplored the murder of Matteotti, still thought that Mussolini was better than the Communists. They therefore chose to believe that Mussolini knew nothing about the murder, and that the Socialists were trying to use it as an excuse to slander him, to bring down his regime, and to plunge Italy again into anarchy.

Mussolini's foreign admirers adopted the same attitude. The London *Times* condemned the murder of Matteotti as another example of the unlawful violence to which some Fascists resorted; but they hastened to add that it would be very wrong of the opposition in Italy to try to use the incident to bring down Mussolini's government. They regretted 'the tragedy of Mussolini's situation' and 'the stunning blow that had fallen upon him', just when he had succeeded in restoring law and order; but *The Times* was confident that Mussolini was handling the situation 'in the only right way' and was 'not the man to go down without fighting a sturdy fight'. The *Daily Mail* hailed Mussolini as 'the Saviour of Italy,' and declared: 'We in England have confidence in Signor Mussolini; so have the Italians.'[13]

Ramsay MacDonald unwittingly helped Mussolini. Curzon had delayed ceding Jubaland to Italy despite repeated warnings from Graham that the delay was causing resentment in Rome and was threatening to harm Anglo-Italian relations. When MacDonald took over from Curzon at the Foreign Office, he in his turn came under pressure from Graham to cede Jubaland. As a Socialist, MacDonald disliked Fascism, but he was also eager to show that he was not a Tory imperialist like Curzon who refused to make concessions for the sake of world peace. After the details of the transfer had been negotiated between British and Italian experts, the treaty ceding Jubaland was initialled at the Foreign Office in London on 9 June 1924, the day before Matteotti was murdered.[14] The news of this Italian diplomatic success came just at the right time to help Mussolini during the furore about the murder.

The Ethiopian prince Ras Tafari, who later became the Emperor Haile Selassie and Mussolini's great enemy, also unwittingly helped Mussolini. On 18 June Ras Tafari arrived in Rome on a state visit. Mussolini used the visit as an excuse to summon the militia in Florence and Perugia to come to Rome, ostensibly to protect and honour Ras Tafari, but in fact to be ready to resist any attempt by the Italian opposition to overthrow the Fascist regime. He entertained Ras Tafari at the Villa Torlonia in Rome. They liked each other, and held friendly talks about the possibility of Italy providing financial and economic assistance in developing Ethiopia.[15]

Even the Soviet ambassador, Konstantin Konstantinovich Yurenev, came to Mussolini's aid. The day before Matteotti was murdered, he had sent Mussolini an invitation to attend a banquet at the embassy on 11 July. At the height of the uproar over the murder, the Italian Communists and Socialists asked Yurenev to withdraw the invitation. He refused to do so. He told the Italian Communists and Socialists that he did not believe their forecasts about the imminent fall of Mussolini, that Italian friendship was important for the Soviet Union, which was confronted with a hostile world, and that he would do nothing to antagonize Mussolini. The dinner at the embassy duly took place, and Mussolini's presence was commented upon by both his supporters and opponents. The government in Moscow approved of Yurenev's conduct. It was not until 1937 that he was arrested and executed by Stalin.[16]

Mussolini survived the storm. Turati wrote about the situation in his correspondence with Anna Kulisciov, who was no longer young and beautiful, but was as mentally alert and as devoted to socialism as she had been fifty years before. 'The day before yesterday,' he wrote to her on 14 June, 'we were the victors almost without knowing it, and he was beaten and knew it. Yesterday they had already taken heart.'[17] On 17 June Mussolini had his first audience with the King since the murder of Matteotti. The King did nothing. On 26 June a vote of confidence in the government was carried in the Senate by 225 votes against 21, with six abstentions.[18]

Mussolini adopted the prescribed Machiavellian policy of sacrificing his subordinates to save himself. De Bono and the prominent Jewish Fascist, Aldo Finzi, were forced to resign as Chief of Police and Under-Secretary of the Interior, for there had been rumours that they had tried to impede the investigation into the murder. But Mussolini had to be careful not to alienate the Fascist rank and file. Balbo advised him to have Dumini and the other murderers shot; but Farinacci strongly opposed this suggestion. At Fascist meetings, the audience were shouting 'Long live Dumini! Long live Volpi! Death to the enemies of Mussolini!'[19]

As week after week went by, and Mussolini was still there, firmly in power, the protest of the Aventines became more and more futile. By the time that Rossi's evidence – that Mussolini had said that the Cheka and Dumini should prevent Matteotti from circulating – was made public in November, it was too late to do Mussolini much harm. He was now almost ready to take the offensive and strike down his opponents.

In December 1924 the police discovered that Giunta had led a group that assaulted a former Fascist who had disagreed with the party. The police asked the Chamber of Deputies to lift Giunta's parliamentary immunity. The Fascist deputies protested loudly. A few days later, the Fascists in Florence organized a great demonstration to protest against the arrest of a number of Fascists who had committed crimes of violence against their opponents. The Fascists wrecked the printing presses of two opposition newspapers in Florence, the masonic lodge, and the houses of several lawyers who had appeared in court on behalf of anti-Fascist defendants. There were smaller outbreaks of violence by protesting Fascists in Bologna, Pisa and elsewhere. They broke into the house of Mussolini's former colleague, the Socialist leader Lazzari, and beat him up. Piero Gobetti, the brilliant young Socialist editor of the journal *Rivoluzione Liberale*, came off worse than Lazzari. He was attacked by the Fascists in Turin in September 1924, and so badly beaten that after escaping to Paris he died there seventeen months later at the age of twenty-four.[20]

The Fascist demonstrators demanded the release of all Fascists from prison. They demanded that Mussolini support them and lead them to complete the Fascist revolution.[21]

On 3 January 1925 Mussolini addressed the Chamber of Deputies. He had seen the King the previous day, and had made sure that there would be no difficulties from the Quirinal. He made the speech that his Fascist supporters wished to hear. 'I, and I alone, assume the political, moral and historical responsibility for all that has happened ... If Fascism has been a criminal association, if all the acts of violence have been the result of a certain historical, political and moral climate, the responsibility for this is mine.' This was a remarkable statement to make only seven months after Matteotti's murder; was that murder one of the 'acts of violence' for which he alone assumed responsibility? But he was now in a position, with the rioting Fascists behind him, where he could say it.

He ridiculed the idea that he had an organization called 'the Cheka' which committed crimes. There was a Cheka in Russia, which terrorized the whole bourgeois class, but not in Italy. He denounced the Socialists who had gone to the Aventine. The Aventine secession was unconstitutional and flagrantly revolutionary. It was republican – and at this point the Fascist deputies shouted 'Long live the King!'[22]

Dumini and his companions who had murdered Matteotti, with

Marinelli and Rossi who had incited them to do it, and Filippelli, the owner of the car, and Naldi, were prosecuted for murder. They were defended by Farinacci, who had recently qualified as a lawyer. The trial dragged on through 1925. In December the Court of Appeal held that there was no case against Marinelli, Rossi, Filippelli and Naldi, who were found not guilty and released from prison. Rossi hastily left Italy, and in due course joined the anti-Fascist refugees in Paris, from where he denounced Mussolini for his part in the murder.

The five men who had been in the car when Matteotti was killed remained in custody till judgment was finally given in their case in March 1926. Viola and Malacria were found not guilty. Dumini, Volpi and Poveromo were found guilty of killing Matteotti, but the court held that the murder was unpremeditated and had been committed under provocation – the 'provocation' being Matteotti's determined resistance to the attempt to kidnap him. They were all three sentenced to six years' imprisonment less ten days. Under a recent amnesty, four years of the sentence were remitted. As they had been in prison for one year and nine months before and during their trial, they had another two months and twenty days to serve before they were released. Dumini afterwards got into trouble for other crimes, and was again imprisoned; but Marinelli, who had been acquitted of all charges, was soon reappointed to the Fascist Grand Council and to Mussolini's personal entourage.[23]

Mussolini's position in Italy had never been stronger; and he was about to be warmly acclaimed by government circles in Britain and by an influential section of opinion in the United States.

# CHAPTER 19

# Consolidating the Dictatorship

USSOLINI had got away with murder – a murder that he
had condoned, though not committed – and had done so
by relying on the most murderous sections of the Fascists.
His first reaction to the news of Matteotti's death, and the storm of
protest that it aroused, was to follow the advice of Federzoni and
the more moderate and Conservative members of his government;
he got rid of Finzi and De Bono and authorized the arrest and prosecution of Marinelli, Dumini and the murderers. But then, as he told
his wife Rachele, he began to fear that Federzoni might be thinking
of also getting rid of him, Mussolini. He turned to Farinacci and the
militia, who were shouting 'Long live Dumini!' He often told Rachele, at the time and in later years, that he was grateful to Farinacci,
who had saved the Fascist regime during the crisis of 1924.[1]

The Socialists in every country of the world expressed their horror
at the murder of Matteotti. The National Executive Committee of
the British Labour Party passed a resolution of protest at a meeting
that was attended by Ramsay MacDonald and his Home Secretary,
Arthur Henderson. The press in Italy were indignant that the British
Prime Minister should have interfered in the internal affairs of Italy
by voting for the resolution. MacDonald hastened to assure the
Italian government that he had attended the meeting in his capacity
as a member of the National Executive Committee of the Labour
Party and not as Prime Minister and Foreign Secretary. Mussolini
said that he accepted this explanation and would make no formal
protest, though he thought that MacDonald would have been wiser
if he had left the meeting before the Matteotti resolution was discussed.[2]

But though the international Socialist movement condemned the
Matteotti murder, no one else did. The Liberal philosopher Benedetto

Croce and Pope Pius XI in Italy, and the Conservative statesmen and press in Britain and other countries, expressed their support for Mussolini against the attempts of the Reds to use the Matteotti case to overthrow him.[3] The Socialists had hoped that Matteotti the martyr would triumph in death over his murderers; but in fact his murder led to the final destruction of socialism in Italy. When Mussolini realized that the Conservatives, the Catholic Church and even the Liberals would forgive him for the murder of a Socialist leader, he knew that he could safely proceed to annihilate the Socialists and that anti-socialism was the banner under which his Fascist revolutionaries and the Conservative Establishment could unite.

Within a few days of his speech on 3 January 1925 his police began harassing the Socialists, raiding their party offices, arresting their activists, and placing restrictions on the publication and circulation of their newspapers, though the Socialist Party and its press continued to function legally as best they could. On 15 February he appointed Farinacci as Secretary of the Fascist Party, though Farinacci was acting as counsel for the defence at the trial of Dumini and the other murderers of Matteotti.[4] The appointment was a fillip for the *squadristi* and a warning to all the enemies of Fascism.

On the same day Mussolini collapsed, falling ill with stomach ulcers.[5] It was the first serious illness he had had in his life. His doctors and his friends all believed it was brought on by the strains of the Matteotti crisis; he had lasted out as long as the crisis lasted, but as soon as he had emerged victorious, the symptoms began. The ulcers may also have been caused by his lifestyle and his eating habits.

Mussolini led an ascetic life, and was very conscious of the need to remain physically healthy. Many forceful political leaders have had large appetites, and were *bons vivants* who indulged to the full in the pleasures of food, wine, brandy and tobacco – among them Henry VIII, Louis XIV, Peter the Great, Bismarck, Mustafa Kemal, Tito, Stalin and Churchill. But Mussolini, like Napoleon, Lenin and Hitler, was not interested in the pleasures of life, and was satisfied with the pleasures of power. He ate very little, and very quickly, rarely spending more than ten minutes on a meal. He hardly ever drank wine, except when toasts were proposed at official banquets, and never spirits or cocktails. As a young man he sometimes smoked cigarettes, and during the First World War, like so many other soldiers, he acquired the habit of smoking heavily in the trenches; but after his discharge from the army he reduced his smoking to an occasional cigarette, and had given up completely by the time of the March on Rome.[6]

Like Napoleon, his only sensual pleasure was sex. He had always had love affairs, perhaps because they satisfied his lust for power. He believed that the masses, like women, admired masterful men. Mussolini enjoyed seducing and mastering women, but he enjoyed even more seducing and mastering the masses.

When he became Prime Minister and moved to Rome, Rachele and the children stayed in Milan, because the children felt more at home there, and were settled in their school. Mussolini lived alone in a flat in the Palazzo Tittoni in the Via Rasella. The flat had a small entrance hall, a dining room, a decent-sized bedroom, and three other small rooms. There was no kitchen, and meals were sent up to him by the cook of a baron who lived in the flat on the floor below. The catering and the cleaning were managed by a woman who had been recommended to him by Margherita Sarfatti;[7] but she could not ensure that he ate at least a frugal meal, as Rachele did when he was at home with her.

As Prime Minister he was too busy to spend time on any relaxation. He had always enjoyed the theatre, and in Milan went regularly to his box at the theatre with Rachele, and sometimes with his daughter Edda. In Rome he also took a box at the theatre, but never had time to go there. He did not even have time to have love affairs with the beautiful society ladies who met him at official receptions and were fascinated by his strong, aloof personality and his hypnotic eyes. 'I do not deny that he had some love affairs,' wrote Rachele, 'but the fanatical devotion he inspired made them readily comprehensible, and he was always the first to tell me about them. Sometimes his contrition was positively comic.'[8]

She would have been more worried if Margherita Sarfatti had been in Rome, for she intensely disliked *la* Sarfatti, and thought her overbearing;[9] but Margherita had remained in Milan with her husband. Rachele seems to have been right in thinking that Mussolini had very little time for gallantry. Perhaps, now that he was ruler of Italy, he did not need to satisfy his lust for power by pursuing women. He may have found it more enjoyable to play the part of the hard, cold, unapproachable god whom women admired from a distance.

\*     \*     \*

The authorities tried to suppress the news of Mussolini's illness. Rachele wished to go to him, but was persuaded by the Chief of Police in Milan not to travel to Rome for fear that it would start rumours that he was very ill.[10] For five weeks, he could not carry on with his work, which gave Farinacci a free hand to encourage the Fascist *squadristi* to commit revolutionary excesses. When Mussolini was well enough to resume the direction of the government on 23 March 1925, he made no attempt to check them.

The militia in Florence were particularly violent. When a Fascist was killed, they attacked and burned Socialist newspaper offices, and the houses of Socialists, Catholic oppositionists and freemasons.[11] During the nineteenth century the freemasons had played an important part in the struggles of the Risorgimento; Garibaldi became the Grand Master of the Italian Grand Orient lodges, and Victor Emmanuel II and many other national leaders were freemasons. But in the twentieth century the Fascists, like the Communists, regarded the freemasons as a rival organization which must be destroyed. The rules of the Fascist Party prohibited Fascists from being freemasons; but several important Fascists secretly retained their membership of their lodges.

Mussolini was not happy that Farinacci allowed the Fascists to burn down the houses of freemasons in Florence. He was even more worried when the Fascists in Rome attacked a Catholic procession in June 1925, and the Pope made a strong protest. It was also embarrassing that Farinacci was vigorously defending Dumini and the other murderers of Matteotti at their long trial throughout 1925. So in April 1926 Mussolini dismissed Farinacci as party secretary, and appointed a far less colourful figure, Augusto Turati – no relation of the Socialist leader – to succeed him.[12]

Mussolini was well satisfied with the developments in foreign policy. In October 1924 the Conservatives in Britain were returned to power at the general election. MacDonald resigned, and Baldwin became Prime Minister with Austen Chamberlain as Foreign Secretary and Churchill as Chancellor of the Exchequer. Mussolini was delighted at MacDonald's resignation, for though MacDonald had given him Jubaland, he had angered him by his protest about Matteotti's murder. Mussolini commented joyfully that the fall of Mac-Donald's Labour government was another defeat for international socialism.[13]

The Conservatives had fought the British general election in a bitter campaign on the issue of relations with Bolshevik Russia, denouncing MacDonald's government for recognizing the Soviet Union and for being soft on Communism. They made great use of the famous Zinoviev letter, which they claimed had been written by Zinoviev as Secretary-General of the Communist International to the British Communists, urging them to vote Labour because it would be to the Communists's advantage to have a Labour rather than a Conservative government in Britain. The Soviet government and the British Labour Party claimed that the letter was a forgery, and we now know it was; although it accurately expressed the line of Zinoviev and the Comintern, it had been forged by White Russian refugees in Berlin. After the Conservatives had been returned to power, they sent a protest to the Soviet government about the letter and set up an inquiry to examine if the letter was genuine or a forgery. The inquiry reported that it was genuine, and the Conservative government accepted the report, despite Labour protests.

Mussolini told Graham how glad he was that the Conservatives had won the general election, and said that he had no doubt that the Zinoviev letter was genuine. Graham tactfully reminded him that when he had exchanged ambassadors with the Soviet Union a few months before, he had said that he hoped that this would lead to a reduction in Bolshevik propaganda in Italy. Mussolini said that he had been mistaken, and that Soviet subversive activity in Italy had increased since diplomatic recognition; he had been reliably informed that Trotsky himself had recently visited Rome in disguise to address a secret meeting of Communists.[14] Trotsky certainly did not go to Rome in 1924, and it is very unlikely that Mussolini really believed that he had been there; but although in January Mussolini had wished to beat MacDonald in the race to recognize the Soviet government, in November he wished to impress on Austen Chamberlain that he was as anti-Bolshevik as the new British Conservative government.

A month later, a meeting of the Council of the League of Nations was held in Rome. Austen Chamberlain came, thus establishing a precedent that the British Foreign Secretary attended in person the meetings of the Council of the League. He met Mussolini, and the two men immediately established a friendly relationship. Chamberlain wrote that Mussolini was 'a wonderful man . . . working for the greatness of his country'.[15]

But things did not always go smoothly between Chamberlain and Mussolini. Two such strong personalities, each so conscious of the need to uphold their country's prestige, could hardly have avoided occasional conflicts. When an Italian company made a bid to obtain a concession to search for oil in Albania, but the Albanian government granted the concession to the British company, Anglo-Persian Oil, Mussolini instructed the Italian ambassador in London, the Marchese di Torretta, to protest against the action of the British government in forcing the Albanians to grant the concession to Anglo-Persian Oil. Chamberlain resented Torretta's language, and reacted strongly. 'These allegations against the honour and the good faith of His Majesty's Government must be definitely withdrawn,' he wrote to Graham. 'No British minister can stomach such a message as Torretta delivered, and if Mussolini proceeds upon the assumption that we can be addressed and bullied like a third rate power he makes a fatal mistake.'[16]

But Chamberlain was prepared to take into account the fact that Mussolini had been ill, and to do all he could to enable him to save face with his Fascist extremists. The matter was settled amicably. Mussolini withdrew his accusations, and Chamberlain persuaded the Albanian government and Anglo-Persian Oil to give the Italians a 33 per cent interest in the oil concession. The French, who had also hoped to obtain a share in the concession, got nothing.[17] Mussolini's tough talking to Chamberlain had paid off.

Chamberlain pursued a consistently anti-Soviet policy during his five years as Foreign Secretary, repudiating the trade agreement that MacDonald's government had signed with the Soviet Union, expelling the Soviet commercial representatives in London after the general strike in Britain, and sending British troops to China to defeat a Communist revolution that had been instigated by agents of the Comintern. But his main project in 1925 was to conduct the negotiations that were to bring Germany back into the comity of nations and end the isolation to which she had been subjected since her defeat in 1918. The negotiations led to the Treaty of Locarno in October 1925 and to Germany's admission next year to the League of Nations from which she had hitherto been excluded. Part of Chamberlain's object was to prevent an isolated Germany from making an alliance with that other pariah state, the Soviet Union. His policy was viewed with great suspicion and hostility by right-wing nationalists in France; but Mussolini supported it.

The Treaty of Locarno replaced the anti-German military alliance of Britain, France, Italy and Belgium with a five-power pact, by which these four powers and Germany agreed not to attack the other parties to the pact and to go to the assistance of any of the five powers that was the victim of aggression. Briand had returned to power in France as Foreign Minister in Paul Painlevé's government, and he agreed to Chamberlain's proposal despite the fierce protests of his critics at home. The German Foreign Minister, Gustav Stresemann, was a moderate Conservative whose attitude was appreciated by Liberals and German sympathizers in the West.

Mussolini pleased Chamberlain and British public opinion by proposing that the treaty should be registered with the Secretary-General of the League of Nations and should expressly state that it was subject to the Covenant of the League.[18] This raised difficulties in Germany, as Germany was not allowed to be a member of the League; but Chamberlain persuaded Stresemann to waive this point and to make other concessions to appease French public opinion, and promised Stresemann that he would do all he could to ensure that Germany was admitted to the League in 1926.

When all the preliminary negotiations had been completed, a conference was held in Locarno in Switzerland in October 1925. The British delegation was led by Chamberlain, the French by Briand, the German by the Chancellor, Hans Luther, and Stresemann, and the Belgian by Vandervelde. Grandi and other delegates represented Italy. The Foreign Ministers of Poland and Czechoslovakia, Count Skrzyinski and Edvard Beneš, attended as observers at some of the sessions. Chamberlain hoped that Mussolini himself would come to Locarno, but was told that this was very unlikely; Mussolini had attended the conferences in Lausanne and London a few weeks after he became Prime Minister, but since December 1922 he had not left Italy. He had not attended any meeting of the Council of the League of Nations, or any international conference, and no one believed that he would lower his dignity by coming to Locarno, especially as Britain and France were represented there by Foreign Secretaries, not Prime Ministers. Chamberlain then wrote a personal letter to Mussolini asking him to come to Locarno for the final session of the conference as a personal favour to himself, as he was so eager to meet him again.

Mussolini told Graham that he would go to Locarno just to please Chamberlain. He left Rome that same evening, arriving in Locarno on 15 October, and attending the final session of the conference next day.[19] Chamberlain was delighted, and his friendship with Mussolini was confirmed. The Treaty of Locarno was hailed as a great achievement by moderate opinion everywhere, and everyone gave Chamberlain the credit for it. He was rewarded with a knighthood and the Order of the Garter.

—————— ◆ ——————

# CHAPTER 20

# The Terrorists

I N Italy the Socialists, unable to gain the support of any of the other parties against Mussolini, found the freedom of their press restricted and their activists in danger of their lives from Fascist *squadristi*. They turned to their old traditional tactics of violence. The Socialist deputy Tito Zaniboni decided to assassinate Mussolini. He would do it on 4 November 1925, the anniversary of the armistice of 1918, when Mussolini came out on to the balcony of the Foreign Office, the Palazzo Chigi in Rome, to take the salute of the army and militia marching past. Zaniboni hired a room in a hotel opposite the Palazzo Chigi, from where he could see and shoot Mussolini on the balcony. He obtained a militiaman's uniform and put it on, so that he would be allowed to enter the area with his rifle and gain access to the hotel. But some weeks earlier he had told an old friend what he intended to do; the friend had told the police; and Zaniboni had been under surveillance ever since.

The police allowed him to enter the hotel, and at 11 a.m., the hour when Mussolini was due to come out on to the balcony, Zaniboni was in position in his room in the hotel, looking through the sights of his rifle, when the police broke in and arrested him. They sent word to the Palazzo Chigi that he was safely in custody, and Mussolini went out on to the balcony ten minutes later than scheduled and took the salute.[1]

The press gave the widest publicity to the attempt on Mussolini's life. Congratulations on his escape came in from all quarters. 'God has saved Your Excellency and Italy,' wrote General Badoglio.[2] In many cities the Catholic Church held a Te Deum to give thanks. The police announced that they had traced a link between Zaniboni and General Castello, a retired general who had often expressed his opposition to Fascism, and that Zaniboni had received money from Socialists in Czechoslovakia as a reward for assassinating Mussolini. Zaniboni was sentenced to thirty years' imprisonment.

In February 1926 trouble flared up about South Tyrol. The northern part of the territory of the Trentino and the Alto Adige, which the Italians had liberated from Austria in 1918, included areas where the majority of the population were German-speaking Austrians, as Mussolini himself had recognized many years before in his book *The Trentino as seen by a Socialist* in 1909. Fascist Italy was now ruling these territories in defiance of the principles of self-determination of peoples which had been proclaimed in President Wilson's Fourteen Points and the Treaty of Versailles. Mussolini pointed out that the benefits of Italian rule were granted to all the inhabitants, to the German-speaking as well as to the Italian-speaking population; but the use of the German language was banned in schools and on all official occasions. The Germans in the Alto Adige resented this, and in Austria and Germany there were loud protests over the sufferings of their brothers in the lost *Süd-Tirol*. Their complaints were also voiced by the Socialist parties throughout Europe, who publicized them as an example of Fascist oppression.

But there was one German nationalist who did not support the cause of South Tyrol. An Austrian who had served as a corporal in the German Army in the First World War, Adolf Hitler, had formed his National Socialist German Workers' Party in 1920. It had seven members, and was one of a number of small nationalist groups in Germany. When Hitler read about the March on Rome, he formed the highest admiration for Mussolini. He championed the cause of all other oppressed German minorities in foreign countries; but he refused to champion the cause of South Tyrol, as this would have meant criticizing his hero Mussolini.

In 1923 Hitler took part in an abortive insurrection in Munich, and was arrested. When the Communists had made an unsuccessful insurrection there in 1919, their captured leaders had been summarily executed by right-wing irregulars; but Hitler was merely sentenced to five years in prison, and was freed after serving ten months. While he was in prison, two prominent members of his Nazi Party, Alfred Rosenberg and Adolf Dresler, published articles and a book denouncing Mussolini for oppressing the people of South Tyrol and also for his links with wealthy Italian Jews, like Finzi, who supported the

Fascist Party. As soon as Hitler was released from prison, he ordered his followers to stop this anti-Mussolini propaganda.[3]

In February 1926 Dr Heinrich Held, the Prime Minister of Bavaria, made a speech in Munich in which he criticized the Treaty of Locarno because it did nothing to liberate the people of South Tyrol from Italian oppression. Held's speech infuriated the Italians, especially the Fascist rank and file, and Mussolini knew that his supporters expected him to make a vigorous reply when he spoke on the subject in the Chamber of Deputies. He warned Held and the Germans and Austrians that if he chose to do so, he could order the Italian Army to move the Italian frontier with Austria a long way north of the Brenner; and he then went on to attack the German tourists who visited Italy in their ridiculous hikers' shorts and socks, which should be worn on the football field, not in Italian city streets and churches.[4]

Mussolini's speech delighted his followers and most of the Italian public, but it aroused as much resentment in Austria and Germany as Held's speech had aroused in Italy. Stresemann felt bound to reply; although he spoke in more moderate language than Held and Mussolini, he criticized Mussolini for his offensive remarks about Germans. The British Foreign Office were dismayed to see Mussolini and Stresemann engaging in this public slanging match so soon after they had shaken hands in friendship at Locarno. Chamberlain, knowing that Mussolini was due to make another speech in the Senate, instructed Graham to urge him to cool the situation by making a moderate speech and offering reconciliation to Stresemann.

Mussolini said nothing in the Senate that showed any desire for reconciliation with Germany; but neither did he inflame the situation any further. The British government was reasonably satisfied with the speech. Graham wrote to Chamberlain that the state of Italo-German relations, though unpleasant, was not dangerous.[5]

Despite these occasional difficulties, both Graham and Chamberlain admired Mussolini. Graham praised his 'attempts to enforce discipline on an essentially undisciplined nation'; he had even succeeded in making motorists and pedestrians in Rome observe the traffic regulations.[6] Chamberlain agreed. 'It is not part of my business as Foreign Secretary to appreciate his action in the domestic politics of Italy,' he wrote, 'but if I ever had to choose in my own country between anarchy and dictatorship, I expect I should be on the side of the dictator . . . I think we might easily go far before finding an Italian with whom it would be as easy for the British Government to work.'[7]

There were some diplomats in the British Foreign Office who did not like certain features of Fascism; but when they wrote reports that criticized the Fascists, these reports were usually shelved by other officials and not passed on to higher authority, whereas reports that were favourable to the Fascists were sent up to the Foreign Secretary and sometimes shown to King George V.[8]

The wives of the British statesmen and diplomats admired Mussolini even more than their husbands did. Graham's wife, Lady Sybil, was a personal friend of Mussolini's, and sometimes invited him to private tea parties at the embassy. In March 1926 Winston Churchill's wife Clementine came to Rome, and Sybil Graham invited her to tea to meet Mussolini. Clementine wrote to Winston that she found him 'most impressive – quite simple & *natural*, very dignified', with a charming smile and 'beautiful golden brown piercing eyes which you see but can't look at'. When he came in, everyone, including the women, rose to their feet as if he were a king – 'it seemed the natural thing to do'. She was sure that he was a very great man, and hoped that nothing would happen to him. He presented her with a signed photograph of himself. 'All the Embassy ladies are dying of jealousy,' she wrote to Churchill.[9] 'No doubt he is one of the most wonderful men of our time,' wrote Churchill in reply; but he reminded her that the Liberal politician, Augustine Birrell, had said: 'It is better to read about a world figure than to live under his rule.'[10]

Mrs Churchill was more fortunate than Hitler, who at about the same time asked the Italian embassy in Berlin to send him a signed photograph of Mussolini. The Foreign Office in Rome told the embassy to refuse Hitler's request in a courteous way.[11] Mussolini wished to have nothing to do with German nationalists.

Not all aristocratic English ladies admired Mussolini. In the spring of 1926 Mussolini decided to go on an official visit to Libya. On 7 April, the day before he was due to sail from Fiumicino, he opened an international medical congress in Rome. As he left the building after his speech and approached his car, a woman standing only a few yards from him fired at him with a revolver. Her shot only grazed his nose, inflicting a slight wound. The doctors who were attending the congress hurried to render him medical assistance, and he was more irritated by the presence of large numbers of them standing all around him than he was by the wound in his nose.[12]

The woman who had fired the shot was arrested, and inquiries revealed that she was a member of the Anglo-Irish aristocracy, the

Honourable Violet Gibson, the daughter of a former Lord Chancellor of Ireland and the sister of Lord Ashbourne. Guido Letti, of Mussolini's secret police the OVRA – the Organizzazione Vigilanza Repressione Antifascismo (the Organization to Watch and Repress Anti-Fascism) – set out to discover who she was and whether she was acting on behalf of some international political organization. Letti was grateful for the assistance he received from the head of the British Passport Control Office in Rome, who as always was most co-operative in investigating subversive political activity against Mussolini's government.

Letti discovered that Violet Gibson was well known to be mentally unstable; she had once had a nervous breakdown in the middle of the Strand in London. She had personal contacts with members of Sinn Fein, but had never played an active part in politics. Her brother, Lord Ashbourne, was an eccentric, living as a recluse in a château near Compiègne in France. Letti sent an agent to rent a house near the château, but none of the neighbours could give him any information about Ashbourne. The OVRA decided that Violet Gibson had not been part of any political conspiracy, but was a solitary, demented individual. Mussolini, who despite his nose wound was fit enough to sail to Tripoli next day, ordered that she was to be released and deported from Italy without any charge being brought against her.[13]

When Mussolini attacked, and virtually destroyed, the Socialist trade unions, he formed Fascist trade unions, and had considerable success in persuading many workers to join them. The Fascist trade unions emphasized that they did not wish to wreck the national economy and bankrupt the employers, as the Socialist trade unions wished to do, but to represent the interests of the workers in a society in which employers and their work-force could collaborate to their mutual advantage. The Fascist trade unions did not completely rule out the use of the strike weapon, but believed that it should only be resorted to exceptionally, as a last resort. They called a miners' strike in August 1924 in support of a demand for a 20 per cent wage increase, and obtained and accepted an offer of a 15 per cent increase. In March 1925 they called a steelworkers' strike.[14]

But after Mussolini had weathered the storm that followed the Matteotti murder, and it was clear that all the Conservative and

Liberal parties would support him against the Socialists, he came down on the side of the employers against the workers. In March 1926 the government introduced a law to establish the Fascist trade unions as the only organizations entitled to represent the interests of employees.

Mussolini spoke in the debate. He said that Fascism recognized the historical mission of capitalism, which was not on the decline; it had not yet reached its zenith, and would remain in existence for many centuries. He said that Fascism was definitely anti-Socialist. The Socialist conception of the capitalist as an exploiter of the proletariat was false and ridiculous; the capitalist of today was a captain of industry, with a full sense of his responsibilities, and the wages and well-being of thousands of his workmen depended on him.[15] Mussolini had certainly moved a long way since 24 November 1914, when he had told the Socialists who expelled him from the party that whatever they might do he would always believe in socialism.

By the law of 3 April 1926, no association of employers or employees, or of artists or members of the professions, could be formed unless the officers of the association could 'give proof of their competence, good moral behaviour, and positive faith in the nation'. Public employees were guilty of an offence punishable by imprisonment from one to six months if there was a strike and they 'fail to do all within their power to continue or restore the regular work of a public service or public utility enterprise'. Anyone who organized a strike or lock-out 'in order to coerce or influence the decision' of the state or of any public official was liable to up to seven years' imprisonment in solitary confinement.

In June 1926 the government abolished the eight-hour working day which had been established soon after Mussolini came to power, and replaced it by the nine-hour working day. The Charter of Labour, after stating that the Italian nation was 'a moral, political and economic unity integrally embodied in the Fascist State' and that labour was a 'social duty', laid down that all labour disputes had to be referred to the Labour Court. 'Infractions of discipline' in the workplace were punishable by fines and dismissal.[16] The first prosecution under this provision took place at Gallarate near Milan in November 1926 when eighty-one workmen who stopped work and asked their employer for more pay were each fined one hundred lire with costs.[17]

\* \* \*

On 11 September 1926 Mussolini was being driven in his car through the streets of Rome when a young anarchist stonemason named Gino Lucetti threw a bomb at his car. It hit the front wheel, ricochetted along the street, and exploded just after Mussolini had passed. He was unhurt, but several bystanders were injured. Lucetti was arrested. He told the police that he had for some years been an anarchist and had taken part in street fights against the Fascists, and had then emigrated to Paris, where he had made contact with Italian anarchist refugees who had sent him back to Italy to assassinate Mussolini. He was sentenced to thirty years' imprisonment. He was released after Mussolini's fall from power in July 1943, but was killed a few weeks later in an Allied air raid.[18]

At the end of September 1926 Sir Austen Chamberlain and his wife Ivy, who were on a Mediterranean cruise in their private yacht, called at Leghorn. Mussolini went to meet them, and ordered the Italian Navy in the port to fire a nineteen-gun salute to Chamberlain. Lady Chamberlain was even more impressed by Mussolini than Mrs Churchill had been. She asked him if he would give her a Fascist Party badge, which she proudly wore in her coat lapel during her stay in Leghorn and on other occasions.

Soon afterwards the Chamberlains sent their daughter to finish her education in Florence. Sir Austen sometimes visited her there, and Mussolini came to Florence to have private talks with him.[19] These talks cemented their friendship, for they agreed on so many things, including the League of Nations. Chamberlain said that the League was excellent when sparrows quarrelled, but was useless when eagles fell out. Mussolini was delighted with the phrase, and often quoted it in later years, with due acknowledgments to Chamberlain.[20]

Chamberlain paid a public tribute to Mussolini when he spoke at the Imperial Conference in London to the statesmen of the British Dominions on 20 October 1926. In his survey of British foreign policy throughout the world, he said that relations with Italy were excellent. Mussolini's methods might sometimes be a little rough, and he was 'apt to fancy a slight and go off at a tangent'; but he was a very remarkable man from very humble origins who had abandoned the Socialist extremism of his youth when he 'felt the call of patriotism' during the war. He had saved his country from 'political corruption, social anarchy, industrial strife and national degeneracy', and had restored Italy's international prestige. But Chamberlain wondered if the Fascist regime could survive his death, and there had been three attempts on his life during the previous year.[21]

There was soon to be a fourth attempt. Young Anteo Zamboni, the sixteen-year-old son of an anarchist typographer, Mammolo Zamboni of Bolgona, decided to assassinate Mussolini the next time he came to the city.[22] Anteo was an ardent anarchist; but although his father had encouraged him to believe in anarchism, Anteo seems to have decided to kill Mussolini on his own initiative without consulting his father or anyone else. He planned it carefully in advance; he joined the Fascist youth movement, the Avanguardisti, because he thought that it would be easier for him to approach Mussolini if he were wearing Avanguardisti uniform.

Mussolini arrived in Bologna on the evening of 30 October 1926 with Rachele and Edda – now aged sixteen – and his brother Arnaldo. He spent all next day inspecting public buildings and taking the salute at Fascist demonstrations. On the evening of 31 October he set off for the station to take the train back to Rome. Rachele, Edda and Arnaldo had gone to the station separately, while Mussolini, with Grandi and the Mayor of Bologna sitting beside him in the car, was driven slowly through the streets lined with Fascists and the general public.

Anteo Zamboni in his Avanguardisti uniform managed to pass through the police cordon and enter the reserved zone. He pushed his way to the front of the crowds lining the Via dell'Indipendenza. The previous evening he had written a note which he left in his room: 'I cannot fall in love, because I do not know whether I will be alive after I have done what I have promised to do. To kill a tyrant who tortures the nation is not a crime, it is justice. To die for the cause of liberty is beautiful and sacred.'[23]

As Mussolini's car passed him, Anteo Zamboni fired at it with his revolver. The bullet missed all the occupants of the car, and only tore the Mayor's uniform. While Mussolini's driver drove on quickly to the station, the crowd threw themselves on Zamboni and lynched him; his body, full of revolver bullets and knife wounds, was torn to pieces, and his arms and legs were carried around the city in triumph by the Fascists.

Mussolini reached the station and told Rachele that he was alive and unhurt. He described for her what had happened. 'The procession was passing along in the ordinary way when I saw someone forcing his way through the crowd and approaching the car. I had just time to notice that it was a pale, shock-headed boy, before he fired a small revolver in my direction. In a second the crowd had got him down and wreaked summary justice on him. It was impossible to stop them. It is monstrous to make a boy the instrument of a crime.'[24]

The Fascists, furious at this fourth attempt on Mussolini's life, reacted violently. In Milan they burned the offices of the Socialist and other opposition parties. In Rome, Genoa, Naples and Cagliari they broke into the homes of Socialist and Liberal oppositionists and threatened them. Anteo Zamboni's father Mammolo and his aunt Virginia Tabarroni, being well-known anarchists, were arrested and put on trial as accessories to the assassination attempt. There was no evidence that they knew about it, but they were convicted on the grounds that they had indoctrinated Anteo with the anarchist doctrines that had caused him to commit the crime. They were sentenced to thirty years' imprisonment, but were soon pardoned and released on Mussolini's orders.

Mussolini's foreign admirers hastened to congratulate him on his escape. In the United States the *Washington Post* wrote that he was a brave man who performed his duty under threat of death. He told the correspondent of the *New York Herald Tribune* that his lucky star had again preserved him from assassination, and confidently predicted: 'I shall die a natural death.'[25]

On 5 November the Council of Ministers promulgated a number of decrees giving the government drastic powers to suppress subversive anti-Fascist activity. The Socialist and opposition press and organizations were suppressed, and their deputies were expelled from the Chamber. Anyone suspected of anti-Fascism could be interned without trial. Capital punishment had been abolished in Italy, but the death penalty was introduced for an attempt to assassinate the King, the Queen, the heir to the throne, or the head of the government. In November 1926 Italy became a Fascist dictatorship.[26]

It was the right moment to deal with the problem of Ida Dalser. She had continued to pester Mussolini after he became Prime Minister. She was not allowed to approach him, but she wrote to him repeatedly, reminding him how he had loved her and claiming that she, and not Rachele, was his lawful wife. Mussolini did not reply; perhaps his secretaries saw to it that he did not read the letters. She also wrote to the Pope.

One day in the summer of 1926 the Minister of Education, Pietro Fedele, was attending a function at a hotel in Trent when Ida appeared and made a hysterical scene which culminated in her falling to the ground in some kind of epileptic fit. She was taken first to a mental hospital at Pergine Valsugana, and then moved in turn to two other mental hospitals in Venice, before being returned to the hospital at Pergine. The doctors who examined her certified her as suffering from paranoia. Her family were not allowed to visit her, but her son Benito Albino – Mussolini's son – wrote her loving letters.

She told the doctors that she was sure that Mussolini did not know what was happening to her, and continued to write letters to him which never left the hospital. 'My dear Benito,' she wrote on 24 July 1927, 'you know nothing, you have given no orders [about me], and as I am sure of this I can defy them all.' She signed it 'Your despairing Ida'.[27]

Her family did not abandon her. Her sister Adele, who had married Riccardo Palcher, a banker in Trent, did all she could; she contacted any leading Fascist or government official who came to Trent, and was eventually granted an interview with members of Mussolini's secretariat; but nothing happened. Then, during the night of 15–16 July 1935, Ida Dalser escaped from the mental hospital at Pergine. She managed to get as far as Sopramonte, but was recaptured there after thirty-six hours of freedom on the afternoon of 17 July and taken to the mental hospital in Venice, where she died in December 1937.

Benito Albino never tried to see his father, who had loved him when he was a few days old, and Mussolini made no attempt to get in touch with him. Mussolini loved his five children by Rachele, but forgot about the existence of Benito Albino. The Duce's bastard son grew up like any other child in Fascist Italy; he did well at school and in the Fascist youth movement. He fell in love with a girl, and they were engaged to be married; but before the wedding, Benito Albino went off on a cruise to China.

What happened then is a mystery. His family are convinced that soon after he returned to Italy he was sent to a mental hospital at Mombello, and died there in 1942 at the age of twenty-six. They believe that he had talked too loudly about being the Duce's son; that like his mother he was wrongly certified insane in order to hush him up; and that he may even have been murdered in the hospital. There are no records of his admission to Mombello mental hospital, or of his death there. His family believe that they were destroyed by the OVRA or by other agents of the government or the Fascist Party.

If Mussolini's secretariat were capable of murdering Matteotti, they would also have been capable of kidnapping Ida Dalser and Benito Albino and incarcerating them unjustly in a mental hospital; and they would have seen to it that Mussolini himself knew no more about the fate of his former mistress and his son than he knew about what they intended to do to Matteotti. His secretariat realized that there were things that he would prefer not to know.

But some of Benito Albino's friends tell a different story. They say that there are no records about his admission to Mombello hospital or his death there because he was never in the hospital. On the contrary, he joined the navy on the outbreak of war in 1940 and served with distinction in a destroyer operating in the Tyrrhenian Sea. He was determined to prove himself a worthy son of Mussolini, and succeeded in doing so. He was lost at sea in the course of naval operations during the war.[28]

It was Ida Dalser's misfortune that she happened to be in Trent in 1909 and met the young socialist Benito Mussolini. The story of Mussolini's other family is not a pretty one.

# CHAPTER 21

—————◆—————

# The Mafia

B Y November 1926 parliamentary democracy had been finally
destroyed in Italy; but Mussolini gave a series of reassuring
interviews to the foreign press – to the Rome correspondent
of the *Deutsche Algemeine Zeitung* of Berlin, by telephone to the
*Chicago Tribune*, and to Shaw Desmond of the London *Sunday
Pictorial*. He told Shaw Desmond that he did not think there would
be another world war, as the memories of the horrors of the four
years of the last war were too vivid in the people's minds; and he
added that England and Italy had never gone to war against each
other, and never would.[1]

In the British Foreign Office, Mr Oliver Harvey of the Central
Department was worried at the suppression of democracy and free
speech in Italy; he thought it was comparable to the suppression of
freedom in Russia. Sir Austen Chamberlain did not agree. 'Are these
generalities very helpful?' he wrote about Harvey's memorandum.
'There is no greater mistake than to apply British standards to un-
British conditions. Mussolini would not be a fascist if he were an
Englishman in England. Is Mr Harvey certain that if he had been an
*Italian* living in pre-fascist Italy he would not have joined a fascio?'[2]

The Chancellor of the Exchequer, Winston Churchill, was more
explicit when he passed through Rome on his return from a holiday
in January 1927, two months after the Fascist dictatorship was finally
imposed in Italy. After meeting Mussolini, he held a press conference
for the Italian and foreign press correspondents in Rome. He said
that he had been charmed, like so many other people, by Mussolini's
'gentle and simple bearing and by his calm, detached poise in spite
of so many burdens and dangers.' He told the Fascists: 'If I had been
an Italian, I am sure I should have been wholeheartedly with you
from start to finish in your triumphant struggle against the bestial

appetites and passions of Leninism.' Churchill said that in foreign affairs the Fascist movement 'has rendered service to the whole world'. Italy 'has shown that there is a way of fighting the subversive forces ... She has provided the necessary antidote to the Russian poison.'[3]

Churchill's statement was warmly welcomed by the Fascist press in Italy. Graham wrote to Austen Chamberlain that he thought Churchill's statement was very good, and that 'Mussolini was perfectly delighted with it, but I cannot say the same as regards the Russian press representative'.[4]

Mussolini was praised not only by British right-wing Conservative politicians, but also by a maverick left-wing genius, George Bernard Shaw. In a letter to the *Daily News*, which was duly quoted in *Il Popolo d' Italia*, Shaw wrote that the Italian people followed Mussolini because they were fed up with lawlessness and parliamentary fatuity, and wanted an efficient tyrant; and Mussolini was their beloved tyrant.[5]

Lord Rothermere's *Daily Mail* had supported Mussolini more consistently than any other British newspaper. Apart from admiring Mussolini as an enemy of Communism, Rothermere had an additional reason for praising him; like Rothermere himself, the Duce was a teetotaller and a non-smoker.[6]

Mussolini had another foreign admirer who was even more fervent than Churchill, Shaw and Rothermere. Richard Washburn Child was the United States ambassador in Italy at the time of the March on Rome. He retired from the post in 1924, but often went to Rome to see Mussolini. He suggested to Mussolini that he should write his autobiography, which was published in English in New York and London in 1928, under the title *My Autobiography, by Benito Mussolini*. It was never translated into Italian.

According to Child, Mussolini dictated the text, and after Child had had it copied, he sent it back to Mussolini, who made a few corrections, in red pencil and in ink, in his own hand.[7] But in 1932 Mussolini wrote a short biography of his brother Arnaldo, who had died in December 1931 at the age of forty-seven. In this *Vita di Arnaldo*, he wrote about his great love for Arnaldo ever since they were children together, and how much his brother had helped him in his political work; and he stated that Arnaldo was chiefly responsible for the autobiography that he wrote in 1928, which could not have been produced without his help.[8] This has led many commentators to believe that Arnaldo wrote the so-called autobiography of Benito Mussolini. Some have gone further, and suggested that Arnaldo wrote most of his brother Benito's articles and speeches. This is obviously untrue, for the articles and speeches that Benito wrote and delivered after Arnaldo's death are in exactly the same vigorous and brilliant style as those written during Arnaldo's lifetime.

But the autobiography of 1928, which was of course very different from the autobiography that Mussolini wrote in prison in 1911–12, does not read as if it were written by Mussolini. It is coarser and more brutal than any of his other writings. Mussolini, in his articles and speeches, never pulled his punches and never spared his opponents; but his denunciations of them were usually flavoured with lively if bitter humour, and with trenchant ridicule as well as menace. In the autobiography, the criticism is often mere vulgar abuse, which is levelled even at the dead Matteotti.[9] The book was a strange way to present Mussolini to his foreign admirers.

This makes it all the more extraordinary that it should have made such a favourable impression on the former United States ambassador. In his preface to the book, Child, after claiming that 'for his autobiography I am responsible', forecast that no man in our time would 'exhibit dimensions of permanent greatness equal to those of Mussolini'. Child thought that a man who administers a state was a statesman, but to 'make a state', as Mussolini had done, was 'superstatesmanship'.[10]

Mussolini's reputation abroad rose still higher when he confronted the Mafia, who had controlled Sicily ever since the beginning of the century. There has been a great deal of argument and speculation, and very little reliable evidence, as to the origin of the name 'Mafia' and the date and circumstances of the formation of the organization. The name is probably derived from an Arabic word; but despite all the attempts to connect it with historical revolutionary movements, there is no recorded reference to the Mafia before 1865.

As the power of the landowning aristocracy declined, the Mafia grew in influence. Its chief object was to control the distribution of agricultural produce by forcing the farmers to sell their grain and fruit to the Mafia, who resold at a high profit to the shopkeepers in the towns and villages. Any farmer or shopkeeper who tried to cut out the Mafia and trade directly with each other ran the risk of being murdered. The chiefs of the Mafia were often leading figures in urban middle-class society in Palermo – lawyers, doctors and other professional men; but the large landowners were against the Mafia, who made a profit at the expense of their tenant farmers and therefore kept down rents. The local authorities' links with the Mafia, the tradition of lawlessness and vendetta, and the reluctance of the ordinary Sicilian to co-operate with the police, prevented any attempt to enforce law and order in Sicily. In the province of Trapani in western Sicily there were seven hundred murders a year.

The Fascists had very little influence in Sicily before the March on Rome; but after Mussolini came to power they made good progress in winning local and national elections. In May 1924 Mussolini visited Sicily, and the local Fascist and ex-servicemen's organizations complained to him about the activity of the Mafia and the amount of crime in Sicily. He decided to crush the Mafia. He chose Cesare Mori for the job, as the local Fascists under their leader, Alfredo Cucco, had not been very successful against the Mafia.

Mori had been hated by the Fascists when he was prefect of Bologna in 1921 because he wished to enforce the law against the Fascists as well as against the Reds. He had been the target of the hostile demonstrations by Balbo's *squadristi*, who had frightened Facta's government into moving Mori from Bologna to Bari, where there was very little Fascist activity. Next year he retired from public service and wrote a book about his experiences when he was a young police officer in Sicily, and his attempts to suppress crime there.

Mussolini thought that Mori, with his determination to enforce law and order, would be the best man to cope with the Mafia in Sicily. He recalled him to public service, and in June 1924 appointed him prefect of Trapani. In October 1925 Mori was promoted to the post of prefect of Palermo, and received orders from Mussolini to act with all necessary vigour against the Mafia. As a Conservative, Mori's sympathies were with the landowners against the Mafia, and though he had opposed the Fascists when they were resorting to illegal violence in Bologna, he supported them now that they were the government and wished to suppress the lawless violence in Sicily. He was prepared to perform the duty that was required of him with all the ruthlessness Mussolini could desire.

Mori began his operations on 28 November 1925. His methods were to arrest hundreds of suspects, including anyone with a criminal record, and also young middle-class men who attended night-clubs, for Mori strongly disapproved of loose sexual conduct. He issued a proclamation warning the *latitanti* – the men on the run who had escaped to the mountains to avoid arrest – that if they did not surrender within twelve hours he would arrest their wives and children. Within five weeks large number of bandits, including some prominent Mafia leaders, had surrendered, and on 6 January 1926 Mussolini sent Mori a telegram congratulating him on his 'magnificent' achievement. Mori continued his operations during the next two years. His opponents accused him of resorting to torture to obtain information, and of ill-treating the women and children who were interned; but he strongly denied this, and persuaded the landowners to make voluntary contributions to maintain the families of the men who had been arrested.[11]

He was certainly very popular with many Sicilians, and he had the full support of Mussolini. In May 1927 Mussolini told the Chamber of Deputies that he rejected the suggestion that Mori's methods had been too drastic, and said that the fight against the Mafia would continue until all memory of it has been blotted out from the minds of the Sicilians.[12]

Mori's proceedings culminated in a number of well-publicized trials of Mafia supporters, though most of the defendants were charged only with 'criminal association', as no evidence could be obtained of their direct complicity in crimes. The most important trial began at Termini Imerese on 4 October 1927. There were 154 defendants in the dock, including two priests and seven women. Over three hundred witnesses were called for the prosecution. Mussolini thought that the trial was taking far too long. After it had lasted for nearly two months, he telegraphed to Mori that it should be given 'a more rapid, in other words more Fascist, rhythm', for otherwise it would not be finished before the year 2000.[13] But the verdict was in fact delivered on 10 January 1928, after the jury had deliberated for three days.

Only eight of the defendants were found not guilty. Seven were sentenced to imprisonment for life, and the others to imprisonment for terms ranging from five to thirty years. They probably received a fair trial, though the official *Giornale de Sicilia* wrote before the verdict was given that none of the lawyers who had been given the painful duty of defending the accused would seek to obstruct the glorious work of the national government in freeing Sicily from crime.[14]

Mussolini was not satisfied. As soon as he heard the verdict, he telegraphed to Mori and again demanded that future trials should be conducted 'with a rhythm more in keeping with the times, in other words, more Fascist'.[15] But the next trial of the Sicilian Mafia, with 161 defendants and five hundred witnesses, lasted even longer, from August 1928 to the spring of 1929.

Mussolini's foreign admirers applauded his proceedings against the Mafia. The *New York Times Magazine* wrote that the Mafia was dead and a new Sicily was born.[16] But Graham was less impressed, for he had noticed that the leading Mafiosi had not been prosecuted. He wrote to Austen Chamberlain on 1 August 1928 that Mori had come to terms with the leaders of the Mafia, and had prosecuted the 'lesser villains' and many people whose only connection with the Mafia was that they had obeyed its orders out of fear. Graham thought that Mori had eliminated many Mafiosi and also 'a number of innocent people by very doubtful means, including fabricated police evidence'.[17] But Graham as usual blamed the subordinate Mori and not his friend Mussolini.

Mori had now become an ardent Fascist, expressing his 'gratitude, faith and love' for Mussolini in a speech to his 'fellow Blackshirts' in May 1928. Mussolini duly appointed him a senator soon afterwards. Next year, Mori rendered another service to Mussolini when a plebiscite was held throughout Italy as to whether the electorate supported the Duce and the Fascist regime. Mori instructed his officials that the result of the plebiscite must be 'totalitarian'. It had always been difficult to get the people of Palermo to vote in elections; they believed in self-help and vendetta, not in electing governments. Before Mussolini came to power, only 25 per cent of the electorate voted in Palermo; in the plebiscite of March 1929, 92 per cent went to the poll, with 190,797 voting Yes and 320 No.

But Cucco and the Sicilian Fascists had never really liked the Conservative Mori; and Mussolini, in the last resort, would never alienate the local Fascists. In June 1929, only three months after Mori had so successfully achieved a 'totalitarian' result in the plebiscite, Mussolini dismissed him from his office as prefect of Palermo on account of his age – he was fifty-seven – while thanking him for his great services to Italy in bringing about the moral, political and social regeneration of the noblest of her islands.[18]

The methods of Mussolini and Mori in prosecuting the lesser fry in the Mafia, while allowing the leading Mafiosi to escape, may have been unfair, but they were effective. The Mafia chiefs gave orders to suspend all operations, though the organization remained secretly in existence. For seventeen years after 1926 there was no Mafia activity in Sicily, until the Mafia was revived and let loose again on the population by the American invaders during the Second World War as a means of weakening Fascist authority there.

CHAPTER 22

## The Concordat

MUSSOLINI'S greatest anxiety in 1927 was the falling birth-rate. He made a long speech about it in the Chamber of Deputies on 26 May. The birthrate in Italy was now 27 per 1,000 per annum, and though this was better than the 18 per 1,000 in France and the 16 per 1,000 in Britain – the lowest in Europe – it was lower than the 35 per 1,000 in Germany and the 40 per 1,000 in Bulgaria, the highest in Europe. It was lower, too, than the 38 per 1,000 in Italy forty years earlier, between 1881 and 1885. Mussolini was worried that the population of Italy had increased by 470,000 in 1925 but only by 418,000 in 1926. It was 'fortunately' still increasing in the slums of Palermo and Naples, but was stationary in Milan and Turin, where any increase in population was solely due to immigration. He reminded the deputies that 1,500 years ago the Roman Empire had declined because of the fall in its population.

As the birthrate was higher in the countryside than in the towns, Mussolini approved of rural life; but as there was unemployment in the country districts, many people moved from the countryside into the towns in the first months of 1928. Mussolini tried to check this by launching a campaign in the autumn under the slogan 'Empty the cities' which emphasized the benefits of rural over urban civilization; and he followed this with legislation that imposed restrictions on mobility of labour and the law against urbanization of 1934.[1]

To counter the threat of a declining population, Mussolini tried to prevent emigration. No one was permitted to leave Italy without a passport, which was refused to any member of the work-force who wished to emigrate. A considerable number of Italians left the country illegally. Some of them walked across the Alps in the snow, and a few were fired on and killed by the border guards.[2]

Mussolini's emphasis on the need to increase the birthrate not only led him to increase the punishment for abortion but also reinforced his belief that women should give birth to children and care for them in the home, and not take employment in factories or offices. When he founded the Fasci di Combattimento in 1919, his programme had included giving women the vote; but he did not carry out this promise when he came to power, and in his conversations with Emil Ludwig in 1932 he said that if he gave women the vote in Italy, people would laugh at him.

He told Ludwig that he repudiated the system in Bolshevik Russia, where men and women could play an equal part in public life. In Italy 'woman must play a passive part', because women could not build constructively. 'During all the centuries of civilization, has there ever been a woman architect? Ask her to build you a mere hut, not even a temple; she cannot do it . . . As far as political life is concerned, they do not count here.' It was different in Anglo-Saxon countries, which would probably end as matriarchies ruled by women. He also told Ludwig that 'women exert no influence upon strong men'.[3] But the Fascist women were among his most enthusiastic supporters. He often spoke to special meetings of Fascist women, and thanked them for their services to Fascism and to Italy.

Mussolini had abandoned, one by one, all the doctrines that he had expounded so vigorously and brilliantly before 1914 – his internationalism, his socialism and his republicanism. It now remained for him also to repudiate his hatred of the Catholic Church. He no longer spoke about the martyrdom of Giordano Bruno on 17 February every year, but on the contrary set out to heal the rift between state and Church in Italy which had continued unabated under every government of both the Left and the Right, since the clashes of the Risorgimento and the invasion of Rome by the Italian Army in 1870 when the city was annexed to the Kingdom of Italy. The Pope remained in the Vatican. No Pope, once elected, had emerged from the Vatican for nearly sixty years.

Mussolini had prepared the way for his conversion shortly before the March on Rome, in an article in *Gerarchia* on 25 May 1922, which he reprinted a week later in *Il Popolo d'Italia*: 'Fascism respects religion, it is not atheist, not anti-Christian, not anti-Catholic.'[4] Five days after he became Prime Minister, on the anniversary of the armistice on the Italian front on 4 November 1922, he, with General Diaz and Admiral Thaon di Revel, took the salute at the tomb of the Unknown Warrior in Rome. For the first time a religious service was held as part of the ceremony. When his Minister of Education, Gentile, introduced his first reforms in 1923, he ordered that the crucifix should be displayed in state schools for the first time since the creation of the Kingdom of Italy.[5]

Mussolini made his private contribution to placating the Church. In June 1923, when he was visiting Rachele and the children in his house in Milan, he arranged for his three children – Edda aged twelve, Vittorio aged six, and Bruno aged four – to be baptized in a private ceremony in the house by his brother Arnaldo's brother-in-law, Father Colombo Bondanini.[6] Two years later, he suggested to Rachele that they should go through a religious marriage ceremony. Rachele thought that it was quite unnecessary, as they had been living together since 1910 and had been through a civil marriage ceremony in 1915. 'To me,' she afterwards wrote, 'our deep attachment to each other, the fact that we had stood together as one in our stormy life together, and above all our children, were a firmer bond than any conventions. But I readily agreed to consecrate our union in the sight of God.'[7] Perhaps what she really meant was that she readily agreed to further Benito's political career and his new line towards the Church. The religious marriage was privately performed in Milan by Monsignor Magnaghi on 28 December 1925.

In August 1926 Mussolini began secret negotiations for a rapprochement between the Kingdom of Italy and the Papacy with Cardinal Pietro Gasparri, the aged Papal Secretary of State, who had been born in the Papal States and lived there for eighteen years before the Italian Army entered Rome in 1870.[8] But there were still areas of conflict between the Fascist state and the Church.

On 3 April 1926 the Fascist youth movement was given official legal status – as the ONB (Opera Nazionale Balilla), named after Gian Battista Perasso, nicknamed the Balilla, a heroic youth who had started the uprising against the Austrian troops in Genoa in 1746; the name of the organization was afterwards changed to the Gioventù Italiana del Littorio. From the age of six the boys and girls, according to age, were in one or other of the youth groups: the Figli della Lupa (the children of the wolf who suckled Romulus and Remus in roman legend) for both boys and girls from six to eight; then the Balilla, the Avanguardisti and the Giovani Fascisti for boys, and the Piccole Italiane and the Giovani Italiane for girls. At twenty-one a man became a Fascista, a Fascist party member; a woman at the age of twenty-five, or earlier if she married, became a Donna Fascista.[9]

Children were not compelled to join the ONB, but were under strong moral pressure to do so, and most of them wished to join in the fun with their schoolmates. If their parents were anti-Fascists and forbade them to join, this made them in many cases more eager to do so.

On 12 January 1927 a law was passed which forbade the formation of any new youth movement, and dissolved all the branches of the Catholic Boy Scouts except in towns of more than twenty thousand inhabitants. It was in the villages, where the influence of the parish priest was strongest, that it was particularly important to ensure that the children joined the Fascist, not the Catholic, youth movement. In December 1927 a government circular ordered the elementary schoolteachers to ensure that all children under fifteen were automatically enrolled in the Balilla; but membership of the Avanguardisti and the Giovani Fascisti remained voluntary for secondary schoolchildren, though here again nearly all of them wished to join voluntarily. Between September 1925 and July 1927 membership of the ONB rose from 100,000 to 1,236,000.[10]

In April 1928 a decree dissolved all youth organizations except the ONB. The Catholic Azione Cattolica was thus suppressed, as were the Italian branches of Lord Baden-Powell's British Boy Scouts. This saddened Mussolini's British admirers, but they still preferred him to the Communists. The Catholic Church in Italy reacted more strongly. They broke off the negotiations with Mussolini which Gasparri had been conducting. Mussolini soon gave way; he allowed the Azione Cattolica to continue to exist, because, unlike the 'semi-military' Boy Scouts, it was concerned only with religious objectives.

His negotiations with the Vatican for a concordat and a reconciliation were then resumed. He had several private meetings with Francesco Pacelli, the brother of the future Pope Pius XII, who was an eminent Catholic lawyer and often acted for the Vatican in complicated legal negotiations.[11] There were many arguments and differences to be settled by compromises on both sides; but everything had been agreed by 11 February 1929, when Mussolini, accompanied by Grandi, Giunta, and other officials from the Foreign Office, went to the Lateran Palace in Rome to meet Cardinal Gasparri with Francesco Pacelli and other Vatican representatives. Gasparri had some difficulty in rising to his feet to welcome Mussolini and take part in the signing ceremony; but he insisted on doing so, though Mussolini begged him to remain seated. Mussolini and Gasparri signed the treaty, and Gasparri presented Mussolini with the golden pen with which he had signed it.

By the Treaty of Lateran, the Pope, for the first time, recognized the Kingdom of Italy and its sovereignty over the city of Rome except for the Vatican City; and the Italian government recognized the Pope as the ruler of the sovereign state of the Vatican. Italy and the Vatican were to exchange ambassadors. Persons permanently residing in the Vatican would be citizens of the Vatican and not Italian subjects. The Vatican would maintain neutrality towards Italy and abstain from intervention in its internal politics. The Italian government would give legal recognition to ecclesiastical corporations, such as monasteries and convents. Religious education would be made compulsory, and extended, in all state schools. Marriages in church would be recognized as valid, even when they had not been accompanied by a civil marriage before the state authorities. Azione Cattolica would abandon all political activity in Italy.

A settlement was reached at last of the disputes between the Kingdom of Italy and the Papacy, which had been going on for seventy years, as to the compensation payable to the Church for the papal property taken over by the state during the Risorgimento. The Italian government, which had always refused to pay compensation for the property, now agreed to pay 750 million lire to the Papacy, and a further one milliard compensation for claims that should have been settled in the past.[12]

Both Pius XI and Mussolini hailed the treaty as a triumph. Next day, on 12 February, a thanksgiving Mass was celebrated in St Peter's Square, with the Pope giving his blessing from the window of his palace. Mussolini and his journalists saw to it that his daughter Edda, now aged eighteen, occupied a prominent position among the crowds in the square. A Te Deum was held in most Italian cities, and the Fascist press praised the Duce's achievement. The Pope declared that Mussolini was 'the man of Providence'.[13]

When Mussolini, immediately after the signing ceremony, telephoned the news to Rachele in Carpena in the Romagna, Father Facchinetti, a friend of the family who afterwards became Bishop of Tripoli, was visiting Rachele. He asked to speak to Mussolini on the telephone, and told him that he had solved a problem that had baffled statesmen like Cavour and saints like Father Giovanni Bosco, the founder of the Salesian Order. Faccinetti said to Rachele that it was 'the holiest achievement of our time'.[14]

There were also the critics. The Socialists condemned the Lateran Treaty, with the *Daily Herald* in Britain and Socialist newspapers in other countries denouncing it as a surrender to Catholic obscurantism. It was condemned by Protestant opinion abroad, and by the liberal humanists in France. *L'Ère nouvelle* wrote that it was an alliance of the two Romes against the France of 1789, the France of liberty, and the France of European security, in support of the new *condottieri*. King Victor Emmanuel was unhappy about it, for it was a repudiation of the anti-Papal traditions of his house since the days of the Risorgimento; but he put a brave face on it. So did Mussolini's friend Ezio Garibaldi and the old Garibaldini, and the Mazzinian republicans.[15]

Mussolini thought that this was the moment, when the Fascists and the Catholic Church were united, to ask the Italian people to vote in a plebiscite as to whether they supported the regime. Having expelled the Communist, Socialist and republican deputies from the Chamber of Deputies, he persuaded Parliament to pass a law abolishing elections to the Chamber; in future the deputies would be nominated by the Fascist Grand Council, and the electorate throughout Italy could then either accept or reject them all. The people were now invited to answer Yes or No to the question of whether they supported the government, Fascism and the Duce Benito Mussolini. As usual Mussolini had calculated correctly. After the press and the prefects had done their job, with the anti-Fascists being denied any opportunity to make their propaganda, and the Church and Catholic Action urging their supporters to vote Yes, 89.6 per cent of the electorate went to the polling stations on 24 March 1929; 8,519,559 voted Yes, and 155,761 voted No.[16]

Among all the paeons of praise for the Lateran Treaty, and the repetitive platitudes of the politicians, the churchmen and the journalists, Mussolini managed to introduce a note of originality and controversy in his speech about the treaty in the Chamber of Deputies on 13 May. He said that it was fitting that the Roman State should be reconciled to the Roman Church, because Christianity had spread throughout the world through its connection with Rome. If Christianity had not come to Rome, but had remained in Galilee, it would have died and passed into oblivion with all the other religious sects that flourished in Palestine at that time. He traced the development of Christianity throughout its 1,900 years' history. In speaking about the Emperor Constantine, that hero of the Church who had made the Roman Empire Christian, Mussolini mentioned that Constantine had killed his rival for the throne, Maximinus, and exterminated the whole family, men, women and children, with great cruelty, just as the Bolsheviks in Russia had recently exterminated the Romanov family.

Mussolini said that the liberal ideal was a free Church in a free state; he did not mention that this was a quotation from Cavour. But this ideal was an absurdity. If the state was free and liberal, the Church would take advantage of the situation to establish an authoritarian Church which would not be a free Church; if the state was strong enough to prevent this from happening, and could control the Church, then the Church would not be free. He traced the history of the conflicts between state and Church, between the Emperors and the Popes, in the Middle Ages. At the Reformation the Protestant nations had ended the conflict by making the same man – the King – the head of both the authoritarian state and the authoritarian Church. In Catholic Europe the authoritarian state had been able to live peaceably with an authoritarian Church, and this would happen again in Fascist Italy.[17]

The Pope thought it necessary to point out to his cardinals that it was heresy to say that the Church of Christ would have passed into oblivion if it had remained in Galilee. But he was not going to reopen the conflict with the Fascist state because of Mussolini's speech in the Chamber of Deputies. On 11 February 1932, the third anniversary of the Lateran Treaty, Mussolini was received by the Pope in a private audience in the Vatican. He knelt and kissed the Pope's hand, and Pius showed him round the Papal library.[18]

# CHAPTER 23

# The Fascist Regime

I N recent times, many political commentators have pointed out that while Fascist Italy, with its plebiscites, its one-party state, its censored press and the imprisonment without trial of political oppositionists, was certainly a dictatorship, it was not a totalitarian state like Nazi Germany or the Soviet Union under Stalin. There is an irony here, for it was Mussolini and his Fascist ideologists who first invented the word 'totalitarian' in 1923 to describe the state in Fascist Italy:[1] unlike the state in the democracies and all previous regimes, the Fascist state was totalitarian because it demanded the total commitment and devotion of all its citizens. But in a number of ways it was milder than Nazi Germany and Stalinist Russia or the royal despotisms of the sixteenth and seventeenth centuries. It resembled more closely Tsarist Russia in the nineteenth century, Metternich's Austria, or the France of Napoleon I and Napoleon III.

After the fourth attempt on Mussolini's life, the authorities adopted new repressive measures against political opponents in November 1926. All the Communist deputies in the Chamber were arrested, along with all the Communist leaders except Palmiro Togliatti, who happened to be in Russia and remained there; he became a member of the Presidium of the Executive Committee of the Communist International, and, under the name of Ercole Ercoli, one of the foremost leaders of the international Communist movement.

The leading Communist theoretician, Antonio Gramsci, who was also a deputy in the Chamber, was arrested in Montecitorio on 6 November 1926, and put on trial in Rome in May 1928 with seven other Communists. They were charged with conspiracy to incite civil war and class hatred. Gramsci was sentenced on 4 June to twenty years, four months and five days' imprisonment, and some of the other defendants received even longer sentences. Gramsci was in poor health, but Mussolini refused all petitions for an amnesty or to allow him to be transferred from prison to a hospital, despite – or perhaps because of – the efforts on Gramsci's behalf by an international committee of intellectuals in Paris. Eventually Gramsci was transferred to a clinic, where he died in April 1937.[2] Although his health was adversely affected by the conditions in prison, he was allowed to write letters and books, as Mussolini had done in prison in 1911–12. Gramsci's prison writings have made an important contribution to Marxist philosophy.

All the Socialist deputies were expelled from the Chamber and their seats declared vacant. Some writers have implied that this was a peculiar perversion of Mussolini's; but it was a measure adopted in the 1920s against Communist and Socialist deputies in several dictatorial regimes of central and eastern Europe, and the example was afterwards followed by the Daladier government in France at the outbreak of the Second World War and by the apartheid regime in South Africa in 1950.

Suspects who could not be proved guilty of any offence, and prosecuted in the courts, could be detained by an order of *confino* for a period not exceeding five years. The order for the *confino* was made by a tribunal presided over by the prefect of the district, usually on an application by the OVRA. The accused person had to be informed of the grounds for the application, and could argue his case before the tribunal, but could not be legally represented. If the order was made, he could appeal to an appeals tribunal appointed by the Under-Secretary for the Interior, but not to the courts of law. The *confino* was enforced against him while his appeal was pending. It was quite a common practice for the appeals tribunal to reduce the period of *confino*, though it was very unusual for them to quash the order completely. Those sentenced to *confino* could be released before the end of their term by administrative order. This was sometimes done after they had agreed to collaborate with the Fascist regime.

The victims of the *confino* were originally interned in the Isle of Lipari off the north coast of Sicily. In later years, places of internment were opened on the Isles of Tremiti off the Adriatic coast and of Ponza and Ventotene in the Gulf of Gaeta, and on the mainland at Amalfi, Cava dei Tirreni and elsewhere.

According to Guido Letti, of the OVRA, the treatment of the internees was much more humane than in dictatorial regimes in other countries. They were not worked to death like the inmates of Stalin's labour camps, or subjected to the calculated cruelties of Hitler's concentration camps or the spasmodic brutalities of internment camps under other regimes. Mussolini's internees were lodged in cottages of their own choice on their prison islands. They were obliged to attend a roll-call twice a day, but otherwise could move at will on the island and do what they wished. They were paid five lire a day, which was later increased to ten lire, which they could spend in buying what they fancied in the shops on the islands. Their family at home were paid two lire a day for their wives and one lira a day for each child. The internees could be granted leave of absence for a few days for compassionate reasons, though some of them took advantage of their leave to escape, in breach of their promise to return to confinement. Several of them escaped to France, and Paris became the main centre for Italian anti-Fascist refugees.[3]

But some of the prisoners told a different story from Letti's. The Socialist Carlo Rosselli escaped to France from the Isle of Lipari. The escape was organized by his English wife, Marion Cave, who sent a motorboat to Lipari to rescue him and two former parliamentary deputies, Emilio Lussu and Francesco Fausto Nitti, who were also interned there. Nitti then wrote an account of the conditions on Lipari, the brutality of the Fascist guards, and the occasional use of torture.[4] In view of the way that the Fascists sometimes behaved in the streets of the cities, it is not surprising that they acted in the same way on Lipari.

The refugees in France sent emissaries back to Italy to organize socialist underground groups, and sometimes to make more unsuccessful attempts to assassinate Mussolini; but the OVRA were vigilant, and caught many of them on the frontier.[5] The Socialists believed that some of their agents were denounced to the OVRA by the Communists,[6] who during the period between 1928 and 1934 considered the Socialists to be their greatest enemies. One of the most sensational operations of the refugees was undertaken by Lauro De Bosis. In October 1931 he piloted a plane which took off from Cannes and flew over Rome, dropping anti-Fascist leaflets; but on his way back to Cannes his plane dived into the sea, and he was killed.[7]

In the first years of the Fascist era, the press was the chief means of propaganda. The first Italian radio stations began broadcasting in

1924, but by 1930 there were only 100,000 radio sets among the forty million Italians. The radio became increasingly important throughout the 1930s, reaching many millions of people in their homes and through the loudspeakers in the public squares. By 1922 cinemas were showing silent films all over Italy, and several private Italian film companies were producing excellent films which competed very successfully with the American films produced in Hollywood and the German UFA productions. The Fascist government produced propaganda newsreels about current events with suitable captions written by official commentators. A law of 3 April 1926 made it compulsory for every cinema to show the official government newsreels, which became much more effective as propaganda after the introduction of talking pictures in 1928.

The Fascist government controlled the press in three ways. The Fascist Party bought shares which gave them a controlling interest in several of the leading national and local newspapers; by 1930 nearly 66 per cent of all newspapers were controlled by the Fascists. Secondly, the newspapers received instructions every day as to the political line that they were expected to adopt, from the government press office, which was at first under the control of Cesare Rossi, who gave the order for the murder of Matteotti.

Thirdly, there were the powers given to the prefects under the decree of 8 July 1924, at the height of the campaign of the Aventines against the Fascist regime. The prefect could issue a warning to any newspaper editor who had 'damaged the credit of the nation at home or abroad' or who published false news. An editor who received two warnings within one year could be dismissed by the prefect, who could then refuse to consent to the appointment of a new editor to succeed him. The prefect could not exercise these powers without the consent of a committee consisting of the prefect, a magistrate and a journalist; but he could order the seizure and confiscation of any issue of a newspaper without consulting the committee, and prefects used this power of confiscation more often than they issued warnings. A stricter control was imposed by the law of 31 December 1925, which set up the Order of Journalists and prohibited anyone from being a journalist unless he was a member of the order.[8]

Subject to these restrictions, independent newspapers could be published, and an editor could express his individual views, and even criticize some aspect of government policy, if he combined this with general support for the government and for Fascism, and especially with lavish praise of the Duce. The newspapers of Farinacci, Giovanni Preziosi and Telesio Interlandi, and various Catholic ultramontane journals, denounced the Jews many years before this became Mussolini's official policy. The *Giornale Italiano*, which was owned by Mussolini's Jewish minister, Finzi, and *Israel*, the official organ of the Italian Jews, replied to this anti-Semitic propaganda.

Arguments as to whether *The Protocols of the Elders of Zion* were genuine, or an anti-Semitic forgery by the Tsarist secret police, were freely carried on in the press for many years.[9] Ezio Garibaldi's weekly journal, *Camicia Rossa* (the 'Red Shirt' of Garibaldi and his volunteers), criticized the pro-German trends that sometimes appeared in Fascist policy, and certain aspects of the Concordat with the Vatican.[10] All these journals inserted passages praising Mussolini, and used quotations from his recent or more distant articles and speeches to justify the line that they were advocating against their opponents.

These differences of opinion and journalistic polemics were particularly marked on questions of art, literature and science. Already, before the First World War, the Futurist movement in art had supported the revolutionary nationalist ideas that afterwards expressed themselves in the interventionist campaign of 1914–15 and the Fascist movement after the war. They claimed that their modern art was revolutionary and Fascist as opposed to the stodgy, conventional art of the old conservative bourgeois parties and classes. But the ideas of the Futurists were opposed, often with great vehemence, by other more conservative elements in the artistic establishment. The Fascist leadership did not give a ruling as to which side was right, or proclaim an official 'Fascist art' which must be adopted by all artists, as a 'Socialist art' was prescribed in the Soviet Union. Both sides were left free to denounce each other year after year, with tactful praise of the Duce intermingled with their criticism of their rivals.

The arguments were particularly bitter among the architects. Did modernistic buildings best express the new revolutionary spirit of the Fascist era? Or was the classical architecture, based on the buildings of ancient Rome, a better expression of the incomparable genius of Mussolini?[11] There were similar arguments among scientists, geneticists, biologists and anthropologists as to the significance of racial as opposed to environmental factors in producing the glories of Fascist Italy.

This freedom of discussion, which was so different from Nazi Germany and Soviet Russia, showed both the strength and the weakness of Mussolini's regime. It was his strength that he was tolerant enough to allow these differences of opinion. The drawback was that his toleration extended to allowing his Fascists from time to time to riot, burn and murder. He might urge them not to do so, but they knew that they could flout his wishes with relative impunity.

Mussolini never exterminated the radical left-wing of the Fascist Party, as Hitler exterminated Ernst Roehm's SA on the 'night of the long knives' on 30 June 1934; still less did he put to death – before 1943 – nearly every other member of the government and party leadership as Stalin did. He played the various local Fascist bosses against each other, and sometimes ordered the OVRA to trail them. Balbo once discovered that the OVRA were tapping his telephone. He telephoned Mussolini in a rage, and protested. Mussolini said that of course the OVRA were tapping his telephone; it was an elementary security precaution. What else did Balbo expect? Balbo realized that there was no answer to this rhetorical question, and that was the end of the incident.[12]

The greatest importance was placed on education, and the indoctrination of youth. This was particularly important in a country where every child was indoctrinated in Catholic Christianity from the very earliest age. Mussolini's first Minister of Education was the philosopher Professor Gentile; and although Gentile resigned from the government in protest after the murder of Matteotti, he was persuaded to rejoin the Fascist hierarchy, although not as a minister, when the repercussions of the murder had died down. He was put in charge of drafting the syllabus and laying down the guidelines of elementary, secondary and university education, and of publishing the *Enciclopedia Italiana*, which was to rival the *Encyclopædia Britannica* and the French *Grand Larousse* in completeness and scholarship.

Gentile's educational theories were very different from those of the Socialists who had exercised great influence in the years before the First World War. The aim of the Socialists had been to spread literacy among the people. Gentile wished to produce excellence, and provide a suitable education for the élite, the meritocracy, the hierarchy, the *gerarchia*. He explained that education was of secondary importance as long as Mussolini was alive, when everything could be left to his infallible wisdom and brilliant leadership. At present, it was only necessary to train children who would obey and follow him without question; but Fascism would survive him, and when he was no longer among them they would have to produce a generation who would be able to fend for themselves.[13]

Along with the state schools, there were many private schools in Fascist Italy, particularly the Church and convent fee-paying schools where many children of the upper classes were educated. They were allowed to run themselves, but were obliged to follow Gentile's national curriculum, just as religious teaching was made compulsory in all state schools, in line with Mussolini's new policy and the Lateran Treaty. Gentile abandoned the system, which had been in force before the March on Rome, of holding consultations with representatives of the teachers' trade unions. He ordered that the teachers' unions were to be ignored. The duty of the teachers, like everyone else, was to obey the Duce and the state, not to argue with them.

But in educational policy, as in other matters, free discussion was tolerated in the press and elsewhere. Scholars were free to criticize Gentile's decision that the schools should teach more about ancient Rome and less about ancient Greece; more about the Risorgimento and less about the history of modern Europe; more about Garibaldi and less about Cavour. The most eminent of these critics was the classical historian Gaetano De Sanctis, who had always opposed the Fascists; he continued to argue that the free governments of ancient Greece were more worthy of study than the military regimentation of ancient Rome. But Gentile appointed him to be the editor of the classical section of the *Enciclopedia Italiana*.[14]

Gentile's successors as Minister of Education, Pietro Fedele and Giuseppe Belluzzo, carried through a purge of teachers and of textbooks after 1925, to eliminate all traces of anti-Fascism in schools and to comply with Mussolini's directive of December 1925: 'The government demands that the schools should be inspired by the ideals of Fascism', and should not be hostile 'or agnostic' about Fascism.[15] In all schools, including the private and convent schools, an hour was devoted every week to physical training. The physical training instructor was a Fascist – a Donna Fascista in the girls' convent schools – who combined the physical instruction with uplifting talk about the role of Fascism and the Duce in elevating the physical and moral health of the Italian people.[16]

The six-year-olds in the schools learned to read and write from the primer that had been made compulsory in all state and private schools; they copied, slowly and laboriously, the sentences in the printed book on to the ruled lines of their copybooks. 'Long live the King! Long live Italy! Long live the army! Long live our Chief Benito Mussolini! Down with Russia! Long live Africa! Long live our soldiers! Long live our King and may he always be victorious! Long live our DUCE, our Chief, and the founder of Fascism! Long live Italian Rome!'

By the age of seven they had moved on to their second exercise book. 'Children love Benito Mussolini. Benito Mussolini has worked and will always work for the good of our country and of the Italian people. You have often heard your Daddy say it, you have heard Mummy say it, you have heard the teachers say it. If Italy is today stronger than before, we owe it to him. Let us salute him altogether *A noi!*' ('Come on!', the Fascist slogan).

At nine they could take more advanced dictation. 'The immediate post-war years were a dark period for Italy. The revolutionary idea came as propaganda from Russia to our country. Industry, commerce and transport were at a standstill. Our country was threatened with utter ruin by the continual strikes and the occupation of the factories by the Communists, when Heaven sent us a man who uplifted our destiny – Benito Mussolini. On 28 October 1922 the Blackshirts entered Rome, and our King confided the government to Benito Mussolini, who immediately restored order all over Italy. During his years in government He has conferred incomparable and great benefits which have made Italy ever more beautiful and ever more powerful.'[17] In the Italian language, capital letters are used less than in English; but references to the Duce were always in capitals, and usually the whole word 'DUCE' was written in capitals.

More subtle forms of propaganda were sometimes adopted with adults, though here too much of the propaganda was crude. A very popular and best-selling calendar, with a page for every month, was published every year for housewives to hang up in their kitchens. Each page contained a recipe for some dish, and the housewife could consult the calendar for instructions while she was cooking the dish. In the middle of each page there was a photograph of Mussolini and a quotation from his speeches.[18] Most housewives did not look at the photograph or read the quotations, but studied only the recipe; but they were nevertheless aware, at least unconsciously, that the Duce and his words of wisdom were in their kitchen.

In the cities, towns and villages of Italy, the slogans issued by the Duce and the party were displayed on the hoardings and painted on

Mussolini aged fourteen

Mussolini in Switzerland
in 1904

Mussolini when editor of the
Socialist newspaper *Avanti!* in 1912

Rachele Mussolini

(*Above left*) Angelica Balabanoff
(*Above right*) Margherita Sarfatti
(*Left*) Leda Rafanelli

Mussolini as a soldier during the First World War

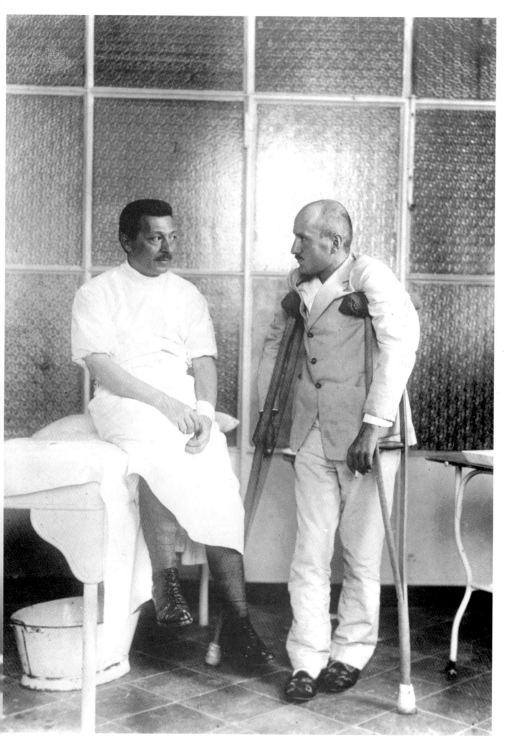

Mussolini walking on crutches after being wounded on the Isonzo front in 1917

Mussolini, his wife Rachele, and their daughter Edda

*Il Popolo d'Italia* of 29 October 1922,
with the proclamation of the Quadrumvirs during the March on Rome

Mussolini welcoming King George V on the King's arrival in Rome on 10 May 1923

(*Above*) Mussolini and Cardinal Gasparri at the signing of the Concordat on 11 February 1929

Mussolini playing the violin

Mussolini and Italo Balbo

Mussolini and Pierre Laval in Rome, January 1935

Mussolini throwing a new type of gas bomb during a demonstration in Rome in May 1935

Mussolini's house at Rocca delle Caminate

Claretta Petacci

Mussolini talking to Neville Chamberlain at Munich on 30 September 1938

Mussolini and Hitler in Hitler's plane
flying over German-occupied Russia on 28 August 1941

Mussolini and General Messe near Uman,
400 miles inside the Soviet Union, on 28 August 1941

The Villa Feltrinelli at Gargnano on Lake Garda,
Mussolini's residence when Chief of the Italian Social Republic, 1943–5

The corpses of Mussolini and Claretta Petacci
hanging from their feet in the Piazzale Loreto in Milan on 29 April 1945

the walls in the streets: '*Credere, obbedire, combattere*' (believe, obey, fight); 'If I advance, follow me; if I stand still, drive me forward; if I retreat, shoot me'; and '*Noi tireremo diritto*', which English commentators have wrongly translated as 'shoot straight', but in fact meant 'Carry straight on regardless'. Another slogan, the most popular of all, was displayed everywhere, and constantly quoted: '*Mussolini ha sempre ragione*' (Mussolini is always right).

The intellectuals beat all the others in their eulogies of Mussolini. The philosopher Ottavio Dinale wrote in *Gerarchia* in July 1930 that all the qualities and virtues of Alexander the Great and Caesar, of Socrates and Plato, of Virgil and Lucretius, of Horace and Tacitus, of Kant and Nietzsche, of Marx and Sorel, of Machiavelli and Napoleon, and of Garibaldi and the Unknown Warrior, had been reproduced in one man – Benito Mussolini.[19]

No wonder that Mussolini, glorified on all sides every day, was not particularly impressed when the King twice offered to make him a duke, the first time after he had induced Yugoslavia to cede Fiume to Italy, and the second after the signature of the Lateran Treaty with the Vatican. It was enough to be '*Capo del governo, Duce del fascismo*'; as head of the government and leader of Fascism, he felt that he did not need a dukedom, and that if he accepted it he would look rather ridiculous. He admitted that he felt like the Rohan family in France under the *ancient régime*, who had adopted the motto '*Roi ne puis, prince ne daigne, Rohan je suis*' (I cannot be a King, I disdain to be a Prince, I am a Rohan).[20]

In view of the fact that the Fascist regime interfered comparatively little with academic and intellectual freedom, nearly all the intellectuals were prepared to subscribe to Fascism and then continue as before in their intellectual and creative work. In 1931 a new law required all university professors to take an oath of loyalty to Fascism. This was the most direct interference with academic freedom which had so far taken place; but only eleven out of 1,200 professors in the whole of Italy refused to take the oath and lost their positions.[21]

Mussolini's old colleague, Arturo Toscanini, was one of the few who refused to compromise. In the general election of 1919 he had stood, together with Mussolini, as a Fascist candidate in Milan; but when the violence, arson and murders began, he turned against Fascism. He always refused to play the Fascist hymn *Giovinezza* at the beginning or end of his concerts and operatic performances. In 1930 he made a successful foreign tour, and received a great ovation when he conducted at the Albert Hall on his first appearance in London. But the Fascists did not forgive him for refusing to play *Giovinezza*.

In May 1931 a Fascist congress was held in Bologna. During the congress, Toscanini conducted at the Giuseppe Martucci memorial concert. The Fascists stormed into the concert hall and demanded that he play *Giovinezza*. He refused. They assaulted him, punching him and his wife, and beating them with canes. Neither he nor his wife was seriously injured, but he was ordered by the prefect to stay in his house for his own protection and to surrender his passport to the authorities. The case attracted much attention in the international press. After a month his passport was returned to him, and he was allowed to travel on foreign tours.[22] Next year, when Mussolini talked to Emil Ludwig, and they discussed music, Mussolini went out of his way to say that Toscanini was the greatest conductor in the world.[23] Toscanini eventually settled in the United States.

As far as the majority of the population was concerned, Fascism did not greatly interfere with their ordinary lives. Young men were liable to be called up for compulsory military service in peacetime, but this applied in most countries of Europe, though not in Britain, which, except during the First World War, had always relied on a small volunteer army, or in Germany, where conscription had been forbidden by the victorious Allies in the Treaty of Versailles. The ladies and gentlemen of Roman society continued to go to balls, night-clubs and theatrical first nights, to expensive hotels in the mountains for winter sports and summer holidays, and to the fashionable golf clubs. The lower middle class and factory workers found that food and minor luxuries could be bought at reasonable prices in the shops and markets, and that they could occasionally take the family to lunch and dine at popular restaurants and to an evening at the cinema.

They all appreciated the fact that Mussolini had made the trains run on time, as was often pointed out by his British admirers. This aroused much ridicule among the left-wing intellectuals: Mussolini was suppressing the fundamental freedoms of the Italian people, and was being praised for so trivial an achievement as making the trains run on time. In Britain in the 1920s trains nearly always ran on time, and Englishmen did not appreciate, as their grandchildren would do and their Italian contemporaries did, the inconvenience of having trains that do not run on time; nor did they realize that if Mussolini had made the trains run on time, it was because he had stopped strikes and other disruptive practices by the railway trade unions. The intellectuals were reluctant to admit that many Italians, like many people in other countries, attached more importance to making trains run on time and causing other things to run efficiently in their humdrum lives than to preserving freedom of speech for opposition politicians, journalists and writers.

The Fascist regime brought some real benefits to the people. For the ordinary Italian, whether he was an industrial worker, a peasant, or a lower-middle-class bank clerk, the Fascist organization, the Dopolavoro (after work), provided recreational and sporting activities and opportunities that most of them had never had before. A month's summer holiday was given, free of charge, to all children in the Fascist youth movement. A doctor examined every child and decided whether a holiday in the clean air of the mountains, or one at the seaside, would be better for his health. The child would then be sent to a holiday centre in some hotel that had been acquired for the purpose. The holiday centre was run chiefly by women in the Donne Fasciste organization who had volunteered to do the work. It was a happy month for the children, who still remember it nostalgically sixty and seventy years later. Nothing like this had been done for the children in the days before Mussolini, and the holiday camps did not survive his downfall and death. No one provides them for the children in post-war Italy.

There were other advantages in belonging to the Fascist Party and its youth movement. Children who were bullied at school, or ill-treated by unkind schoolmasters, appealed for help to the leader of the local Balilla, who spoke to the schoolmaster and the parents of the bully. A law provided that wounded ex-servicemen must be offered work if they asked for it, and in the Trentino the law applied to those inhabitants who had been conscripted into the Austrian Army in the First World War as well as to those who fought in the Italian Army. When Fortunato Pangrazi, a wounded ex-serviceman who had fought for Austria, went to an employer and asked for a job, the employer refused to employ him; he said that he sympathized, but it would not be profitable for him to employ a man whose incapacity made him a less productive worker than other employees; and that in any case the law did not apply in favour of soldiers who had fought on the Austrian side. Pancrazi went to the local branch of the Fascist Party. They told him that the law did apply to ex-servicemen who had served in the Austrian Army, and they visited the employer, who made no further difficulties about employing Pancrazi.[24]

It was certainly a way of enforcing a worker's rights without being impeded by bureaucratic red tape. No intervention by government inspectors, no delay, no form-filling, no hearings before industrial tribunals, no appeals and prolonged litigation in the courts. Instead, the local Fascist Party secretary called on the employer and made it clear that if he did not play fair by his employee, some Fascists would come and beat him with cudgels, or burn down his house. The warning was nearly always effective.

# CHAPTER 24

———— ◆ ————

# The Duce at Work

IN March 1925 Rachele and the children moved from Milan to Carpena in the Romagna, and in November 1929 they came to live with Mussolini in Rome. He had at last been persuaded to leave the flat that he had occupied since becoming Prime Minister and accept the offer from Prince Giovanni Torlonia to live in the Villa Torlonia in the Via Nomentana, which was then on the outskirts of Rome. Mussolini had stayed there for a few days in 1924 in order to have a suitable residence in which to entertain Haile Selassie; but he moved back to his flat after Haile Selassie left Rome. He now made it his permanent family home. He took up residence there on 15 November 1929, with Rachele and their five children[1] – Edda aged nineteen, Vittorio aged thirteen, Bruno aged eleven, Romano aged two, and Anna Maria, two months old.

Despite all his preoccupation with state affairs, he found time to play with his children, for he loved them all. Like many other great men, he enjoyed the company of children and animals who accepted his leadership and authority without question. He loved horses and the more bizarre animals – the cheetahs and lion cubs – that he received as gifts from Asian and African potentates, including a lion cub from Haile Selassie, now Negus of Ethiopia. He passed them on to the zoo in Rome, and visited them there, and his public relations men arranged for him to be photographed with them.

But he loved his children more. He went riding with them on horseback and on bicycles in the grounds of the Villa Torlonia, and played lawn tennis with them. He was good at tennis, and could give a game to the Italian lawn tennis champions. When he had time he would take the children to the seaside and go swimming with them.[2]

In 1930 the town council of Forlì gave him a country house, the castle of Rocca delle Caminate in Emilia, not far from the Mussolini family home. It was about a four-hour drive from Rome in the fast cars that Mussolini enjoyed driving. He spent as much time as he could at the Rocca delle Caminate with his family.

Edda now had boyfriends. She was not a beautiful girl, being fat and unshapely, and found it hard to compete with the other girls in a country so famous for its glamorous women. But what she lacked in looks she made up for in character, courage and intelligence. Rachele thought that she resembled her father in many ways. She had several suitors. Mussolini was very conscious that this might be due to the fact that she was his daughter. He had always insisted that all the children should go to state schools and mix with other boys and girls of their age;[3] and he was equally determined that Edda should not marry a man who was eager to become the Duce's son-in-law.

Edda fell in love with a young Jew who was the son of a colonel in the army. Mussolini was strongly opposed to the idea of her marrying a Jew. He warned Edda that mixed marriages usually ended in failure; but he was probably more worried about the adverse effect that her marriage to a practising Jew might have on his new allies in the Catholic Church. Edda soon lost interest in her Jewish admirer, and fell for the son of a wealthy industrialist; but the young man's father refused to agree to the marriage when he discovered that Mussolini was not wealthy enough to give Edda a suitable dowry.[4]

It was third time lucky for Mussolini as far as Edda was concerned. She fell in love with Count Galeazzo Ciano, the son of Admiral Count Costanzo Ciano, who had been a loyal Fascist for many years and had been at Mussolini's right hand in the days before the March on Rome and during the withdrawal of the Aventines after the murder of Matteotti. Ciano's son Galeazzo was aged twenty-seven and had entered the consular service. Mussolini strongly approved of the match.

He arranged a splendid wedding for Edda and Galeazzo. On 23 April 1930, the day before the wedding, he gave a reception in the grounds of the Villa Torlonia. It was the society event of the year, for Mussolini abandoned all his Spartan simplicity and frugality when it was a question of his daughter's wedding. The four thousand guests included everybody who was anybody in Rome, with the diplomatic corps there in strength. The ladies wore their most elegant dresses and their most expensive jewellery. Rachele noticed that the wife of the Soviet ambassador wore more jewellery than anyone else, and was dressed in her best fur coat, although it was a warm spring day in Rome.

Galeazzo and Edda were married next day. It was of course a religious wedding in the local parish church of San Giuseppe in the Via Nomentana. Mussolini gave the bride away, and Prince Torlonia and Grandi signed as witnesses for Edda.[5]

The journalists and the photographers turned the bride into a national and international figure; but once Edda had got out of her wedding dress, she made no attempt to dress fashionably or adopt a striking hairstyle. She was the despair of the fashion houses and magazines. She was glad to escape from the publicity a few months after the wedding, when Ciano was appointed Italian consul in Shanghai; but Mussolini was sad to see her go, for even when the family were living in Milan and Carpena while he was in Rome, he was in much closer touch with her than it was possible in 1930 to be with Shanghai. He was pleased when he received a telegram on 1 October 1931 with the news that Edda had given him his first grandson, Fabrizio, who had been born in Shanghai.

At the Villa Torlonia, Mussolini led his well-regulated life. Unlike many great statesmen, such as Bismarck, Churchill and Stalin, Mussolini did not work most of the night, taking a siesta in the afternoon or a number of short five-minute sleeping spells. Rachele has described how he rose at 6 a.m., performed physical exercises, drank a glass of orangeade or grape juice, and went out for a ride on horseback in the grounds. When he came back, he had a shower and then ate a breakfast of fruit, milk and wholemeal bread, and a little coffee, though in later years he gave up coffee completely. He then left for the Prime Minister's office, and had started work there by 8 a.m. He worked all the morning, taking a short break at 11 a.m. to eat a little fruit, and came home at 2 p.m. for his lunch. This consisted of a little spaghetti with tomato sauce, some fresh or cooked vegetables, and a good deal of fruit.

He spent the afternoon in his study, reading the Italian and foreign newspapers and some recently published books, or his favourite classical authors. He went back to his office, where he worked from 6 to 9 p.m., and then returned to the Villa Torlonia for a supper of plain soup, vegetables and fruit.[6] Although he spent only a few minutes eating, he sometimes remained at the table for a little time to talk to the children while they finished their meal at greater leisure.[7]

After supper he drank another glass of orangeade, or some camomile tea, and went to bed at 10.30 p.m. for his seven and a half hours' sleep. He gave orders that he was not to be disturbed during the night unless there was bad news that he ought to hear at once; if it was good news it could wait till the morning. He told Emil Ludwig in 1932 that in the previous ten years he had only three times been wakened to be told bad news: when the post office in Rome burned down, when the members of the Italian mission 'were murdered in Albania', and when the Queen Mother fell ill.[8] But as General Tellini and his officers were murdered early in the morning, Mussolini must have heard the news before he went to bed; and it is remarkable if he said that they were 'murdered in Albania', since the justification for his bombardment of Corfu was that they had been murdered in Greece by Greeks. According to the sculptress Clare Sheridan, who after sculpting Lenin in Moscow came to Rome to sculpt Mussolini, he was told the news of the murder of Tellini while he was trying to rape her;[9] but it is difficult to believe that her account of this incident is accurate.

He went to his Prime Minister's office every day of the week except Sundays; but on Saturday mornings he was less busy than usual. This was therefore a good time for his friend Ezio Garibaldi to come, sometimes accompanied by his little daughter Anita. Ezio Garibaldi came every Saturday to tell him what the people were saying about him, and the latest jokes that were circulating.[10] Like those other autocratic rulers, Harūn-al-Rashid in eighth-century Baghdad and Louis XI in fifteenth-century France, Mussolini wanted to know what the people really thought, not what his courtiers and propagandists were saying that they thought. A twentieth-century dictator, whose photograph was known to all his subjects, could not emulate Harūn and Louis and go unrecognized into the bazaars of Baghdad or the inns of Paris to discover the state of public opinion; he had to find out from Ezio Garibaldi. He knew that he could trust Ezio to tell him the truth.

Rachele's account of Mussolini's daily routine must in fact have been the exception rather than the rule. Most days there were receptions and meetings at which he made speeches to the party secretaries and other members of the *gerarchia*, to enthusiastic women of the Donne Fasciste, and to delegations of workers in industry or to peasants from the countryside. His lunch and supper did not always consist of Rachele's frugal meals, for he often attended banquets for visiting foreign rulers and statesmen at which he proposed the health of the guests or responded to their toast to him and his government. He often travelled outside Rome, making short visits to nearby factories and military establishments, as well as going to the North, the South, to central Italy, or the islands for a tour of several days or longer. He usually travelled in a chauffeur-driven official car or by special train; but sometimes he went by air, piloting his own plane, for he had held an air pilot's licence since 1921.

As well as his speeches in Parliament and to meetings of the *gerarchia*, Mussolini also addressed the larger rallies of the militia and other groups of Fascists who assembled in the square outside the Palazzo Venezia in Rome to hear him speak from the balcony or to see him appear at a window, as they raised their right arms in the Roman salute and roared again and again 'Duce, Duce, Duce!' – a chant that the writer Ignazio Silone ridiculed as a meaningless 'Cedu, Cedu, Cedu, Cedu!'[11] It has been stated that many members of the cheering crowds were Mussolini's secret policemen in plain clothes. Some of them may have been; but there were thousands who were not, and were enthusiastic Fascists or interested onlookers. They filled the square, not only in the city where he was speaking, but also in all the other cities in Italy, where his more important speeches were broadcast over the radio and by loudspeakers erected on the decorated lamp-posts in the squares.

His style of speaking had not changed in the last thirty years. He was still the same spellbinding orator who had thrilled the left wing Socialists at the congress of Reggio Emilia in 1912; it was only the opinions he expressed which had changed into almost their exact opposite. He spoke in the same short sentences, slowly and vigorously, with his left arm motionless at his side or resting on the rostrum, and the right arm moving straight up and down to emphasize his points. When the crowd cheered, he would pause for as long as he wished, and then command them to silence with an imperious gesture with his right arm. When he had said all that he wished to say, he would end quite suddenly and unexpectedly, turning his back on his audience and walking away, back into the Palazzo Venezia or down from his pedestal. And a pedestal it always was; once, at Reggio Calabria in 1938, it was a medieval tower rising high above the admiring audience.

He never spoke to them as an equal speaking to his comrades, but as a ruler to his subjects, as the leader to his followers. With every phrase, every inflexion of his voice, every gesture, he expressed his contempt for them. He knew that they expected and enjoyed it that way. It was different when he spoke in the Chamber or the Senate, or at smaller indoor gatherings, when it was a question of reviewing the achievements of the past year and of giving statistics and other detailed information. He then read his speech, and was much less effective, speaking quite flatly and more quickly than in his extempore speeches to large crowds in the open air, as if he were bored with the proceedings, and wished to get it over as soon as possible.[12]

These theatrical displays, with the cheering crowds, the marching militia, and Mussolini's harsh features and intemperate words, and his pose of superiority, had a double advantage from his point of view: not only did they impress the Italian masses, but his contrasting behaviour in private pleased his foreign visitors. Nearly all the British statesmen and journalists and their wives who praised him began their tributes by commenting how different he was in private from his public image. They were already half won over in the first moment they met him, when they found him charming, smiling, and soft-spoken. It convinced them that his public image was not his true self, but was only put on for the benefit of the Italian public. This further convinced them that Italians were different from Englishmen, that Mussolini would not behave like this if he were a politician in England, that he knew best what went down well in Italy, and that it was not for them to tell him how to govern Italians.

Sir Oswald Mosley had admired Mussolini ever since he had got the better of Mosley's father-in-law, Lord Curzon, during the Corfu crisis in 1923; but he did not agree with Austen Chamberlain and Churchill that Mussolini's methods, though admirable in Italy, would not work in Britain. Mosley, after beginning his political career as a Conservative MP, left the Conservatives in disgust and joined the Labour Party, becoming a minister in Ramsay MacDonald's second Labour government in 1929 and the hero of the Labour left wing; but when he found that he could not shift the Labour leadership to the left, he resigned from the government and soon afterwards from the Labour Party and formed his New Party in 1931. Next year he turned the New Party into the British Union of Fascists, and put himself forward as the English Mussolini.

Mosley visited Mussolini several times in Rome. As they both spoke fluent French, they could talk without difficulty until Mussolini, who had always prided himself on being a good linguist, told

Mosley that he had now learned to speak English. After this, he always insisted on speaking English to Mosley, but Mosley found it much more difficult to understand Mussolini's English than his French. Mosley was greatly impressed by Mussolini. He was sure that Mussolini was not taken in by his own rhetoric and theatrical postures, but had deliberately adopted them in order to impress his followers.[13]

Mussolini himself adopted a cautious and ambivalent attitude towards Fascists in other countries. In March 1928 he pleased the British Conservatives by stating that 'Fascism is not an article for export';[14] but when right-wing movements began to develop in other countries, based on violent anti-communism – and in many cases also on anti-Semitism – and the leaders of these movements expressed their great admiration for him, he encouraged them without openly associating with them. In October 1932 he said that in ten years' time all Europe would be 'Fascist or fascisized'.[15]

He developed semi-secret links with Mosley in Britain; with Charles Maurras and Léon Daudet's Action Française and other Fascist groups in France; with Léon Degrelle's Rexists in Belgium; with General Sacanell Sanjurjo and with Antonio Primo de Rivera's Falangist movement in Spain; with the National Socialists in Hungary; with Ante Pavelić's Ustaše in Croatia; and with Konstantin Vladimirovich Rodzaevsky's Russian Fascists operating from their exile in Harbin in Manchukuo.[16] But there was always one exception; he would have nothing to do with Adolf Hitler's Nazi Party in Germany. Hitler's admiration for him was not reciprocated.

While refusing to encourage any German nationalists, Mussolini was very pleased to grant a series of interviews to the eminent German author Emil Ludwig, although some Italian Fascists were already calling him 'Abraham Cohen, alias Emil Ludwig'. Ludwig had written very successful biographies of Napoleon and Bismarck. He had two interviews with Mussolini in March 1929, and followed this with a series of longer interviews between 23 March and 4 April 1932.[17] His book *Talks with Mussolini* was published later that year in German and in an English translation, and with a few minor deletions in Italian by Mondadori in Milan.

Mussolini received him in the Palazzo Venezia in the large fifteenth-century room that is called the Hall of the Mappamondi, because the first globe of the world ever made was installed in the room. Mussolini sat at his desk facing the window at the end of the room, and when his visitors entered at the other end and began their long walk towards him, he would rise from his desk and come to meet them. Mussolini, who wore a dark lounge suit and a black tie, gave Ludwig an hour of his time every day, and resumed the interview at the appointed time next day.

Ludwig spent the rest of his time in Rome looking at various aspects of the city under Fascism. When he went to the first night of a new production of Donizetti's *Don Pasquale* he noticed that the *toilettes* of the ladies in the audience were more elegant and expensive than anything he had seen at first nights at the Metropolitan in New York or the Opéra in Paris. One day he had lunch with Balbo at the canteen in the Air Ministry. When he was in Moscow and lunched in government canteens there, the officials sat in three groups according to their rank in the ministries and the party, with the higher-ranking members eating more and better food than the other groups. In the canteen at the Air Ministry in Rome all the staff sat together and ate the same food, for which the higher officials paid seven lire and the lower-paid staff paid two lire.

Mussolini and Ludwig talked about Mussolini's life, his ideas, the books he had read – Dante, Byron, Leopardi, Nietzsche – and how he liked parts of Wagner's *Tristan, Tannhäuser* and *Lohengrin* but hated his *Parsifal*, and preferred Beethoven to all other composers. They talked about great men in history – Bismarck, Napoleon and Julius Caesar. When Ludwig said that Mussolini had often been compared to Napoleon, Mussolini said that it was a false comparison, because Napoleon had put an end to a revolution and he himself had started one; but he said that he admired Napoleon. He was in fact the joint author with the playwright Gioacchino Forzano of a play about Napoleon during the Hundred Days, *Campo di Maggio*, which was performed at the Argentina Theatre in Rome on 20 December 1930. It dealt with Napoleon's effort to enlist the support of the French Liberals against the Allied armies by granting a Liberal constitution on the *champ de mai* on 1 June 1815. The moral of the play was that this was an error on Napoleon's part, because, in Mussolini's version, the Liberals betrayed Napoleon after Waterloo, and only his old soldiers remained loyal to him.[18]

Mussolini told Ludwig about his great admiration for Julius Caesar. This was a departure from the tradition of the Risorgimento, for Mazzini had praised Caesar's murderer, Brutus, as an example of justifiable tyrannicide. Ludwig asked Mussolini if he modelled himself on Caesar. Mussolini said that he did to some extent, but added that Caesar should have looked at the paper that was handed to him on the Ides of March which contained the names of the conspirators who were plotting to murder him.

Ludwig said that many people condemned Napoleon for having had the Duke of Enghien shot. Mussolini said that this was as absurd as blaming Caesar for having executed the defeated leader of the Gauls, Vercingetorix; great men should not be criticized for having committed an occasional crime. Ludwig and Mussolini touched on the subject of anti-Semitism. 'Anti-Semitism does not exist in Italy,' said Mussolini. 'Italians of Jewish birth have shown themselves good citizens, and they fought bravely in the war.'[19]

In 1932 Fascist Italy celebrated the tenth anniversary of the March on Rome. The greatest event of the celebrations was the opening of the Via dell'Impero, the imperial boulevard that commemorated the glories of ancient imperial Rome and emphasized its link with Fascist Italy. At the opening ceremony on 28 October Mussolini rode along the Via dell'Impero on horseback. Maps in coloured marble, showing the frontiers of the Roman Empire at its height, were cemented into a wall near the Forum. Mussolini decreed that 21 April should be celebrated every year as the anniversary of the traditional date on which the city of Rome had been founded by Romulus in 753 BC. He abolished the annual celebrations on 20 September of the entry of Italian troops into Rome in 1870, in order to please the Pope. He also abolished May Day, which had been celebrated by so many Socialists all over the world, including Benito Mussolini, since it was proclaimed by the Second International in 1889. In his English autobiography he – or his brother Arnaldo – wrote that May Day 'had foreign origins, and a print of Socialist internationalism', and he had therefore abolished it and given the workers an alternative day for their holiday, 21 April, 'a gay and glorious date in Italian life . . . the birthday of Rome'.[20]

Like other revolutions, the Fascist revolution revolutionized the calendar. The French revolutionaries in 1793 introduced a completely new calendar which did not survive Napoleon and lasted only twelve years. The Bolshevik revolution in 1917 abolished the Julian and introduced the Gregorian calendar in Russia several centuries after the rest of Europe had adopted it. It was typical of Mussolini to make a more modest reform. The days of the week and the months remained unchanged, but the years were dated both from the birth of Christ and from the Fascist revolution of 28 October 1922, the Fascist year being given, in all official documents, in Roman numerals after the Christian year had been given in Arabic numerals. Thus Mussolini's fiftieth birthday, 29 July 1933, was given as '29 July 1933 XI', as the eleventh year of the Fascist era ran from 29 October 1932 to 28 October 1933.

Italy moved into the front rank of international sport. Italian athletes won nine gold medals at the Olympic Games in Los Angeles in 1932. In lawn tennis Baron de Stefani, who never played a backhand stroke but passed his racket whenever necessary from his right to his left hand, regularly reached the last rounds at Wimbledon and in the French championships. Primo Carnera won the world boxing heavyweight title. Tazio Nuvolari was ranked first in the world in motor racing. Italy was even able to challenge the invincible English team at football, drawing 1-1 with England in Rome in May 1933 in a match that Mussolini attended. Next year Italy won the football World Cup, in which England did not compete. Mussolini was present at the final in Rome, when the Italian team, after being a goal down, defeated Czechoslovakia 2−1 in extra time. It was a great triumph for Fascist sport.

Italy's greatest international success was in the air. As soon as Mussolini came to power he set up the air force as a separate defence department, and continually increased its share in the defence budget. In November 1926 he appointed Balbo as Minister for Air, and Balbo's energy and charisma increased the strength of the air force and its international prestige. Balbo believed in the strategic theories of Giulio Douhet, who was convinced that if there was another war it would be won by strategic bombing against which there was no defence. By 1929 Italy had become the fourth strongest air power in the world after France, Britain and the United States.[21]

Mussolini's press made great propaganda out of the achievement of General Umberto Nobile, who flew over the North Pole in his airship *Italia* on 24 May 1928. Unfortunately Nobile crashed into the ice next day on his homeward flight; he was uninjured, but his airship became encrusted in the ice. Aviators from all countries set out to rescue him. The famous Norwegian explorer Roald Amundsen, who had been the first man to reach the South Pole in 1911, lost his life when his plane crashed while he was trying to locate and rescue Nobile.

For six weeks the rescue attempts were front-page news in the world press. It was publicity of a kind that Mussolini did not relish; and it was aggravating that Nobile was eventually rescued on 12 July by a Soviet ice-breaker. Mussolini may have been irritated, but he was generous both in his praise of Nobile and in his thanks to the Soviet Union for the rescue.[22]

Balbo was much more successful than Nobile.[23] In 1927 he obtained his pilot's certificate and led a number of long-distance flights in person. Mussolini could present to the world the spectacle of a Minister for Air who was not a middle-aged or elderly politician, whose only connection with flying was his ability to answer questions in Parliament on which he had been briefed by his civil servants, but a handsome, dashing ex-serviceman in his early thirties, piloting his own plane as he flew halfway across the world at the head of his squadrons. The international press and public were impressed, and admired Balbo the aviator, forgetting about his earlier exploits with castor oil, arson and the murder of Father Minzoni.

After leading a flight over England, France and the western Mediterranean in the summer of 1928, Balbo flew at the head of thirty-five aircraft in June 1929 by Athens, Istanbul and Varna to Odessa. He was lavishly fêted in Odessa, and got on very well with the officers of the Red Air Force and the other Soviet officials whom he met. He wrote to Mussolini that the strains of the *Internationale*, which he had always found so hateful when he heard it sung after the war by 'subversive' peasants in Emilia, sounded much better when it was sung in Odessa to express the Russian nationalist will to power. When he returned to Italy he wrote a book, *Da Roma a Odessa*, about his flight. He wrote that although the Bolsheviks were blood-thirsty Orientals, 'they have made a revolution and they defend it. Whoever strongly professes a political faith respects that of others, most of all when he opposes it.' And Communists and Fascists had one thing in common: they were opposed to the Western democracies, which were 'rotten to the bone'.[24]

On his way home he stopped at Varna in Bulgaria and made a speech at a dinner in which he referred sympathetically to the Bulgarian claims to Macedonia. This annoyed the government of King Alexander in Yugoslavia, and was adversely commented upon in the Yugoslav press. Relations between Italy and Yugoslavia were always sensitive.[25]

On 17 December 1930 Balbo set off on a third great flight with fourteen planes by Spain, Morocco and Dakar to South America, arriving in Rio de Janeiro on 15 January 1931. He crowned his achievements with his greatest flight in July 1933 when he led twenty-five planes by Amsterdam, Londonderry, Reykjavik, Labrador and Newfoundland to Montreal and on to Chicago, where he arrived fourteen days after leaving Orbetello airport in Tuscany.

He received a tremendous reception in the United States. He was greeted by several high-ranking army officers, including Colonel Dwight D. Eisenhower. He had a ticker-tape reception in New York, and a street in Chicago was named after him. He had tea at the White House with President Franklin D. Roosevelt, who told him how greatly he admired Mussolini for reviving the fortunes of Italy and for the part he was playing in international affairs. Roosevelt sent a message of congratulation to the King of Italy, and his Secretary of State sent one to Mussolini. Balbo sent a telegram to Mussolini: 'In the name of the Duce we reach all goals.'

The Socialists and the other anti-Fascist groups among the Italians in the United States organized protest meetings and demonstrations, and Balbo was guarded by a large force of police; but he was not worried. He telegraphed to Mussolini that his visit had exploded the myth that Italians abroad were anti-Fascist.[26]

Stories were told by anti-Fascists at the time and afterwards of Mussolini's jealousy of Balbo, that he demanded that Roosevelt should send a congratulatory telegram to him, and had to be told that as the President was head of state his message must be sent to the King. He is also said to have demanded that if a street in Chicago was named after Balbo, one in New York should be named after him.[27] These stories, like so many other tales about Mussolini, are almost certainly untrue. Mussolini was not a vain man; he wanted to dominate his followers, his people and his century, but that is a different matter from resenting the fact that Balbo had a street named after him or that the King, and not he himself, received a telegram from Roosevelt. Mussolini wanted the realities, not the trappings, of power. Like Stalin, he accepted the eulogies of his journalists, writers and the public, not out of vanity, but because he knew that this was the best way to retain the devotion of the masses and to maintain his power and the power of the Fascist state.

# CHAPTER 25

# Depression and Disarmament

I N December 1931 M.K. Gandhi – the Mahatma to his followers
– came to Rome on his way home to India after attending the
round table conference on India in London. His civil disobedience
campaign and the passive resistance to the British attempts to suppress it had aroused great admiration throughout the world. Mussolini received him as an honoured guest, probably in order to impress
pro-Gandhi popular opinion in the United States and elsewhere, and
perhaps also to embarrass the British government. He gave a reception for Gandhi in the Palazzo Venezia, and invited him to stay for
a few days at the Villa Torlonia. Gandhi arrived with the goat that
went everywhere with him, on a long lead. Gandhi's outlook and
character always led him to take a rosy view of everybody's actions
and motives, and he praised Mussolini, as he was later to praise
Hitler, as a well-meaning man who was trying his best to perform
the mission entrusted to him by God. He told Mussolini that he was
sure that he would live to see the liberation of India.

Mussolini said to Rachele that Gandhi was a holy man, a genius,
and unique in being able to use goodness as a weapon. He thought
Gandhi was probably one of the few men in the world who knew
how to handle the British; if India ever became free, she would owe
this to Gandhi.[1]

By 1930 the world economic depression was under way, and it
reached its peak in 1932 and the first months of 1933. It caused
monetary deflation, a fall in wages and prices, great poverty, and
unemployment on an unprecedented scale, particularly in Britain,
the United States and Germany. It shook the people's faith in capitalism and democratic government. The Communists claimed that it
was the final crisis of capitalism which Marx had foretold, and that
until capitalism was overthrown by the international Communist

revolution, the standard of living of the masses would never be restored to the level it had reached before the depression began in 1929. The depression brought down the second Labour government in Britain, President Herbert Hoover and the Republican Party in the United States, and the Weimar Republic and parliamentary democracy in Germany; but Mussolini emerged from the depression with an enhanced reputation.

Italy did not escape the effects of the depression. Even according to Mussolini's official figures, which his opponents said were distorted, unemployment had risen by February 1933 to its peak of 1,229,000. If the figures were correct, they compare favourably with the peak figure of 2,700,000 in Britain in January 1933, the eleven and a half million in the United States, and more than five million in Germany. But Mussolini's reputation for dealing with unemployment and the depression owed more to propaganda than to any action on his part.

He did take certain steps to alleviate the situation. He changed his policy on stopping emigration. On 13 August 1930 he ordered that anyone who wished to emigrate was free to do so, and was to be given a passport. Like Roosevelt in the United States, but unlike the Conservative National government in Britain, and the governments in most other countries, he accepted the economic theories of J.M. Keynes and his followers, who thought that a government could spend its way out of the depression, and instead of cutting public expenditure should increase it in order to provide work for the unemployed and give the slumping national economy a kick-start. Mussolini launched a number of public works; the most publicized was the cleaning of the Pontine Marshes near Rome. The Duce was photographed wielding a pick and spade and helping personally with the clearance work. He was also photographed on several occasions helping with the harvest in the fields.

Mussolini's trump card for dealing with the depression was to announce that he was introducing the Corporate State. In 1926 he had stated that the Socialists were wrong when they said that capitalism was in decline, and that he believed that it would flourish for several centuries to come. He changed his line during the depression. In a speech in the Chamber on 14 November 1933 he said that 'the capitalist method of production has become out of date'.[2] The world depression was not merely one of the slumps that came regularly in industrial countries and was always followed by a boom and renewed prosperity; this depression was caused by a fundamental defect of capitalism. The Fascist revolution would therefore abolish capitalism and replace it, not with Bolshevism or international socialism, but with the Corporate State.

On 20 March 1930 an Act of Parliament established the Corporate State by creating the National Council of Corporations which was to direct twenty-two Corporations covering all forms of economic and social life, from the Corn Corporation and the Vegetable Corporation in agriculture and the Steel Corporation and the Chemical Corporation in industry to the Corporation of Sea and Air Travel and the Corporation of the Stage. But it was not very clear exactly what the corporations were supposed to do. Mussolini's critics said that they existed only on paper; and in fact none of the corporations was actually established. It was eight months before any members of the corporations were appointed, or any premises made available for them; and after the Corporation of the Stage was set up on 6 December 1930, and entrusted with the task of animating the theatre and the film industry, no other corporation came into existence for another four years until 9 December 1934, when Mussolini – who was nominally the president of every corporation – appointed the vice-presidents and members of the committees of the other twenty-one Corporations. The first corporation actually to begin functioning was the Corporation for Cattle-breeding and Fisheries on 7 January 1935.[3]

But from the point of view of Mussolini's prestige, this did not really matter. The fact that he had announced that he had created the Corporate State was enough to show that he was doing something; he was not waiting helplessly for things to remedy themselves, as the governments in other countries seemed to be doing. The Communists and Socialists blamed 'the capitalists' for the world depression; but many more people of all parties blamed 'the old gang', and turned to anyone who put forward a new idea for ending the crisis and ending unemployment – Keynes, Major Douglas of 'Douglas Credit', Professor Frederick Soddy, or Silvio Gesell. And they turned to Mussolini, who was not merely writing books about how to put things right, but was actually creating the Corporate State to replace the capitalist system which had failed the world. No one could accuse Mussolini of being one of the old gang; he was not yet fifty, and his Fascist song, which had become the unofficial Italian national anthem, was *Giovinezza* (Youth). In Germany, too, many people were looking for a youthful leader – not to the eighty-five-year-old

President von Hindenburg, but to the young Adolf Hitler, aged only forty-three.

In Britain, Mussolini was praised not only by the young Sir Oswald Mosley but also by the veteran elder statesman, David Lloyd George, the former radical leader and wartime Prime Minister. He had been out of office for ten years, but at the age of seventy was putting forward new and unconventional ideas on how to restore prosperity. In January 1933 the Italian press reported that he had said that only two men, Stalin and Mussolini, had been able to save their countries from the depression.[4]

In April Mussolini opened the eighteenth Interparliamentary Commercial Congress in Rome. The delegates from all parts of the world expressed their admiration for his achievements in saving his country from her political and economic crises. The American writer Charles Spencer Hart said that Italy had found a Moses, 'Benito Mussolini, who belongs to the family of giants'.[5]

Franklin D. Roosevelt had just become President of the United States, and had promised the American people a New Deal. Here was a third national leader, apart from Mussolini and Stalin, who seemed to the admiring world to be doing something to surmount the depression. When the United States Congress voted Roosevelt emergency powers to deal with the economic situation, Mussolini said that Roosevelt, too, was a dictator, and that the United States had realized that democracy had failed and that only a dictator could save them.[6]

Mussolini followed closely the purge that Stalin was conducting in the Communist Party of his Trotskyist and other opponents, and thought that this proved the failure of communism. When Trotsky, in his exile in France, formed his Fourth International in 1934, Mussolini mocked it, and predicted that the Fourth International would fail like all the others. 'We await the Fifth.'[7]

The despair and anger generated by the depression increased the pacifism that spread at this time in the Western democracies, and particularly in Britain. In 1918 Lloyd George had spoken about creating a land fit for heroes to live in – the heroes who had won the war. Now that the heroes were living on their meagre unemployment benefit only just above starvation level, it reinforced the resentment against war, because it emphasized that all the sufferings and the heavy loss of life in the trenches had been in vain.

In Britain the Reverend Dick Sheppard, Rector of the fashionable

Church of St Martin's-in-the-Fields in London, formed the No More War movement. He asked his supporters to sign a declaration, 'I renounce war and will never take part in another', and obtained over three million signatures. Books like the German author Erich Maria Remarque's *Im Western nichts neues* (*All Quiet on the Western Front*), and Henri Barbusse's *Le Feu* in France, showed the horrors of the First World War; so did plays like the French Paul Raynal's *Le Tombeau sous l'Arc de Triomphe* (produced in Britain under the title *The Unknown Warrior*) and the English playwright R.C. Sherriff's *Journey's End*. The pacifist propaganda appeared in the most improbable places. The fans of the international film star Greta Garbo, who flocked to see her film *Queen Christina*, heard Garbo, in the part of Christina, denounce the pro-war policy of her father Gustavus Adolphus and her successor Charles X, and make a plea for pacifism. On the London stage, the very successful play by Gordon Daviot, *Richard of Bordeaux*, starring the young John Gielgud, which became 'London's longest run' in 1933, glorified the fourteenth-century King Richard II of England as a pacifist, who was deposed and murdered by baronial warmongers because he wished to end the Hundred Years' War.

The famous comedian George Robey, well known for his chorus line 'I'm more than surprised, I'm amazed', which he introduced into all his songs, received a rousing ovation when he inserted a topical verse into a song at a gala performance which was broadcast over the BBC radio:

> But quite the most curious thing of the lot
> Is the way that our statesmen behave . . .
> When you ask for more pay they say they're hard up,
> But for armaments millions they've raised;
> If it's all to take part in a war that won't start,
> Then I'm more than surprised, I'm amazed.

Left-wing writers were very successful in making the British public believe that if there was another war, it would lead to the extermination of the whole population by poison gas. The Socialist author Raymond Postgate, writing in 1934 as a member of the British Labour Party to denounce the Communist theory that the next war would lead to a successful Communist revolution, stated that, if there was another war, within 'the very first few weeks . . . where any survive in the poison-laden, burnt and wrecked streets, half will be crippled or raving', while the other half would be fighting savagely for what scraps of food could be found. In the countryside, the farmers would join together to shoot at sight 'the savage bands of town refugees roaming the country-side. Whole areas will pass out of human occupation as the winds change and the low-lying, long-waiting, heavy clouds of poison gas shift about.'[8]

On 25 January 1933 – five days before Hitler came to power in Germany – that most prestigious debating society, the Union at Oxford University, passed by a large majority a resolution that 'this House will under no consideration fight for its King and country'. The British people were startled; some were pleased, some contemptuously tolerant, some disgusted. Churchill did not agree with *The Times* that it could be dismissed as 'the children's hour' (the radio programme for children). Speaking to the Anti-Socialist and Anti-Communist Union at the Queen's Hall in London on 17 February 1933, he called it a 'disquieting and disgusting symptom' which would arouse the contempt of the 'splendid clear-eyed youth' of Germany marching eagerly to join the army, and in 'Italy with her ardent Fascisti, her renowned Chief, and a stern sense of national duty'. He then went on to praise 'the Roman genius of Mussolini', who was 'the greatest lawgiver among living men', and a zealous enemy of communism.[9]

The renowned chief of the Italian Fascisti was certainly putting over a very different line from the pacifists in Britain. In 1929 the first volume of Gentile's *Enciclopedia Italiana* was published, and in 1932, Year X of the Fascist revolution, volume F had been reached. Gentile asked Mussolini to write the article on 'Fascism: the Doctrine'.

Mussolini wrote that Fascism stood for the supremacy of the state. It rejected liberalism, which exalted the rights of the individual above the state; for the state was composed of many individuals, and the whole was greater than the part. The individual could only realize his full potential by serving the state. Fascism likewise rejected socialism, which put loyalty to a class above loyalty to the state; and Fascism rejected Marx's doctrine of historical materialism – that the struggle between economic classes was the decisive influence in history. Fascism did not deny that these material class interests existed, but believed that in great nations selfish class interests would give way to the glorious ideal of service to the state.

In a passage dealing with the Risorgimento, Mussolini rejected the idea that the liberals had been responsible for uniting Italy. They had played no part in it. Garibaldi and Mazzini were not liberals; Lombardy had been liberated thanks to the assistance of Napoleon III, who was the enemy of liberalism, and the anti-liberal Bismarck had helped Italy to liberate Venice.

Fascism was against democracy and democratic lies. Fascism was against pacifism, 'believing neither in the possibility nor the usefulness of permanent peace. It rejects Pacifism, which conceals a flight from struggle and cowardice in the face of sacrifice. Only war brings out the maximum expression of human energy and prints a mark of nobility on those peoples who have the courage to affront it.' Fascism supported religion in general and Italian Catholicism in particular; it did not seek to create its own God, as Robespierre did, or vainly to eradicate God from men's souls, as Bolshevism did. The Fascist state sought power and domination, and aspired to create an empire, not from eagerness to gain a square kilometre of territory but because the expansion of a nation was an expression of its vitality.[10]

No wonder that Churchill was worried. If the youth and people of Britain believed that war would lead to the extermination of the whole population and was an evil that must be avoided at all costs, while the Italians believed that only war could bring out the full glory of a nation that was brave enough to start a war, this gave the Italians a winning advantage over the British in the game of bluff that has always been such an important ingredient of international diplomacy.

During the winter of 1933–34 there were two parliamentary by-elections in the London area, East Fulham in November being followed by North Lambeth in February. Labour won them both, reversing a Conservative majority of over 15,000, which in view of the smaller number of voters on the electoral register was a higher percentage swing than a similar result would be today. The Labour candidates had fought on an out-and-out pacifist programme of opposition to all wars and rearmament.

Immediately after the North Lambeth by-election, the Lord Privy Seal, the thirty-six-year-old Anthony Eden, was sent to Rome to discuss the international situation with the Italian government. On 26 February he had his first meeting with Mussolini. He spent most of the time answering Mussolini's questions, especially his question about the North Lambeth by-election result. Mussolini knew the exact voting figures, and asked Eden the reason why the Conservatives had lost.[11] We can be sure that he already knew the reason, and had drawn his own conclusions.

The pacifists and Socialists in Britain believed that the ultimate horror, war, was caused by armaments, and by armament manufacturers who sold armaments to their own and foreign governments for profit. If one nation rearmed, this would frighten other nations, who would also rearm; an arms race would take place, and one day the nation that had a temporary lead in the arms race would start a preventive war before the other nations caught up and overtook it. War could be avoided only if all nations disarmed, and reduced their armaments step by step by international agreement until they retained only the minimum amount of arms necessary to maintain internal order.

Mussolini was disappointed when the British Labour Party won the general election in May 1929 and his friend Austen Chamberlain left the Foreign Office. Ramsay MacDonald became Prime Minister in a minority Labour government relying on Liberal support, and chose the veteran Arthur Henderson as his Foreign Secretary. Henderson's principal aim was to convene an international disarmament conference at which the nations would agree to reduce their armaments. The service chiefs in every country were suspicious of disarmament; they feared that if their country disarmed, other nations would cheat and gain an advantage that would endanger national security. In Italy, Balbo was particularly hostile to any plan to reduce the size of his air force.

Mussolini sympathized with Balbo, and was contemptuous of international Socialists who had pacifist illusions; but once again he was going to ride two horses at the same time. While he glorified war in his articles and speeches, he paid lip service to the idea of disarmament in his conversations with foreign statesmen. In April 1931 Henderson came to Rome with A.V. Alexander, the First Lord of the Admiralty, to try to persuade Mussolini to support the idea of a disarmament conference. Mussolini gave them a warm welcome, and told Henderson that he approved of a disarmament conference and would do all he could to secure an agreement to reduce armaments.

By the time the Disarmament Conference met in Geneva in February 1932, the British Labour government had resigned; MacDonald had joined the Conservatives and had become Prime Minister in a National government that was completely dependent on the Conservative MPs; and the Labour Party, which bitterly denounced MacDonald as a traitor, had been routed at the general election of October 1931 at which nearly all the Labour leaders, including Henderson, lost their seats in Parliament. The new Foreign Secretary was the brilliant Liberal barrister Sir John Simon; but the National government sent Henderson to represent Britain and take the chair at the Disarmament Conference.

Mussolini sent Grandi to Geneva to make speeches at the conference in support of the principle of disarmament; but very little progress was made, because all the powers insisted on retaining those arms on which they especially relied. The proposal to agree to a ban on bomber planes fell through because of the objections of the British delegate, Anthony Eden, who very reluctantly carried out his instructions from the British government to insist on retaining the right to bomb from the air troublesome Indian and Arab tribesmen.[12]

The Socialists and liberals in Britain and other countries were strongly in favour of improving relations with Germany. They had a guilty conscience about the way in which the defeated Germans had been treated in 1919, when the whole German people and their new Socialist government were made to pay the penalty for the crimes of the Kaiser, although they had made a revolution and had driven him out. Liberal opinion in Britain sympathized with the demands of the democratic and liberal Weimar Republic in Germany for a revision of the Treaty of Versailles which would remove the injustices that had been inflicted on Germany. This idea was viewed with great suspicion in France and by France's allies in the Little Entente of Czechoslovakia, Yugoslavia and Romania.

Again Mussolini adopted a double policy. He was conscious of the threat from a strong Germany, and vigorously opposed any suggestion that he should grant concessions to South Tyrol. He continued to declare that the German-speaking population in the Alto Adige were well treated and had no cause for complaint, that the agitation about their sufferings was stirred up by international socialism with the object of discrediting Fascism, and that all Italy – her living and her dead – would arise to defend her frontier on the Brenner.[13] But in other respects he was conciliatory towards both

Austria and Germany. In February 1930 he signed a treaty of friendship with Austria; and he pleased the British government by hinting
that he would be prepared to support a revision of the Treaty of
Versailles in Germany's favour.

On 23 October 1932 he made a speech in Turin[14] in which he put
forward a plan for a Four Power Pact of friendship between Italy,
Britain, France and Germany, and clearly implied that this could
lead to the revision of old treaties. His speech alarmed the French
government and the Czechoslovakian Foreign Minister, Beneš, who
said that treaties must be observed. Mussolini agreed, but said that
they could be revised by agreement between the parties.[15]

His speech was welcomed in Britain, and in March 1933 Ramsay
MacDonald, his daughter Ishbel, and his Foreign Secretary Sir John
Simon came to Italy to discuss the international situation with Mussolini. They went first to Genoa, where Balbo met them and flew
them to Rome in his plane, which he piloted himself. Mussolini met
them at the airport. MacDonald and his daughter saw all the sights
in Rome, visited the Pope in the Vatican, and were lavish in their
praise of the achievements of Fascist Italy. Mussolini put aside all
the old disagreements he had had with MacDonald in the days when
MacDonald was a Socialist. Their relations were most cordial, and
they agreed about the necessity of revising the Treaty of Versailles.
Mussolini said to Rachele: 'MacDonald's views and mine are almost
completely identical.'[16]

# CHAPTER 26

— ◆ —

# Hitler

ON 30 January 1933 President von Hindenburg appointed
Adolf Hitler to be Chancellor of Germany. At the end of
February, Hitler used the burning of the Reichstag building
in Berlin by a demented Dutch anarchist as an excuse to suppress
the Communist Party, to throw the Communist leaders into concentration camps, and to rule by emergency powers. He attacked the
Jews, and on 1 April his Nazi SA (Storm-Troopers) organized a
boycott of Jewish shops throughout Germany. The international
Communist, Socialist and liberal press launched a passionate anti-
Nazi campaign. They accused the Nazis themselves of burning the
Reichstag in order to have an excuse to suppress democracy and the
left-wing parties; and they described the beatings and other brutalities
inflicted by the Nazi SA and SS on the Communists, Socialists and
Jews in their concentration camps.

The Nazis replied by denouncing Jewish Bolshevism. In May Hitler
sent Alfred Rosenberg on a goodwill mission to London. Rosenburg
told Sir John Simon that if foreign pressure brought about the fall
of Hitler's government, 'Bolshevism would take its place'.[1]

Mussolini had ambivalent feelings about the Nazi regime. He had
recently realized that he must take Hitler and the Nazis more seriously than he had done in the past, and now that they had come to
power he welcomed their suppression of the Communists and the
Socialists, and their repudiation of the principles of parliamentary
democracy and liberalism. But he had no sympathy with their anti-
Semitism, and feared their designs on Austria, for he was convinced
that a union between Germany and Austria would constitute a threat
to Italy.

Hitler's coming to power did not deflect Mussolini from his policy
of a Four Power Pact and a possible revision of treaties. At the

beginning of March 1933 he suggested to the French ambassador in Rome, Henry de Jouvenel, that German resentment about the 'Polish Corridor' which cut off East Prussia from the rest of Germany might be removed if the city of Danzig was ceded to Germany with a strip of land not more than ten or fifteen kilometres from the coast.[2] This idea did not appeal to either the French or the British governments.

On 24 March Graham discussed with Mussolini the events in Germany. Mussolini said that he deplored the Nazi violence, and the Italian ambassador in Berlin had made this clear to the German government on several occasions; but the Nazis had for so long been fed on anti-Jewish propaganda that now they had come to power there was no way of controlling them. He hoped that the situation in Germany would soon quieten down; but in any case Hitler would remain in power for some considerable time.[3]

In April Hermann Goering, who had played the leading part in suppressing the German Communists and in opening the concentration camps, came on a visit to Rome. Simon suggested to Grandi, who had been appointed Italian ambassador in London, that Mussolini might take the opportunity, while Goering was in Rome, to urge him to restrain the anti-Jewish campaign in Germany, as this would have a favourable effect on Anglo-Jewish opinion. 'Not only on Anglo-Jewish opinion,' said Grandi.[4]

Mussolini continued to adopt a dual policy towards Hitler and the Nazi regime. On the one hand he repeatedly told the British government how he disapproved of their anti-Semitic excesses and that he was trying to use his influence with Hitler to restrain the Nazis; but on the other he tried to dissuade Britain and France from taking any action against them. On 11 May 1933 Lord Hailsham, the Lord Chancellor, said in the House of Lords that even if Germany withdrew from the Disarmament Conference the Allies would be entitled to compel her to observe the clauses in the Treaty of Versailles which restricted German rearmament. Two days later, Mussolini and Graham attended the international football match between Italy and England in Rome, and during the match they had a private talk about the German problem. Mussolini said that he had tried hard to be friendly with Germany, but that the German attitude made this very difficult. He said he strongly approved of Hailsham's speech, for this was the only kind of language that could make the Germans see sense.[5]

But on 15 July he was discouraging the suggestion that Britain,

France and Italy should take any steps to deter German action against Austria. Graham reported that when he raised the matter, Mussolini was evasive; and Fulvio Suvich, who had replaced Grandi as Mussolini's Under-Secretary for Foreign Affairs, said that it would be inappropriate, on the eve of concluding a Four Power Pact, if three of the powers were to take precautionary measures against the fourth power.[6]

In October 1933 Hitler threatened to leave the Disarmament Conference. This caused alarm in diplomatic circles and in the international press. Mussolini again combined tough talking with opposition to tough action. On 10 October he told Graham that German policy was controlled by two men, Hitler and Goering; the one was a dreamer and the other a former inmate of a lunatic asylum. But Britain, France and Italy must be realistic. Did they really want to take effective action to stop Germany and send troops to invade the Rhineland? For the Germans had told him that they would resist and go down fighting, and 'the outcome could only be world chaos'. Would it not be better to make a few minor concessions to keep Germany in the Disarmament Conference?[7] Perhaps Germany could be allowed to have a few anti-aircraft guns.

On 14 October the German ambassador informed Mussolini that Germany would leave the Disarmament Conference. That evening Mussolini gave a farewell dinner party for Graham, who was being replaced as ambassador by Sir Eric Drummond. As they were sitting down to dinner, the news came that Germany had left not only the Disarmament Conference but also the League of Nations. Mussolini said that the Germans seemed to be burning down their house to cook an egg. But he thought it was essential to keep calm and avoid any violent comment.[8]

On 21 October Graham had his last talk with Mussolini. Graham had never seen him so angry and disgusted. Mussolini said that he had told Suvich to warn the German ambassador to keep out of his way, because if he met the ambassador he might be rude to him. Germany had wrecked the Disarmament Conference, the League of Nations and the negotiations for a Four Power Pact, and he would do nothing more about it.[9]

Mussolini had worked out his own way of checking Hitler's aims in Austria. The peace treaty had deprived Austria of 86 per cent of her pre-war territory and reduced her population from forty-seven million to six and a half million. Nearly two million lived in Vienna.

Like Paris in the nineteenth century, Vienna was a Red stronghold in a country of Catholic peasants who hated the Reds. The Socialists had 70 per cent of the votes in Vienna and 40 per cent in the whole of Austria. They had made Vienna a showpiece of Socialist planning, with the model workers' flats in the Karl Marx Hof, and the most modern health and social services. But they were just short of a majority in the national Parliament, and the government was a right-wing coalition led by the Christian Democrats.

Opinion in Austria was divided about union with Germany. On the one hand there was the feeling of German solidarity and the tie of language; but against this was the permanent antagonism between Germany and Austria. The Germans despised the Austrians for being lazy, happy-go-lucky and incompetent, and the Austrians resented German arrogance. There were also Austrians who favoured a union with Hungary under a restored Habsburg emperor. Neither France and the Little Entente, nor Mussolini, would agree to this.

Mussolini wanted to have an independent Austria that was anti-Socialist, anti-German, and which did not cause trouble about South Tyrol. The right-wing dictatorship in Hungary of Admiral Horthy and his Prime Minister, General Gömbös, agreed with him. It was the Hungarian government who first advised Mussolini to support the Austrian right-wing party, the Heimwehr, who were anti-Socialist and anti-German, and Mussolini gave them financial help after 1929.

In May 1932 the Christian Democrat politician, Engelbert Doll-fuss, succeeded in forming a government. He was aged forty, only four feet eleven inches in height, a shrewd and able politician who had practised as a lawyer and been a university lecturer in economics, a devout Catholic, and a strong opponent of socialism and of a union with Germany. His government obtained a vote of confidence in Parliament with a majority of one.

In May 1933 Dollfuss visited Mussolini in Rome. Mussolini advised him to suppress the Socialists and parliamentary democracy, and convert Austria into a Fascist state. Dollfuss said it was not easy to do this with a majority of only one. On 1 July Mussolini wrote to Dollfuss that he appreciated his difficulties, but that it was essential for him to suppress the Socialists and democracy as soon as possible, for otherwise those right-wing forces who wished to do this would join the Austrian Nazis and invite Hitler to come in and crush the Reds. Dollfuss visited Mussolini again in August 1933, and agreed to follow his advice if he could rely on Mussolini's moral support and his military support if Germany invaded Austria. Mussolini suggested to Dollfuss that it might be advisable to adopt 'a touch of anti-Semitism' which would be popular in Austria and would steal the thunder of the Austrian Nazis; but he later changed his mind about this and discouraged Dollfuss from pursuing an anti-Semitic policy.[10]

In September the Heimwehr held a party rally in the Hippodrome in Vienna at which they declared that their aim was to establish a German-Christian-Social state in Austria based on corporations and opposed to the Nazis and the Socialists. A few days later Dollfuss appointed Major E. Fey, the leader of the Heimwehr, to be his Vice-Chancellor. Dollfuss obtained a small majority in Parliament for a motion that sent Parliament into indefinite recess, and gave Dollfuss power to legislate by decree. The Socialists became alarmed. Their left-wing extremists and the Communists called for armed resistance to Dollfuss; but their leaders were reluctant to resort to violence and launch a civil war. In October the Socialists held a conference at which they decided to resort to armed resistance if the government suppressed parliamentary government, violated the constitution, or suppressed the Socialist Party. Dollfuss decided to follow Mussolini's advice and strike first.

In February 1934 Dollfuss issued a decree dissolving the Socialist city council in Vienna. The Socialists called for a general strike and their defence organization, the Red Guards, prepared to resist any attempt by the Heimwehr to enter the Karl Marx Hof or the workers' districts of Vienna. Fey called up the army artillery and shelled the workers' districts, doing substantial damage to the Karl Marx Hof and other blocks of workers' flats. After four days' street fighting the Socialists were crushed, and many of their defence fighters were shot. The Socialist Mayor of Vienna and several other Socialist leaders were arrested.

While the fighting was going on in Vienna, rumours circulated that Hitler might seize the opportunity to invade Austria. At Mussolini's suggestion, the British, French and Italian governments issued a declaration on 17 February guaranteeing the independence of Austria.[11] In April the Austrian Parliament met; the Socialist deputies were deprived of their seats. The deputies of Dollfuss's party moved a resolution abolishing Parliament and voting supreme powers to Dollfuss and his government. In the absence of the Socialist deputies the resolution was carried with only the Nazi deputies voting against.

Hitler was eager to meet Mussolini. In April 1933 the German

Vice-Chancellor, Franz von Papen, came to Rome and suggested that a Hitler–Mussolini meeting should take place. Mussolini did not respond beyond saying that he would think about it. But in March 1934 von Papen again came to Rome on what was officially called a private visit. On 29 March he met Mussolini at the opera. In the course of their conversation he told Mussolini how much Hitler wanted to meet him. This time Mussolini agreed, provided that their ministers could arrange a suitable agenda. After further Italo-German discussions, it was agreed that the meeting should take place in Venice on 14 and 15 June 1934, and that they should discuss disarmament, economic relations, the situation in central Europe, and Austria.[12]

The foreign journalists who went to Venice to report the meeting thought that Mussolini had deliberately tried to downstage and humiliate Hitler at the meeting; but this impression may have been partly due to the fact that they had already made up their minds that Mussolini was the dominant figure among the two dictators. Ever since Hitler had become prominent on the international scene, Mussolini's British and American admirers had been saying that 'Hitler is not a Mussolini'. When Mussolini arrived at Venice airport dressed in a well-fitting and bemedalled grey uniform of an Italian general, and Hitler emerged from the plane wearing civilian dress, a rather shabby belted raincoat and a crumpled hat, they thought that the costume of the two leaders reflected the picture of the powerful Mussolini and the insignificant Hitler. The caricatures in the foreign press showed a giant Mussolini towering over Hitler the pygmy. In fact, Mussolini and Hitler were both small in stature, about five feet five inches; but Hitler was marginally taller than Mussolini.

They went to the Villa Pisani at Stra between Venice and Padua for their first talk on the afternoon of 14 June. They were alone together and spoke without interpreters in German, the only language that Hitler could speak and one of the foreign languages that Mussolini spoke well. They discussed Austria, and reached a broad measure of agreement, because Hitler agreed to most of Mussolini's demands. Hitler said that he did not contemplate an Anschluss (union) between Germany and Austria in the foreseeable future. They agreed that they would both support Dollfuss and his government. New elections should be held in Austria as soon as possible. Dollfuss would invite a few Austrian Nazis to join his government. Hitler suggested to Mussolini that in view of their general agreement about

Austria, Italy should dissociate herself from the Franco-British guarantee to Austria; but Mussolini would not commit himself to this. They then discussed Italo-German trade relations, and agreed to do all in their power to increase economic co-operation between their two nations.

Next day they went to Venice, where they visited places of artistic and cultural interest, and then had a second discussion in a building on the Lido. This time their advisers were present, but their talks were less constructive than on the previous day. They discussed disarmament, the League of Nations, the relations between France and the Soviet Union, the internal situation in Germany, the Nazi doctrine, the Jews, and the relationship of their two governments with the Catholic Church. They agreed to disagree on most of these matters. Hitler said he would prefer to remain outside the League of Nations, and Mussolini said that he was not intending to put forward any new proposals about disarmament. Hitler showed no interest in Mussolini's suggestion that the Four Power Pact might be extended to include Poland, and perhaps the United States and Japan.[13]

Hitler was delighted with his visit to Venice. He told his entourage how greatly he had been impressed by Mussolini, and the pleasure the meeting had given him. Mussolini was much less enthusiastic about Hitler. He thought that Hitler talked too much, and was too doctrinaire; instead of getting down to discussing how to solve concrete problems, he had quoted long extracts from his book *Mein Kampf*.[14]

After Hitler had left Venice, Mussolini addressed a Fascist rally in the Piazza San Marco. He said very little about his meeting with Hitler. Most of his speech was devoted to reminding his audience that he had last visited Venice in 1923, and in pointing out how greatly the prosperity of the city had increased during the intervening eleven years of Fascist rule. It was only towards the end of his speech that he dealt with the question of the day. 'I wish to tell you Italians and all those beyond the frontier that Hitler and I are determined not to alter the political map of Europe or of the world, or to add to the anxieties which are already disturbing all countries from the Far East to the Far West.'[15]

A fortnight after Hitler returned home, he had Roehm and a substantial number of his SA supporters shot on the 'night of the long knives' on 30 June. Mussolini was shocked; this was not the way he treated his Fascist extremists. In July, Dollfuss's wife and children

came to Riccione near Rimini for a holiday. It was not far from the
Rocca delle Caminate, where Mussolini and his family were staying.
Dollfuss's little daughter fell ill, and when Dollfuss heard this, he
telegraphed Frau Dollfuss that he would come to Riccione to see
them, which would give him the opportunity to talk to Mussolini.
But next day some Austrian Nazis broke into the Chancellery in
Vienna and shot Dollfuss. As he lay bleeding to death on the floor
of his office, the killers refused to allow a doctor to come to him,
and they refused his request to send for a priest who could give him
the last rites before he died.

The news was telegraphed to Mussolini at Rocca delle Caminate.
He asked Rachele to come with him to Riccione to break the news
to Frau Dollfuss. They drove there through a thunderstorm, and told
her that her husband had been assassinated. Mussolini provided her
with a private plane to fly her back to Vienna and a detective to
accompany her.[16] Was the assassination the prelude to a Nazi coup
in Austria, and would Hitler send in the German Army and unite
Austria to the German Reich? Mussolini ordered four army divisions
to go into the Alto Adige and take up positions near the Austrian
frontier on the Brenner. If Hitler sent German troops into Austria,
Mussolini would send in the Italian troops to drive the Germans out.

But as soon as Dollfuss was assassinated, Major Fey sent men of
the Heimwehr to surround the Chancellery and the Austrian Nazis
who occupied it after killing Dollfuss. The Nazis surrendered after
Fey had promised them that if they did, their lives would be spared;
but he immediately ordered them all to be executed without trial by
a firing squad. Hitler disowned them. He told Mussolini that they
had acted without his knowledge, and perhaps on orders that Roehm
had given them a month earlier, just before Hitler had shot Roehm.
Hitler was probably speaking the truth when he said that they had
murdered Dollfuss and planned a coup without his knowledge; but
Mussolini was not sure of this.

Dollfuss was succeeded as Chancellor not by Fey or the Foreign
Minister, Prince Ernst Rüdiger von Starhemberg, but by a less high-
profile minister, Kurt von Schuschnigg, who promptly came to Florence to discuss the situation with Mussolini. The British government,
who wished to preserve the independence of Austria from Germany,
suggested to Mussolini that he should advise Schuschnigg to form a
united anti-Nazi front in Austria by making concessions to the Socialists. Simon did not suggest that Schuschnigg should invite the Social-

ists to join his government, but that he should ease the repression that had been directed against them since February. Mussolini replied that he was sure that Schuschnigg wished to unite all the people of Austria, but that if he followed Simon's suggestion and advised Schuschnigg to relax his suppression of the Socialists, he would be accused of interfering in the internal affairs of Austria; and if people thought that Schuschnigg was abandoning his firm anti-Socialist policy, many Heimwehr supporters, who hated the Socialists, would join the Nazis, and would invite Hitler to come in and suppress them.[17]

On 9 October 1934 King Alexander of Yugoslavia arrived at Marseilles on a state visit to France which was intended to strengthen the ties between France and the countries of the Little Entente. As he was driven through the streets of Marseilles at the side of the French Foreign Minister, Louis Barthou, a man broke through the police cordon and fired a number of shots which killed both the King and Barthou. The assassin was a Croatian nationalist, a member of the Ustaše party which resented the domination of Croatia by the Serbs under King Alexander's dictatorship. He was one of many Croatian Ustaše who had taken refuge in Hungary, though the leader of the party, Ante Pavelić, had moved from Hungary to Italy some years before. The Yugoslav government had sent a protest to Hungary six months earlier, complaining that Hungary was granting asylum to terrorists and that Hungarian officials were helping to arm the terrorists and were giving them facilities to commit terrorist acts against Yugoslavia.

The Yugoslav government and press accused Hungary of responsibility for King Alexander's murder, and they were strongly supported by Czechoslovakia and Romania, their allies in the Little Entente. France backed them, but Italy supported Hungary. The inquiries conducted by the police in France seemed to implicate Pavelić, and the French authorities began extradition proceedings against him in Turin. Mussolini intervened, and refused to extradite Pavelić. Yugoslavia, Czechoslovakia and Romania raised the matter before the Council of the League of Nations, demanding that the League take action against Hungary; but on 19 November Grandi informed Simon that if Hungary were attacked by Yugoslavia and the Little Entente, Italy would go to her defence.[18]

As the world waited for a bitter argument at the Council of the League on 7 December 1934, there were widespread fears that a new European war was about to break out. The First World War had been caused by the assassination of an Austrian prince at Sarajevo in the Balkans; would the assassination of a Balkan king at Marseilles start the Second World War? Tension increased when the Yugoslav government expelled the Hungarian population from the Vojvodina district of Yugoslavia.

But as Beneš told the British minister in Prague, 'wars on a large scale are not started by the small powers, but by the interference of great powers'.[19] Italy and France did not wish to go to war with each other; so the threatening language of the Yugoslav Foreign Minister and Beneš in Geneva counted for nothing. Eden was appointed as mediator, and used his influence to take the heat out of the situation. The Little Entente denounced Hungary, but used much milder language about Italy; Yugoslavia stopped the expulsions of the Hungarian minority; the Hungarian government admitted that some of their subordinate officials had been negligent in allowing the Croatian Ustasě to operate on their territory and promised to censure them; and by Christmas the crisis had passed.

Mussolini had never been alarmed about the situation. He had confidently told his ministers and generals that there was no danger of war breaking out between Hungary and Yugoslavia. He had decided to begin a war in a different continent. On 5 December 1934 Ethiopian troops attacked and killed some Italian soldiers at Walwal on the frontier between Ethiopia and Italian Somaliland. This was what Mussolini had been waiting for.

# CHAPTER 27

◆

# Ethiopia

O N 1 February 1934 Mussolini told General De Bono that he intended to conquer Ethiopia,[1] which in Britain, and sometimes in Italy, was still called by her old name of Abyssinia. It was the only country in Africa, apart from the republic of Liberia, which was not a colony or protectorate of a European power. It was backward, with slavery still in force in many parts of the country; and it was ripe for economic development by a European nation. The Italians had had their eye on Abyssinia since the 1880s, but their tentative attempts to seize it had been defeated by the Emperor Menelek's forces at Adowa in 1896.

Mussolini could have developed Ethiopia economically, to Italian advantage, without conquering it. He had established friendly relations with the Negus (Emperor) of Ethiopia, Haile Selassie, when Haile Selassie stayed with him at the Villa Torlonia in 1924, and the Negus would have welcomed Italian help in Ethiopia's economic development. In the nineteenth century the Italians had been afraid that if they did not conquer Abyssinia, Britain or France would conquer it first and exclude Italian economic penetration; but Mussolini knew very well that there was no likelihood of Britain, France or any other European power annexing Ethiopia in 1934.

Mussolini intended to conquer Ethiopia because he wanted Italy to have an empire. He had reminded the Italians of the glories of imperial Rome in ancient times. He had written in the *Enciclopedia Italiana* that 'the Fascist State is a wish for power and domination. In Fascist doctrine, Empire is not only a territorial, military or commercial expression, but also a spiritual and moral one.'[2] He saw imperialism as the logical sequel to nationalism. He had rejected Socialist internationalism in 1914 because he realized that the masses would be inspired by the call of national superiority, not of international solidarity. He knew that the Italian people would respond if he told them that he would make *them*, the white Italian race, the masters ruling over an inferior black race of Ethiopians, just as the people of Britain and France had responded in the nineteenth century during the Boer War and the French conquest of Algeria.

In the spring of 1934 the Italians were reading a novel, *Amore nero* (Black Love), about a young Italian's love affair with a black girl. Mussolini banned the novel, which was withdrawn from circulation. He told Baron Pompeo Aloisi, the Chief of his Cabinet, whom he had recently appointed as the Italian delegate to the League of Nations, that he had banned the book because the theme of sexual relations between an Italian and a negress was 'inadmissible in a nation which wishes to create an empire in Africa'.[3]

He did not have to wait long to find an excuse to attack Ethiopia. By the Italo-Ethiopian treaty of 1928, the precise frontier line between Ethiopia, Italian Somaliland and British Somaliland was to be settled by representatives of the three nations on the ground. In November 1934 British and Ethiopian officers were examining the frontier at Walwal when the Italians arrived in strength and adopted a threatening attitude, with their aircraft flying overhead. The British officer decided it would be wiser to withdraw to avoid the risk of incidents; the Ethiopians stayed, and, according to the Italians, attacked and killed some Italian soldiers. The Italians then counter-attacked in some strength, using aircraft, and drove back the Ethiopians, killing more than a hundred of them.[4]

Mussolini demanded an apology and compensation from Ethiopia, and the punishment of the Ethiopian officers responsible for the incident. He rejected all suggestions that the dispute should be referred to arbitration, still less to the League of Nations. From the beginning he adopted the attitude that Ethiopia was a barbaric, uncivilized country where slavery existed, and should not be treated as an equal of a great civilizing power like Italy; and he instructed the Italian representatives in Somaliland and Geneva to refuse to negotiate with the Ethiopians, and to walk out whenever they were admitted to a meeting.

Would Britain and France take action to prevent the Italian conquest of Ethiopia? Mussolini did not think so. Britain had no economic interests in Ethiopia. France had invested in the railway from Addis Ababa, the capital, to the port of Djibouti in French territory; but he was sure that he could persuade the French that if Italy conquered Ethiopia she would not interfere with French interests in the railway. As public opinion in Britain was so strongly pacifist, the British government would not go to war to stop Italy from conquering Ethiopia; and nor would the French government, because they wanted to have Italy as an ally against Germany. Mussolini had only one anxiety: would Hitler take advantage of the situation and invade Austria while the Italian army was away fighting in Ethiopia? But here again, Mussolini thought not. Britain and France, as well as Italy, would oppose a German invasion of Austria, and Hitler was not yet ready to take a step that might involve him in a conflict with Britain and France.

But Mussolini had first to make sure of the French position. On 5 January 1935 the French Foreign Minister, Pierre Laval, came to Rome. Laval, a brilliant lawyer who came from a peasant family in the Auvergne, was aged fifty-one. Like Mussolini, he had begun his political life on the extreme Left and had moved almost to the extreme Right. He had been Prime Minister for a year in 1931 and had handled the situation competently and pursued a friendly policy towards Italy. He was famous for his skill in fixing things, his sly look, his cynical humour, the crumpled white tie he always wore, and the hundred Gauloise cigarettes he smoked every day. He became Foreign Minister in November 1934 in Pierre Etienne Flandin's moderate Conservative government.

Laval had come to Rome in the hope of ending the strains in Franco-Italian relations that had followed the assassination of King Alexander of Yugoslavia, and he and Mussolini succeeded in doing this in their three days of talks. Mussolini agreed to abandon any claims that Italy might have put forward to any rights in French Tunisia. Laval told him about the negotiations that were proceeding between him and the Soviet Foreign Minister, Maxim Maximovich Litvinov, for a pact between France and the Soviet Union which would obviously be a defensive military alliance against Germany. Mussolini, who had signed a treaty of friendship with the Soviet Union in September 1933 and had met Litvinov in Rome two months later, had no objections at all to the proposed Franco-Soviet Pact. Mussolini and Laval agreed not to allow Italian support of Hungary and French support of Yugoslavia to lead to a European war or to friction between Italy and France.

On the question of Germany, Mussolini said that there were three ways of dealing with Germany: to make war against her, to do nothing, or to negotiate a settlement acceptable to her. Laval said that he preferred this last choice, and Mussolini agreed.[5]

On the first evening, Mussolini gave a dinner for Laval, who proposed a toast to Mussolini. 'You have written the finest page in the history of modern Italy,' said Laval. The dinner was followed by a reception for the press, including the French journalists who had come to report the Laval–Mussolini meeting. Among them was Madame Geneviève Tabouis, the diplomatic editor of *L'Oeuvre*, and one of the most famous and well-informed journalists. People said that whenever there was an important diplomatic conference, Madame Tabouis was always hiding under the table. She was one of the most outspoken critics of Mussolini, and had already accused him in *L'Oeuvre* of planning a war in Ethiopia. At the reception, Mussolini spoke briefly to all the journalists who were lined up to meet him. He said to Madame Tabouis: 'That's a nice dress you're wearing; your name is Geneviève; but your articles on Italy are unfair.'

On the following evening there was another brilliant reception at the French embassy, and on 7 January the treaty of friendship was signed by Mussolini and Laval at a splendid ceremony in the Palazzo Venezia. In the evening there was a gala performance at the opera of Ambroise Thomas's *Mignon*. The whole house rose to their feet when the *Marseillaise* was played, and as the last strains ended, Mussolini came into Laval's box and warmly shook his hand amid loud applause. The government organized a great display of pro-French feeling, with penny whistles and concertinas playing the *Marseillaise* and *La Madelon* under the windows of the houses where the French delegates and journalists were staying.[6]

Mussolini and Laval signed a secret agreement about Ethiopia, and Mussolini wrote a secret letter to Laval on the subject. The wording of both the treaty and the letter was deliberately ambiguous. The French government recognized that, subject to any British interests secured by treaties, 'Italy has preponderant interests on all the territory of Ethiopia' except for French interests in the Addis Ababa – Djibouti railway. The French government agreed that 'even if there should be modifications of the *status quo* in the region', France would seek no further interests there; and the Italian government agreed to protect in all possible circumstances French interests in the Addis Ababa–Djibouti railway. In Mussolini's secret letter to Laval, he alleged that Laval had written to him that France would not seek to further any interests 'in Central Africa and especially in Ethiopia and Somaliland' except for her interests in the railway as granted by the treaty of 1906.[7]

Laval was afterwards accused of having agreed in Rome in January 1935 to allow Mussolini a free hand to invade Ethiopia. He always denied this, and said that he had acknowledged only Italy's economic interests in Ethiopia and not her right to invade and annex the country. Strictly speaking, this is no doubt true; but Laval had convinced Mussolini that he would do nothing to stop him from going to war with Ethiopia.

While the Council of the League of Nations considered the Ethiopian complaint at their leisure, they placed an embargo on the export of arms to both Italy and Ethiopia. This did not harm the Italians, who were already well armed and could manufacture more arms, but seriously impeded the attempts by the Ethiopians, with their primitive weapons, to modernize their armaments and build up their defences. They were obliged to try to obtain arms from Germany and the United States, who were not members of the League; but the British and French embargo prevented the arms from being sent legally to Ethiopia through British or French Somaliland.

Meanwhile Mussolini proceeded with his preparations for war. On 23 February 1935 the first Italian troops sailed for Africa; but Hitler then upset Mussolini's calculations. On 16 March he announced that Germany would introduce compulsory military service. This was a breach of the Treaty of Versailles – the first time that Germany had ventured on such a step. What would the Allies do? The British government sent a protest to Germany, but at the same time announced that the Foreign Secretary (Sir John Simon) and Eden would visit Hitler in Berlin. The French and Italian governments had not previously heard of this intended visit, and it produced a very bad effect in France and Italy. The Italian Under-Secretary for Foreign Affairs, Suvich, told the British ambassador, Sir Eric Drummond, that he thought that the visit would be viewed as a breach of the united front of France, Italy and Britain; but Mussolini immediately proposed that the Foreign Ministers of the three powers should meet at Stresa on Lake Maggiore in Italy to restore their unity and take concerted action against Germany.

Meanwhile the negotiations for a Franco-Soviet pact were nearing completion. The British government strongly opposed the pact, and criticized France for making an alliance with the Soviet Union. This was another point dividing the anti-German alliance. In all the discussions between Britain, France and Italy as to how to react to Hitler's breach of the Treaty of Versailles, Simon was the most pro-German and Mussolini the most anti-German. From Mussolini's point of view there were two reasons why it was essential to restore unity between the three powers. It would deter Hitler from invading Austria while Mussolini was invading Ethiopia; and it would make Britain and France eager to gain Italian goodwill in order to preserve the alliance, and therefore willing to acquiesce in the Italian conquests in Africa.

MacDonald announced that he would lead the British delegation to Stresa, so it became a conference of Prime Ministers, not merely of Foreign Ministers. Britain was represented by MacDonald and Simon, with Sir Robert Vansittart, the chief permanent official at the Foreign Office. Flandin and Laval represented France, and Mussolini headed the Italian delegation. The conference opened in the Palazzo Borromeo on the Isola Bella at Stresa on 11 April 1935, and lasted four days. At the end they issued a communiqué which did not say very much, but did at least present a façade of unity. When they discussed the possibility of imposing economic sanctions against Germany, Mussolini said that economic sanctions looked simple, but were often double-edged, doing more harm to those countries who imposed them than to the country against whom they were directed.[8]

Mussolini's chief concern was what MacDonald and Simon, and Flandin and Laval, would say about his plans in Ethiopia. He thought it better not to raise the subject himself, but to wait and see what they would say when they raised it, as they were sure to do. To his great surprise, none of the British or French delegation referred to Ethiopia, though Vansittart thought that this was a mistake.

On the fourth and last day of the conference, they discussed their final communiqué. The proposed draft stated that the three powers 'find themselves in complete agreement in opposing . . . any unilateral repudiation of treaties which may endanger peace'. Mussolini proposed that 'endanger peace' should be changed to 'endanger the peace of Europe'. Vansittart at once saw the point; but MacDonald and Simon looked at each other, and said nothing. After a few moments of silence, Mussolini's amendment was accepted. He was now certain that Britain and France would not stop him in Ethiopia.[9]

On 14 May he spoke in the Senate and publicly committed himself to taking action in Ethiopia. He said that if Italy were to play her part in keeping the peace in Europe, she would have to safeguard her back in Africa – in Eritrea and Somaliland, four thousand kilometres from Rome.[10]

On 2 May 1935 France and the Soviet Union signed their treaty of alliance. The British government was displeased. In June, without consulting France or Italy, Simon signed a naval treaty with Hitler. It was agreed that Germany could build a navy up to 35 per cent of the strength of the British Navy. The British argued that they had made a good bargain by limiting the size of the German Navy by a treaty that Hitler did in fact observe up to the outbreak of war in 1939; but the French saw it as a betrayal of Allied anti-German solidarity, and were all the more determined to remain on good terms with Italy.

In June MacDonald resigned as Prime Minister, and the government was reconstituted with Baldwin as Prime Minister and Sir Samuel Hoare as Foreign Secretary. MacDonald remained in the government, and a new office of Minister for League of Nations' Affairs was created for Eden. The situation was complicated for Baldwin by the fact that he would have to go to the country in a general election within sixteen months, and that the British people had developed an enthusiasm for the League of Nations and the principle of collective security. This was chiefly due to the propaganda of the League of Nations Union and its President, Viscount Cecil of Chelwood, who as Lord Robert Cecil had opposed Mussolini at the time of the Corfu incident in 1923. Their Peace Ballot asked the British public if they would support economic sanctions, and if necessary the use of military force, against the aggressor. The replies to the questions by more than ten million people were announced in June 1935. Ninety-four per cent supported economic sanctions; a smaller majority, but more than 74 per cent, supported the use of military force.[11]

The British government wished to support the League of Nations and collective security, and hoped to win the general election by doing so; but they did not wish to antagonize Italy. This was particularly true of the anti-German section in the government and the Foreign Office. There was a deep disagreement among the Establishment about the policy to be pursued towards Germany. Some, like Lord Rothermere, thought that Hitler's splendid young storm-troopers were defending Europe against communism; others, like Baldwin, hoped that Nazi Germany and Communist Russia would go to war with each other. But others believed that Germany was the greatest threat to peace, and that the traditional British policy of preserving the balance of power in Europe made it necessary to oppose Germany, if necessary by going to war against her, in alliance with any useful ally, including both Italy and the Soviet Union.

The chief exponents of this line were Churchill, now out of office but an influential backbench Conservative MP, and Sir Robert Vansittart in the Foreign Office. Churchill and Vansittart, though determined to stop any aggression by Hitler, were prepared to allow Mussolini to commit aggression in Africa, though they hoped that he would do this in a way that would save the reputation of the League of Nations and the Conservatives in the general election.

But Mussolini, realizing that this was their policy, did not wish to save the reputation of the League of Nations nor of the British government; he preferred to conquer Ethiopia in the face of opposition from the League and Britain, and to win a victory over them all. When Drummond spoke to Mussolini on 21 May, there was blunt speaking, and also bluff, on both sides. Drummond said that in the last resort, Britain might have to sacrifice her traditional friendship with Italy in order to preserve the League of Nations. Mussolini replied that he had not spent so much money and sent so many troops to Africa merely in order to settle the dispute that had arisen about the frontier clash at Walwal; he must obtain security against Ethiopia, and if he could obtain this only by going to war, he would do so.[12] The Italian delegate to the League of Nations, Aloisi, put it even more forcibly at a private dinner with Eden in Geneva. He said that a man like Mussolini would not spend six hundred million lire in order to change his mind at the request of the League of Nations. In this situation, Simon could only tell the British Cabinet that while he expected Italy to go to war with Ethiopia in September, the matter must be handled in a way that would not adversely affect Anglo-Italian relations.[13]

The British government thought of a compromise solution at their own expense. Ethiopia would cede a substantial part of her territory to Italy, and Britain would compensate her by granting Ethiopia a strip of territory at Zeila in British Somaliland which would give Ethiopia an outlet to the sea; and British capital would be provided to build a new port for Ethiopia in the ceded territory. On 25 June 1935 Eden went to Rome to put the proposal to Mussolini. Almost as soon as he arrived, a story was circulating in Rome which has now become an accepted legend. When Eden was ushered into the large Hall of the Mappamondi, Mussolini continued working at his desk without taking any notice of Eden while Eden walked all the way across the room to Mussolini. Eden deeply resented this, and also other examples of Mussolini's rudeness; and all the anti-Italian actions of successive British governments during the next ten years until May 1945 were due to Eden, although other members of the governments, including Churchill during the Second World War, wished to pursue policies that were more friendly to Italy.

But many years later Eden told Lord and Lady Gladwyn that there was no truth in this story. When he entered the Hall of the Mappamondi, Mussolini rose and walked halfway across the room to greet him, and treated Eden with perfect courtesy throughout his visit to Rome.[14] It is true that at the time, Eden advocated a more anti-Italian policy than his Prime Minister and Foreign Secretary, Baldwin and Samuel Hoare, and that during the next three years he opposed the policy of appeasing Italy pursued by Baldwin's successor, Neville Chamberlain; but this was not because Mussolini had been rude to him in Rome in June 1935. By the time of the Second World War there was no difference of opinion between Eden and Churchill about the policy to be adopted towards Italy.

Although Eden found Mussolini courteous and charming when they were alone together, he noticed a change in his manner when they attended public functions. As soon as there were two or three other persons present, Mussolini abandoned his quiet, relaxed manner; he thrust out his jaw and adopted his hard, dominating pose. Eden afterwards wrote, in his memoirs, that they attended a lunch at which there were many guests, including ladies. 'When luncheon was announced, Mussolini made an imperious gesture towards me and marched on. I hung back, English fashion, waiting for the ladies, and the Duce strode in alone.'[15]

Eden presented the British government's plan as a disinterested British sacrifice to preserve peace, emphasizing that while Italy would gain territory at Ethiopia's expense, and Ethiopia would be compensated at Britain's expense, Britain asked for no compensation from anyone for her loss of territory. But Mussolini rejected the proposal. He said that from Italy's point of view it had two grave drawbacks. It would strengthen Ethiopia economically, and therefore politically, by giving her a port; and the corridor to be granted across British territory would enable Ethiopia to import arms more easily.[16] He did not tell Eden his real objection: Italy would have acquired territory on condition that she did not go to war. Mussolini did not want a piece of territory that was not very valuable. He wanted to conquer all Ethiopia; he wanted an empire; he wanted a war.

◆

# CHAPTER 28

# Defying the World

E DEN left Rome convinced that there was no point in trying to appease Mussolini; and Mussolini sensed correctly that Eden would oppose his aims in Ethiopia. 'We felt we were enemies,' he told Rachele. 'I temporarily, but he is a sworn enemy of Italy.'[1]

In July the Council of the League of Nations again discussed the Ethiopian crisis, and asked Britain, France and Italy to hold talks to try to reach a settlement. The exclusion of Ethiopia from the talks perturbed the Labour opposition in Britain and the supporters of the doctrine of collective security. Eden, Aloisi and Laval, who had become Prime Minister as well as Foreign Minister, met in Paris for a few days during a very hot August, when most Parisians were on holiday in the country. Laval and Eden offered Mussolini a larger slice of Ethiopia than Eden had offered him in June, with a mandate and exclusive economic rights over the rest of Ethiopia; but Mussolini turned down the offer.

Stalin had at last realized that Hitler was a greater threat than the Social Democrats to the Soviet Union. In September 1934 the Soviet Union joined the League of Nations, which Lenin had denounced as an imperialists 'thieves kitchen'. The military alliance with France followed, and Stalin's friendly talk with Eden in Moscow. In France, the Communists and the Socialists formed the People's Front to resist the threat of a coup by the French Fascists.

The policy of supporting a People's Front with the Socialists against Fascism was confirmed at the Seventh Congress of the Communist International in Moscow in August 1935. When the Communists denounced Fascism they used the word to include all right-wing dictatorships, but they had Nazi Germany particularly in mind. Mussolini wrote in *Il Popolo d'Italia* that the Communists had abandoned all their other doctrines and now concentrated only an anti-Fascism. He declared that he was proud that they should consider the Fascists to be their chief enemy.[2]

The People's Front in France under the Socialist leader Léon Blum – the German Nazis and the French Fascists always pointed out that he was a Jew – grew in strength throughout 1935. They became the main opposition to Laval's government. They hated Mussolini, who was still for them the murderer of Matteotti, and demanded stiff sanctions to prevent his aggression in Abyssinia.

In Britain the Labour opposition led the campaign in favour of sanctions against Italy, and were supported by the Liberal Party and Lord Cecil's League of Nations Union; but the pacifist tradition in the Labour Party was strong enough for them to combine their vociferous demand for sanctions, and their criticisms of the government's hesitation, with opposition to rearmament – even to the inadequate amount of rearmament that Baldwin had undertaken.

The supporters of sanctions realized that there was one step above all which should be taken to stop Mussolini. The Suez Canal was owned by a consortium in which the British government held the majority of the shares, and continual dredging operations were necessary to keep the canal navigable for shipping; it would be perfectly possible for the British government to close the Suez Canal, which would prevent Mussolini's troop-ships from sailing through on their way to Eritrea and Italian Somaliland. But when Drummond said to Mussolini on 17 August that there was pressure in Britain to close the Suez Canal, Mussolini replied that if they closed the canal he would order the Italian Navy to reopen it. The British government took no steps to close the canal, for they were sure that this would mean war.

On 22 August the British Cabinet discussed the situation for five hours. They were agreed that British public opinion would not allow them to give in to Mussolini and abandon the League of Nations; but if the Council of the League imposed sanctions against Italy, would the other nations enforce them, or would they leave it to Britain to take action alone? What would be the position if sanctions led to war with Italy? How strong was the British Navy compared with the Italian Navy and Air Force? They consulted the Admiralty, who advised that if there was a naval war against Italy in the Mediterranean, Britain would ultimately win, but not before they had lost four capital ships. The service chiefs, who were more worried about the threat to British interests in the Far East from Japan than about Italy's plans in Abyssinia, were strongly against taking any action that might lead to war with Italy. Admiral Hughes-Hallett believed that their opinion was influenced by the admiration that many senior naval officers felt for Mussolini.[3]

The Cabinet therefore decided to drift, to do nothing for the moment, but to wait and see what happened when the Council of the League met in a fortnight's time. MacDonald thought that they were facing the most dangerous situation since 1914, and Baldwin gave instructions to Hoare: 'Keep us out of war, we are not ready for it.'[4] Hoare complained to the Chancellor of the Exchequer, Neville Chamberlain, about Baldwin. 'Stanley would think about nothing but his holiday and the necessity of keeping out of the whole business at almost any cost.' He deplored 'Stanley's attitude of indifference' and 'Ramsay's alarmist and pusillanimous surrender to the Italians'.[5]

While Ethiopia was still denied the right to buy arms, and the British and French governments took no steps against Mussolini, the British banks, for their own business reasons, suspended the granting of credit facilities to Italy. This caused Mussolini some inconvenience and anxiety, and on 13 August he complained about it to the French ambassador, and warned him that if Britain and France took any step that seriously threatened Italy, he would not hesitate, in desperation, to declare war on Britain and France.

Throughout August, Italian troop-ships continued to sail through the Suez Canal as the army build-up continued. De Bono, in command in Eritrea, and General Rodolfo Graziani in Italian Somaliland in the south-east, now had 150,000 men under their command. On 24 August Vittorio and Bruno Mussolini left for East Africa. Vittorio was aged eighteen and had joined the air force. Eighteen was the minimum age for the air force, so Bruno, who was only sixteen, was ineligible; but Mussolini granted his entreaties to be allowed to join, and pulled the necessary strings to obtain a commission for him.[6] He was by no means the only young Fascist Avanguardista who succeeded in enlisting when under age. Galeazzo Ciano, who had returned with Edda and their family from Shanghai and had taken a post in the Foreign Office in Rome, also volunteered for the air force and left for East Africa.

On 28 August Mussolini presided over a Cabinet meeting. After the meeting a press statement was issued which explained the government's position. Ethiopia was a barbaric state which did not deserve to be treated as a civilized nation or granted any consideration in international affairs. Italy's aims in Ethiopia did not threaten British interests in any way, and there was no justification for Britain inciting the League of Nations against Italy. Nothing would be allowed to prevent Italy's civilizing mission in Ethiopia.[7]

Early in September the Council of the League of Nations met in Geneva, and heard the arguments of the Italian and Ethiopian representatives. Ethiopia was represented by a rather pompous French lawyer; as soon as he began to speak, Aloisi walked out on Mussolini's instructions. The Council of the League referred the dispute to a Committee of Five – Britain, France, Poland, Turkey and Spain. The Committee of Five offered Italy even more concessions in Ethiopia; but Mussolini again turned down the offer.

In the British Cabinet Eden and Neville Chamberlain were in favour of strong action against Italy; but Baldwin, Hoare, MacDonald and Simon wished to make concessions to Mussolini; and Laval was even more strongly in favour of concessions. He might have been more ready to offend Mussolini if he had believed that Britain could be trusted to support France against any German aggression; but Simon's visit to Hitler, the British opposition to the Franco-Soviet Pact, and the British naval treaty with Germany had shaken French trust in the British alliance and persuaded them of the importance of an alliance with Italy.

In Britain the Labour Party, the Liberals and the League of Nations Union were becoming more and more contemptuous and suspicious of the sincerity of the British government when they declared that they would uphold the League of Nations and stop Mussolini. The brilliant satirical poet Sagittarius, writing in the left-wing London journal, the *New Statesman*, was at her best in her analysis of the League's attitude in the Abyssinian crisis:

> While Laval looked to Hoare and Hoare looked to Laval
> To sanction joint Sanctions or shut the Canal,
> While the Five with acute international tact
> Offer protacol, treaty, agreement or pact,
> And ministers ended preambles sublime
> With 'Let us do nothing while yet there is time!'[8]

On 11 September Hoare addressed the General Assembly of the League of Nations in Geneva. He made a surprisingly strong speech in support of the League, and promised that Britain would join in enforcing any sanctions that were imposed against Italy. The Belgian delegate, Paul Hymans, after hearing Hoare's speech, commented: 'The British have decided to stop Mussolini, even if that means using force.'[9] Next day Laval caused even greater surprise by speaking almost as strongly as Hoare in support of sanctions. Were the League and Britain and France at last about to take effective steps to stop Mussolini's aggression against Ethiopia?

But the day before Hoare addressed the General Assembly he had two private talks with Laval in their hotels. They agreed that they must try to keep Italy on the side of the Allies and to preserve the Stresa front and that they would under no circumstances go to war with Italy. Hoare said that all that the British government had in mind was to ban the importation of certain Italian exports, and no one could consider that this was an act of war. Laval passed this encouraging news on to Aloisi. He told him that neither he nor the British government had ever considered the possibility of closing the Suez Canal; and he did not think that Mussolini could seriously object if the English decided that they did not wish to buy gorgonzola or chianti.[10]

The Italian press had begun a violent campaign against Britain. They wrote that the whole trouble with Ethiopia and the League was stirred up by Britain for her own ends. They wrote about the thirty thousand Boer women and children who died in British concentration camps in South Africa during the Boer War, and the massacre of Amritsar in India in 1919. But the British Foreign Office used their influence with the British press – not always successfully – to prevent any denunciation of Italy or Mussolini. Whenever the *Giornale d'Italia* accused Britain of planning to make war against Italy, the British government hastily assured them that they had no such intention.[11]

But Baldwin allowed himself to be persuaded, chiefly by Eden and Vansittart, to reinforce the fleet in the Mediterranean. Two additional battle-cruisers, with three other cruisers and some smaller craft, were sent to Gibraltar, Malta and Alexandria to join the four battleships, two aircraft carriers, forty destroyers and eleven submarines in the Mediterranean. The Italian press angrily denounced the British, and in Rome war was expected at any moment; but Mussolini kept his nerve. When Drummond informed him that the British ships had entered the Mediterranean, Mussolini said that it would be up to the Italians to decide whether they were allowed to leave the Mediterranean.[12]

Drummond was worried. On 17 September he wrote to Hoare that he was sure that once Mussolini had begun the war, he would be satisfied with nothing less than the conquest of all Ethiopia, or at least with the entry of the Italian Army into Addis Ababa, unless the Negus surrendered unconditionally. Drummond reported that Mussolini had the enthusiastic support of the great majority of the Italian people, especially the youth; both Mussolini and the Italian people, in their present mood, were capable of committing suicide rather than climb down. The Italian press were suggesting that Italy would declare war on Britain, and boasting of how easy it would be for the Italian Air Force to bomb Malta and destroy the British fleet. Baldwin decided that it would be safer to move the fleet to Alexandria. Mussolini replied by sending troops from Italy to Libya, where they would be ready to invade Egypt.[13]

Raffaele Guariglia had been recalled from his post as ambassador in Madrid to become the head of the Foreign Office in the Palazzo Chigi. He organized a highly efficient intelligence network in London, Paris and Geneva; on one occasion he succeeded in obtaining a copy of a very secret report from the British representative at the League of Nations to the Foreign Office in London. He informed Mussolini that if Italy invaded Ethiopia, the British would press for economic sanctions to be imposed by the League against Italy; that France would reluctantly agree, but would do all in her power to postpone the application of sanctions and weaken their effect; and that neither Britain nor France would go to war with Italy over Ethiopia or propose the closure of the Suez Canal.[14]

Mussolini asked the British government whether the movements of the fleet meant that Britain was intending to attack Italy or close the Suez Canal. On 23 September Hoare instructed Drummond to give Mussolini 'a personal message from myself, a Foreign Minister who is both a conservative and an old friend of Italy'. He was to tell Mussolini that it was untrue that the British government wished to destroy the Italian fleet; they wished 'to see Italy strong and prosperous and its government stable, as it now has been for years ... I have been most careful to avoid the word sanctions and there has been no discussion of closing the Suez Canal or military sanctions'; but if the League agreed on collective action, Britain would play her part as a faithful member of the League.[15] This was good enough for Mussolini. He would chance it.

On 29 September he sent this order to De Bono: 'No declaration of war. I order you to begin the advance in the early hours of 3 repeat 3 October.'[16] On the evening of 2 October he addressed the crowds from the balcony of the Palazzo Venezia. 'Blackshirts of the Revolution! . . . At this solemn moment in the history of our country twenty million men are occupying the piazzas all over Italy', to show the world the strength of Italy and Fascism in this year 1935, Year XIII of the Fascist era. 'Proletarian and Fascist Italy, Italy of Vittorio Veneto and the Revolution, arise! Let Heaven hear your shouts of encouragement to our soldiers who are waiting in Africa, so that they are heard by our friends and enemies in every part of the world, the cry for justice, the cry of victory!'[17]

That day he was visited by his old friend Giuseppe Prezzolini, whose writings he had so much admired when they were both Socialists before the First World War. Prezzolini knew that he could talk frankly to Mussolini; he asked him whether he knew what he was doing in risking war with England. The British fleet in the Mediterranean would be able to strike at all the vital centres of Italy, although Italy would not be able to strike at London or the vital centres of Britain. 'Yes,' said Mussolini, 'but England will not be willing to sacrifice the life of a single English soldier for Ethiopia.'[18]

# CHAPTER 29

———— ◆ ————

# Victory

I N June 1936, after the Italians had conquered Abyssinia, Churchill wrote an article in the *Evening Standard* in which he ruefully analysed British policy during the Abyssinian war.[1] British public opinion had demanded that Britain should uphold the authority of the League of Nations, prevent the Italians from conquering Abyssinia, and show the world that aggression does not pay; but they also demanded that the government should at all costs keep Britain out of war. The government knew that the only measures that would seriously impede Italian aggression were the closure of the Suez Canal and an embargo on the export of oil to Italy; but Mussolini had announced that if either of these two steps were taken, he would go to war with the League of Nations and Britain. So the League and the British government imposed only those other economic sanctions which did not seriously inconvenience Italian aggression, with the result that Italy conquered Abyssinia and humiliated the League and Britain.

It was a correct and brilliant analysis of what had occurred; but while the Abyssinian war was in progress, Churchill himself had not been able to suggest any alternative policy. He believed that Germany, not Italy, was the threat to world peace and British interests, and he hoped that Mussolini, whom he still admired, would be a useful ally of Britain against Hitler; but, quite apart from British public opinion, he thought it necessary to uphold the prestige of the League of Nations because of the role that the League could play in preserving peace; and a defeat for the League would be an encouragement to that other and far more dangerous aggressor, Hitler. Churchill was also very concerned about the deficiencies in British military strength, and thought that very little could be done to deter an aggressor until the country had rearmed. 'Be on your guard', he wrote to Hoare, 'against the capital fault of letting diplomacy get ahead of naval preparedness ... Where are the fleets? Are they in good order? Are they adequate?'[2]

At 5 a.m. on 3 October 1935 the Italians, without declaring war, began military operations against Ethiopia by bombing Adowa from the air and moving forward with their ground troops. The air raid inflicted heavy casualties on the civilian population. The British minister in Addis Ababa reported that the first bomb fell on a building that was being used as a store for hospital equipment and was marked with a red cross.[3] The Italians captured Adowa, avenging the defeat they had suffered there in 1896.

The war aroused great enthusiasm in Italy and had the full support of the Catholic Church. At the beginning of September, before the war began, the Pope told a friend that if Italy went to war in Ethiopia it would be 'deplorable', for he could not understand how a civilized nation could set out to seize another country.[4] But when the fighting had begun, the Church in Italy gave it their full support. 'O Duce!' said the Bishop of Terracina, 'today Italy is Fascist and the hearts of all Italians beat together with yours. The nation is ready for any sacrifice to ensure the triumph of peace and of Roman and Christian civilization ... God bless you, O Duce ... and will ensure the inevitable victory of the Italian armies.'[5] The Bishop of Vicenza was nearly as enthusiastic. On 28 October Cardinal Ildefonso Schuster, preaching in his cathedral in Milan, said that he would not be mixing the sacred with the profane if he pointed out that today was not only the feast of St Simon and St Jude, but also the thirteenth anniversary of the March on Rome, which had opened a new chapter in the history of this peninsula and of the Catholic Church in Italy.[6]

The League of Nations condemned Italy as the aggressor, raised the embargo on the supply of arms to Ethiopia, and appointed a committee to consider how to apply economic sanctions against Italy. Fifty of the fifty-two nations who were members of the League agreed to enforce sanctions; only Austria and Hungary refused. Within a month the sanctions had been agreed, and nearly all the fifty nations began operating them on 18 November. It was decided to ban the importation of all Italian exports, but to forbid the export to Italy of only a limited number of goods; these included arms, rubber, tin and scrap iron, but not oil. These measures seem to us today very mild and ineffectual, compared with the sanctions imposed in recent years against Yugoslavia, Iraq and Libya; and we also know that if economic sanctions are ever effective, it is only after they have been enforced and continued for several years. But the statesmen in Geneva in 1935 hoped that if no nation would purchase Italian exports, Italy would not have enough foreign currency to pay for the imports that she needed for making war.

Things were not going well for the Italians in Ethiopia. After six weeks De Bono's army in the north had advanced only forty miles beyond Adowa, and in the south-east Graziani was unable to make any progress from Somaliland. The gold reserves of the Bank of Italy were falling, and the League of Nations' ban on Italian exports might make them fall still further. On 27 November the lire was devalued by 25 per cent.

In Britain, Baldwin decided to call a general election a year earlier than necessary and to campaign on his government's record in standing by the League of Nations against aggression. The Labour opposition criticized the government's delaying tactics and reluctance to apply sanctions, and demanded oil sanctions, while at the same time opposing rearmament; but the government won the general election on 14 November, losing only 80 of the 556 seats in the House of Commons that they had won in the landslide election of 1931, and being returned to power with a majority of 249. But in France, the right wing opposed sanctions against Italy. The right-wing Henri de Kérillis was a strong opponent of Germany, and in the Chamber of Deputies opposed any concessions to Hitler; but he wrote an article in L'Écho de Paris on 9 October 1935 under the heading 'No war against Fascism', in which he argued that France should never have joined the international crusade against Fascism which England and the League of Nations had launched in order to enable the British government to win an election.[7]

At the beginning of November, Ezio Garibaldi suggested to Mussolini that Ezio should go to England for talks with Sir Samuel Hoare, whom he had known when Hoare was serving in Italy during the First World War. Mussolini agreed; he said he could never trust his diplomats to give him truthful reports,[8] and that he would welcome any initiative by Ezio to improve relations with Britain. He authorized Ezio to put, unofficially, proposals to the British government for a compromise settlement in Ethiopia. It involved the cession to Italy of a larger slice of Ethiopia than Hoare and Laval had so far offered her. Italy would be granted nearly half of Ethiopia and a mandate authorized by the League of Nations over most of the other half; and Ethiopia would disarm. Mussolini now said that he would not object, as he had done in June, to the British plan to compensate Ethiopia for the loss of her territory by granting her a strip of territory across British Somaliland to the sea.[9]

On 22 November Ezio Garibaldi met Ramsay MacDonald, who had just lost his seat in the House of Commons at the general election, but had remained a member of the government. MacDonald said that he appreciated Italy's desire for expansion, that Abyssinia was a barbaric state, and that Britain would not oppose Italy's aspirations; but these aspirations could not be satisfied at a time when Italy had been condemned as an aggressor by the League of Nations. 'So it is a question of saving the face of the League?' asked Garibaldi. 'Is it for this that you are prepared to set the world on fire?' 'Yes,' said MacDonald, 'because for Britain the League is the last defence of peace.'[10]

On 28 November Garibaldi discussed the situation with Hoare, who said that he would carefully study Mussolini's proposals, but that he thought they would be unacceptable to the British government and to Ethiopia. Mussolini was demanding too much territory from Ethiopia, and the Negus had to be allowed to have an army. Grandi and Vansittart were also meeting to discuss very similar proposals.[11]

On 7 December Hoare met Laval in Paris, and they agreed to offer Italy and Ethiopia the Hoare–Laval plan.[12] This was very similar to the proposals that Mussolini had made through Ezio Garibaldi. Ethiopia would cede about half her territory to Italy, who would have a trusteeship over the other half. The proposals aroused a storm of protest in the British press and in the House of Commons, and Hoare was forced to resign.

Mussolini summoned a meeting of the Fascist Grand Council to consider the Hoare–Laval plan. There was general agreement in the Grand Council that it was a basis for negotiation, and that they should propose amendments to the plan; only Farinacci and one other member of the Grand Council wished to reject it outright. The Grand Council agreed to reconsider the matter two days later; but by that time Hoare had resigned, and it was clear that the British government and Ethiopia would reject the plan. The Grand Council then decided that Italy, too, should reject it.[13] The opportunity for compromise had gone, and Italy would defy Britain, the League of Nations and the world.

Guariglia always believed that the collapse of the Hoare–Laval plan was a tragedy that changed the course of history. If the British government had not repudiated the plan, Mussolini would have accepted it; Italy's alliance with Britain and France would have been restored; the Rome–Berlin Axis would never have been formed; Germany would not have begun the Second World War; and the Fascist regime would have survived in Italy.[14] But this analysis perhaps ignores the fundamental nature of Mussolini's regime and character.

Mussolini decided on a move that could help the gold reserves and do even more for patriotic morale. He called on all the men and women of Italy to sacrifice their wedding rings and other gold objects for the national cause. They were invited to come on 18 December and bring their rings to depots in the cities, towns and villages all over the country. There they were received by Fascist volunteers; many of them were members of the older sections of the youth movement. These devoted young men and women waited there from seven o'clock in the morning till ten o'clock at night and accepted the wedding rings that the Queen, the Princesses, Rachele Mussolini, Edda Ciano and nearly all the society ladies and so many middle-class, working-class and peasant women handed in, with their husbands' rings, to help Fascist Italy as she stood alone, heroically defying the unjust and illegal sanctions imposed by a hostile world at the instigation of Britain and international anti-Fascism.

Thousands of women came, although it rained all day. The Fascists called it the *Giornata della Fede* (the day of faith), a phrase that had a double meaning, as *'fede'* in Italian means 'wedding ring' as well as 'faith'. The young members of the Fascist youth who received the rings still remember that day with pride and emotion, though they are now more than sixty years older and in many cases are quite disillusioned with Fascism and with Mussolini.[15]

When Hoare was forced to resign, Eden became Foreign Secretary; at the age of thirty-eight he was the youngest British Foreign Secretary for many years. In France, Laval just survived a vote of censure in the Chamber of Deputies, but his government fell a month later. When he left office, he wrote a personal letter to Mussolini, claiming that he had succeeded in holding up the imposition of sanctions against Italy for as long as possible;[16] but Mussolini was not very impressed.

The new French Prime Minister was the Radical Albert Sarrault, who appointed Flandin as Foreign Minister. But Eden and Flandin did not make much further progress with imposing oil sanctions against Italy than Hoare and Laval had done. The Labour Party newspaper, the *Daily Herald*, which had welcomed Eden's appointment as Foreign Secretary, now wrote that he might not be a good man going wrong, but he was certainly a good man going slowly.[17]

Eden wished to impose oil sanctions, but encountered serious difficulties in doing so. Forty per cent of Italy's oil imports came from Romania, 13 per cent from the Anglo-Persian Oil Company's oilfields in Persia, 12 per cent from the Soviet Union and 6 per cent from the United States. After the Italian invasion of Ethiopia, the Anglo-Persian Company reduced their supplies from 13 to 4 per cent of Italy's oil imports.[18] Romania and the Soviet Union expressed their willingness to ban all oil exports to Italy if the League of Nations called on them to do so; but what would the United States do?

The Italian attack on Ethiopia, one of the last remaining independent black states in the world, had aroused great indignation among the black populations everywhere, including the United States, where black demonstrators hanged Mussolini in effigy;[19] but most of the white population in the United States, and the Senators and Congressmen, were not very interested in what was happening in Ethiopia. At the beginning of the Italo-Abyssinian war, President Roosevelt and his Secretary of State, Cordell Hull, invoked the United States Neutrality Acts against the supply of arms to Italy, and hinted that they might be prepared to extend the embargo to include oil; but between October 1935 and February 1936, United States oil exports to Italy rose from 6 per cent to 17 per cent of Italian oil imports,[20] and Roosevelt knew that he would be unable to persuade Congress to pass the necessary legislation to prevent the American oil corporations from increasing the supply if Romania and the Soviet Union banned the export of oil to Italy.

There was the further difficulty that Flandin was firmly opposed to oil sanctions. He told Eden that the French ambassador in Rome was sure that if oil sanctions were imposed, Mussolini would leave the League and perhaps declare war on Britain and France. Flandin eventually went so far as to tell the British government outright that France would vote against oil sanctions and would refuse to enforce them.[21]

On 16 November Mussolini dismissed De Bono as Commander-in-Chief on the Eritrea front and appointed General Badoglio to replace him. Reinforcements to Badoglio, and ships carrying oil to his air force, had been passing through the Suez Canal ever since the outbreak of war, and by February 1936 Badoglio had 200,000 men and 4,000 aircraft. During February he won several decisive victories, and annihilated two Ethiopian armies. His air force played a vital part in the victory against the Ethiopian forces, who were still organized on primitive feudal lines, and had no planes or anti-aircraft defences.

Public opinion in foreign countries was becoming increasingly shocked at the Italian way of waging war. After the rejection of the Hoare–Laval plan, and Badoglio's assumption of the supreme command, the Italians started to wage unrestricted warfare in breach of several international conventions that they had signed; they repeatedly bombed hospitals marked with the red cross and used mustard gas. On Sunday 22 December Badoglio first used mustard gas against the Ethiopian army opposing him. On 30 December the air force with Graziani's army bombed the Swedish Red Cross at Dolo in the south. The Ethiopian Red Cross was bombed at Amba Aradam in the north and at Daggahbor in the south.[22]

Mustard gas played a useful part in Badoglio's advance in February and March. It caused havoc among the Ethiopian forces, many of whom fought barefoot. The British Red Cross team under Dr John Melly on the northern front were treating between eighty and a hundred cases a day of Ethiopian soldiers and civilians who were suffering from the effects of poison gas. On 4 March the Italian Air Force bombed the British Red Cross hospital at Alomata. The planes flew in very low, as they knew that the Ethiopians had no anti-aircraft defences, and the red cross marked on the hospital was clearly visible. Vittorio Mussolini was one of the pilots who took part in this attack.[23]

The Red Cross were convinced that the Italians were deliberately targeting them, and that it would be safer not to display the red cross. After his experience at Alomata, Melly treated the victims of gas at secret locations hidden in the forests. Some commentators believed that the attack on Melly and his doctors was an attempt by the Italians to kill all the British Red Cross team who could have told the world that the Italians were using gas on a large scale. But the Rome correspondent of the *Morning Post*, George Martelli, who had often interviewed Mussolini and admired him, dismissed this idea as ridiculous, because the Italians would have known that it was impossible to kill every European witness to the use of gas.

He thought the raid on the British Red Cross was just a piece of 'frightfulness' to show that Fascist Italy would wage total war, and was also inspired by hatred of the English, the instigators of sanctions against Italy.[24]

The Italians saw it differently. They thought that the Ethiopians were barbarians who had used the terrible dum-dum bullets that they had bought from the 'sanctionist powers', although these had been banned by international conventions. The press cartoons, including those in children's magazines, showed one tall, smiling, clean-limbed Italian soldier firing a machine-gun at hundreds of ridiculous little black piccaninnies who ran away in panic, or surrendered with their hands above their heads.[25] The popular songs mocked the Negus, Haile Selassie, and the black savages. Vittorio Mussolini wrote that while flying over Ethiopia he had realized the beauty as well as the horrors of war. He had found it 'magnificent sport'. When he saw a group of Ethiopian horsemen blown up by a bomb it had reminded him of a budding rose unfolding as they were blown in all directions. 'It was exceptionally good fun.'[26]

The Italians at home enjoyed the popular songs about the war, *Poor Selassie*, *The Lion of Judah* [Haile Selassie] *and the Little bitch*, and the favourite of them all, *Faccetta Nera*, written by the very prolific songwriter Mario Ruccione. It told the story of a beautiful Ethiopian girl held as a 'slave among slaves' by the barbarian slave-owners; she dreams of being liberated by Italian soldiers who will carry her off as their war booty to Rome, where she will become a Roman, wear a black shirt, and march past the King and Mussolini. But later in the war Mussolini banned the song, and ordered Badoglio to punish any white Italian soldier who had sexual relations with black women in Ethiopia. Songs like *Faccetta Nera* were not the way to inculcate in the Italian people a belief in their racial superiority over the conquered black savages. The cartoons in the papers, which at first had shown Italian soldiers having fun with black beauties, now showed a slinky black seductress offering herself to a handsome young Italian soldier, but being firmly told 'No, thank you, my dear; I prefer my Italian girl-friend back home'.[27]


On 7 March Hitler sent his troops into the Rhineland, in breach of the Treaty of Locarno, which had stipulated that it should be a demilitarized zone. Hitler had now broken, not the hated Treaty of

Versailles which had been imposed on Germany by force, but the treaty that Stresemann had freely negotiated in 1925. But Britain was as reluctant to act against Germany over the Rhineland as France was to act against Italy over Ethiopia. When Eden asked his taxi driver what he thought about the entry of German troops into the Rhineland, the driver replied: 'I suppose Jerry can do what he likes in his own back garden, can't he?'[28]

Eden and Flandin and the Council of the League of Nations now discussed the Rhineland, not Ethiopia. Mussolini took no part in their discussions, but happily received reports of the continued advance of Badoglio's army in Ethiopia. Haile Selassie took personal command of his army at Ashangi, but made the fatal mistake of launching an offensive instead of retreating into the forests and waiting until the rainy season put a halt to Badoglio's operations. Haile Selassie was decisively defeated on 31 March. His forces suffered very heavy losses, and lay wounded and dying, and suffering from the poison gas, without any medical attention, for most of the international Red Cross teams had been withdrawn because of the Italian air raids on their hospitals. In Italy enthusiasm for the war had never been greater as victory was imminent. When acquaintances greeted each other in the street, one would ask 'A chi l'Abissinia?' (To whom does Abyssinia belong?), and the other would reply 'A noi!' (To us).[29]

In desperation, Haile Selassie now made secret peace overtures to Mussolini, sending a former Ethiopian minister in Rome to contact the Italian consul in Djibouti. He offered to sell a large part of Ethiopia to Italy for one and a half milliard lire and to appoint six Italian advisers to direct the policy of his government if Italy would recognize the independence of Ethiopia. Mussolini sent a courteous reply to the intermediary, expressing his pleasure that the Negus had at last decided to negotiate directly with him without the intervention of the League of Nations or of any foreign government; but he said that the offer was unacceptable.[30]

It was now clear in British government circles that Mussolini had won. On 20 April Eden in Geneva demanded that the existing sanctions against Italy should be continued; but three days earlier Churchill had written, in an article in the *Evening Standard*, that the British government should do nothing do discourage Haile Selassie from accepting any terms that he might obtain from Mussolini, even if they were worse than those offered in the Hoare–Laval plan.[31] On

29 April Churchill suggested to the Conservative Foreign Affairs Committee that sanctions against Italy should be lifted.[32]

That evening, Grandi had a private meeting with King Edward VIII, who had succeeded his father George V in January. The new King had always been an admirer of Mussolini. He agreed with Grandi that sanctions should be lifted, and friendly relations between Britain and Italy restored. When Grandi said that some people were still suggesting that the Suez Canal should be closed, the King asked: 'Why? To stop the victorious Italian troops from returning home?'[33]

On 1 May Haile Selassie told his ministers that he was leaving the country. The British legation in Addis Ababa arranged for him to be brought to England on a British warship. On 3 May Mussolini, in an article in *Il Popolo d'Italia* headed 'Towards Addis Ababa!', denounced the 'pacifist warmongers' who wished to make war in the name of peace.[34] Badoglio's vanguard entered Addis Ababa at 4 p.m on 3 May. Mussolini announced the news in a speech from the balcony of the Palazzo Venezia on the evening of 5 May, to 'the Blackshirts of the Revolution, the men and women of all Italy'. This was one of the great events in thirty centuries of Italian history. Ethiopia was Italian; civilization had triumphed over barbarism; the empire of the Lion of Judah had been destroyed.[35]

The businessman Alberto Pirelli, who was President of the Italian Exports Association, was in London, and on 7 May he called on Churchill to discuss the situation. Churchill said that in the House of Commons, and in private approaches to ministers, he would propose that sanctions against Italy should be lifted, but that it would be more difficult to persuade the world to accept the position if Mussolini proclaimed the annexation of Ethiopia to Italy. Churchill suggested that it would be wiser if the Italians agreed to rule Ethiopia through native princes, as the British did in parts of India; but he added that if Mussolini insisted on annexing Ethiopia, he had better do it quickly and confront the League of Nations with a *fait accompli*.[36]

Mussolini had in fact been thinking of ruling Ethiopia indirectly through native princes. He told Rachele that if Haile Selassie had not run away he would have appointed him to rule Ethiopia as an Italian viceroy.[37] But things had worked out differently. Italy had defeated Ethiopia, the League of Nations and Britain, and he was determined to have his empire. He was ready to make a concession on this point by merely proclaiming Victor Emmanuel as 'King Emperor' without a specific reference to Ethiopia; but Victor Emmanuel would not agree. He insisted that he must remain 'King of Italy', not King Emperor.[38] So on 9 May he was officially proclaimed as King of Italy and Emperor of Ethiopia.

At 10.30 that evening Mussolini spoke again from the balcony of the Palazzo Venezia. Today on 9 May, Year XIV of the Fascist era, Italy had finally acquired a Fascist empire, because for fourteen years she had harnessed the energy and discipline of youth. After fifteen centuries an empire had again been established on the hills of Rome. He ended his speech: 'Blackshirts, Legionaries, salute the King!'[39]

On 11 May the Council of the League of Nations decided to maintain sanctions against Italy; but everyone knew that this was just a face-saving fiction. In France the People's Front had won the general election and Léon Blum became Prime Minister of a coalition government of Socialists and Radicals, which the seventy-two Communist deputies in the Chamber supported, but would not enter. But it was too late for Blum to do anything to save Ethiopia. In Britain the Chancellor of the Exchequer, Neville Chamberlain, who had hitherto been one of the most determined supporters of sanctions in the British government, changed his mind in the new situation. On 10 June he told a Conservative meeting in London that to continue to maintain sanctions would be 'the very midsummer of madness'. Eden was compelled to agree. When the Labour MPs denounced him in the House of Commons for having failed to impose oil sanctions against Italy, he replied by criticizing them for having opposed rearmament. He said that they had supported the League and confronted Mussolini not with horse, foot and artillery, but only with threats, insults and provocations.[40]

On 30 June, in the General Assembly of the League, Eden proposed that sanctions should be lifted, and Blum agreed. Haile Selassie went to Geneva and addressed the Assembly on behalf of Ethiopia. Some Italian Fascist journalists in the audience heckled and catcalled him, and had to be thrown out. But the League decided that all sanctions against Italy should be lifted on 15 July.

Mussolini announced the end of sanctions from the balcony of the Palazzo Venezia. 'Today, 15 July, in Year XIV, the sanctionist world raised the white flag on its battlements. The merit of this great victory is due to the Italian people, to the men, to the women, to the young girls of all Italy.' The crowd roared back: 'To you, Duce!'[41] Two days later, civil war broke out in Spain.

# CHAPTER 30

## ◆

# The Spanish Civil War

I N his hour of triumph, Mussolini – Head of the Government, Duce of Fascism, Founder of the Empire – was desperately worried. His youngest child, Anna Maria, aged six, fell ill in May 1936. At first she was diagnosed as having whooping cough, but this developed into poliomyelitis. Mussolini always worried when his children were ill, and now he sat at her bedside night after night, for she wanted either him or Rachele to be there. She was an intelligent child, and insisted on knowing what was the matter with her. When they told her that she might be paralysed, she cried out: 'If I can't move for the rest of my life, I'd rather die.' On 2 June the four doctors who were treating her told Mussolini and Rachele that she was at the point of death, and during the next few days Mussolini hardly slept and was almost out of his mind. When the wind blew open the window in Anna Maria's room, he cried out, 'Shut the window, or the wind will carry off my child.'

He carried on his work as Prime Minister in the room next to Anna Maria's, but found it difficult to concentrate on the political situation, though by 8 June she had begun to recover. When they brought him reports about the preparations in Geneva to lift the sanctions against Italy, he said: 'They might leave me in peace at my child's bedside.' But by 12 June the doctors said that she was definitely improving, and on 20 June they announced that she had been saved.[1] She recovered from the polio, but she died of cancer at the age of thirty-eight in 1968.

One of the matters in which Mussolini was involved when he was most worried about Anna Maria was a meeting with the Austrian Chancellor, Schuschnigg, at Rocca delle Caminate on 5 June, at which Schuschnigg told him that Austria would be the first foreign government to recognize Victor Emmanuel as Emperor of Ethiopia.[2]

The second nation to do so was Germany. When the trouble with Ethiopia first arose, Hitler did not pursue a friendly policy towards Italy. As Germany had left the League of Nations, she was not bound by the decisions of the League; and when the League imposed the embargo on the export of arms to both Italy and Ethiopia, which caused such difficulties for Ethiopia, Germany sold arms to Haile Selassie. After war had broken out, and the League imposed sanctions against Italy, the German government announced in November 1935 that they were banning the export to Italy of tin, aluminium and other war material. This would win British goodwill at a time when Hitler was thinking of reoccupying the Rhineland, and would show Mussolini that German friendship was worth acquiring.

But in November 1935 Mussolini sent his daughter Edda on a goodwill visit to Germany. She was warmly received by the Nazi leaders, and when she came home she impressed on Mussolini the importance of improving relations with Germany. Soon afterwards Hitler agreed to supply Italy with coal, which she badly needed after British coal exports to Italy were banned.[3]

On 11 July 1936 Mussolini had another meeting with Schuschnigg at Rocca delle Caminate. He advised Schuschnigg to make a treaty of friendship with Germany and to offer the Austrian Nazis a few seats in his government. Schuschnigg agreed, and three Austrian Nazis became ministers.[4] In 1934 Mussolini had rejected the British government's advice to urge Schuschnigg to offer concessions to the Austrian Socialists in order to win their support against Hitler. Now he had persuaded Schuschnigg to make concessions to the Nazis and to accept Hitler as his ally against socialism.

For some years Mussolini had been closely watching the position in Spain. When he first came to power, Spain had been ruled by the right-wing military dictator, King Alfonso XIII's Prime Minister General Miguel Primo de Rivera. But in 1930 King Alfonso dismissed Primo de Rivera and relaxed the dictatorship, and this was soon followed by a revolution in 1931 which drove Alfonso into exile and led to the proclamation of a republic and the establishment of a left-wing liberal government. The traditional right-wing forces in Spain – the alliance of the landowners, the army and the Church – strongly opposed the republican government. Mussolini also opposed the republican regime in Spain. He regarded the revolution of 1931 as a victory of international socialism; and the man who had been a revolutionary Socialist and an enemy of the Catholic Church before 1914, and who in 1931 still considered himself to be a Fascist revolutionary, supported conservative militarism, royalism and clericalism in Spain. This increased his popularity with the Vatican and with the Catholic Church in Italy.

In 1932 General Sacaneli Sanjurjo planned a military coup d'état to overthrow the Spanish liberal government. Sanjurjo secretly contacted Guariglia, who was then the Italian ambassador in Madrid, and asked Mussolini to support his coup d'état; and his emissary contacted Balbo. Mussolini instructed Guariglia to maintain secret contacts with Sanjurjo and to encourage him, but to refuse to give him aid or public support.[5] In August 1932 Sanjurjo attempted a coup which was a complete failure.

Mussolini made a more serious commitment to the Spanish right wing in 1934. On 31 March he had a secret meeting in Rome with the Spanish General Emilio Barrera and two aristocrats who were the leaders of an extreme right-wing organization in Spain. Although a conservative government had come to power, Barrera and his colleagues wished to overthrow the republic by a military coup which would place power in the hands of a regent who as soon as possible would restore the monarchy. Mussolini promised to supply them with money and arms if they attempted a coup,[6] but they were never strong enough to do this.

In February 1936 the Liberals, Socialists and Communists, who had formed the People's Front, won the Spanish general election. The liberal government was too weak to prevent anarchists and other left-wing revolutionaries from committing acts of violence against churches and monasteries, and assaulting right-wing politicians. Matters came to a head when the brilliant right-wing leader, the former minister Calvo Sotelo, was murdered by the left-wing Assault Guards in the streets of Madrid in July 1936. On 17 July a right-wing revolt broke out. The leader of the revolt, General Sanjurjo, was killed on the third day when his aircraft crashed, and his second-in-command, General Francisco Franco, replaced him as leader. In the Red stronghold of Barcelona the anarchist and Socialist workers rose and defeated the attempted coup, and the general who was leading it was shot. The people pledged themselves to defeat Fascism, and launched the slogan 'No *pasarán!*' (They shall not pass).

On 21 July General Franco sent an envoy to Mussolini and asked him for help, reminding him of the encouragement that he had given to the Spanish right-wing plotters in 1934. Franco particularly wanted aircraft to transport his Moorish troops from Spanish Morocco to the Spanish mainland, because the navy, as he put it, 'was in the hands of the Communists' – that is to say, was loyal to the liberal government. Mussolini wished Franco success, but said that he could not give him aid and intervene in an internal civil war in Spain unless Socialist governments intervened on the other side.[7] Franco then turned to Hitler. His envoys to Berlin saw Goering, who persuaded Hitler to order on 26 July that German aircraft should be sent to transport Franco's troops from Morocco to Spain.[8]

During the first fortnight of the war, the Spanish republican government purchased arms and planes from France; but on 2 August Blum proposed that France, Britain and Italy, and later all other European powers, should agree to pursue a policy of non-intervention in Spain and ban the supply of arms to either side. The British government supported the proposal. The Spanish republican government and its supporters complained bitterly that it deprived them of the right, under international law, of any lawful government to obtain arms to suppress a revolt; and the Socialists in Britain and elsewhere have always accused the British government of putting pressure on Blum to propose non-intervention, by informing him that Britain would remain neutral if France became involved in a war with Germany and Italy as a result of supporting the republican government in Spain. Eden denied it, at the time and ever after. He stated that non-intervention was Blum's idea, because when the news leaked out that his government was supplying arms to the Spanish republicans, he was fiercely criticized by the French right wing, and he feared that this would lead to a right-wing rising and a civil war in France.[9]

Churchill used his private influence in support of non-intervention. His hatred of communism and his suspicion of Germany led him to be neutral between the two sides in the Spanish Civil War. He told his friend Flandin that there was great sympathy for Franco in the British Conservative Party, and that if, as a result of helping the republican government, France became involved in a war with Germany and Italy, it would be difficult to persuade Britain to intervene on France's side.[10]

After it was known that France had sent aircraft and other military help to the republican government in the last fortnight of July, Mussolini began sending aircraft and war material to Franco at the beginning of August. Throughout August he sent supplies to Franco on a large scale, and he also alarmed the British government by sending aircraft and troops to Majorca.[11] He told Rachele that he had decided to help Franco because if the republican government won the civil war, it would lead to communism being established in Spain. 'There's no alternative,' he told her. 'Bolshevism in Spain means Bolshevism in France, which means Bolshevism next door, and in fact a serious threat to bolshevize Europe.'[12] He may have had other motives as well, and thought perhaps that if Franco won with Italian help, Italy would control Spain and would be in a position, in the event of war with Britain, to capture Gibraltar and control the western end of the Mediterranean; but there is no doubt that his chief motive was to prevent Spain from going Communist, and to defeat Bolshevism, Socialist internationalism and anti-Fascism in Spain.

The Spanish Civil War was fought with the savagery that has always marked the civil wars between the Right and the Left in Spain, and it divided public opinion in other countries. The Communists, Socialists and liberals saw it as a revolt by a military caste against a democratically elected government; the right-wing parties believed that it was a rising by patriots who were determined to prevent a weak government from allowing Spain to fall into the hands of the Communists. Both sides committed atrocities and in their propaganda reported and exaggerated the atrocities of their opponents. The right wing spoke about the destruction of churches and convents in republican territory, and the storming of the prisons by anarchist mobs who murdered the Franco supporters who were confined there; the left wing spoke about the large-scale executions of republican soldiers and civilian sympathizers by Franco's firing squads whenever his forces captured a town or village. The Spanish Civil War was not only a war between Spaniards, but also part of the international struggle between what both Mussolini and his enemies called the forces of Fascism and anti-Fascism.

After sending supplies to Franco for three weeks, Mussolini on 21 August accepted Blum's proposal for non-intervention in Spain and agreed to stop all aid to Franco.[13] He also agreed to co-operate with the Non-Intervention Committee which was established in London to supervise the observance of the non-intervention agreement. He thought that he had done enough to ensure Franco's victory, and that if no more supplies were sent to either side in Spain, Franco would be certain to win because of his superiority in arms. Franco's armies were advancing; in August they captured Badajoz, where they massacred some two thousand Republican prisoners; by the end of September they had captured Toledo, relieving their garrison who had held out for more than two months in the Alcázar fortress there, and seemed poised to advance on Madrid and capture it. On the Non-Intervention Committee the Soviet ambassador in London, Ivan Maisky, accused Portugal, Italy and Germany of breaking the agreement and sending arms and men to help Franco, a charge denied by Grandi and Joachim von Ribbentrop, the German ambassador in London.

On 23 October Maisky announced that in view of these breaches the Soviet Union would no longer be bound by the non-intervention agreement, and Stalin immediately began sending money and arms, including aircraft, to help the republican government. He sent only a few hundred Soviet technicians and secret police agents to Spain, but the Comintern organized an International Brigade of Communist volunteers from many countries in Europe and from the United States. The 3,350 Italians were the third-largest national group in the International Brigade.[14] They were formed from Communist, Socialist and other anti-Fascist refugees in France, and organized by Carlo Rosselli, the Socialist leader who had escaped from *confino* in the Lipari Islands. They called themselves the Garibaldi Brigade – an appropriate name, as Garibaldi had fought for the cause of freedom in several foreign countries in two continents. This did not please Garibaldi's grandson Ezio, who tried to prove that if Garibaldi were alive he would have been a Fascist, not a Communist, by quoting the criticisms that Marx had made of Garibaldi in 1864.[15] The International Brigade arrived in Madrid in time to play an important part in repulsing Franco's attack on the city in early November.

The support that Mussolini and Hitler were giving to Franco drew them closer together. They decided to forget their old differences about Austria and form an Italo-German alliance. This was strongly supported by Galeazzo Ciano, whom Mussolini had appointed Foreign Minister.[16] For many years Mussolini had held the Ministry of Foreign Affairs himself, and many other ministries as well; for a time in 1929 he had held nine ministerial portfolios, with the assistance of under-secretaries. But while Grandi and Suvich had been Under-Secretary for Foreign Affairs to Mussolini, Ciano was given the title of Foreign Minister.

In September 1936 Hans Frank, the German Minister of Justice, came to Rome; he was an able lawyer who during the Second World War became an exceptionally brutal Governor of Poland. He invited Mussolini to come on an official visit to Germany at some future convenient date. Mussolini accepted the invitation, and he and Frank agreed that it would be desirable to establish a Rome–Berlin Axis, a close diplomatic and military alliance.[17]

In November 1936 Hitler and Mussolini both recognized Franco's government in Burgos as the legal government of Spain, and in view of the intervention of the International Brigade on the republican side they both stepped up their aid to Franco. Mussolini decided to send substantial ground forces as well as several air squadrons; Germany gave technical assistance and aircraft with German crews, but no ground forces. By the spring of 1937 Mussolini had sent fifty thousand Italian troops to Spain. They took part in the attack on Malaga, which Franco captured in February, and in the massacre of nearly four thousand republican prisoners after their victory.

In February the republican army, including the International Brigade, attacked Franco's forces at Jarama outside Madrid, and won their first major victory of the war, though at a heavy cost in casualties. In March, Mussolini's Italians attacked the republicans at Guadalajara to the north-east of Madrid, and were defeated and repulsed. The anti-Fascist Italians in the Garibaldi Brigade fought valiantly, and made an important contribution to the republican victory.

Their leader, Carlo Rosselli, was unable to take part in the battle because he was suffering from phlebitis. In May he went to Bagnoles in France to take a cure. His routine at Bagnoles was to take the cure in the mornings and go for a drive in his car in the evenings along a quiet lane through the park. On the evening of 9 June 1937 he and his younger brother Nello were driving along this lane when they found the road blocked by a car which appeared to have broken down. When they got out of their car to see if they could help the stranded driver, they were set upon by four men who attacked them with knives. The murderers' target was Carlo Rosselli, and he was killed by one knife thrust; his killer was an expert who knew how and where to strike. Nello was probably killed only because he happened to be in the car with his brother; the men detailed to kill him were less expert than their colleague, and several knife wounds were necessary to finish him off.

After killing the two brothers, the murderers drove off in their car and abandoned it a few miles away. They were never caught, but there is little doubt that they were members of the OVRA acting on orders from the Italian government, though perhaps, as in the case of Matteotti, they knew that Mussolini would prefer not to know in advance. Farinacci wrote in the newspaper *Regime Fascista* that the killing of the Rossellis was an 'act of justice' which he 'would not hesitate to uphold'.

The funeral of Carlo and Nello Rosselli in Paris was attended by 200,000 mourners. The anti-Fascists also held a protest meeting at Toulouse where they heard Silvio Trentin, a former Italian Socialist deputy, accuse the Fascists of the murder. Farinacci wrote that some-one should 'pay Trentin back in his own coin'.[18] But the Fascists never succeeded in getting Trentin.

Mussolini was not pleased at the defeat of his troops at Guadala-jara, but they did better later in the year when they played an impor-tant part in the capture of the republican territory in the Basque country in the north. Mussolini no longer denied that he was intervening in Spain, and his congratulations to his troops on their victory in the Basque territory were prominently published in the Italian press.[19]

The Italian Air Force took part in air raids on the cities and towns in republican territory, including Madrid and Barcelona. These air raids caused much more damage to life and property than had been done by the air raids in the First World War, and were the foretaste of what air raids would be like in the Second World War. Franco declared that he would continue the air raids until every building in Madrid had been destroyed rather than allow the city to remain in the hands of the Marxists.[20]

The almost total destruction of the little town of Guernica in April 1937, which particularly shocked public opinion in Britain, the United States and other democratic countries, was carried out by German, not Italian, aviators; but the Italian airmen played a prominent part in the campaign, and were highly respected and feared by the enemy. Bruno Mussolini volunteered to serve with the air force in Spain. After he had distinguished himself in twenty-seven aerial engagements, Franco's agents discovered that the republican airmen, in their Soviet planes, were trying to target Bruno. Franco insisted that it was too dangerous for Bruno to continue serving in his air force, and that he had done enough for the cause and for his own glory; and he insisted that Bruno return to Italy.[21]

Vittorio Mussolini, unlike his brother, did not volunteer to fight in Spain. After returning from Ethiopia he got married and began a career as a film director. He worked with famous directors in Germany and in Hollywood. In the summer of 1937 he was in Washington D.C., and Roosevelt invited him to tea at the White House. Roosevelt told Vittorio that he would like to meet his father. It was very difficult for the President of the United States to visit a foreign country – Wilson in 1919 was the only President who had ever done so – and Roosevelt realized that it would be difficult for Mussolini to visit the United States; but would it not be possible for them to meet on a ship in mid-Atlantic?

When Vittorio returned to Italy he told Mussolini what Roosevelt had said. Mussolini laughed, and said that he was sure that Roosevelt did not mean it seriously.[22] Today Vittorio, and other political commentators, speculate as to whether the course of history would have been changed if the meeting had taken place; but it is much more likely that Mussolini's own comment was correct.

In December 1937, Italy left the League of Nations, although the League had done nothing new to annoy Mussolini; it was a gesture of contempt for liberalism and internationalism and of solidarity with Nazi Germany. But Mussolini was adopting a more conciliatory policy towards Britain. The British government did not object if Mussolini's troops crushed the Reds in Spain, but they were worried that he might stay in Spain after Franco's victory and threaten Gibraltar, and were also worried that his submarines in the Mediterranean were endangering British shipping, for they sometimes sank merchant ships that were trading with ports in Spanish republican territory. The British government were relieved when Mussolini satisfied them on both these points by agreeing to the pact that was drawn up at a conference at Nyon in Switzerland in September 1937, and in giving assurances on several matters that had disturbed the British government.

Churchill was pleased, for he still admired Mussolini. He paid tribute to him, to his great role in world history, and to 'the amazing qualities of courage, comprehension, self-control and perseverance which he exemplifies'. By establishing Fascism he had defeated the hammer and sickle of Asiatic communism. 'Liberty was lost, but Italy was saved.'[23]

Baldwin resigned in June 1937 and was succeeded as Prime Minister by Neville Chamberlain, who he was eager to improve relations with Italy. His Foreign Secretary, Eden, did not oppose this policy, but was more suspicious of Mussolini than Chamberlain was. Eden also resented the fact that Chamberlain sometimes wrote personal letters to Mussolini that he did not show to Eden, and also kept up contacts with Mussolini through his sister-in-law, Lady Chamberlain, Sir Austen's widow. She had a house in Rome, where she spent several months in the year, and continued her personal friendship with Mussolini which had begun when her husband was Foreign Secretary.[24]

In February 1938 Eden resigned as Foreign Secretary because of his disagreements with Chamberlain. Mussolini and his journalists were pleased, for ever since the Ethiopian war they had considered Eden to be an enemy of Italy and a bar to improving relations with Britain.

———— ♦ ————

# CHAPTER 31

# The Racial Laws

USSOLINI had appointed Marshal Graziani to be Viceroy
of Ethiopia. After the fall of Addis Ababa the Ethiopians
had continued a guerrilla resistance to the Italians in some
parts of the countryside. On 5 June 1936 Mussolini sent an order
to Graziani that all captured guerrillas must be executed. Three days
later he ordered Graziani to use poison gas to end the rebellion. On
8 July he told him to conduct a systematic policy of 'terror and
extermination' against the rebels and their supporters among the
population.[1]

Mussolini had moved from nationalism to imperialism and from
imperialism to racism. He encouraged Graziani and the Minister for
the Colonies, Alessandro Lessona, to pursue a policy that would
inculcate into the Italian settlers in Ethiopia a sense of their superiority over the black subject race. A royal decree of 19 April 1937 made
it an offence punishable by between one and five years' imprisonment
for any Italian to have sexual intercourse with an inhabitant of East
Africa. An Italian who had unsuccessfully asked the King's permission to marry an Ethiopian woman, but who nevertheless had
sex with her, was sentenced in 1939 to thirteen months in prison.
Laws were introduced which enforced segregation, and required
whites and blacks to travel in separate trams and eat in separate
restaurants and cafés. Whites were forbidden to take jobs under
black employers.[2]

Building projects had been a feature of Mussolini's Fascist regime
at home, and they were now to feature equally prominently in the
Empire. In Addis Ababa, as in Rome, a great new boulevard was
built through the centre of the city. Only whites were allowed to
drive or walk along this boulevard; the blacks had to go along
another parallel street which was narrower and less impressive.[3]

On 19 February 1937 Graziani attended a ceremony in Addis Ababa in honour of the birth of Prince Umberto's only son, at which alms were distributed to the native poor. During the ceremony two men from Eritrea, who were in the crowd, threw seven or eight bombs at Graziani and his entourage. No one was killed, but Graziani and some thirty other people were wounded. After the two Eritreans had been shot down by Graziani's guards, the army and police began a search of the houses in the native quarters, and burned down any house in which weapons were found; but the secretary of the local Fascist Party in Addis Ababa, Guido Cortese, called on the Fascists to take more drastic action.

For forty-eight hours, the Fascists avenged the attempt on Graziani's life by massacring Ethiopians and burning down their primitive houses. The action continued for three days and two nights until midday on 21 February, when Graziani, from his hospital bed, ordered it to end; but neither he nor Mussolini condemned it, or criticized Cortese and the Addis Ababa Fascists. According to Graziani's report to Mussolini, about one thousand Ethiopians were killed and one thousand houses burned; but journalists in Addis Ababa believed that this was a serious underestimate, and that about three thousand Ethiopians were killed.[4]

As the Ethiopian rebellion still continued, Mussolini ordered Graziani to adopt the policy that had been pursued in Libya between 1930 and 1932 after a native uprising, and deport whole populations of the rebellious districts to far-distant internment camps. Thousands of men, women and children were rounded up. Those who survived the long forced marches lived and died in conditions of terrible squalor in the insanitary camps.[5]

Things were quieter now in Libya. Mussolini appointed Balbo to be Governor. Many Libyans approved of Balbo, and were grateful to him for preserving order. He would not tolerate any disobedience to his decrees. Wishing to encourage the tourist trade, he ordered that all shops should stay open on Saturdays. Some members of the local Jewish community refused, on religious grounds, to open their shops on the Sabbath day. Balbo ordered that three of the ringleaders of the disobedient Jews should be publicly whipped, each to receive ten lashes. The sentence on one of them was commuted on medical grounds to three months in prison. But on several occasions Balbo praised the Jews for their service in the army in wartime and as good members of the community.[6]

In March 1937 Mussolini visited Libya; it was the first time that he had been there since his visit in 1926. The Italian press and radio gave great publicity to the visit. Mussolini rode on horseback through the city centres at the head of a band of horsemen; he was presented with a ceremonial sword by the native chiefs, and was proclaimed the Protector of Islam.[7]

But Mussolini imposed his racialist ideas in Libya. A decree of 30 December 1937 extended to Libya the laws against sexual intercourse between Italians and Ethiopians. When two Arab youths in Libya 'touched' an Italian girl in the street, they were sentenced to eight years in prison for having 'insulted racial prestige'. In 1938 an Italian woman who had lived for six years with her Arab lover and had two children by him was sentenced to five years' imprisonment under the decree of 30 December; but the Court of Appeal in Rome quashed the conviction because she had committed the offence before the decree came into force.[8]

Mussolini's long-awaited visit to Germany took place in September 1937. The Nazis put on a great display to welcome him in Berlin. The boulevards were decorated and floodlit, and the best German film directors and government administrators saw to it that it was a brilliant spectacle that passed off without a hitch. On the evening of 28 September Hitler and Mussolini addressed a mass rally on the Maifeld in Berlin, which was part of the complex built for the Olympic Games in 1936. It was reported that there were nearly a million people present, but this was an exaggeration as the Maifeld held only 250,000. Their enthusiasm was unabated despite the fact that they were thoroughly drenched by a thunderstorm.[9]

After the Minister of Propaganda, Joseph Goebbels, had introduced him, Mussolini spoke in German. He said that Fascism and Nazism were two forms of the same phenomenon. What the world called the Rome–Berlin Axis had originated in the autumn of 1935, when Italy, facing the sanctions imposed by fifty-two nations, found a friend in Germany. Italy and Germany were waging a common struggle in Spain against Bolshevism; the unity of two nations of 115 million people could never be broken.[10]

But one thing worried the Nazis leaders: Mussolini was not anti-

Semitic. Anti-Semitism seemed to the Nazis to be an indispensable part of the struggle against Jewish Bolshevism. In nearly all other countries their Fascist and right-wing allies were anti-Semitic; the National Socialists in Hungary, the Iron Guard in Romania, the Action Française and the other right-wing pro-Fascist groups in France were all anti-Semitic, as was Sir Oswald Mosley in Britain, who had transferred his allegiance from Mussolini to Hitler; but Mussolini never said or did anything against the Jews.

Some of the Nazis thought that Hitler should speak to Mussolini about this and urge him to be anti-Semitic. Hitler did not agree He did not wish Mussolini to feel that he was trying to interfere in internal Italian affairs, for Mussolini would resent this, and it would be counter-productive. Hitler was sure that if Mussolini were left to himself, he would become anti-Semitic in his own good time, because it was in the fundamental nature of every Fascist and nationalist movement to be anti-Semitic.[11]

Despite Hitler's attitude, some Nazi officials did raise the matter with Mussolini during his visit to Germany. On 28 September, a few hours before he spoke on the Maifeld, they asked him why he was not conscious of the Jewish menace in Italy. Mussolini said that he was far less worried about Italy's seventy thousand Jews* than about the millions of blacks in Italy's new Empire in Africa. The important thing was to make Italians realize the supremacy of the white race over the black race. He thought that he was succeeding in this, for only three Italian women had disgraced themselves by having sexual intercourse with blacks. He had given orders that they were to be beaten and sent for five years to a concentration camp.[12]

In March 1938 Hitler ordered German troops to march into Austria, and proclaimed the Anschluss of Austria with Germany. Schuschnigg was imprisoned. Jews were rounded up in Vienna and forced to scrub the pavements in the streets; some of them fled to Berlin, where the people were less violently anti-Semitic than in Vienna. Mussolini had warned Schuschnigg shortly before that he would do nothing to help him if Hitler invaded Austria. The Anschluss was supported by

---

* There were 33,000 Jews in Italy in 1911. When Trieste was acquired in 1918, the Jewish population increased by 6,000. The arrival of Jewish refugees from Germany raised the number of Jews in mainland Italy to 47,000. There were also 24,000 Jews in Libya.

a large majority in a plebiscite which followed. The Germans rejoiced that the Führer's homeland had been included in the German Reich, and that they had now *Ein Volk, ein Reich, ein Führer* (one people, one state, one leader).

Four days later, on 16 March, Mussolini spoke about the situation in the Chamber of Deputies. As usual when he found it necessary to change his policy, he made no attempt to hide the fact, but fully explained the reasons for the change. He reminded the deputies that in 1934, after the assassination of Dollfuss, he had sent troops to the frontier on the Brenner to prevent the Anschluss; but he now realized that the great majority of the Austrian people favoured union with Germany, and it was politically foolish to try to thwart the will of a majority of the population. The international situation had completely changed during the last four years, because the Western Powers had tried to strangle the Italian people by imposing sanctions against Italy during the war in Ethiopia; so in October 1936 Italy made an alliance with Germany and formed the Rome–Berlin Axis. Germany was now Italy's friend and ally, and they would not allow any disagreements over Austria to disrupt their unity. Italy would soon have a population of fifty million and Germany of eighty million and they would form an invincible bloc in central Europe.[13]

In April 1938, after Lady Chamberlain had talked to Mussolini and written to Neville Chamberlain, Mussolini signed the Anglo-Italian treaty by which he agreed to withdraw all Italian troops from Spain as soon as the civil war ended. Chamberlain hailed the agreement as the restoration of Anglo-Italian friendship.[14]

After Mussolini's visit to Berlin it was Hitler's turn to go to Rome, and he arrived on 3 May 1938. During his six days in Rome there were banquets and speeches that emphasized the solidarity of the Rome–Berlin Axis. Hitler was annoyed that protocol required him, as head of the German state, to stay in the Quirinal Palace with King Victor Emmanuel and not with Mussolini, and he did not like either the food or the conversation in the palace; but he had several talks with Mussolini about the international situation. Hitler and Mussolini agreed to continue their aid to Franco until he had defeated the Bolsheviks in Spain; and Hitler told Mussolini that he had taken up the cause of the Germans in the Sudetenland in Czechoslovakia, and that this might well lead to an international crisis later in the year.

Mussolini promised Hitler that Italy would not oppose his actions against Czechoslovakia. At no time, during his talks with Mussolini in Rome, did Hitler refer to the Jews or urge Mussolini to adopt an anti-Semitic policy.[15]

On 14 July 1938 the *Giornale d'Italia* published an article with the title 'Fascism and the Problem of Race'.[16] The article soon became known as the Manifesto on Race. It was officially said to be the work of a group of scholars of the Ministry of Popular Culture; but Mussolini told Ciano that he had drafted most of the manifesto himself. It was in fact written by a twenty-five-year-old anthropologist, Guido Landra, after an interview with Mussolini, at which Mussolini had told him what to write.[17] The Manifesto on Race stated that the Italians had for two thousand years been an Aryan race, and that Jews were not members of the Italian race. The Nazi newspapers in Germany welcomed the manifesto.

Mussolini was in jocular mood when he discussed with Ciano on 30 August what to do about the Jews. He said that they might be sent to the northern tip of Italian Somaliland, which had natural resources that the Jews might develop, including a shark fishery, 'which has the great advantage that, to begin with, many Jews would get eaten'.[18]

Margherita Sarfatti became alarmed about the new anti-Semitic policy. She went to see Ciano, who told her not to worry; he was sure that she would come to no harm. But she decided to emigrate to the United States.[19] She had been to see Ciano, not Mussolini, because her love affair with Mussolini had ended some years before. Mussolini had now fallen in love with Claretta Petacci.

They first met in September 1933, when Claretta was nineteen and Mussolini was fifty. He was being driven along the road from Ostia to Castel Fusano; she was also being driven along the same road by her fiancé, Lieutenant Federici of the air force. As Mussolini's car overtook Federici, Mussolini noticed Claretta, and he turned round to look again at the pretty girl. She caught his eye, and waved to him. He stopped the car, and directed Federici to stop, and he got out and talked to Claretta. She told him of her unbounded admiration for him, the Duce, and they arranged to meet again in Rome, where Claretta lived.[20]

She was the daughter of a doctor, Francesco Saverio Petacci. All Dr Petacci's children were gifted and ambitious. His son Marcello studied medicine like his father, and became a major in the Army

Medical Corps; he also engaged in a number of successful business ventures. His daughter Myriam became a singer and a film actress, and married a marquis, the Marchese Boggiano. It was not long before his daughter Claretta became the mistress of a dictator, though she married Lieutenant Federici in June 1934, nine months after she first met Mussolini. It was a big society wedding. The Papal Secretary of State, Cardinal Eugenio Pacelli, who later became Pope Pius XII, was one of the guests.[21]

Lieutenant and Signora Federici soon fell out, and agreed to separate. They could not get a divorce, because Mussolini, to please the Pope, had refused to allow divorce in Italy; but Major Marcello Petacci usually managed to fix things, and he worked out a way by which Claretta and her husband could get a divorce in Hungary which would be valid by Italian law. Mussolini was deeply in love with Claretta; but the Duce, the favourite of the Pope, the champion of the Church against godless communism, no longer wrote autobiographical books in which he boasted of all his sexual conquests. He managed his affair with Claretta very discreetly; she visited him in the Palazzo Venezia, using a secret staircase.[22]

Their relationship was not generally known, and Rachele knew nothing about it;[23] but a few people in Mussolini's entourage realized what was happening, and did not approve. They particularly disapproved of what they considered to be the pervasive influence of the Petacci family. When Mussolini went to some provincial town to address a meeting or to inspect a factory, it so happened that Claretta was often on holiday in the neighbourhood; and she was usually accompanied by Dr Petacci, Major Petacci and the Marchese and Marchesa Boggiano. Mussolini's officials thought that the Petaccis were a pushy lot.[24]

Unlike Margherita Sarfatti, the Petaccis were not Jews, and were unaffected by Mussolini's new racial policy. On 1 September 1938 the Council of Ministers, 'on the proposal of the Duce and the Minister of Information', ordered that all foreign Jews who had taken up residence in Italy, Libya or the Dodecanese Islands since 1 January 1919 were to leave Italian territory within six months. This was aimed particularly at the eight thousand Jewish refugees who had fled to Italy from Germany and Austria after the Nazis came to power; it included those who had become naturalized Italians, whose naturalization was to be revoked. A person was to be considered a Jew if both his parents 'are of the Jewish race', even if he was not a Jew by religion. Next day another decree of the Council of Ministers laid down that no 'persons of Jewish race' could be teachers or could be admitted as students at any school or university, but those who had already begun their studies would be allowed to complete them.[25]

There was considerable opposition in Italy to the racial laws. The Pope publicly condemned them, the King disapproved, and many Fascists did not like them. Many people said that Mussolini had given in to German pressure. The Fascist press strongly denied this, and repeatedly emphasized – quite truthfully – that there had been no German pressure, and that the racial laws were the natural consequence of Fascist doctrine.[26]

On 6 October the racial laws were discussed at a meeting of the Fascist Grand Council. Balbo, Federzoni, De Bono and Giacomo Acerbo criticized them, but the other members supported them,[27] and the Grand Council issued a statement approving them. It declared that the measures now taken against the Jewish race were a development in Fascist policy which logically followed the March on Rome and the ban on sexual relations between Italians and blacks in Ethiopia. It recommended amendments and clarifications of the government decrees, which were duly implemented by the government.

Jews were defined as those who had either two Jewish parents or were the children of a Jewish father and a foreign Aryan mother. The children of mixed marriages were also to be considered as Jews if they had adopted the Jewish religion, but not if they had adopted another religion before 1 October 1938. The decree expelling foreign Jews from Italy was not to apply to Jews who were over sixty-five or who had married an Italian before 1 October 1938. Jews were exempted from the laws if they had fought in the First World War, in Libya, Ethiopia or Spain, or had joined the Fascist Party between 1919 and 1922, or in the last six months of 1924 – during the crisis that followed the murder of Matteotti; but even these exempted Jews were forbidden to be teachers in any school or university. All other Jews were not only prohibited from being teachers, but also from joining the Fascist Party or the army, from employing more than one hundred employees, or owning more than fifty hectares of land. The Grand Council also ruled that no Italian could marry a Jew or other non-Aryan, and no civil servant or member of the armed forces could marry any foreigner, whatever her race.[28]

The Germans were far from satisfied. On 5 September Friedrich von Strautz, of the German embassy in Rome, wrote to the Foreign Office in Berlin that the decrees showed how half-hearted the Italians were in their anti-Semitism. Unlike in Germany, where anyone with one Jewish grandparent was classified as a Jew, the Italian definition of a Jew as someone both of whose parents were Jews meant that anyone with any trace of non-Jewish blood would be exempt from the legislation, which would apply to very few people. Strautz thought that part of the trouble was that the Minister of Education, Giuseppe Bottai, had a Jewish mother; but Strautz was wrong, for Bottai was in fact one of the strongest supporters of the racial laws at the meeting of the Fascist Grand Council.[29]

The German ambassador, Baron Hans Georg von Mackensen, gave a more comprehensive explanation in his report to Berlin on 18 October. He wrote that the anti-Jewish campaign had been frustrated by the Fascist Grand Council because of the widespread sympathy for Jews in Italy, which was a much more serious problem than those officials in Germany who knew one good Jew. Mackensen thought that it was because of the anti-racist doctrines of the Catholic Church, whose influence was as strong as ever after sixteen years of Fascism. It would be unfair to blame Mussolini; for however much he might deplore this sentimental humanitarianism, he understood the Italian people, and realized that their feelings could not be ignored.[30]

Mussolini was quite content. He told Ciano that the exact provisions of the legislation against the Jews were unimportant; the essential thing was that a start had been made in inculcating anti-Semitism into the Italian people. When the time was opportune, he would enforce very severe measures against the Jews.[31]

Hitler was right. Mussolini had become anti-Semitic, without any pressure from the Germans, because it was in the nature of Fascism to be anti-Semitic. It is true that until 1938 Italian Fascism, unlike nationalist and anti-Communist movements in most other countries, was not anti-Semitic, because there was virtually no feeling against the Jews in Italy; but when the alliance with Nazi Germany gave Mussolini a reason for being anti-Semitic, he eagerly seized the opportunity. He moved from nationalism to imperialism, from imperialism to white racism, from white racism to anti-Semitism. He told Ciano that one of the advantages of his racial laws against the Jews was that they had outraged public opinion in the Western democracies, thereby consolidating his alliance with Germany.[32] He had often stated that Fascism rejected the doctrines of 1789 – they were also the American doctrines of 1776 – which had led, in the nineteenth century, to liberalism, democracy, human rights and the liberation of the Jews from persecution; Fascism had destroyed liberalism, democracy and human rights, and now renewed the persecution of the Jews.

### ◆

# CHAPTER 32

# Munich

As soon as Hitler had annexed Austria he began his preparations to seize the Sudetenland district of Czechoslovakia. He could make out a plausible justification for this by arguing that the three and a half million Germans in the Sudetenland wished to be united with Germany, though the Communists, Socialists, liberals and Jews among them emphatically did not want this. But he was in fact aiming at the destruction of Czechoslovakia, a democratic state, allied to France and, in recent years, friendly towards the Soviet Union, with a President, Beneš, who was one of the leading European liberal statesmen.

Ever since 1919 there had been tension between Czechoslovakia and Hungary, and Horthy's government in Hungary was willing to be Hitler's ally against the Czechs. Hitler also had the support of the right-wing government in Poland, and of a nationalist movement for independence in Slovakia under the leadership of a right-wing Catholic priest, Father Josef Tiso. The international anti-Fascist movement believed that after Ethiopia and Spain, Hitler's threat to Czechoslovakia was another Fascist assault on democracy; but from the start of the Czech crisis, in the spring of 1938, the British government was secretly sympathetic to Hitler's designs, and thought that the cession of the Sudetenland to Germany was the best solution.[1]

The British government sent Lord Runciman to Prague, and throughout August 1938 he put pressure on the Czechs to make more and more concessions to the Sudeten Germans; but Hitler was satisfied with nothing less than the cession of the Sudetenland to Germany. He demanded that a plebiscite should be held in the Sudetenland on the question of union with Germany. This demand was supported in an unsigned article with the title 'Letter to Runciman' in *Il Popolo d'Italia* of 15 September which was in fact written by Mussolini.[2] But the French government objected to a plebiscite, for they were afraid that it might be a precedent for demanding a plebiscite in Alsace to decide if people preferred to be under Germany or France. So the French Prime Minister, Edouard Daladier, and his Foreign Minister, Georges Bonnet, told Chamberlain that France would prefer an outright cession of the Sudetenland to Germany rather than a plebiscite.[3]

On 12 September Hitler addressed the Nazi Party annual rally in Nuremberg, and made a violent attack on Czechoslovakia, and especially on Beneš; he said that behind the three and a half million 'tortured' Sudeten Germans stood the German nation in arms.[4] But the British ambassador in Berlin, Sir Neville Henderson, thought that Hitler had 'made a good debating speech which showed no signs of mania with which he is credited in some quarters', and that he had 'emphasized his sacrifices for and love of peace'. Henderson thought that Beneš, not Hitler, was to blame for the crisis.[5]

Hitler inserted a short passage in his speech praising the Italian Fascists for their new anti-Semitic policy. He said that Italy, solving her own internal problems in her own way without asking advice from anyone, had taken the necessary steps to deal with the Jewish menace.

Hitler was threatening to begin a European war if he were not given the Sudetenland. Chamberlain became thoroughly alarmed, and asked Hitler if he could come to Germany immediately to discuss the situation with him. They met at Hitler's country residence at Berchtesgaden in Bavaria on 15 September. Chamberlain told Hitler that if Germany refrained from invading Czechoslovakia, he would persuade Beneš to cede the Sudetenland to Germany.

Mussolini kept calm during the crisis. He instructed Ciano to make it clear to Drummond (who had succeeded to his father's title of Earl of Perth) that if there was a European war, Italy would fight on Germany's side; but he was confident that there would be no war, and that Czechoslovakia would agree to cede the Sudetenland. It would be a bitter pill for Beneš to swallow, but 'swallowing bitter pills is what democracies are made for'.[6] When he heard that Chamberlain had offered to go to Berchtesgaden, he was astonished, but delighted. He said to Ciano: 'There will be no war, but this is the liquidation of English prestige. In two years England has twice been floored.'[7]

Mussolini was visiting north-east Italy. While Europe was waiting anxiously, expecting war, the international statesmen and journalists were speculating on what Mussolini would say in a speech he was to make in Trieste on 18 September. The speech confirmed the fears of the Foreign Offices in London and Paris. He emphasized the unity of the Rome–Berlin Axis. His comments on Chamberlain's visit to Berchtesgaden were very different from his remarks in private to Ciano. He congratulated Chamberlain on his initiative, and said that it showed that, despite all the propaganda from Moscow, the peoples of Europe wanted peace. He spoke about the recent racial laws against the Jews, and said that they were the logical consequence of the ideas about race that the Italian people had developed as a result of acquiring an empire. For sixteen years, ever since Fascism came to power in Italy, the Jews throughout the world had been anti-Fascist, but during this time Fascist Italy had taken no steps against the Jews. They had been patient, too patient, but now they were hitting back at the Jews.[8]

After going to the Yugoslav frontier, and exchanging salutes and courtesies with the commander of the Yugoslav garrison,[9] Mussolini spoke at a meeting in Treviso on 21 September. He said that the so-called Czechoslovakia ought to be called 'Czecho-German-Polish-Magyar-Slovakia'. It was a polyglot state which could not survive in its existing form.[10]

At 2 a.m. on 19 September the British and French ministers in Prague went to Beneš and told him that they would allow Hitler to destroy Czechoslovakia unless Beneš agreed immediately to cede the Sudetenland, but that if he did agree, Britain and France would guarantee Czechoslovakia against any further German aggression. Beneš gave way, and informed them that 'under pressure of urgent insistence' from Britain and France, 'Czechoslovak Government sadly accept French and British proposals'.[11]

On 22 September Chamberlain again flew to Germany and met Hitler at Bad Godesberg in the Rhineland. He told him that Beneš had agreed to cede the Sudetenland; but Hitler was not satisfied. He said that he did not trust Beneš to keep his promise, and that unless all his demands were accepted, he would order the German army to invade the Sudetenland in six days' time, at 2 p.m. on 28 September. Chamberlain went back to London convinced that this meant war, and ordered air raid precautions to be put into operation; shelters were dug in Hyde Park in London, and balloons erected over London as a protection against German aircraft. In Britain and France and throughout Europe, there was fear that at 2 p.m. on 28 September the Second World War would begin and would lead to the immediate destruction of civilization.

On 24 September Mussolini told a meeting at Padua that the commander-in-chief of the Czechoslovak Army was much too friendly to Moscow, and that he thought that Germany had behaved with great moderation throughout the crisis. At this point his audience broke into shouts of 'Hitler! Hitler!'; when he said that Hitler had given the Czechs a six-day respite before his troops invaded, they shouted 'Too long!' It would be absurd and criminal, said Mussolini, to cause the death of millions of Europeans to enable Master Beneš to maintain his mastery over eight different races (*per mantenere la signoria del signor Benès su otto razze diverse'*). Later that day he spoke at Belluno. He reminded his audience that Beneš had presided at the meeting of the General Assembly of the League of Nations when fifty-two nations had imposed sanctions against Italy. Now Beneš was in trouble; everyone who confronted Italy would be in trouble.[12]

At 10 a.m. on 28 September, with four hours to go before the outbreak of war, Lord Perth called on Ciano and gave him a letter from Chamberlain to Mussolini, imploring Mussolini to try to persuade Hitler to postpone the invasion of the Sudetenland by at least twenty-four hours, to give the statesmen time to save the world from war. Ciano said that he would tell Mussolini at once, as the question of peace or war would be decided in hours, not days. Mussolini immediately telephoned instructions to Bernardo Attolico, the Italian ambassador in Berlin, to go at once to Hitler and ask him to postpone the invasion for twenty-four hours. At 3 p.m. Attolico telephoned Mussolini that Hitler had agreed, and had invited Chamberlain, Daladier and Mussolini to meet him in Munich next day, on 29 September. The news reached Chamberlain while he was speaking in the House of Commons, and he told the House that he had accepted the invitation. He received a great ovation from the MPs. Ciano told Perth that Hitler had agreed to postpone the invasion and to hold the meeting in Munich only because Mussolini had asked him, and that in the case of war, Italy would be Germany's ally.[13]

Mussolini and Ciano caught the night train to Munich. They met Hitler at Kufstein, and went on to Munich in his train. Chamberlain and Daladier flew in from London and Paris, and landed at Munich airport at midday on 29 September, and the conference opened in the Führerhaus half an hour later. Ten men were present. Germany was represented by Hitler, his Foreign Minister von Ribbentrop, and Ernst von Weizsäcker, the permanent head of the German Foreign Office; Britain by Chamberlain and Sir Horace Wilson, the civil servant whom Chamberlain employed as his personal emissary in international diplomacy, though he was not attached to the Foreign Office; France by Daladier and a professional diplomat; and Italy by Mussolini and Ciano. Hitler's interpreter, Dr Paul Schmidt, was also present, as only Mussolini could speak all the four languages.

They adjourned at 3 p.m. for lunch in their hotels, and resumed at 4.30 p.m., continuing their discussions, with a short break for dinner. They were agreed that they would compel Czechoslovakia to cede the Sudetenland to Germany, that the Czechs would begin to evacuate the territory in two days' time on 1 October, and that the evacuation would be completed by 10 October. Czechoslovakia would be held responsible for ensuring that no damage was done to any property or installations, and Britain, France and Italy guaranteed to Germany that Czechoslovakia would accept the agreement. The discussions were only on questions of detail, what villages would be evacuated and occupied on the various dates.

The text of the agreement was drafted by Mussolini and Ciano, and after discussion was signed shortly before 2 a.m. Chamberlain and Daladier then saw the Czech representative, Dr Mastný; he had not been admitted to the conference, but was waiting at Chamberlain's hotel to hear the fate of his country. Chamberlain and Daladier told him at 2.15 a.m.

Next morning Hitler, Chamberlain and Mussolini had informal talks before they left for home. Hitler and Chamberlain signed a statement in which they agreed that Germany and Britain would never again go to war with each other. Chamberlain spoke to Mussolini about improving Anglo-Italian relations, and expressed his profound gratitude for the part that Mussolini had played in calling the conference and preserving world peace. Ribbentrop, too, had a private talk with Mussolini, and urged him to sign a military Three Power Pact with Germany and Japan; but Mussolini was evasive, as he did not wish to commit himself irrevocably.

Mastný flew to Prague, accompanied by a British diplomat who was to ensure that Beneš accepted the agreement. He accepted, and on 1 October Hitler's troops marched into the Sudetenland. A few days later Beneš resigned as President of Czechoslovakia and went into exile. Hitler, Mussolini, Chamberlain and Daladier had agreed at Munich that if the claims of Hungary and Poland to Czechoslovakian territory had not been settled between the parties within three months, they would meet again to dictate a further dismemberment of Czechoslovakia; but this was unnecessary, as the new Czechoslovak government ceded the province of Ruthenia to Hungary and the town of Teschen to Poland.[14]

Chamberlain was cheered by the crowds in London when he proudly showed them the document that Hitler had signed, and assured them that it was 'peace in our time'. Mussolini received an even more rapturous welcome from the Italians who flocked to see him on his journey back to Rome. Great crowds cheered him at the station in Bologna. The King, who was on holiday in the neighbourhood, came to the station in Florence to greet him. When Mussolini reached Rome, he came out on to the balcony of the Palazzo Venezia and was cheered by the crowds in the square. The secretary of the Fascist Party called to them: 'Salute the Duce, the Founder of the Empire!' When Mussolini withdrew from the balcony, the crowds called on him to come out again. They called him back ten times, and cheered, and cried 'Duce, Duce, Duce!'[15]

Mussolini was delighted with what had happened at Munich; Britain and France had joined with Germany and Italy to dismember democratic and liberal Czechoslovakia, to compel the Czechs to agree, and to redraw the map of central Europe without consulting the Soviet Union. On 25 October he told a meeting of the National Council of the Fascist Party that Prague had been the headquarters of democracy and of Bolshevism, but 'what happened at Munich was colossal'. It was 'the end of Bolshevism in Europe, the end of Communism in Europe, the end of any political influence of Russia in Europe'.[16]

At the beginning of November, the German government expelled several hundred Jews from Germany and drove them across the Polish frontier. Poland refused to admit them, and they remained for days stranded between the German and Polish frontier posts without food or shelter. Their sufferings so outraged a Polish Jew in Paris that he shot and killed an attaché at the German embassy there; the attaché was not in fact a Nazi supporter. Hitler thereupon launched an anti-Jewish reprisal throughout Germany on 9 November, on what became known as the *Kristallnacht* (Crystal Night). Nazi stormtroopers wrecked Jewish shops and other property in every town, doing a great deal of damage. The Jews had insured most of the property, but a government decree ordered the insurance companies to pay the insurance money, not to the Jews, but to the state; and in addition a collective fine of one thousand million marks was levied on the entire Jewish population. Goering cheerfully commented: 'I would not like to be a Jew in Germany now.'

Liberal opinion throughout the world was shocked by the *Kristallnacht*, which was the worst anti-Semitic outrage that the Nazis had hitherto committed; but Mussolini was pleased. 'He approves unconditionally the reprisals carried out by the Nazis,' wrote Ciano. 'He says that in their position he would have gone even further.' But he thought that the collective fine imposed on the Jews was excessive, as seven thousand million lire (one thousand million marks) placed too high a value on the life of a murdered German diplomat.[17]

Mussolini followed up his friendly talk with Chamberlain at Munich by instructing Ciano to make a formal approach, through Perth, to the British government. He told them frankly that if Anglo-Italian relations did not improve he would be obliged to commit Italy irrevocably to a military alliance with Germany against Britain and France; it might be different if Britain were prepared to take an immediate step towards improving relations by recognizing the Italian conquest of Ethiopia. Chamberlain replied that he would like to do so, but it would be difficult to persuade British public opinion to accept this unless Italy gave something in return; could Mussolini not agree to withdraw some troops from Spain?

Franco had made great advances during the summer of 1938, and had succeeded in reaching the coast north of Madrid and splitting the republican territory into two parts; and Stalin persuaded the republican government to send the International Brigade home in the hopes of winning the goodwill of Britain and France. So Mussolini decided that as Franco was winning, he could safely withdraw ten thousand Italian troops from Spain, leaving twenty thousand still fighting for Franco. Chamberlain agreed to recognize Victor Emmanuel as Emperor of Ethiopia, but asked Mussolini to keep this secret until after a debate on foreign affairs in the House of Commons.[18] On 16 November Perth presented his letters of accreditation to the 'King of Italy and Emperor of Ethiopia'.

The British government were disconcerted when on 30 November the deputies in the Chamber in Rome rose to their feet shouting 'Nice! Tunisia! Corsica!', and demanded that France cede these territories to

Italy, though Italy had not put forward claims to Tunisia since 1881, had ceded Nice to France in 1860, and Corsica had not been Italian since France captured it in 1769. Churchill was very disturbed, and it shook his faith in Mussolini. He did not mind very much if Mussolini captured Ethiopia and defeated the Communists in Spain, but he thought that this demand on France, Britain's ally, must be firmly resisted.[19]

The demonstration in the Italian Chamber did not affect Chamberlain's resolve to improve Anglo-Italian relations, which culminated in a visit to Rome by Chamberlain and his Foreign Secretary, Lord Halifax. The international press had made Chamberlain's umbrella, which he always carried, into a mascot, and it featured in gossip columns and cartoons; in his hour of triumph, after Munich, there had been a popular song in Britain, 'The Umbrella Man'. Mussolini told Rachele that Chamberlain and his umbrella would be coming to Rome. When Chamberlain arrived on 11 January 1939 his umbrella featured in the press reports. Once, during his visit, Mussolini telephoned to Rachele from the Palazzo Venezia: 'Rachele, it's happened at last! Chamberlain has lost his umbrella!' The umbrella had disappeared during a reception, but the police succeeded in finding it and returning it to Chamberlain.[20]

Mussolini wore full evening dress, with white tie and tails, when he went to the opera with Chamberlain, and at the dinner in Chamberlain's honour, at which Chamberlain proposed Victor Emmanuel's health with the words 'I raise my glass to His Majesty the King of Italy, Emperor of Ethiopia'. In their political talks, Mussolini said that while the Rome–Berlin Axis would remain the basis of Italian foreign policy, this need not prevent the development of Anglo–Italian friendship or of Franco–German friendship; and he did not exclude the possibility that the Rome–Berlin Axis might develop into a Four Power Pact. In their discussions on Spain, Mussolini said that the Italian volunteers were only 3 per cent of Franco's total forces. Chamberlain expressed his anxiety about the demonstration in the Italian Chamber when the deputies had called for Corsica, Nice and Tunisia. Mussolini said that it was a spontaneous demonstration by the deputies for which he and his government were not responsible.[21]

Chamberlain was very satisfied with his visit to Rome, and believed that it had been valuable in improving Anglo-Italian relations; but Mussolini was not impressed by Chamberlain and Halifax. He said to Ciano: 'These men are not of the stamp of Francis Drake and the other magnificent adventurers who created their Empire.'[22]

The Spanish republicans were facing final defeat. On 26 January 1939 Franco's troops entered the republican stronghold of Barcelona, and the beaten republican armies streamed across the French frontier to be interned in camps in terrible conditions by Daladier's government. Mussolini announced the news on the same evening in a speech from the balcony of the Palazzo Venezia. 'The splendid victory of Barcelona is another chapter in the history of the new Europe that we are creating.' It was a victory for the splendid troops of Franco and 'our intrepid legionaries ... The slogan of the Reds was *No pasarán* [they shall not pass]. We did pass, and we shall pass again.'[23]

# CHAPTER 33

◆

# Non-Belligerency

ON 10 February 1939 Pope Pius XI died. His Secretary of State, Cardinal Pacelli, was elected as his successor, and took the name Pius XII. Mussolini always denied that he had exerted any influence in Pacelli's favour,[1] but there is no doubt that he welcomed his election. Pius XI had often praised Mussolini, especially for his intervention against the Reds in the Spanish Civil War; but he had publicly condemned the racial laws against the Jews. Pius XII, who was even more anti-Communist than his predecessor, never publicly criticized the racial laws.

The decree of September 1938 had ordered all foreign Jews to leave Italy within six months. The time limit expired on 12 March 1939, and Jewish and humanitarian organizations throughout the world became alarmed about the eight thousand Jews who had fled to Italy from Nazi persecution: would they be expelled and handed over to the Nazis on 12 March? President Roosevelt, who had congratulated Mussolini, after the Munich agreement, on the part that he had played in preserving the peace of Europe, sent William Phillips to Rome to intercede with Mussolini for the Jews.

Phillips had an interview with Mussolini on 3 January 1939. He urged him not to expel the Jews, but to collaborate in a scheme to settle them in Africa, which would be financed by American money. Phillips asked if Mussolini would allow them to settle in Jubaland. Mussolini said that Jubaland would not be a suitable place, as they would find no means of subsistence there; he had suggested some months ago that they should settle in the northern tip of Italian Somaliland, but they had not welcomed the proposal. He foretold that ultimately every country in Europe would expel its Jews, as there was 'no room for Jews in Europe'. He thought that there was plenty of room for them in North America and in Russia, and they should emigrate there.[2] But Ciano promised Phillips that the Jews would not be expelled from Italy on 12 March, and would be given more time to find somewhere to go; and this promise was kept.

On 30 January 1939 Hitler addressed the Reichstag in Berlin on the sixth anniversary of his coming to power. He declared that he had no intention of attacking any other country and stressed his friendship with Italy. His speech was generally regarded as concili-atory by foreign governments. One sentence in his speech attracted less attention at the time than it did in later years. He said that if international Jewry started a war, the result would be not the triumph of Bolshevism throughout the world, but 'the annihilation of the Jewish race in Europe'.* There have been arguments as to whether these words show that Hitler had already decided in 1939 to murder all the European Jews and to carry out the holocaust of 1942–5, or whether it was just tough talk. Mussolini told Ciano to ask Ribben-trop to congratulate Hitler on the speech, which had particularly pleased him;[3] but it was presumably Hitler's favourable references to Italy, not his sentence about the annihilation of the Jews, which had delighted Mussolini.

On 14 March the clerico-Fascist movement of Father Tiso pro-claimed the independence of Slovakia, and next day German troops invaded Czechoslovakia and entered Prague. Hitler proclaimed that Germany had established a protectorate over the provinces of Bohemia and Moravia, and recognized Tiso's Slovakia as an indepen-dent state. Chamberlain thought that this was a flagrant breach of the Munich agreement, as Hitler had stated publicly and privately in Munich that he would not invade Czechoslovakia beyond the Sudetenland. Chamberlain denounced Hitler's action in a speech in Birmingham, and abandoned his appeasement policy. Hitler was demanding that Poland cede Danzig and the Polish Corridor to Ger-many; but Britain prepared for war, and on 31 March signed a treaty with Poland promising to go to war in defence of Poland if Hitler attacked the Poles.

Chamberlain wrote to Mussolini, his co-signatory of the Munich agreement, and suggested that Mussolini should use his influence with Hitler on behalf of peace. Hitler had not informed Mussolini in advance of his intention to annex Czechoslovakia, and it was

---

* Hitler's word 'Vernichtung' can be translated as either 'destruction', 'annihilation' or 'extermination'.

rumoured at the time, and has often been stated since, that Mussolini resented Hitler's action, and was so angry that he contemplated breaking the Rome–Berlin Axis; but there is no reliable evidence of this. Publicly, at least, Mussolini supported the German invasion of Czechoslovakia. He wrote in an unsigned article in *Il Popolo d'Italia* on 18 March that the government in Prague had not succeeded in getting rid of the legacy of the 'Beneš system', and that the separation of Slovakia and the break-up of the Czechoslovak state might have created a dangerous instability in central Europe which had been prevented by the establishment of the German protectorate over Bohemia and Moravia. If Fascist Italy had faced a similar situation, she would have acted as Germany had done. As to the 'great democracies', they had not hesitated to establish protectorates over other countries in various parts of the world.[4]

On 21 March Mussolini presided at a meeting of the Fascist Grand Council. He said that the Czechs had only themselves to blame for losing their independence, because they had failed to throw off the influence of Jews, freemasons, democrats and Bolsheviks. He emphasized that it was now more necessary than before that Italy should adhere loyally to the alliance with Germany.[5]

On 28 March Madrid surrendered to Franco, and the Spanish Civil War ended in his victory. He disregarded the friendly advice, given to him by Churchill and other British commentators, that he should show moderation in victory, and many thousands of supporters of the republican government were sentenced to death or to long terms of imprisonment. Franco asked Mussolini what he suggested should be done with the Italians who had fought on the republican side and who had been captured by the nationalist forces. Mussolini urged Franco to shoot them all.[6]

Mussolini and Franco exchanged messages congratulating each other on their great contribution to the victory in Spain. Mussolini said that Madrid, which the Communists had hoped would be the grave of Fascism, had instead been the grave of communism.[7]

Today, Mussolini's supporters in Italy – and in other countries too – claim that whatever faults he may have had, he deserves the credit for his great achievement: he defeated communism in Spain. They argue that if Spain, as well as eastern Europe, had been Communist after 1945, it would have been impossible even for the United States to have prevented all Europe from going Communist. Certainly Mussolini played an important part in Franco's victory in Spain, and triumphed there. Spain was the only sector of the battlefield between Fascism and anti-Fascism where Fascism was victorious. Within six years Fascism had been defeated in Ethiopia, the Soviet Union, the Balkans, central Europe, France, Germany and Italy; but in Spain the Fascists retained power for nearly forty years. When Fascism finally passed away, it was followed, not by communism, but by a constitutional and democratic monarchy, and communism in Russia only survived Franco's regime in Spain by a few years.

But many believed in 1939, and still believe, that Mussolini overthrew a democratically elected liberal and Socialist government in Spain. At the beginning of the civil war, the Communists were a small minority among the government supporters; it was only after Mussolini's intervention had led to Soviet intervention that the Communists gained influence in republican territory. Mussolini's triumph over communism in Spain was also a triumph over parliamentary democracy and human rights.

On Good Friday, 7 April, Italian forces, without warning, invaded Albania and overran the country within twenty-four hours. Albania had for many years been under Italian economic and political influence, but Mussolini had only recently decided to drive out King Zog and annex it. He did not tell Hitler in advance, just as Hitler had not told him about his intention to invade Czechoslovakia; but Hitler accepted it as happily as Mussolini had accepted the German annexation of Bohemia and Moravia. Ribbentrop assured Mussolini that Germany would always welcome any Italian victory.[8] It has been suggested that Mussolini decided to seize Albania out of pique at the German action in Czechoslovakia, and from a determination not to be upstaged by Hitler. It is more likely that he wished to strike another blow that would expose the impotence of the Western democracies and their inability to maintain peace and uphold their principles of international law. A delegation of Albanian notables duly arrived in Rome to offer the crown of Albania to Victor Emmanuel, who was proclaimed 'King of Italy and Albania, Emperor of Ethiopia'.[9]

On 22 May Ciano and Ribbentrop in Berlin signed the 'Pact of Steel' which created a military alliance between Italy and Germany. Britain and France, on their side, had guaranteed to defend Poland against German aggression. But Chamberlain hesitated to follow the advice that he was given by the Labour opposition and by a small group of Conservative MPs led by Churchill, to make an alliance with the Soviet Union against Germany. On 26 May Chamberlain wrote in his diary: 'I must confess to the most profound distrust of Russia. I have no belief whatever in her ability to maintain an effective offensive, even if she wanted to.'[10] Apart from their hatred of communism, the British government were influenced by the advice of their military advisers that Stalin had greatly weakened the Red Army by the drastic purge that he had conducted in 1937, when most of his leading generals had been executed as traitors. The British General Staff advised the government that the Soviet Army would be unable to fight for more than a few weeks, whereas the Polish Army was the second strongest in Europe after the French Army. Eden wrote in later years that throughout the crises of the 1930s, the British government were grossly misled by the information and advice that they received from their military advisers.[11]

In June Hitler decided to attack Poland in the autumn. He kept his intention very secret, and did not tell Mussolini; nor did he tell him that he was conducting secret negotiations for a pact with the Soviet Union, as Stalin became convinced that the British government would not support him in an anti-German alliance. On 11 August Ribbentrop informed Ciano about the German plans against Poland, though he still did not tell him about the negotiations with the Soviet Union.[12]

There was a difference of opinion between Hitler and Mussolini about war. Hitler wanted a war against Poland and the Western powers immediately, before Britain had completed her rearmament programme. In the summer of 1939 he frankly told the French ambassador in Berlin that he was now aged fifty and preferred the idea of war at fifty to war at fifty-five. Mussolini believed that a war of the Axis powers against the Western democracies was ultimately inevitable, but that Italy was not yet ready for it; he wished to postpone the war until 1942 at the earliest, and had announced his intention of holding an international exhibition in Rome in 1942. He hoped to settle the Danzig crisis in 1939 by another Munich conference, at which Britain and France would agree, at the last moment, to sacrifice Poland, as they had sacrificed Czechoslovakia, to preserve peace.

On 23 August Ribbentrop flew to Moscow and signed the German–Soviet Non-Aggression Pact. The secret clauses of the pact, by which Germany and the Soviet Union agreed to partition Poland, were not disclosed. Mussolini congratulated Hitler on a brilliant diplomatic manoeuvre which had double-crossed Britain and France and left Germany free to invade Poland without any fear of being involved in a war with the Soviet Union;[13] but, unlike Hitler, Mussolini hoped to avoid a European war; and he suggested a Four Power Conference, another Munich. But Chamberlain no longer trusted Hitler to observe any agreement that he might make at a Four Power Conference.

On 1 September German troops invaded Poland. Britain and France immediately sent an ultimatum to Germany stating that they would declare war unless German troops withdrew within forty-eight hours to the German frontier. Hitler did not reply. Next day Mussolini proposed to Chamberlain that they should urgently open negotiations with Hitler;[14] but Chamberlain insisted that there could be no negotiations unless the German Army withdrew from Poland. On 3 September Britain and France declared war on Germany. Mussolini surprised international diplomatic circles by not entering the war on Germany's side, but declaring that Italy would adopt a policy of 'non-belligerency'. She was not 'neutral' in a war in which her German ally was involved, but for the moment, at least, she would not engage in hostilities.

Although Mussolini had congratulated Hitler on the German–Soviet Pact, many Italian Fascists were disconcerted that their Nazi ally had made friends with the Bolshevik enemy. The German armies quickly overran western Poland, and on 17 September the Red Army invaded eastern Poland. Polish resistance collapsed under this double invasion, and within a few days German and Soviet officers had met and saluted each other on the demarcation line that had been agreed in the secret clauses of the German–Soviet Pact. This increased the opposition to the pact, and to Hitler's policy, in Italian Fascist circles.

The Italian press published a series of articles attacking Bolshevism, exposing the horrors of life in the Soviet Union under the rule of the secret police, the NKVD. The Fascist journalists in Italy had been indulging in anti-Soviet propaganda for many years; but now it acquired a new significance. Their articles made no reference to Germany, but the German Nazis were not pleased, as they interpreted the articles as a veiled criticism of the German–Soviet Pact. The German ambassador in Rome raised the matter with Ciano.

Mussolini and Ciano made no apology for the articles, but they were soon discontinued.

By the beginning of October, Poland was conquered, and Hitler, in a speech in the Reichstag, invited Britain and France to make peace. Mussolini had every hope that Chamberlain and Daladier would be forced to accept Hitler's peace offer, for the British and French armies would be unable to attack the Germans on the Western Front without suffering very heavy losses. He blamed Britain and France for the outbreak of war. He said that it would have been possible to have reached a peaceful solution of the Danzig dispute, through his mediation, in September 1939 if Britain and France had not imposed the unreasonable, humiliating and unacceptable condition that the German armies in Poland must withdraw to the German frontier before any negotiation could take place.[15] Surely Chamberlain and Daladier would not be so obstinate as to continue the war when nothing could be done to save Poland and the war in the west must inevitably end in stalemate.

Farinacci and Preziosi, who for many years had been the leading anti-Semite in Italy, were strongly supporting Germany, denouncing Britain and France, and accusing the Jews of being responsible for the war. At the meeting of the Fascist Grand Council on 7 December 1939 Farinacci proposed that Italy should immediately enter the war on the German side; but Mussolini opposed this, and said that the time was not yet ripe for intervention.[16] On 5 February 1940 Farinacci wrote to Mussolini that there were 'honorary Jews' in the Fascist Party leadership who were preventing Italy from fighting at the side of her German ally: these honorary Jews were Balbo, De Bono, De Vecchi and Federzoni.[17] But Mussolini issued a directive to the press to praise the Germans but not to attack Britain and France.[18]

Roosevelt sent his Under-Secretary of State, Sumner Welles, to Europe to attempt to mediate between the belligerents in the hope of ending the war. Sumner Welles went first to Rome, and had a meeting with Mussolini on 26 February 1940. Mussolini said that the responsibility for the continuation of the war rested with Britain and France, who refused to accept the fact that they could not defeat the Germans on the Western Front, where for the last six months the Allied and German armies had faced each other while hardly firing a shot. Mussolini thought that the Allied war aims of insisting on the restoration of the independence of Czechoslovakia and Austria were absurd. Sumner Welles went on to Berlin, Paris and London for talks, before returning to Rome for a second meeting with Mussolini on 16 March on his way home to Washington. He had not succeeded in persuading the British and French governments to modify their war aims or to accept any other peace terms.[19]

During the seven months from September 1939 to April 1940, the period that commentators in Britain called the 'phoney war', Germany and the Allies did not engage in any serious military activity, either on land or in the air. There was fighting only at sea; the Germans sank a British battleship in the harbour at Scapa Flow in the north of Scotland, and the British sank a German battleship off the coast of South America. The British Navy enforced a blockade, preventing shipments to and from Germany. Britain also engaged in an intensive propaganda war against German Nazism over the radio, and in the press in neutral countries; but they adopted a very different attitude towards Fascist Italy. They did not want to annoy Mussolini, and hoped to encourage him to remain neutral by contrasting him favourably with Hitler.

In December 1939 a semi-official pamphlet, *The British Case*, was published in London. It was written by Lord Lloyd, a former colonial governor and right-wing Conservative MP who had become a hate figure to the left wing because of his severity in suppressing unrest in India and Egypt. The Foreign Secretary, Lord Halifax, wrote the preface. Lord Lloyd stated that in this war Britain was fighting for the principles of Christian civilization against Nazi Germany and her ally, godless communist Russia. He stressed that German Nazism and Russian Communism had nothing in common with Italian Fascism, which was based on the principles of Christianity.[20] But from Mussolini's point of view the British government, though they might be friendly and pro-Fascist in words, were less friendly in their actions, for the British fleet stopped Italian merchant ships from trading with Germany, and prevented the transport of coal by sea from Germany to Italy.[21]

On 30 November 1939 the Soviet Union invaded Finland, after the Finnish government had refused to cede to the Soviet Union some territory that Stalin thought was too close to Leningrad for the city's safety, in exchange for a larger area of worthless territory further north. Nothing could more clearly illustrate the antagonism of the British and French governments to the Soviet Union, and the different way in which they regarded communism and Fascism, than their reactions to Mussolini's aggression in Ethiopia in 1935 and Stalin's aggression in Finland in 1939. The British government sent two air squadrons to help the Finns, and allowed serving British soldiers in wartime to leave the British Army in order to fight for Finland. Britain and France were on the point of large-scale military intervention in support of Finland when a Soviet military breakthrough induced the Finns to make peace.

Public opinion in Italy strongly sympathized with the Finns, and increased the Fascist criticism of their German allies for having made the pact with the Soviet Union. Mussolini broke off diplomatic relations with the Soviet Union and sent forty planes to help the Finns; he wished he could have done more for that gallant little country whose resistance to the Red Army had aroused great admiration in Fascist Italy.[22]

On 3 January 1940 Mussolini wrote a long letter to Hitler about the German–Soviet Pact. He wrote that after nearly forty years of political experience he well understood the need for tactical manoeuvring, but this must always be accompanied by a determination to adhere to fundamental principles as a long-term objective. He had congratulated Hitler on his pact with Stalin, which had safeguarded Germany against attack from the Soviet Union while she was going to war with Poland and the Western democracies; and he himself had recognized the Soviet government in 1924. But they must never forget that their fundamental objective was the destruction of Bolshevism, against which he and Hitler had fought in Spain. He thought that he must point out that the German–Soviet Pact had aroused great misgivings in Italy, and also, he believed, among many National Socialists in Germany. He came close to urging Hitler to attack the Soviet Union, for he wrote that the great spaces in Russia provided more than twenty-one million square kilometres of fertile territory where Germany could settle her surplus population.[23]

Hitler waited for two months before replying to Mussolini, but then wrote him a long letter on 6 March. He wrote that, in considering the question of relations with Russia, he had to take into consideration the general European situation, and also the fact that Stalin was transforming the nature of Bolshevism in the direction of Russian nationalism. The Jewish and internationalist influence in Bolshevism was diminishing. As soon as Litvinov left the Soviet Foreign Office, the Russians had made friendly overtures to Germany, and Russia seemed now to be developing into a state with a nationalist ideology.

Hitler believed that it would be possible for Russia and Germany to work together in friendship for peace.[24]

A few days later Ribbentrop came to Rome, and Mussolini repeated to him the warnings about the German–Soviet Pact that he had expressed in his letter to Hitler. His own government had been the first in Europe to recognize the Soviet Union in 1924; but diplomatic recognition and pacts must be combined with continued ideological opposition to communism. He said that he had been interested in the passages in Hitler's letter about the changing nature of Bolshevism, and asked Ribbentrop if his experiences during his two visits to Moscow had confirmed the view that Stalin had abandoned his plans for world revolution. 'Do you really believe it?' asked Mussolini. Ribbentrop said that he did believe it, that Lazar Mosseiyevich Kaganovich was the only member of the Politburo of the Communist Party of the Soviet Union who was a Jew, and that after the dismissal of Litvinov from the Foreign Office the Jewish influence in the Soviet government had ceased to exist. Ribbentrop had been surprised at how well he got on with the Soviet leaders at their banquet in the Kremlin.

Mussolini and Ribbentrop discussed the internal situation in Britain and France, and agreed that there was much opposition to the war in both countries. In France the Communists were distributing illegal newspapers in which they denounced the war as an imperialist war. Ribbentrop said that some of these French Communist newspapers were printed in Germany. Mussolini mentioned that there were 24,000 conscientious objectors in Britain who had refused to obey the call-up for the army, and Ribbentrop referred to the number of votes cast for the anti-war candidate at a recent by-election in Britain.[25]

On 18 March Mussolini met Hitler on the frontier on the Brenner. Mussolini explained that he had always intended to bring Italy into the war on the German side at the appropriate moment; he had not yet declared war because he knew that the German Army could crush the Poles without Italian aid, and thought that he could, at present, do more to help Germany as a non-belligerent. Hitler accepted this argument, and said that he was sure that Mussolini would declare war at the appropriate time.[26]

On returning to Rome Mussolini, on 31 March, wrote a memorandum for the King, in which he considered the policy that Italy should pursue with regard to the war. Only eight copies were made of this highly secret document: one each for the King, Marshal Badoglio, Marshal Graziani, Ciano, the Ministry of Italian Africa, the chiefs of the navy and air force, and one to be retained by Mussolini. After stating that it was difficult to forecast what was likely to happen in the war, Mussolini wrote that, as Sumner Welles had realized, there was no possibility of a negotiated peace, because Britain and France insisted on restoring the independence of Poland, Czechoslovakia and Austria, and Hitler would never agree to this. The French and British would remain on the defensive on the Western Front, and would try to attack elsewhere, perhaps in the Balkans or the Caucasus, but would rely mainly on action at sea and enforcing the blockade against Germany. Nor would the Germans attack the Maginot Line on the Western Front, as this would be too risky, and a defeat would have disastrous consequences on German morale.

Italy would never be truly free while she was imprisoned in the Mediterranean; to be free she must do away with the British strongpoints at Gibraltar and Suez. Italy could not achieve this by remaining neutral throughout the war; if she remained neutral she would count for nothing in the post-war world, like Switzerland. It was unthinkable that Italy should enter the war against Germany; therefore the only possibility was for her to join in on the German side. But Italy could not afford to fight a long war; so she must enter the war at just the right moment, not too early and not too late. After declaring war, Italy must stand on the defensive on her frontier with France, and only attack there if the French Army had collapsed under a German offensive, which seemed unlikely to happen. Italy would also stand on the defensive in Libya, both against the French in Tunisia and against the British in Egypt. If the situation arose, Italy might take the offensive in the Balkans, against either Yugoslavia or Greece; and she should definitely take the offensive in Ethiopia, against the British in Somaliland and the French at Djibouti, and at sea.[27]

Mussolini said nothing in his memorandum of 31 March about the date on which Italy should enter the war; but at the beginning of April 1940, Hitler invaded Denmark and Norway to forestall the British plan to mine Norwegian waters to prevent Norwegian trade with Germany. Mussolini wrote to Hitler congratulating him on his preventive strike. The German success in Norway convinced Mussolini that the Germans would win the war sooner than he had hitherto expected, and he decided that Italy should declare war before it was all over. On 1 May he told his ministers that in the nineteenth century France had been victorious because she was revolutionary. Now France and England were conservative. Germany was no longer the Germany of the Prussian Junkers, but a Germany of the people that had put an end to plutocracy.[28]

On 10 May Hitler launched his attack on the Western Front through Belgium and Holland – the attack that both Mussolini and Hitler's generals had thought would be suicidal. Within three weeks the German armies had conquered Holland and Belgium, and had forced the British to evacuate their forces from Dunkirk. The German newsreels, which were seen in the Italian cinemas, showed the devastating air raids on Rotterdam, the flight of the French civilians along the roads before the advancing German armies, the old women wringing their hands and the little children wandering helplessly amid the ruins of the bombed cities. The German commentator in the newsreels ended by saying: 'We must thank the Führer and his soldiers that nothing like this can ever happen to us.'[29]

On the day of the German attack in the west, Churchill replaced Chamberlain as Prime Minister at the head of a coalition government of Conservatives, Labour and Liberals. At the meeting of the War Cabinet on 15 May Lord Halifax, who had remained Foreign Secretary, suggested that Churchill should make a personal appeal to Mussolini to stay out of the war.[30] Churchill agreed, and wrote the letter next day. He reminded Mussolini of their very friendly meeting in Rome some years before, and assured him that he valued the traditional Anglo-Italian friendship. Britain and Italy could no doubt 'inflict grievous injuries upon one another and maul each other, and darken the Mediterranean with our strife'; but he hoped that Mussolini would not give the signal for war, which 'will never be given by us'.[31]

Mussolini replied on 18 May. He wrote that the long tradition of Anglo-Italian friendship had been ended by Britain when she took the lead in persuading the League of Nations to impose sanctions against Italy during the Ethiopian war, although Italy's action in Ethiopia had not caused any harm to British interests. If Britain had gone to war to honour her treaty obligations to Poland, Churchill would understand why Italy would go to war to honour her treaty obligations to Germany.[32]

As the German armies advanced through France, Paul Reynaud, who had succeeded Daladier as French Prime Minister, suggested to

Churchill that Britain and France should ask Mussolini to mediate with Hitler in the hope of obtaining a negotiated peace. The French proposal was discussed at the meeting of the British War Cabinet on 27 May. Halifax wished to accept Reynaud's proposal, but it was strongly opposed by Churchill, Chamberlain, Sir Archibald Sinclair (the Liberal leader), and by the two Labour ministers, Clement Attlee and Arthur Greenwood. After a heated discussion Halifax threatened to resign, but Churchill persuaded him not to do this.[33]

The German success in France, which Mussolini had not expected, convinced him that he must hurry and enter the war before it had ended in a German victory. On 26 May he informed his generals that he would declare war on Britain and France on 5 June. They persuaded him to give them a few more days in which to make the necessary preparations.[34] On the evening of 10 June Mussolini spoke to the crowds from the balcony of the Palazzo Venezia. Arrangements had been made to broadcast his speech to the people in all the other cities of Italy.

He told the men and women of Italy, the Empire and Albania that 'the declaration of war' – and he could not proceed because the crowd cheered and cheered, and shouted 'Duce! Duce! War! War!' for nearly two minutes before he held up his hand to command them to silence, and continued: 'was delivered to the ambassadors of Great Britain and France', the two states who had incited fifty-two nations to impose sanctions against Italy, and who had rejected the Führer's peace offer of 6 October. 'People of Italy, to arms, and show your tenacity, your courage and your valour.'[35]

# CHAPTER 34

# The War between Blood and Gold

T HE day after war was declared, the King appointed Mussolini as commander-in-chief of all the Italian armed forces. Mussolini immediately ordered Badoglio to launch an offensive against France; but the British Air Force was quicker off the mark, and on the second day of the war bombed Turin, killing fourteen civilians and wounding thirty.[1] On 26 June Mussolini wrote to Hitler and asked him, when the time came to bomb London, to allow some Italian air squadrons to take part in the raids in revenge for the British air raid on Turin.[2] The Italian Air Force at once made repeated and heavy air raids on the British naval base in Malta, and the civilian population in the island. Bruno Mussolini distinguished himself in the air raids on Malta.

Within a week of the declaration of war, the Italian Army had invaded France and captured Menton and other places on the French Riviera; and the German armies had entered Paris. The eighty-four-year-old Marshal Pétain, the hero of the First World War, became Head of State in France; he established his capital in Vichy, and signed an armistice with Germany and with Italy. On 18 June Mussolini went to Munich to meet Hitler and to stake his claim to a share of the spoils of the victory over France. He asked Hitler to make the French cede Nice, Corsica, Tunisia and Djibouti to Italy. Ciano suggested to Ribbentrop that Italy might also be given Algeria and Morocco. But Hitler was non-committal, and told Mussolini that he had not yet decided what peace terms to impose on France.[3]

In Libya, small-scale operations began at once against the British forces in Egypt. Balbo himself took part in air operations, leading his squadron as they flew over the desert looking for British armoured cars to attack. On 28 June Balbo flew off with his squadron from the airfield at Tobruk to search for the British. While he was engaged on the operation, some British planes flew in low over the airfield, dropping their bombs as they flew off. When Balbo and his squadron returned to the airfield, the anti-aircraft gunners there thought that Balbo's planes were the British making a second attack. They opened fire. Balbo's plane was shot down, and Balbo was killed – by the 'friendly fire' of his own men.[4]

The RAF respected Balbo as a brave enemy. Some British planes flew over the Italian airfield and dropped a wreath with a message paying tribute to him. Mussolini ordered the Italian press not to report this; he wanted the Italians to hate the British, not to respect them for an act of chivalry.[5]

Some members of the hierarchy thought that Mussolini had not shown any signs of grief when he heard of Balbo's death, and that his official condolences were cold. It helped spread the rumours that circulated at the time, and ever since, that Mussolini was jealous of Balbo's popularity. But it was probably nothing more than another case of Mussolini adopting his pose of the hard man who never thanked anyone for loyal service, but accepted it as a simple performance by his subordinates of their duty.

He was certainly much more distressed two months later, when Claretta Petacci underwent an urgent operation for peritonitis. The peritonitis had been caused by a miscarriage – or that, at least, is what the records say; but although it is possible for a miscarriage to lead to peritonitis, it is very unlikely. It much more frequently follows an abortion. Mussolini had banned abortion in Italy, partly to please the Church, and also because, like Stalin, he worried about a falling birthrate, and needed soldiers to fight in twenty years' time. But there are exceptions to every rule, and Mussolini's entourage, whether or not they deserved the name of 'the Cheka', were certainly prepared to break the law in the interests of Italy and of Fascism. And what better reason could there be to perform an illegal abortion than to prevent the birth of the Duce's illegitimate child and the scandal that might ensue?

Claretta was operated on in her home in a villa in the Camilluccia district of Rome on 27 August 1940. The urgent calls of government and of the war did not prevent Mussolini from going to the villa and anxiously remaining there while the operation was performed. It appeared to be going well, and then Claretta's condition worsened, and on 1 September Mussolini was told that her life was in great danger; an operation for peritonitis carried a 40 per cent risk of death. But the crisis passed, and Claretta was restored to full health. The miscarriage, or abortion, did not prevent the rumours; when Claretta's sister-in-law gave birth next year to Major Marcello Petacci's son, the story spread that the baby, Ferdinando Petacci, was the illegitimate son of Claretta and Mussolini.[6] But Rachele heard nothing about the rumours, or about Claretta's abortion and Mussolini's visit to her villa.

Nearly everyone in Europe believed that Germany had won the war; but when Hitler in July offered to make peace, Churchill did not reply, and in August and September the Luftwaffe tried unsuccessfully to destroy the RAF as a prelude to the invasion of Britain. As Mussolini had requested, a squadron of Italian planes joined the Luftwaffe in France and took part in the air raids on London. On 11 November some Italian bombers escorted by some sixty fighters attacked British shipping in the Medway; eight of the bombers and five fighters were shot down.[7]

On 4 October Hitler and Mussolini met on the Brenner. Hitler told Mussolini that he was going to meet Franco at Hendaye on the Spanish frontier and Pétain at Montoire. He hoped to persuade Pétain's Vichy regime to collaborate with Germany, and Franco to enter the war on the side of the Axis. Mussolini was not happy about Hitler meeting Pétain; the better Hitler got on with Pétain, the less chance there was of his agreeing to give Italy the French territories of Nice, Corsica, Tunisia and Djibouti.

Mussolini tried to persuade Hitler that he should not trust Pétain. He said that he was sure that Pétain's Vichy government was in secret contact, through the British embassy in Lisbon, with Charles de Gaulle, the leader in London of the Free French Forces who were fighting on the side of the British. Hitler said that his intelligence services had informed him that they had no reason to believe that the Vichy government was in touch with de Gaulle or the British. He told Mussolini that he would settle the future of the French colonies in the peace settlement after the war, and would then give full consideration to Italy's claims; but he was too busy for the moment fighting the war, and the French colonies would remain under French control until the war was won.[8]

Hitler and Mussolini agreed that they would meet again in Florence on 28 October to discuss the results of Hitler's meetings with Franco and Pétain. Soon afterwards Ribbentrop informed Mussolini that German intelligence had discovered that the Greek government had agreed to grant Britain naval and air bases in Greece to assist them in their operations against Italy in the Mediterranean. Mussolini decided to forestall them by invading Greece, and ordered the army to launch the invasion on 28 October, the anniversary of the March on Rome. On 19 October he wrote to Hitler and explained that he faced the same situation that had confronted Hitler six months earlier in April, when Hitler had invaded Norway as a pre-emptive strike to prevent the British from occupying the country.[9]

On 28 October the Italian Air Force raided Salonika, and Italian troops in Albania invaded Greece. Hitler first heard about the Italian invasion when he reached Bologna the same day on his way to meet Mussolini in Florence; but the story that he was angry, because Mussolini had given him no intimation of his intention in advance, is untrue. It was only the date which Mussolini had not revealed to Hitler in his letter of 19 October.

The Italians at first advanced against the Greeks, but were hampered by bad weather. Then the Greeks counter-attacked, and invaded Albania. The six thousand Albanian troops serving in the Italian Army mutinied, refused to fight, and deserted in large numbers. After three weeks of campaigning, Mussolini wrote to Hitler on 22 November and told him that after an initial success the Italians had been forced to retreat. He wrote that there were three reasons for this: firstly, the sudden onset of bad weather; secondly, the mutiny by the Albanians; and thirdly because the Bulgarians, who were supposed to be allies of Germany and Italy, had withdrawn their troops from the Greek frontier, thus enabling the Greeks to transfer eight divisions, who had been facing the Bulgarians in Thrace, to the Albanian front and send them into action against the Italians.[10]

From Libya Graziani invaded Egypt in September 1940, and advanced against the British; but in December the British launched a counter-attack, drove back the Italians, and invaded Libya. They rapidly advanced, and captured Sidi Barrani, Bardia, Tobruk and Benghazi. Only in East Africa were things going well for the Italians. Their army of 300,000 Italian and native soldiers in Ethiopia and Italian Somaliland invaded British Somaliland and Kenya in the south and the Sudan in the north.

On the night of 11–12 November the British bombed the naval

base of Taranto on the heel of Italy, with devastating effect. It was a heavy blow to Italian morale.[11]


Hitler had been pleased with his meeting with Pétain, but was very annoyed with Franco. He had completely failed to persuade Franco to enter the war on the side of the Axis. Franco had said that Spain had not yet recovered from her losses in the civil war, and as the harvest had failed there was a food shortage in Spain; Hitler would have to send food supplies to Spain and give her large-scale financial aid before Franco could contemplate declaring war on Britain. Hitler had hoped that, if Franco joined in, he would be able to send German troops into Spain from where they could attack Gibraltar; the troops who had been selected for this operation were already training in France for the attack on the rock.

Hitler thought that Franco was being most ungrateful, in view of the aid that he had given to Franco during the civil war, and that the financial demands Franco was making as a condition for joining in the war were quite unreasonable. He considered the possibility of invading Spain and ordering his troops to march from the Pyrenees to Gibraltar and attack the rock; but if he did this, and the Spanish Army resisted, they would be able to hold up the Germans for long enough to allow the British to send reinforcements to Franco and to Gibraltar; and the result would be that Franco would be converted from a friendly neutral into an enemy and ally of Britain.[12]

When Mussolini visited Hitler at Berchtesgaden on 19 January 1941, Hitler suggested that Mussolini might attempt to persuade Franco to enter the war; as Mussolini had helped Franco even more than Hitler had done during the Spanish Civil War, Mussolini might be able to exercise more influence on Franco than Hitler himself could do. On 12 February Mussolini and Franco met at Bordighera on the Italian Riviera, a popular holiday resort in summer but almost deserted in February in wartime. Their Foreign Ministers Ciano and Serrano Suñer were in attendance.

Mussolini told Franco that when he had met Hitler at Berchtesgaden, Hitler had expressed his profound admiration for Franco, but was disappointed that Franco had not entered the war on the side of the Axis. Hitler had asked Mussolini to speak to Franco about this. Mussolini then surveyed the war situation in an attempt to convince Franco that Britain could not win the war. She had no potential ally left in Europe except perhaps Russia; but Hitler had 235 divisions ready to repulse a Russian attack. Mussolini thought that Stalin was too shrewd to allow himself to be persuaded by the Jews to attack Germany. It was true that the British were advancing in North Africa; but Hitler had decided to send German troops to Libya, and Italian reinforcements were also on their way there. The Italians had been repulsed by the Greeks in Albania because they had launched an attack with only six divisions against fifteen Greek divisions. He admitted that he had committed the same mistake that the Austrians had committed against the Serbs in 1914 and the Russians against the Finns last year: he had been over-confident and had initially attacked with insufficient forces.

Mussolini said that Hitler believed that it was because of these Italian setbacks that Franco had not entered the war; but Franco hastened to say that he was profoundly grateful for the help that Mussolini had given him during the civil war, and had no doubt that the valiant Italian soldiers would defeat the British in North Africa and the Greeks in Albania. He deeply regretted that he was unable to bring Spain into the great war that was being fought for the cause of international Fascism; but unfortunately Spain had not yet recovered from the effects of the civil war, and faced an acute short-age of grain; only eight of the Spanish provinces had enough grain to last three months. There was also the question of Spain's claims for colonies, and Franco feared that Hitler would not satisfy these claims as long as he was pursuing his policy of friendship with Vichy France.

Mussolini asked Franco: If Germany satisfied Spain's colonial aspirations, would he then come into the war, and when? Franco said that if his conditions were fulfilled, Spain would come into the war, but he could not say when; and he added, rather cryptically, that the timing of Spain's entry into the war depended more on Germany than on Spain. This was all that Mussolini could get out of Franco, who never replied to Mussolini's question as to when Spain would enter the war, although Mussolini asked him three times.[13]


The British continued their air raids on Italian cities. On 9 February 1941 the British Navy and Air Force bombarded Genoa from the sea and bombed it from the air. It was hoped that this would have a strong effect on Italian morale, which, Churchill noted, 'was said to be low'. Mussolini replied defiantly when he spoke to the Fascist *gerarchi* in Rome on 23 February. If the British attack on Genoa had been designed to interrupt communications and damage industrial installations in Genoa, he could understand the reason for the operation; but if the object had been to terrorize and demoralize the population, this proved that Churchill did not have the slightest understanding of the spiritual force of the Italian people and of Fascism.[14]

At the beginning of March Mussolini went to Albania to encourage his troops, but the Italians continued to retreat. In England the public chortled delightedly over the Italian discomfiture, and the people were singing a popular song about it:

> O what a surprise for the Duce, the Duce, he can't put it over
> the Greeks;
> O what a surprise for the Duce, they do say he's had no
> spaghetti for weeks.

Edda Ciano had joined the Italian Red Cross, and sailed to Albania to play her part in nursing the soldiers. This time it was the turn of the British to bomb the Red Cross. They attacked the hospital ship in which Edda was sailing to Albania in the middle of the night, and sank the ship. Edda and the other nurses had to clamber out of their cabins and take to a raft; she was rescued and brought ashore after she had been in the water for five hours. By the time that Mussolini visited her at Valona she had fully recovered from her experience without suffering any physical or psychological injury.[15]

Hitler sent his general Erwin Rommel with German troops to reinforce the Italians in Libya, and the Germans and Italians drove the British towards the Egyptian frontier, recapturing Benghazi and passing Tobruk, which held out as an island of British resistance behind the Axis lines. In the Balkans the decision of the government of Yugoslavia to sign a pact with Germany caused a popular revolution against the pact in Belgrade. Hitler responded by making a devastating air raid on Belgrade and invading Yugoslavia. Italian troops joined in the invasion.

The Croatian Ustaše Fascists under Pavelić welcomed the Germans as liberators. Although Pavelić had for some years been living as a refugee in Italy, Mussolini had taken care not to meet him; now he welcomed him as an honoured guest in Rome and installed him as dictator in Zagreb. The Croats were obliged in return to cede Dalmatia to Italy, and install King Victor Emmanuel's cousin as King of Croatia with Pavelić as Regent and Poglavnik (Leader). Italian troops also occupied Montenegro, where another of Victor Emmanuel's cousins was proclaimed as King. Neither the King of Croatia nor the King of Montenegro ever visited his kingdom.

As German troops had now intervened in the Balkans, they came to the rescue of the Italians who were fighting the Greeks in Albania. Churchill, against the advice of his generals, took the decision, on political grounds, to withdraw troops from North Africa to help the Greeks; but they were unable to prevent the Germans from overrunning Greece. The Germans handed over Athens to the Italians, who shared with the Germans the task of occupying Greece. In May the Germans gained another success when their paratroopers captured Crete from the British, although they were outnumbered by the British.

In Croatia Pavelić's Ustaše proceeded to arrest, intern and massacre large numbers of Serbs and Jews in the concentration camp of Jasenovać and in the villages of Croatia. Mussolini had intensified the persecution of the Italian Jews after Italy entered the war. He ordered that they were to be regarded as enemy aliens, because international Jewry had always been anti-Fascist; their radio sets were confiscated, their bank accounts were frozen, they were subjected to all kinds of persecution, and many of them were arrested and interned in camps or sent to forced labour.[16] But in Croatia the Jews looked to the Italian Army to protect them against the Ustaše. Many Jews escaped to the Italian zone of occupation and to Italian Dalmatia. The Italian authorities saved them from being massacred, and in some cases sent them across the Adriatic to comparative safety in Italy.[17]


In January 1941 the British in East Africa launched an offensive against the Italians both in Kenya and in the Sudan, and advanced on Ethiopia from both south and north.[18] They incited the Ethiopian resistance groups to rise against the Italians. The Emperor Haile Selassie came from his refuge in Bath to the British headquarters in

Khartoum, and by the beginning of January was again on Ethiopian soil. The Italians put up a fierce resistance, particularly at the Keren Pass, and the British Army with their Indian troops suffered substantial losses; but by the beginning of April they had occupied all Ethiopia, the Italian armies there had surrendered, and Haile Selassie was reigning as Emperor in Addis Ababa. On 9 May Churchill wrote to him: 'Your Majesty was the first of the lawful sovereigns to be driven from his throne and country by the Fascist-Nazi criminals, and you are the first to return in triumph.'[19] Churchill was speaking a different language in 1941 than he had spoken in 1927, 1935 and May 1940.

On 28 March a British fleet of thirteen warships sailing out from Alexandria attacked, with the support of aircraft, the Italian battleship *Vittorio Veneto* in a night engagement off Cape Matapan in Greece. The *Vittorio Veneto* was damaged, and in the course of the next few days the Italians lost three of their thirteen destroyers and five of their eight carriers, the British losing only two aircraft and no ships; 2,400 Italian sailors were killed or drowned. The British commander-in-chief, Admiral Sir Andrew Cunningham, reported that he had taught the Italian fleet a lesson that would keep them out of action for the rest of the year.[20]

After meeting Hitler on the Brenner, Mussolini addressed the Chamber on 10 June 1941, the first anniversary of Italy's declaration of war. It was no longer an elected Chamber of Deputies, but a body appointed by Mussolini, the 'Chamber of the Fasces and the Corporations'. He had a series of disasters to report, but he adopted a very confident tone, telling them that they had achieved victory in the war against Greece at a cost of 13,502 men killed, and they had agreed with their German allies that Athens and most of Greece should be under Italian occupation. The British success in Ethiopia was a chapter in the personal vendetta between Italy and Britain, but had had no significant effect on the general course of the war. It did not alter the fact that however long the war lasted, Britain could not win it because she had no allies and no foothold in Europe, and the United States could not help her in this respect.

He hailed the creation of a Croatian state once again after nine hundred years under the Poglavnik Ante Pavelić, who had lived for many years in Italy. He paid tribute to Franco; he understood why it was impossible for Spain to come into the war, and Italy asked only for her moral support in their fight against plutocracy, Judaism and freemasonry. After denouncing the 'totalitarian' regime of 'Delano Roosevelt' in the United States, he said that the war was a struggle between blood and Jewish gold. The Axis, the revolutionary expression of the new Europe, would be victorious. 'The just God, who lives in the souls of young nations, has decided: we shall win.'[21]

◆

# CHAPTER 35

# Marching on Moscow

ALTHOUGH Mussolini had given orders that he was only to be woken in the middle of the night on very exceptional occasions, and then only when there was bad news,[1] they woke him in the early hours of the morning of 22 June 1941 to tell him that Hitler's armies had invaded Russia.[2] Hitler had not told Mussolini that he was planning this when they met three weeks before. When Hitler, just before he committed suicide, wrote his last justification for his actions, he explained why he had attacked Russia before first defeating Britain. He wrote that he had realized that it would be impossible to invade Britain, and that Britain would never agree to make peace as long as she had any potential ally on the Continent. Russia was the only European power who could conceivably go to war against Germany, and if he defeated Russia, Britain would realize that she had no hope of victory and would make peace.[3]

According to what Rachele wrote in later years – was she writing from hindsight? – when Mussolini heard that Hitler had invaded Russia he said that it was a great blunder.[4] If he did in fact say this he soon changed his mind, because he wrote to Hitler congratulating him on having invaded Russia and having once again become the leader of the struggle against Bolshevism. He urged him not to be alarmed if people pointed out that throughout history invaders of Russia had come to grief and that it had often led to their ultimate downfall, because today the situation was quite different. Unlike the invaders of Russia in earlier times, Hitler had the advantage of modern transport, tanks, planes, and the incomparable and invincible German Army.[5]

He asked Hitler's permission to send an Italian expeditionary force to fight under the Germans in Russia. He promised Hitler that they would perform well, because his soldiers never fought better than when they were fighting against the Bolsheviks. He sent 230,000

Italian troops to Russia under the command of General Giovanni Messe. The first units left within three days, after he had inspected them at Verona on 25 June.[6]

Next day he spoke at an airport near Verona which was renamed in honour of Balbo. He made special reference to Balbo's role as one of the Quadrumvirs during the March on Rome. 'If today we are marching on Moscow – a march which is certain to end in our victory – this has been made possible only because twenty years ago we marched on Rome.'[7] He inspected more regiments who were leaving for Russia at Mantua on 29 July. He told them that for twenty years the choice confronting Europe had been Fascism or Bolshevism, Rome or Moscow.[8]

Two million German soldiers, with their Italian, Hungarian, Romanian and Finnish allies, and the Spanish Blue Legion that Franco had sent to help them, advanced along the whole breadth of Russia. Stalin had ignored the many warnings that he had received from his spies, and from Churchill, that Hitler was about to attack him, and had been caught completely off his guard. The Soviet Air Force, which was the largest in Europe, was almost totally destroyed within twenty-four hours on the ground. In the first week the Germans advanced more than a hundred miles without catching sight of their retreating enemy. By the middle of August they had almost reached Leningard in the north; in the centre they had captured Smolensk and were halfway to Moscow; and in the south they were deep into the Ukraine.

Mussolini now suffered a great personal tragedy. His son Bruno was killed when his plane crashed during exercises near Pisa on 7 August.[9] He was twenty-two. Mussolini was utterly shaken, as he always was when there was a tragedy that involved his children. He expressed his feelings in an emotional piece of writing that he wrote soon after Bruno's death and which was later published under the title *I talk to Bruno*. Bruno, who had been the hero of his young contemporaries; Bruno, whose feats in the air, whose flights to South America and elsewhere, whose achievements in the wars in Ethiopia, Spain and over Malta had been an example to so many young Italian men; Bruno, whom thousands of Italian girls had dreamed of marrying; Bruno was dead. Mussolini wrote that he could not accept that Bruno was dead, and often in his imagination talked to him, confiding to him his innermost thoughts.[10]

\*      \*      \*

At the end of August Mussolini visited Hitler at his headquarters at Rastenburg in East Prussia, which the Germans had nicknamed 'The Wolf's Lair'. He travelled by train from Rome with his eldest son Vittorio, aged twenty-five, who was acting as his secretary. After Hitler had expressed his condolences for Bruno's death, he told Mussolini about his strategy in Russia. He was sure that the Russians would put up a desperate defence in Leningrad, the birthplace of the Communist October revolution; but he would not sacrifice the lives of thousands of his soldiers by sending them in to capture Leningrad street by street. He would surround Leningrad and bombard and starve it into submission.[11]

Hitler invited Mussolini to fly with him in his four-engine Condor on a visit to the headquarters of Field Marshal Günther von Kluge and Field Marshal Albert Kesselring at Brest-Litovsk. They flew on to Goering's headquarters at Rostken before returning to Rastenburg for the night. Mussolini slept in his train and next day went in the train to the headquarters of the southern front near Lvov in Poland, with Hitler following in his own train.

On 28 August, a hot and brilliant summer day, Mussolini and Hitler flew from Krosmo airport in southern Poland to Field Marshal von Rundstedt's advance headquarters near Uman in the Ukraine. With them in the plane were Ribbentrop, Heinrich Himmler (the head of the SS), his assistant, SS leader Sepp Dietrich, the Italian ambassador in Berlin (Filippo Anfuso), Dino Alfieri and Vittorio Mussolini. As they flew at a height of 2,500 metres for several hours over the great Russian plain, it brought home to Mussolini the vast expanse of territory that the Germans had captured. Mussolini asked if he could take over the controls, and he piloted the plane for more than an hour. They had no fighter protection, for no Soviet plane had been seen anywhere in the area for several weeks. Mussolini whispered to Vittorio that if a Soviet fighter plane came along and succeeded in shooting them down, bagging him, Hitler, Ribbentrop, Himmler and Dietrich, it would be quite a hit for the enemy. But they saw no sign of any Russian, either in the air or on the ground after they landed near Uman.

The German soldiers had been drawn up on the airfield in ranks waiting for their arrival; but when the soldiers saw that the Führer had come, the famous German discipline completely gave way. They broke ranks and ran towards Hitler, cheering him loudly, swarming around him, and trying to shake his hand. Mussolini was then driven by car to Takuska, a few miles away, to meet General Messe and the commanders of the Italian corps. Mussolini was photographed with Messe, standing on Russian soil, some four hundred miles inside the Soviet Union. He then flew back to Rastenburg with Hitler, and travelled home to Rome with Vittorio by train through Cracow and Vienna.[12]

The German advance continued for the next two months. By the beginning of November they had surrounded Leningrad, they were within forty miles of Moscow, and in the south they had captured Odessa, Kiev, Kharkov and Rostov. They had taken three-quarters of a million Russian prisoners-of-war. They did not give them the honourable treatment prescribed for prisoners of war which they extended to the French and British prisoners whom they captured in the west and in North Africa, using the excuse that the Soviet Union had not signed the Geneva Convention on the treatment of prisoners of war. The Russian prisoners were sent to forced labour in factories in Germany and German-occupied territory, where many thousands of them were worked and starved to death. Hitler had given orders that all the captured Communist political commissars in the Red Army were to be immediately shot. The Germans, and their sympathizers in the Ukraine and the Baltic states, massacred the Jews behind the German lines.

Edda Ciano joined the Red Cross in Russia and worked in an Italian army hospital at Stalino in eastern Ukraine.[13] It was nearly six hundred miles into Soviet territory and only a hundred miles from the furthest point that the Germans had reached at Rostov.

By the end of November Mussolini knew that the Germans had been checked in front of Moscow and driven back, as the winter set in, by a Russian counter-attack. It was clear that the war would continue into 1942. In North Africa the British advanced again in November 1941 and won back some of the territory that Rommel had captured in April.

In Croatia, Dalmatia and Montenegro the Italian army of occupation were confronted with two conflicting resistance movements – the Serbian nationalist Chetniks under Colonel Draža Mihailovich, the Minister of War in King Peter's government in London, and the Communist partisans of Josip Broz Tito. Mussolini had no doubt which of these two movements was the greater enemy, and he supported Mihailovich against Tito, 'Stalin's man'.[14] He sent arms to Mihailovich's Chetniks, and sometimes the Italian troops in Montenegro fought in alliance with them against the partisans. Hitler did not approve of this tactic; he told Mussolini that it was not their business to go in for clever politics by playing off the Chetniks and the partisans against each other, but to exterminate them both.[15] Under pressure from Hitler, Mussolini ordered his generals to stop helping Mihailovich; but they continued to do so surreptitiously, and Mussolini made no serious attempt to stop them. He also had trouble in Albania. As soon as the Soviet Union came into the war, the Albanian Communists under Enver Hoxha began waging a guerrilla war against the Italian Army.

In the United States Roosevelt was doing as much to help Britain and her allies as an isolationist public opinion would allow him to do. In February 1941 he announced the 'Lend-Lease' programme of military aid to Britain, and declared that the United States would be the arsenal of democracy. In June he froze all German and Italian assets in the United States. In August he met Churchill in mid-Atlantic and they issued the Atlantic Charter; and he authorized United States warships to attack German U-boats which were interfering with the merchant ships taking arms to Britain. Mussolini denounced this as the action of a plutocracy controlled by Jewish big business in the United States. Roosevelt also took steps to prevent Japan from acquiring oil and other essential war materials.

On 3 December 1941 the Japanese ambassador in Rome told Mussolini that war between Japan and the United States would break out within a matter of days, and on 7 December the Japanese Air Force bombed Pearl Harbor, sinking most of the American Navy in their base. The United States and Britain declared war on Japan, and Hitler told Mussolini that he would declare war on the United States. Mussolini was pleased; he thought that if the Axis declared war, the United States could not do them much more harm than they were already doing under the pretence of remaining neutral.[16]

Hitler and Mussolini agreed to declare war on the United States at the same time, at 3.15 p.m. on 11 December. After the declaration of war had been delivered to the American ambassador, Mussolini spoke to the crowd from the balcony of the Palazzo Venezia. Fascist Italy and National Socialist Germany had now been joined in the struggle by heroic Japan, forming a bloc of 250 million men who were determined to conquer. Neither the Axis nor Japan had wished to extend the war; the responsibility for this rested with one man alone, the democratic despot who had resorted to an infinite series of provocations, against the interests of his own people. He had wanted war, and prepared for it day after day with diabolical pertinacity.[17] Mussolini was developing an intense hatred of Roosevelt. Rachele noticed that he never spoke of either Churchill or Stalin with the bitterness with which he referred to Roosevelt.[18]

Mussolini was encouraged throughout the rest of the winter by the news of the remarkable Japanese successes in the Far East and the series of defeats that they had inflicted on the American and British armies. But he had his problems with food shortages at home. Bread rationing was introduced, and the people grumbled about their daily ration of two hundred grams. Mussolini told them that in Spain the ration at one time had been down to one hundred grams, and in Greece the population was starving; and people at home should remember the sufferings of the heroic Italian soldiers in Russia, who had endured a temperature of forty-one degrees below zero better than the Germans, and at Christmas had slaughtered four Bolshevik divisions in a temperature of twenty-one degrees below zero.[19]

When spring came and the Axis prepared for another summer offensive, Mussolini went to see Hitler at Castle Klessheim in Salzburg on 29 and 30 April 1942. This time it was Hitler, not Mussolini, who had to explain to his ally why his troops had suffered a setback. Hitler said that the failure to take Moscow in 1941, and the success of the Russian counter-attack during the winter, could not be blamed on his soldiers; they had fought magnificently and had bravely endured all the hardships of the winter, and so had the Italian soldiers who were fighting valiantly at their side in Russia. The failure had been due to the coldest Russian winter for 140 years. His soldiers had endured a temperature of fifty-two degrees below zero, whereas Napoleon had faced only twenty-two degrees below zero, and Hitler had been warned to prepare for a temperature of twenty to twenty-five degrees below zero. But the setback in Russia was only temporary; now that the summer was coming they would advance again.[20]

It did indeed turn out to be a good summer for the Axis. In May the Russians launched an offensive near Kharkov which was repulsed after several weeks' hard fighting. In June the Germans began their counter-offensive which broke through the Russian defences at Rossosh and continued with a two-pronged attack that carried them even further than their advance in the south in 1941. One army group reached the River Volga at Stalingrad, and the other penetrated deep into the Caucasus.

In the middle of June a naval engagement took place in the eastern Mediterranean when an Italian fleet attacked some British ships sailing from Alexandria to Malta. It was the Italian revenge for their defeat off Cape Matapan fifteen months before. In the fighting on 14 and 15 June 1942 the Italians sank five British warships for the loss of only one of their own ships. Mussolini, piloting his own plane, flew over the Mediterranean to watch the battle from the air, avoiding the British fighters that were in the neighbourhood and were taking part in the battle with the Italian fleet. After watching the battle, Mussolini flew his plane to Sicily, were he landed and spoke at a number of meetings about the great naval victory.[21]

From Sicily Mussolini flew back to Rome, and a few days later left on a visit to North Africa, where Rommel launched another offensive in June 1942. For the fourth time in eighteen months the coastal towns changed hands as he advanced into Egypt. This time the British did not succeed in holding Tobruk as a fortress behind the Axis lines; Rommel captured it on 20 June, and was made a field marshal by a grateful Hitler. At the beginning of July he reached El Alamein, only sixty miles from Alexandria. But here the British made a successful stand, and Rommel's attack was repulsed.

Mussolini arrived in Libya on 29 June, just as the battle at El Alamein was about to begin, and stayed for twenty days before flying back to Rome on 19 July. He visited several Italian army units and military hospitals, and a prison camp for New Zealand and South African prisoners of war. He made the commander-in-chief, General Ugo Cavallero, a field marshal. He twice visited the captured town of Tobruk; but he did not go into Egypt and to the front at El Alamein, and he did not meet Rommel.[22]

Mussolini fell ill the day after he returned to Rome from Libya; he complained of stomach pains. It was the same complaint that he had had in 1925, and again the trouble was caused as much by his anxieties as by his sparse diet.

Rommel got no further than El Alamein, and the Red Army held out in Stalingrad. Then on 23 October Lt-General Bernard Montgomery launched an attack on the Axis forces at El Alamein, and after twelve days' fierce fighting Rommel was in full retreat. Although relations between the German and Italian soldiers in North Africa had hitherto been excellent, Rommel now seized Italian vehicles and used them to evacuate his German troops, leaving the Italians behind to be taken prisoner in their thousands. He said that it was his duty to evacuate and preserve his best troops, and his Germans were better soldiers than the Italians.[23] He retreated rapidly through Libya until he reached Tunisia, leaving Bardia, Tobruk and Benghazi to be captured by the British.

Meanwhile, on 8 November, British and American forces landed in Algeria. The French governor, Admiral Jean François Darlan, though he had been an ardent supporter of Marshal Pétain and the Vichy regime and very pro-German, went over to the Allies and ruled Algeria on their behalf until he was assassinated by a supporter of General de Gaulle's Free French movement on 24 December. Mussolini said that the disasters in North Africa were entirely due to the treason of the French Vichy rulers; if Hitler had given the French colonies and Algeria to Italy, the Italian officials would not have gone over to the Anglo-Americans and allowed them to land in North Africa.[24]

On 23 October the British RAF made a very heavy air raid on Genoa. On 18 November the Red Army launched a great offensive to the north and south of Stalingrad which encircled the German Army. Hitler ordered his troops to withdraw from the Caucasus but to stand firm at Stalingrad. The Red Army wiped out the surrounded Germans at Stalingrad after two and a half months' fierce fighting, and on 2 February 1943 the German commander at Stalingrad, Field Marshal Friedrich von Paulus, surrendered the remnants of his army and went over to the side of the Russians. Hitler lost four hundred thousand men at Stalingrad.

Mussolini's stomach ulcers continued. The doctors said that he must reduce the amount of milk in his diet, a difficult prescription to follow, as he ate and drank very little except fruit and milk. They gave him injections, which he did not like and which seemed to make him worse. Rachele thought that the best medicine which the doctors could give him would be news of a victory;[25] but this was a medicine that they could not provide for him.

The stomach ulcers slowly improved. Mussolini, though not yet cured, was able to carry out his engagements, receiving a deputation of German Nazis in the Palazzo Venezia on the twentieth anniversary of the March on Rome on 28 October 1942. He told them that Italy and Germany were engaged in a common struggle against Bolshevism, plutocracy and the Jews.[26]

On 2 December he addressed a meeting of the Chamber. He said that important military events had occurred since he had last spoken to them on 10 June 1941, and proceeded to give them many statistics of the numbers killed and houses destroyed in the Allied air raids on Italian cities. He referred to the enormous losses suffered by the Russians; they had been forced to evacuate a large part of their territory in European Russia, losing between eighty and ninety million of their population, nearly half the total population of the Soviet Union.

He attacked the anti-Italian role of the British throughout history, referring to the hanging of the Italian Jacobin leader Prince Francesco Caracciolo by Nelson in 1799 and to the interception of Mazzini's correspondence in London, and the betrayal of the Bandiera brothers, by Sir Robert Peel's government in 1844. He referred to Churchill's radio broadcast to Italy in which he said that Britain was not fighting against the Italian people but against one man, Mussolini; and he said how proud he was that Churchill should have singled him out as the enemy. He said that if there was one man in the world who had diabolically wanted war, that man was the President of the United States of America.[27]

He again attacked the British and Roosevelt when he spoke to the National Executive Committee of the Fascist Party on 3 January 1943. He said that the great majority of the British people were very stupid; but this stupidity was in some ways their strength, for they were too stupid to realize that they could not win the war. He denounced Roosevelt as a man who was filled with a bitter hatred of all humanity because he had been struck down with poliomyelitis at the age of forty-three. He said that today, 3 January, was a special day every year, because it was the anniversary of 3 January 1925 when the Socialist deputies who had left the Chamber during the Matteotti crisis, 'the Aventines', were finally defeated; but today they faced a threat from other Aventines who were more dangerous than the Aventines of 1924.[28] He was certainly right on this point. It had been easier to murder Matteotti than to defeat the armies of Roosevelt, Churchill and Stalin.

The Nazis had begun to deport the Jews to the death camps in Poland. In January 1942, at a conference on the Wannsee near Berlin, the SS leader Reinhard Heydrich – he later became the German governor in Prague and was assassinated by Czech agents sent from Britain – revealed to a small group of Nazi leaders his plan to murder all the Jews in Europe in gas chambers in Poland. The deportations to Auschwitz and the other camps soon began throughout German-occupied territory, and were well under way in France by the summer of 1942. Apart from Denmark, where the Danes were able to save the Jews by sending them to safety in neutral Sweden, the only country where the Jews were not deported to the gas chambers was Italy. The Jews in Italy were interned, but not deported.

In October 1942 Himmler came to Rome. He urged Mussolini to send the Italian Jews to Poland. He assured him that the Jews would be humanely treated there. Only subversive Jews had been sent to concentration camps. The majority had been set to work building roads in Poland, and the elderly ones were cared for in rest homes in Theresienstadt (Terezín) in Bohemia, which in fact was a transit camp on the way to the gas chambers. Mussolini gave no indication that he knew that Himmler was lying. But on 17 August 1942 Prince Otto von Bismarck, a diplomat at the German embassy in Rome, had told an official at the Italian Foreign Office that the deported Jews were being killed in Poland; and four days later, on 21 August, the Foreign Office had passed on the information to Mussolini.[29]

In France the Vichy government agreed to deport the Jews; but in the Italian zone of occupation in the south, the Italian Army prevented the local French civilian officials from carrying out the deportations. The Germans in Salonika rounded up all the Jews and deported them to the Polish death camps; but the Italian occupation authorities in Athens, despite the protests of the Germans, refused to enforce the regulations that made the Jews wear the yellow star of David as an identification mark.[30]

When Ribbentrop came to Rome on 25 February 1943 he complained to Mussolini about the action of the Italian officers in France who were preventing the Vichy officials from deporting the Jews. Ribbentrop said that obviously these officers, like some German officers, lacked a proper understanding of the Jewish question. Mussolini agreed, and said that he would order them to stop protecting the Jews. He wrote to Hitler that Judaism was 'a disease to be cured by fire and sword'.[31] On 18 March the German ambassador, Baron Hans Georg von Mackensen, raised the matter again with Mussolini, who said how much he regretted the 'sentimental humanitarianism' of his generals, and promised that there would be no more interference by the Italian Army in the actions of the French police;[32] but the Italians in their occupation zone in France continued to protect the Jews.

It has been suggested that Mussolini agreed with Ribbentrop and Mackensen in order to deceive them, and that secretly he ordered his generals to save the Jews; but Mussolini so often used the phrase 'sentimental humanitarianism' as a term of contempt that it is impossible to believe that on this one occasion he did not mean it. When he was told that his generals were saving the lives of Jewish men, women and children out of pity for them, his first reaction was to despise them and condemn them for this act of weakness when they should have been prepared to carry out the deportation of the Jews with admirable ruthlessness. On the other hand, he was not particularly keen on deporting Jews, and having expressed his contempt for the generals' 'sentimental humanitarianism' he did not go to any trouble to prevent them from continuing to save the Jews.

◆

# CHAPTER 36

# The Twenty-Fifth of July

I N North Africa the Italian and German armies were attacked on both sides, by Montgomery's Eighth Army from the east and the Anglo-American forces in Algeria from the west. In March strikes broke out in the war production factories in Milan; they were certainly encouraged, if not instigated, by the underground Communist groups among the factory workers. The situation was therefore serious when Mussolini travelled to Salzburg at the beginning of April 1943 for another meeting with Hitler at Klessheim Castle.

Mussolini proposed to Hitler that they should open negotiations with Stalin for a separate peace with the Soviet Union. It may have been Goering and some of the German generals who asked Mussolini to suggest this to Hitler.[1] But Hitler did not favour it, and it was in fact very unlikely that Stalin would have accepted any such proposal. Stalin, Churchill and Roosevelt had all decided that whatever differences between themselves might arise in the future, they were not going to quarrel with each other until after they had destroyed Hitler and Mussolini.

By May, the German and Italian forces in North Africa were trapped in an area around Tunis, and could not escape by sea because the British Navy was in control of the Mediterranean. Rommel himself and a few of his officers escaped by air to Germany, but 150,000 Germans and Italians were taken prisoner. The Allies then attacked the Italian island fortress of Pantelleria in the Mediterranean between Tunisia and Sicily. Mussolini ordered the general in command on Pantelleria to fight to the last man, but he surrendered it to the Allies after a few days' resistance.[2] On 15 July the Anglo-American armies invaded Sicily.

The Americans enlisted the support of the dormant Mafia in Sicily. After Mussolini suppressed the activities of the Mafia there, they transferred their activities to the Italian-speaking population in the United States. During the Second World War the American Federal Bureau of Investigation used the American Mafia to help them catch the German agents who were carrying out sabotage in the American Atlantic ports. The Mafia, in return for a promise of immunity from prosecution for their crimes, revealed the names of the saboteurs. Having found the Mafia useful in the United States, the American government decided to use the Mafia organization in Sicily, which had been forced into inactivity by Mussolini and Mori but was still in existence.[3] The role of the Mafia in the Allied invasion of Sicily was certainly not decisive, but they helped to hamper the resistance of the Italian Army to the invaders.

Mussolini had committed the one unpardonable crime of a dictator: he was losing a war. The Italian people reacted as the people of every nation react in such circumstances. They cheered him when he defeated the sanctions imposed against him by Britain and the League of Nations and when he gave them an empire in Ethiopia; they turned against him when the empire in Ethiopia was lost, when Libya was lost, when over 150,000 Italian soldiers had been taken prisoner, when Italian towns were being heavily bombed, when Sicily had been successfully invaded by the enemy, and when it seemed as if the invasion of the Italian mainland was imminent.

A young officer, Lieutenant Salvatore Spinello, who was on leave from the army, had become friendly with a very attractive aristocratic girl. She invited him to lunch at her father's house, and he found himself sitting down at the lunch table with counts, generals and admirals. He was surprised at their conversation, for though they never mentioned the name 'Mussolini', he realized at once to whom they were referring when they spoke about the 'cavaliere' – a title that the King had granted to Mussolini. They were all agreed that the cavaliere had made a hash of things, that he was losing the war, that it was time to get rid of the cavaliere; and they did not hesitate to say so in the presence of a stranger like Spinello.[4]

Today Mussolini's supporters still believe, as they believed in 1943, that the coup d'état that overthrew Mussolini was planned by the freemasons, including those prominent Fascists who had secretly remained freemasons after members of the Fascist Party were forbidden to have links with them. But it was not only the freemasons who realized that Mussolini was losing the war. Some of the leading Fascists, including Mussolini's Foreign Minister and son-in-law, Ciano, made secret contacts with the British embassy in the Vatican.[5]

On 19 July Mussolini, piloting his own plane, flew to Treviso for a meeting with Hitler at a country house in San Fermo between Feltre and Belluno, near Trent. He asked Hitler if he could send German troops to reinforce the defenders of Sicily. Hitler said that his experts were inventing a new and very powerful secret weapon, which he would soon be able to use against the enemy in Sicily.[6] Hitler's armies in Russia were engaged, at Kursk to the south of Moscow, in the biggest tank battle that had ever been fought anywhere in the world. Hitler had thrown in all his forces in an attempt to break the Red Army at the beginning of another summer campaign. After a fortnight of fierce fighting the Germans had advanced thirteen miles. Then the Red Army counter-attacked and routed the Germans. During the next three months the Germans retreated four hundred miles, and by the autumn were on the point of being driven out of all the territory of the Soviet Union.

While Mussolini was talking with Hitler at San Fermo, Allied planes bombed Rome for the first time. The fires from the raid were still burning when Mussolini arrived home in the evening. For many months the Allies had been bombing Genoa, Turin, Milan and other Italian ports and cities; but people were saying that they would not bomb Rome so as not to offend the Pope and the Catholics throughout the world. The air raid on Rome on 19 July was not as heavy as those on other Italian cities. No bombs were dropped on the city centre, but the marshalling yards in the working-class district of San Lorenzo were heavily bombed, causing some loss of life among the civilian population; and much damage was done to the historic Basilica of San Lorenzo and to many of the graves in the nearby cemetery. The Pope came out of the Vatican to walk among the people of San Lorenzo and offer them his sympathies. It was now clear to everyone that Rome would not be spared.[7]

A meeting of the Fascist Grand Council was to be held in the Palazzo Venezia at 5 p.m. on Saturday, 24 July. Mussolini had no idea of what was in store for him, though rumours were circulating. Rachele had heard the rumours. As Mussolini left the Villa Torlonia on his way to the meeting she called out to him to have them all arrested.[8] He thought she was joking and did not take her seriously.

Grandi moved a resolution at the meeting. He had a bomb in his pocket; he had decided that if he were arrested he would blow them all up.[9] His motion, after praising the valour that had been shown by all ranks of the Italian Army, Navy and Air Force, respectfully asked His Majesty the King to take personal command of the armed forces and the government. This meant, of course, that the King should dismiss Mussolini as Commander-in-Chief and Prime Minister.

They discussed Grandi's resolution from 5 p.m. till after midnight, with a break for refreshments at supper time. The discussion was conducted in a cool and almost friendly fashion, with Mussolini and his opponents all remaining quite calm. Farinacci and other members of the Grand Council moved amendments to the resolution which supported Mussolini, but it was finally agreed to take a vote first on Grandi's resolution. It was carried by nineteen votes to seven, with one abstention, apart from Farinacci, who supported Mussolini and refused to vote as a protest against the resolution. The nineteen who voted for the resolution included Grandi, the two former Quadrumvirs De Bono and De Vecchi, Marinelli (who had organized the murder of Matteotti), Bottai, Federzoni, Acerbo, and three men whom Mussolini had particularly trusted – Umberto Albini, Giuseppe Bastianini and Ciano. The seven voting against included Scorza and Guido Buffarini-Guidi.

Mussolini said that as Grandi's resolution had been carried, there was no point in voting on the other resolutions, and declared the meeting closed.[10] He was then driven home just after midnight from the Palazzo Venezia to the Villa Torlonia. When he got home he said nothing except that from time to time he repeated: 'Ciano, Albini and Bastianini too!'[11]

He still had not fully taken in what had happened. Next morning, on Sunday, 25 July, he went to his office at the Palazzo Venezia, where he was to receive the new Japanese ambassador, Shinrokuro Hidaka. He congratulated Hidaka on the Japanese victories in the war.[12] While he was at the Palazzo Venezia he received a telephone call from Scorza, who told him that Tullio Cianetti, who had voted in favour of Grandi's resolution, had just notified him that he had changed his mind and asked that he should be recorded as having voted against the resolution. Mussolini then visited the San Lorenzo district, which had suffered in the air raid of 19 July.[13] When he returned home he received an invitation from the King to come at once to his residence at the Villa Savoia. Rachele was suspicious, and urged him not to go; but he went.[14]

Victor Emmanuel came in person to the front door of the villa to greet Mussolini. He was friendly and very sympathetic. He said that Mussolini had performed great services to Italy, but that it was now time for him to resign. Mussolini did not agree, and his discussion with the King was inconclusive.

When Mussolini left the King's presence, a captain of the King's guard came up to him in the anteroom and said that he had been ordered by the King to drive him home in a military ambulance for his greater safety. Mussolini said that he had come to the Villa Savoia in his own car, and that his chauffeur had waited for him and could drive him home. The captain insisted that Mussolini should travel in the military ambulance, and after the captain had finally said 'It is an order, Duce,' Mussolini agreed, and they drove off at great speed. They went to an army barracks, where they waited for three-quarters of an hour. By now, Mussolini had realized that they were not driving him home.

He was taken from one barracks to another, and was eventually handed a letter from Marshal Badoglio, informing him that the King had appointed Badoglio Prime Minister, and that Mussolini would be taken to a place where he could be held in safe custody for his own protection. Badoglio may have been justified in thinking that Mussolini needed protection, for as soon as the news spread that he had fallen from power and had been arrested, anti-Fascists began demonstrating against him and against Fascism, and in some cases attacked Fascists in their houses.

For three days Mussolini was held in custody at various places, and on 28 July was taken by sea from Ponza to the island of La Maddalena off the coast of Sardinia.[15] It was used as a prison for other detainees. One of the prisoners on the island was the former Socialist deputy Zaniboni, who had been sentenced to thirty years' imprisonment for attempting to assassinate Mussolini in 1925. He was released a few days after Mussolini arrived.[16]

Rachele was informed by an anonymous telephone call that Mussolini had been arrested. Her friends urged her to leave the Villa Torlonia at once, because they feared that anti-Fascists would attack the house. No attack on the Villa Torlonia took place, but Rachele moved to the doorkeeper's house nearby. The doorkeeper's wife Irma, who was the chambermaid at the Palazzo Venezia, tried to comfort Rachele; but in the course of their conversation she mentioned the name of Claretta Petacci. Rachele had never heard of Claretta, and asked who she was. When she had induced the bewildered and embarrassed Irma to tell her that Claretta was Mussolini's mistress, she was very angry, and reacted as violently as she always did about Benito's love affairs.[17] She was much more upset about Claretta than about the fall of the Fascist regime.

Rachele joined Romano and Anna Maria at their country house at Rocca delle Caminate, where they were guarded by courteous and friendly police officers.[18] They were allowed to write to Mussolini. He, too, was treated with consideration by his guards, and allowed to write to Rachele.


The King appointed Marshal Badoglio as Prime Minister, and he chose a Cabinet composed of civil servants. Guariglia, who was the ambassador in Turkey, was recalled and appointed Foreign Minister. Badoglio's government announced that Italy would continue the war at the side of her German ally. Hitler was sorry that Mussolini had been overthrown and suspicious of Badoglio, but he did not wish to resort to force against Italy and drive Badoglio into an alliance with the Allies. He therefore announced that he would not intervene in Italian internal affairs, but trusted that Badoglio's government would perform Italy's treaty obligations towards Germany. Badoglio retained all the Fascist laws, including the racial laws; but many anti-Fascists and Jews were released from prison and internment, though no Communists were released.[19]

On 29 July, four days after Mussolini was arrested, he celebrated his sixtieth birthday. He received a birthday telegram from Goering, which was forwarded to his prison. Goering wrote that he had hoped to visit Mussolini on his birthday, but events had made this impossible. A few days later Mussolini received a birthday present from Hitler – a magnificently bound de luxe edition of Nietzsche's *Collected Works*.[20]

While Badoglio's government publicly declared that Italy would continue the war as Germany's ally, Guariglia secretly opened peace negotiations with the Allies through the British embassy in Lisbon.

The British told him to send a representative who could meet the British representative in Tangiers, where their meetings were less likely to be noticed than in Lisbon. Guariglia tried to negotiate the best terms he could for Italy, but the Allies insisted on Italy's unconditional surrender.

On 6 August Guariglia met Ribbentrop at Tarvisio. Ribbentrop asked Guariglia if he would promise, on his word of honour, that he was not conducting secret peace negotiations with the Allies. Guariglia afterwards wrote in his memoirs that he hesitated only for a moment before giving the promise.[21]

Meanwhile the British and American air forces stepped up the air raids on Italian cities. On 12 August the British made heavy air raids on Milan and Turin. The Socialists and left wing in Britain protested against these air raids, because the Allies were bombing and killing Italian anti-Fascist workers who had recently made illegal strikes against Mussolini's regime; but the air raids put pressure on Badoglio's government to accept the Allied demand for unconditional surrender, and might persuade the Germans that the Allies and Badoglio were not on the point of making peace. When Mussolini, in his prison, heard about the air raids on Milan and Turin, he said that he hoped that this would show the Italian people that the Anglo-Americans wished to make war on them, and not only on Fascism and on him; for they were intensifying their air raids now that he and the Fascist regime had fallen.[22]

One of the peace terms on which the Allies were insisting was that Badoglio's government should hand over Mussolini to them. The Badoglio government realized that when the peace terms were announced, Italian Fascists, or the Germans, might try to rescue Mussolini and save him from falling into the hands of the Anglo-Americans. On 28 August they suddenly moved Mussolini, without warning and in great secrecy, from La Maddalena, and after travelling for several days he arrived at a safer prison in a disused hotel on the highest point of the Gran Sasso mountain range near L'Aquila, north of Rome.[23]

Badoglio's government accepted the Allied peace terms, and on 8 September it was publicly announced that an armistice had been signed. Hitler immediately ordered the German Army to occupy Italy. The Allies also landed forces on the Italian mainland, but did not move quickly enough to prevent the Germans from occupying Rome and all Italy north of the River Volturno. The King and Badoglio hastily left Rome and established the government at Brindisi. The Allies held Naples and the South, but most of Italy was under German occupation.

The Germans were indignant; they accused the Italians of betraying them for the second time, as they had done in 1915 when they repudiated the Three Power Pact and entered the First World War on the side of the Allies. In Italy, in the Balkans, and in the Dodecanese Islands, the Germans called on the Italian garrisons to surrender and hand over their arms. Where the Italians resisted, the Germans treated them like rebels, and, after capturing them, put them to death on Hitler's orders. Other Italian prisoners were deported to Germany and treated with great harshness in internment camps.[24]

But Hitler had not lost faith in his friend Mussolini. He sent the dashing paratroop commander, Otto Skorzeny, to find and rescue him. Skorzeny discovered that he was on the Gran Sasso, and decided to land with his paratroopers on the mountain top. By now the German army had occupied all Italy north of Rome, including the Gran Sasso area, and it has therefore been suggested that Skorzeny's rescue of Mussolini was a propaganda exercise staged at Hitler's orders; for it would have been possible to send a German army unit by road to the Gran Sasso to liberate Mussolini without any of the real risks involved in landing a plane on the mountain top. But Hitler had good reason to fear that British paratroopers might reach Mussolini and capture him before Skorzeny arrived. The officer in command on the Gran Sasso afterwards stated that Badoglio, at Churchill's insistence, had ordered him to shoot Mussolini if any attempt were made to rescue him; but other officers at the Gran Sasso stated that they had never been informed of this order.

When the armistice terms were announced on the radio, Mussolini became alarmed that he would be handed over to the British. He confided his fears to the officer who was guarding him. The officer said that he himself had been taken prisoner by the British at Tobruk, that they had ill-treated him, and that he would never surrender any Italian to the British. The officer's experience was unusual, for very few Italian prisoners of war complained of ill-treatment at the hands of their British captors.

On 12 September, Skorzeny and his men landed on the Gran Sasso. They were accompanied by General Soleti of the Italian Police; Skorzeny thought that his presence might be useful. They ran towards the hotel with their machine-guns at the ready. Skorzeny led them, with General Soleti at his side. Mussolini's guards were preparing to fire on them when Mussolini looked out of the window. At first he thought that the British had come for him, but then he recognized the German uniform of Skorzeny's men and saw Soleti in his Italian uniform. He shouted to his guards not to fire, as there was an Italian general there. The guards put up no further resistance.

Skorzeny entered the hotel and found Mussolini. 'Duce, the Führer had sent me to rescue you,' he said. Mussolini replied: 'I always knew that my friend Adolf Hitler would not let me down.' They took off immediately, although this was not easy on the mountain top, and the plane had to taxi down the slope, and only just cleared the rocks in the ravine below; but within an hour of landing they were again airborne. Skorzeny flew Mussolini to the Pratica di Mare airport near Rome, and from there to Vienna. Mussolini went on by train from Vienna to Munich, and flew to Rastenburg to thank Hitler for having rescued him.[25]

The Germans had occupied the area round Forlì and Rocca delle Caminate. A German officer dismissed the Italian police who were guarding Rachele, and Hitler sent a plane to fly her, with Romano and Anna Maria, to Munich, where they were reunited with Mussolini. Rachele was very grateful to Hitler, and when she wrote her memoirs five years later she thanked him for his kindness in sending the plane for her.[26] She was a simple soul who always saw things in personal terms. At this very time when Hitler sent the plane for Rachele and her family, he was sending thousands of Jewish men, women and children in cattle trucks, without food or water for the children, from all over Europe to the gas chambers at Auschwitz; but for Rachele, Hitler was a very kind man who had sent a plane to bring her from Rocca delle Caminate to Mussolini in Munich.

# CHAPTER 37

———— ◆ ————

# The Italian Social Republic

MANY of the Nazi leaders, including some of the generals, wished to treat the Italians as enemies and Italy as a conquered country. But Hitler trusted Mussolini, and decided to install him as the head of an Italian Fascist government in opposition to the government of Badoglio. He gave instructions that Mussolini was to broadcast to the Italian people from the broadcasting station in Munich, and Mussolini made the broadcast on the evening of 18 September.

He was nervous, for he had broadcast only once before.[1] His great speeches to the crowds from the balcony of the Palazzo Venezia had often been relayed over the radio throughout the world; but he had only once before sat alone in a broadcasting studio and spoken into a microphone a message that was to go out to millions of listeners. He performed well, and his message was regarded as a success by his friends and supporters. He said that the King and Badoglio had betrayed Italy to the enemy, and that he would preside over an Italian Social Republic which would continue the war at the side of their German allies.[2]

Mussolini had hoped to establish his government in Rome; but though the German generals had to accept the Führer's decision to rule Italy through Mussolini's government, they persuaded Hitler not to allow him to come to Rome and get in the way of the German military administration, as Rome was not far behind the front line where the Germans faced the enemy. Mussolini had to set up his government in the far north of Italy at Salò on Lake Garda. His residence and office were to be at the Villa Feltrinelli in Gargnano, also on Lake Garda, a few miles from Salò. He summoned the parliament of the republic to meet in Verona.

Before Mussolini and Rachele left Munich, Ciano arrived there in the middle of September. The anti-Fascists were beginning to take over in the South in the territory under Badoglio's government and in Allied occupation; and Ciano had discovered that his action in voting against Mussolini at the meeting of the Fascist Grand Council on 24 July had not been enough to make the anti-Fascists forget that he had for many years been a leading Fascist and Mussolini's Foreign Minister. He therefore thought that he had better rejoin Mussolini in the North. It was an embarrassing family reunion, and the atmosphere over lunch was frigid.[3]

When Mussolini and Rachele went to Rocca delle Caminate and on to Gargnano, Ciano remained in Munich. Five of the other members of the Fascist Grand Council who had voted against Mussolini on 24 July – De Bono, Marinelli, Luciano Gottardi, Carlo Pareschi and Cianetti – also came into German-occupied territory. The others stayed in the South, or, like Grandi, went to Spain, where Franco granted them political asylum. The Fascist extremists, like Farinacci, thought that Ciano and the other traitors who had betrayed Mussolini should be put on trial, and the Germans supported their demand. Mussolini's government at Salò set up a Special Tribunal to try the traitors.

On 17 October the German authorities in Munich informed Ciano that he would be extradited to the Italian Social Republic to face trial. Two days later he was flown under guard to Verona, where he was imprisoned along with De Bono, Marinelli, Gottardi, Pareschi and Cianetti, to await trial on a charge of high treason.[4]

In November 1943 a Fascist congress assembled in Verona. It abolished the monarchy and adopted a constitution for the Italian Social Republic.[5] In all his propaganda Mussolini emphasized the fact that the Italian Social Republic had repudiated the monarchy of the bourgeoisie. Some people thought that he had returned to his old socialism.

He denounced the monarchy, and 'Victor Savoy', as he called the King. He asked the question: Was the March on Rome an insurrection? Yes, it was an insurrection, because it was something more than a constitutional change of government; if it had not been an insurrection, he could not have become Prime Minister when he was the leader of a party with only thirty-eight deputies in a Chamber of more than five hundred deputies. Was the March on Rome a revolution? No, it was not a revolution, because it had not swept away the monarchy.[6] That had been their mistake in 1922; but now the monarchy had been swept away in the Italian Social Republic.

Throughout his life, he had always adapted his dress to the role that he was playing. He no longer wore the wing collar and bowler hat that he had worn as the King's Prime Minister, or the white tie and tails that he had put on when he went to the opera with Neville Chamberlain, but always the Fascist black shirt, without collar or tie. Together with his shaven head, it presented a picture of austerity and harshness. He had developed an intense hatred of beards.[7] Was this because, in his Socialist days, he himself had worn a beard? Or because Balbo, Grandi, and other prominent Fascists had beards?

The constitution of the Italian Social Republic was drafted by Nicola Bombacci, who had known Mussolini when they were both schoolmasters in Gualtieri in 1902. After the First World War Bombacci became a leading Communist in the Chamber of Deputies, where he engaged in several fights with the Fascist deputies when they assaulted the deserter Misiano and on other occasions. He went several times to Moscow for meetings of the Third International. In later years he said that both Lenin and Trotsky had told him that the greatest mistake that the Italian Communists made was to lose Mussolini, for Mussolini was the only man who might have led a successful Communist revolution in Italy; but he did not say this until after he had become a Fascist. When Mussolini began arresting Communists after the March on Rome, Bombacci escaped to Moscow and was assigned a prominent place at Lenin's funeral.

Bombacci became friendly with Kamenev, and associated with the Left Opposition in the Soviet Communist Party. In 1927 he was expelled, as an Opposition sympathizer, from the Italian Communist Party. He decided that he would be safer in Mussolini's Italy than in Stalin's Russia, and returned to Italy. He persuaded the authorities that he was no longer a Communist or politically active, and on Mussolini's instructions was allowed to live in Italy unmolested by the police. When Mussolini's brother Arnaldo died in December 1931, Bombacci wrote Mussolini a letter of sympathy, in which he referred to their old friendship thirty years before, but made no reference to politics.

It was Mussolini's success in defying the sanctions imposed against Italy during the Ethiopian war which converted Bombacci, like so many other Italians, into an enthusiastic supporter of the Duce. He applied to join the Fascist Party, and was accepted as a member. After the armistice of 8 September 1943 he joined Mussolini in the

Italian Social Republic.[8] Mussolini warmly welcomed him, despite the fact that he had a long, bushy white beard.

In the South, the Socialists and liberals were unhappy at having Badoglio as Prime Minister; they thought that Badoglio, with his Fascist past and his war crimes in Ethiopia, was not a suitable leader of the new anti-Fascist Italy that was fighting in alliance with the Western democracies against Hitler and Mussolini. They demanded that the liberal philosopher Benedetto Croce, or some liberal or Socialist politician, should replace Badoglio. The Italian Communist Party did not support this demand: on Stalin's instructions, they supported Badoglio, for Stalin wanted political stability in southern Italy and an efficient general who could assist in the only immediate task – the military defeat of Germany and Mussolini's Fascists.

Bombacci thought that this was the final Communist betrayal of revolutionary socialism. While the Italian Communist Party supported Badoglio, the King, and the British and American imperialists, Bombacci would support Mussolini's Socialist republic.

Bombacci was not deterred from supporting Mussolini by the racial laws against the Jews – had not international Jewish finance capital always supported the American imperialists? – although the Italian Social Republic intensified the campaign against them. All Jews were officially declared to be enemy aliens.[9] For the first time, the Italian Jews in German-occupied territory were deported to the camps in Poland. But the Germans in Himmler's special detachments, who were given the duty of rounding up the Jews, did not find it easy to carry out their task.

On Saturday, 16 October 1943, they tried to arrest all the Jews in Rome. Herbert Kappler, the German Chief of Police in Rome, and his assistant Theodor Dannecker, were in charge of the operation. Dannecker, who had experience in rounding up Jews in Paris and Sofia, waited for the local anti-Semites to come forward and volunteer information about where the Jews were hiding; but no local anti-Semites helped him in Rome. On the contrary, many of the inhabitants helped the Jews to escape. Kappler and Dannecker caught only 1,007 Jews in Rome. They reported to Himmler that for every Jew seized, eleven had escaped.[10] Afterwards another six thousand Jews were arrested in Northern Italy, including nine hundred in Milan; but during the twenty months of German occupation, only seven thousand of the Italian and foreign Jews in Italy died in the gas chambers in Poland[11] – about 15 per cent of the Jews in Italy, a far lower number than in any other country, except Denmark, in German-occupied Europe.

Many Catholics urged the Pope to broadcast a statement publicly condemning the deportation and extermination of the Jews. They said that the effect of such a statement on Hitler's Catholic soldiers would force the Nazis to abandon their extermination programme. The Pope refused to condemn it publicly, but hid Jews in the Vatican, and many more in the monasteries in Rome.[12] He thought that if he publicly denounced the extermination of the Jews, Hitler would send troops into the Vatican, imprison him, and catch and murder the Jews who were hiding there.

Some Italian Fascists willingly and actively helped the Germans round up the Jews; and Mussolini authorized, and indeed ordered, them to do so. The Italians, like the population of every other German-occupied country, knew about this, and photographs of the Jews being deported were shown on the newsreels in the cinemas. It is much more difficult to prove that the people knew that when the Jews reached the camps in Poland, they were murdered there, for this was not revealed to the public. Those Italians who listened illegally to the broadcasts on the Allied radio stations, or who heard the rumours about the gas chambers from other sources, thought at first that it was lying enemy propaganda; but some of them, who knew soldiers and officials who had been in Poland, discovered that the stories were true.[13]

Several of the Fascist leaders knew. Prince Bismarck had told the Italian Foreign Office in August 1942, and they had passed on the information to Mussolini. In May 1943 Gauleiter Wilhelm Kube, the Nazi Regional Commissioner for Byelorussia, told an Italian Fascist delegation who visited him in Minsk that Jews in his district were being killed in the gas chambers.[14]

According to Rachele, Hitler once said to Mussolini that he was too kind to be any good as a dictator.[15] It is a remark which Hitler might well have made to Mussolini, just as Mussolini might have said it to Hitler – banter between friends in which an apparent censure conceals a compliment. But Mussolini approved of the deportation of the Jews to Poland, although he had known since 21 August 1942 that they were being killed there.[16] He knew, and he did not care, believing it to be an example of the brutality that inevitably occurred in wartime. He may not have realized the scale on which the murder of the Jews was being carried out methodically and systematically; but he was certainly not prevented by sentimental humanitarianism from helping his German allies to proceed with their final solution of the Jewish problem.

Many Italians in the territory of the Italian Social Republic joined the partisan forces and carried on guerrilla activity against the Germans and the Fascists. The most active were the Communists in their Garibaldi Brigades, though there were also non-Communist anti-Fascist partisan groups. When Badoglio's government signed the armistice with the Allies, many army officers addressed their men, told them what had happened, and gave them a free choice: to remain in the South and serve in Badoglio's army, to go to the North and join Mussolini's forces, or to go home. Some of them who chose to go to their homes in the North afterwards joined the partisans rather than be conscripted to serve in Mussolini's Republican Militia.[17]

Many of them joined the Communist resistance groups. As they became disgusted with Fascism they turned to the Bolsheviks whom the Fascists had always denounced as their greatest enemy; and many of them had been very favourably impressed by the victories of the Red Army on the Russian front.[18] To Mussolini's disgust, one of the generals who joined Badoglio's army and fought on the side of the Allies was General Messe, the commander-in-chief of the Italian Expeditionary Force in Russia.[19] But Graziani joined Mussolini, who made him commander-in-chief of the forces of the Italian Social Republic.

The surrender *en masse* of the Italian troops in North Africa had led people in Britain and elsewhere to believe that Italians did not know how to fight. The Italian partisans, fighting bravely against overwhelming odds, knowing that if captured they faced instant death, and perhaps torture, proved that Italians could fight as well as Mussolini had boasted. But now they wanted to fight against Fascism, not for Fascism.

The Fascist rank and file, with Farinacci in the lead, were demanding the death sentence for Ciano and his five fellow-defendants. Edda Ciano expected her father to save her husband's life; but Mussolini was in a difficulty here. He was as fond of Edda as he was of all his children; but he felt that he had to do his duty, like Brutus in ancient

Rome 2,500 years before, who had killed his own son when he discovered that he had betrayed the city. How could Mussolini show favour to a traitor, and fail to do his duty sternly and impartially, because the traitor was his own son-in-law? It has often been said that it was German pressure which forced Mussolini to execute Ciano; but while Hitler, Himmler and the SS General Karl Wolff in Verona certainly used their influence in favour of executing Ciano and the other traitors, the strongest pressure on Mussolini came from Farinacci and the Fascist rank and file.

Edda tried to save her husband. She escaped to Switzerland, taking with her the diaries that Ciano had kept for several years and in which he had written comments that Mussolini had made to him, some of which might be embarrassing to Mussolini and to the Germans. She contacted Himmler and offered to hand over the diaries if Ciano was allowed to escape and join her in Switzerland; but Hitler said: No deal.[20]

On 23 December 1943, a fortnight before Ciano's trial was due to begin, he wrote a letter to Churchill from his prison in Verona. He wrote that as the hour of his death was approaching, he was writing to Churchill, 'whom I profoundly admire as the champion of a crusade'. He denied that he was ever 'Mussolini's accomplice in that crime against our country and humanity' of fighting in alliance with the Germans. After referring to the 'daily martyrdom' and the 'barbarous treatment' that he was suffering at the hands of the SS in his prison in Verona, he denounced 'this loathsome clique of bandits' who had plunged the world into war, and 'that tragic and vile puppet Mussolini'. He ended by stating that 'the misfortune of Italy was not the fault of her people but due to the shameful behaviour of one man'.[21]

Ciano's letter was smuggled out of his prison, and Edda gave it to the minister in Berne of Badoglio's government. He gave it to the British minister in Berne, and after some delay it reached Churchill in London. Churchill was eager to publish it in order to embarrass Mussolini, but the British Foreign Office was opposed to this; after giving various excuses against publication, they ultimately put forward the real objection: that it would make a bad impression among the Italian anti-Fascists if they believed that the British government were praising Ciano's conduct.

After consulting his Cabinet, Churchill accepted their advice not to publish the letter. He was probably chiefly influenced by his Minister of Information, Brendan Bracken, who wrote a devastating denunciation of Ciano's past record.[22] Ciano's letter has never been published, perhaps because Mussolini's critics are not eager for its contents to be known. If Mussolini had known about the letter, it would have helped the case for the prosecution at Ciano's trial, because it shows a clear intention to assist the enemy.

Ciano, De Bono and their colleagues were put on trial on 8 and 9 January 1944. Ciano, De Bono, Marinelli, Gottardi and Pareschi were sentenced to death. Cianetti, who on the morning after the meeting of the Grand Council had changed his mind and asked for his vote to be rescinded, was sentenced to thirty years' imprisonment.[23] After the sentences had been passed, Marinelli, while awaiting death, stated that Mussolini had not known about the plan to murder Matteotti, which Marinelli himself had arranged without Mussolini's knowledge.[24]

The sentence of the court had to be confirmed by a magistrate, and the prosecution hurried to find one who would do this and allow them to execute Ciano before Mussolini could pardon him. After several magistrates had refused, giving some plausible excuse, one was found who was ready to oblige them, and the five men were shot by a firing squad next morning. When Mussolini was told the news he said that as far as he was concerned, Ciano was already dead;[25] but Rachele knew that it was a personal tragedy for him, because of the effect that it would have on his relations with Edda.

Some months later he wrote to Edda in Switzerland and told her that he would always love her. But she regarded him not as a loving father, but as the murderer of her husband; she told him that she was proud to be Ciano's wife, the wife of a traitor, and to tell this to his German masters. He sent a priest to visit her in Switzerland, but she rejected any suggestion of a reconciliation. It was not until ten years after Mussolini's death that she agreed to be reconciled to her mother, and they went together to Mussolini's tomb.[26]

———— ♦ ————

# CHAPTER 38

# Mussolini At Bay

MUSSOLINI was usually at Gargnano, but sometimes went to Rocca delle Caminate, which was in the area under German occupation. All his family, except Edda, were with him at Gargnano. Vittorio was acting as his secretary, sharing the duties with Giovanni Dolfin. Romano and Anna Maria were aged sixteen and fourteen. Claretta Petacci was also at Gargnano, and this caused trouble with Rachele. From time to time Rachele protested about Claretta; on one occasion she confronted her, going to Claretta's house and demanding to see her, and telling her that it was her duty to sacrifice her love and to give up seeing the Duce; but Claretta would give no such undertaking.[1]

There were occasionally disagreements between Mussolini and the Germans. Mussolini got on well with Rudolf Rahn, the German ambassador to the Italian Social Republic, and saw him regularly at Gargnano; but there were issues that caused trouble with the Germans. The Italian soldiers who had remained loyal to the King and Badoglio after the armistice of 8 September 1943, and who had been taken prisoner by the Germans in the Balkans and the Dodecanese Islands, had been sent to Germany where they were employed as forced labourers. They were harshly treated by the Germans, who thought that the Italians had betrayed them, and Mussolini on several occasions intervened on their behalf, writing to Hitler and asking him to ensure that their conditions improved. His intervention did not have very much effect. Sometimes Hitler did not reply to his letters.[2]

After Mussolini's death and the Allied victory, several members of his staff wrote books, and gave interviews to Italian newspapers, about their experiences when they were working for him at Gargnano.[3] They tended to paint a picture of Mussolini as a pathetic victim of the Germans, who objected to the way in which the Germans were behaving in Italy, but who was powerless to do anything about it. These writers had a motive to present this picture of Mussolini: if he was an unwilling collaborator with the Germans, this made their own conduct in supporting him more excusable in the eyes of Italians after 1945.

Many of Mussolini's complaints in private about the Germans were no stronger than the acid comments that allies in wartime often make about each other – no stronger than what British generals were saying about their American allies, and American generals about their British allies, in 1944. But sometimes the disagreements were more serious. There were conflicts when the Germans arrested Mussolini's chief of police, and Mussolini's police arrested officials of whom the Germans approved;[4] but the disputes were rapidly settled.

On one matter, Mussolini strongly objected to the action of the German military authorities. The anti-Fascist resistance movements in German-occupied Italy killed German soldiers when they got the chance. The Germans responded in the same way that they did in other occupied countries – by taking hostages, and announcing that they would shoot fifty or a hundred hostages for every German who was killed by the resistance. These hostages were often selected at random by the German commanders; fifty of the local inhabitants were shot for every German killed in the district. Mussolini was indignant. To shoot fifty Italians for every German implied that Italy was an enemy nation; and Mussolini insisted that the Italian people were Germany's loyal allies, and that it was only the traitors who murdered German soldiers. He thought that the Germans should take reprisals only against the Partisans and their political sympathizers.[5]

On 23 March 1944 Partisans threw bombs at a column of German soldiers in an SS unit who were marching along the Via Rasella in the centre of Rome. They killed thirty-two of the Germans and wounded many more; all the Partisans escaped. As a special concession to the Italians, Hitler was persuaded to agree that only ten hostages should be shot for every German soldier killed, though another fifteen were added to the total of 320 after another German soldier died of his wounds. Next day, on the orders of Field Marshal Kesselring and Kappler, the 335 Italian hostages were brought to the Ardeatine caves – the disused underground sandstone quarries just outside Rome – and shot. Seventy-seven of the 335 were Jews; they included Finzi, the Jew who had been a member of Mussolini's first government in 1922, and was now living in retirement in Rome.[6]

According to Rachele, Mussolini was indignant at the shooting of the hostages in the Ardeatine caves; he complained to her that the Germans were treating the Italians as if they were Poles,[7] a remark which shows that Mussolini's racism had now gone to the length of including Poles among peoples who were inferior to the Italians. He protested to Kesselring against the German method of selecting hostages to be executed. His protests were effective. On 21 August 1944 Kesselring issued an order that reprisals were to be taken only against the Partisans and their supporters, and not indiscriminately against the local Italian population. This order was not always observed, and on several occasions Mussolini complained about brutalities committed by German troops against Italian civilians.[8]

But when it was a question of dealing with the Partisans, Mussolini was as pitiless as any of the Germans. He and Graziani issued orders that captured Communists in the Garibaldi Brigades, and other anti-Fascist Partisans, were to be shot. As usual in guerrilla operations, negotiations occasionally took place between the authorities and the guerrillas for an exchange of prisoners. When Mussolini was told about these negotiations, he angrily forbade them, and ordered that captured Partisans must always be shot.[9]

Despite all his disagreements with the Germans, Mussolini had no doubt that the Italian Social Republic must remain united with their German ally. He repeatedly emphasized this in his public speeches and in the signed and unsigned articles which he wrote regularly for the *Corrispondenza Repubblicana*, the new official newspaper of the republic. He believed that if the Allies won the war, the United States and the Soviet Union would dominate Europe and the world, and that Italy would be finished as an independent power; her only chance of survival would be if the Axis won the war. When Churchill and Roosevelt, at their meeting at Casablanca in January 1943, issued a declaration that the war would continue until the unconditional surrender of the Axis, Mussolini wrote that the slogan of unconditional surrender meant that Italy would be enslaved under the domination of Anglo-American Jewish capitalism.[10]

As the Communist partisans in Italy increased in strength, Mussolini shifted his propaganda a little with a view to influencing them, referring less to the struggle against Bolshevism and more to the threat from Anglo-American plutocracy and Jewish capitalism. Did the Communist partisans, who were risking their lives in supporting

Badoglio's government and helping the Anglo-American armies, really believe that if the Anglo-Americans won the war, they would allow a Communist regime to be established in Italy?[11]

In March 1944 strikes broke out in northern Italy. On 3 March 207,000 workers were on strike, 119,000 of them in Milan; and within a few days the number had increased to 350,000. Hitler ordered the German SS General Wolff to arrest every fifth striker and send them to forced labour in Germany. Wolff explained to Hitler that to arrest seventy thousand strikers was easier said than done, and Mussolini asked Hitler to wait for a short time and let him see if he could persuade them to return to work.

Mussolini issued an appeal to the strikers, which was broadcast over the radio and was printed and distributed in Milan and the other northern cities and towns. He told them that the strikes had been organized by the leading agent of the now dissolved Third International, Ercole Ercoli, alias Palmiro Togliatti, born in Turin but resident for many years in Moscow, who in January 1944 had slipped across the frontier from Switzerland and had organized the strikes to coincide with a planned offensive by the Anglo-American armies that was intended to capture Rome. Mussolini was sure that the workers in Milan and Turin did not realize that they were the unwitting agents of the enemy who were bombing Italian workers and killing thousands of Italian civilians, and were planning to subject Italy to the rule of Anglo-American plutocracy. He appealed to their patriotism and their intelligence. The strikes collapsed; within a week the strikers had returned to work.[12]

He took comfort from the fact that there were strikes in Britain too, for as usual he was well informed about events abroad. He wrote mockingly in the *Corrispondenza Repubblicana* about the strike of the Kent miners, which was illegal in liberal England, and the anti-war activities in Britain of the Trotskyist Fourth International.[13]

The British and American air forces intensified their raids on Italian cities. Mussolini, who had applauded the Italian air raids in Ethiopia and in Spain, indignantly denounced the slaughter of Italian women and children in the Anglo-American raids. He wrote that the continuing air raids were causing such heavy casualties among the civilian population that they could only be described as a daily holocaust.[14] In fairness to Mussolini, we must remember that the word 'holocaust' had not yet been applied to the murder of the Jews by the Nazis in the gas chambers; but Mussolini might have noticed that the deaths of the Italian civilians in the Allied air raids were not the only holocaust that was taking place in Europe in 1944.

The anti-Fascist partisans were increasingly active. By May 1944 they were tying down sixteen thousand German troops whom they were engaging in the north, and many of Mussolini's Fascist forces.[15] They were carrying out acts of terrorism in the territory of the Italian Social Republic. Several prominent Fascist leaders were assassinated by the partisans.[16] Professor Gentile, Mussolini's first Minister of Education and the editor of the *Enciclopedia Italiana*, had continued to adhere to him after the armistice of 8 September 1943. In April 1944 four Communist partisans waited on their motor-cycles for Gentile at the corner of the Viale del Salviatino in Florence and shot him dead. Mussolini denounced the murder of this eminent intellectual and loyal Fascist. He wrote that Gentile had been assassinated not only because he was a Fascist but also because he was a great Italian patriot, for anti-Fascism was also anti-Italianism.[17]

The news was bad. As the military situation grew worse, Mussolini had taken comfort in the fact that the Anglo-American advance was held up south of Rome, and that he did not believe that they would succeed in launching an invasion of France across the Channel. But they captured Rome on 5 June, and landed in Normandy the next day. The fall of Rome hit Mussolini hard; he promised to recapture it, and issued Garibaldi's slogan of 1862: 'Rome or death!'[18] He was particularly indignant that the army which had captured Rome included black American soldiers, that blacks were marching under the arches and along the streets that had been built to exalt the glories of ancient and modern Rome. His propaganda emphasized the horror of the black invasion of Italy. Garish posters were displayed on the hoardings, and cartoons were published in the newspapers, showing black American soldiers stealing sacred ornaments from churches and raping Italian women.[19]

He still hated 'Delano' – his usual name for Roosevelt – more than any of the other Allied leaders, but also denounced those Americans of Italian origin who were actively supporting the war in the United States. He castigated Fiorello La Guardia, the Democratic mayor of New York, who was vigorously campaigning against Fascism and Mussolini.[20] He also singled out for criticism his old Fascist supporter, Toscanini, when Toscanini conducted at a concert in Carnegie

Hall in New York to raise money to pay for two Flying Fortress bombers and two merchant Liberty ships. Mussolini wrote that if Toscanini was such an ardent anti-Fascist, why did he not have the courage to come back to Italy and join the Communist partisans? Mussolini had more respect for the partisans who had murdered Gentile than for Toscanini. The murderers of Gentile had risen early in the morning, had waited for some hours in the dark and cold on their motor-cycles, and had risked arrest and death; but what risk had Toscanini run as he stood on his conductor's rostrum in his evening dress? Yet by raising money for the purchase of the bombers he had murdered many more Italians than the bandits who had killed Gentile. Toscanini's white evening shirt was stained red with Italian blood.[21]

On 19 July 1944 Mussolini left by train to visit Hitler at Rastenburg. When he arrived there on the afternoon of 20 July, he was met at the station by Hitler with his arm in a sling. Hitler had been slightly wounded a few hours earlier when a bomb exploded in his map room at Rastenburg; it had been placed there by one of his officers, Major Claus von Stauffenberg, in an attempt to assassinate him; but no one was killed, and though the bomb severely wounded four officers who were in the room, Hitler was only slightly wounded. Mussolini congratulated Hitler on his escape, and said that it proved that Hitler was under the special protection of Providence.[22]

The assassination attempt had been the prelude to a planned coup d'état to overthrow the Nazi regime and make peace with the Allies. After the failure of the plot of 20 July the conspirators were executed. Mussolini admitted to his friends that he could not help being pleased to discover that German, as well as Italian, officers were capable of committing treason.[23]

Hitler was well enough to discuss the military situation with Mussolini on 20 July.[24] Next day Mussolini returned to Gargnano. He and Hitler never met again.

Mussolini refused to consider the possibility that the Axis might lose the war. In March 1944 he rejected out of hand the suggestion of his Chief of Police, Tullio Tamburini, that they should keep a submarine available at Trieste in which he could escape, if the Allied armies overran all Italy, either to the Malacca Islands, to Greenland, to Brazil, to Patagonia or to South Africa.[25] One day his son Vittorio asked him if he now thought that he had backed the wrong horse when he brought Italy into the war on the side of Germany. Mussolini reprimanded Vittorio for talking in sporting metaphors when the destiny of Italy was at stake; but then he softened, and said with a smile: 'But who would have backed the English horse after Dunkirk?'[26]

In the autumn of 1944 the Allies advanced in Italy; by November, before the onset of winter stopped the advance, they had captured Forlì. It was now no longer possible for Mussolini to go to Rocca delle Caminate. The Germans prepared for a determined defence of Florence, and they were helped by Mussolini's Fascist militia, including a detachment of Fascist women. Mussolini warmly praised the patriotism and military prowess of the Donne Fasciste.[27]

Sometimes British and American planes flew over Salò and Gargnano. Once there was an air raid warning. Mussolini's staff left their offices and went into the air raid shelter in the grounds, though Mussolini himself refused to go to the shelter; but no bombs fell.[28] Today Mussolini's son Romano wonders why the Allies never launched pinpoint air attacks on Gargnano in an attempt to kill Mussolini, as they were later to attack Colonel Mu'ammar al-Gaddafi in Libya and Saddam Hussein in Baghdad; but precision bombing was not as accurate in 1944 as it had become forty years later.

Romano Mussolini may also be viewing things with hindsight when he wonders why his father did not surrender to the Americans in the last days of the war.[29] He believes that the Americans would have saved Mussolini from the fate that he suffered at the hands of the Italian Communist partisans. But Romano overlooks his father's hatred for the Americans, and above all for Roosevelt. Mussolini could feel some sympathy for an imperialist warlord like Churchill and a Communist dictator like Stalin. Roosevelt was one of the hated and despised 'sentimental humanitarians', yet he had succeeded in his aim of enlisting Might on the side of Right. Roosevelt was also a cripple, a fact to which Mussolini referred on several occasions. Was it this which so exasperated Mussolini, with his admiration for strength and his contempt for weakness – that his splendid, healthy, strong young Fascists were being trounced by an army of soldiers, including black soldiers, whose commander-in-chief was a cripple?

It has been said in recent years that Mussolini hoped to reach some agreement with Churchill, and carried on a secret correspondence with him throughout the war. It is said that in 1940 and 1941 Churchill wrote to Mussolini and asked him to use his influence with Hitler to obtain favourable peace terms for Britain if Hitler won the war, and that Churchill and Mussolini continued their correspondence in 1943 and 1944 when they were writing about the possibility of Britain and Italy making an alliance against the Soviet Union. Some of this alleged correspondence has been published,[30] but the letters are certainly forgeries. We can be confident that Churchill's letter to Mussolini of 16 May 1940 and Mussolini's reply two days later was the last time they wrote to each other. All the later letters are clever forgeries.

One of the letters is supposed to have been written by Churchill from his country house at Chartwell in Kent, on his Chartwell notepaper, on 22 April 1940. The forger had discovered that Churchill's telephone number at Chartwell was Westerham 93, but printed it in the wrong position on the notepaper. In the letter, Churchill writes that Mussolini's 'counter proposals' had been considered by the Privy Council, whereas in fact they would have been considered by the Cabinet. On 22 April 1940 Churchill was not at Chartwell, but in Paris.[31]

The letter alleged to have been written by Churchill from 10, Downing Street, on 31 March 1945 is equally suspect, though in this case the forger has correctly forged the notepaper. It contains typing errors which no English writer would have left uncorrected. Churchill would never have addressed Mussolini as 'Chief of the Italian Social Republic', thereby recognizing the Italian Social Republic; and the letter is quite inconsistent both with Churchill's style of writing and with his political thought in 1945.

It has been suggested that the authenticity of the letters is confirmed by the fact that Churchill, after losing the general election and resigning as Prime Minister, spent seventeen days painting on Lake Como from 2–19 September 1945. There was some reason to believe that before Mussolini was captured near Como, he might have thrown into the lake a bag containing his confidential papers, including Churchill's letters; and in the summer of 1945 the Italian authorities had conducted an unsuccessful search for these documents in the Como area.[32] Many commentators, including Vittorio Mussolini, think it is a remarkable coincidence that Churchill should have chosen Como, of all places, to indulge in his favourite pastime of painting.[33]

It may be a remarkable coincidence, but coincidence it certainly was. Churchill went to Como because Field Marshal Alexander invited him to spend a holiday in a large mansion on the lake, which had been requisitioned by the Allies for use as the headquarters of a British army division; the division had recently moved out, leaving the mansion empty. Churchill was accompanied in Como by his daughter Sarah, his doctor Lord Moran, his secretary Miss Layton, his detective, his valet, two ADCs, and two officers and twenty-four men of his old army regiment who had been detailed to protect him. He painted nine pictures at Como, which must have occupied most of his seventeen days there; he was accompanied everywhere by his escort; and he wrote regularly to his wife, from whom he had no secrets, telling her in one of his letters that he had no worries of any kind during his holiday.[34] These facts are quite incompatible with the story that he spent his time at Como wandering around by himself searching for his incriminating letters to Mussolini.

The idea that Churchill and Mussolini were contemplating collaborating with each other between 1940 and 1945 rests on a misunderstanding of their characters and of the political situation at the time. Churchill had admired Mussolini in the past, and still admired him. He found time, during the war, to sit for his cousin, the sculptress Clare Sheridan, who had sculpted the head of Mussolini in the 1920s and has alleged, probably incorrectly, that Mussolini tried to rape her. While she was sculpting Churchill in December 1942, she said to him: 'Winston, didn't you at one time rather approve of Mussolini?' 'It's true,' replied Churchill, 'and I regard him as a very able man. He should never have come in against us.'[35] But it is one thing to admire a formidable enemy and quite another to let him off the hook when you have him at your mercy. Churchill had no intention of letting Mussolini off the hook in 1944. He regretted that they had become enemies, but enemies they now were.

Nor did Churchill consider in 1944 making an alliance with Mussolini against Stalin. He knew that there would be difficulties with Stalin after the war, but had decided to face these difficulties after Hitler and Mussolini had been completely defeated. Mussolini realized this. He believed that the Allied victory would mean the end of Italy as an independent state, by which he meant the end of Italy as a great power whose leader could play his part in settling the fate of central Europe, as he had done at Munich in 1938. He did not believe that Britain would be able to play a leading role in international affairs and retain her empire for long; the world would be dominated by the two super-powers, the United States and the Soviet Union. He warned the Italian people that if the Anglo-Americans won the war, the Italians would be used as cannon-fodder and sent to fight in the Pacific, not for the glory of Italy but for the United States against Japan. They might also be used to fight for the United States against the Soviet Union.[36]

On 16 December 1944 Mussolini addressed a meeting in the Teatro Lirico in Milan. The meeting had been announced by loudspeakers in the city only a few hours in advance, to lessen the chances that the Anglo-Americans would make an air raid on Milan to disrupt the meeting; but despite the short notice the audience filled the theatre, and thousands who could not get in stood in the square outside, listening to the speech which was relaid to them by loudspeakers. Mussolini denounced the betrayal of 8 September 1943 by the 'ex-King', the bourgeoisie and the freemasons; it had not led to peace, because forty days later, on 13 October, Italy declared war on her ally Germany; and if Italy now made peace with the Anglo-Americans, she would be forced to declare war on Japan, and Italians would be fighting for the United States in the Pacific until 1947.

The only hope for Italy was that she would win the war in alliance with her gallant German ally. It was known that the Germans were developing new secret weapons. New weapons could not be produced overnight by pressing a button, but they would be ready for use against the enemy with devastating effect in 1945.[37] He was referring to some new weapon far more deadly than the flying bombs and the rockets, the V1s and the V2s, that had fallen on London in 1944; but it was the Americans, not the Germans, who developed the nuclear bomb in 1945.

In the afternoon Mussolini addressed a meeting in the Piazza San Sepolcro in Milan. He received an enthusiastic welcome from the crowd, who were not disturbed by any bombs, either from the Allied air forces or from the Communist partisans.[38]

CHAPTER 39

◆

# Nemesis

THE Allied advance was held up by the winter weather. In January 1945 Mussolini left the mild climate of Gargnano to join his troops in the bitter cold in the Apennines. He was now in good health once again at the age of sixty-one, and seemed to thrive as he tramped around in the snow among his soldiers. But the Red Army was on German soil, and the British and Americans were preparing to cross the Rhine and invade Germany from the west.

In March Mussolini sent Vittorio to contact Cardinal Schuster in Milan and ask him to urge the Vatican to approach the British and American governments with a view to opening negotiations for an alliance with Germany and the Italian Social Republic against the advancing Russians. It was a last, desperate chance and worth a try, but Mussolini cannot have had any hope that his offer would be accepted; and the Vatican refused to transmit the message to the Allies, realizing that it would be rejected out of hand.[1]

The German ambassador to Mussolini, Rahn, was also in secret contact with the Anglo-Americans. He told them that Mussolini could play 'a useful role in the future in the fight against Bolshevism'.[2] But Churchill informed Stalin of all the negotiations. In 1927 he had said that if he had been an Italian he would have stood shoulder to shoulder with the Fascists in their fight 'against the bestial appetites and passions of Leninism'.[3] But Churchill was not standing shoulder to shoulder with them now, as the Leninist guerrillas, thirsting for revenge and armed with the weapons that Churchill had sent them, were closing in on Mussolini.

The Allied advance in Italy began again in April 1945. They captured Bologna on 21 April, and continued to advance. Bombacci tried to console his comrades by pointing out that their predicament was no worse than the situation that Lenin had faced in October 1919 when General Yudenich's White army had reached the suburbs of Petrograd. Bombacci's words reminded Vittorio Mussolini that this old friend of Lenin's was now a Fascist leader.[4]

There was one item of good news to comfort Mussolini. On 12 April Roosevelt died. Mussolini wrote that it was a proof of the justice of God that he had died amid the curses of the mothers of all the world, including the United States. But Mussolini's joy at Roosevelt's death was countered by the fact that Togliatti was a prominent member of Bonomi's government and that he had announced that the government's object was to destroy Fascism.[5]

Nearly all the leading German generals and diplomats in Italy were now making secret contacts with the British and Americans. The Germans had one bargaining counter: they could agree to evacuate Milan and other Italian cities without setting fire to them and destroying the industrial installations. Cardinal Schuster hoped to save Milan from destruction by arranging an agreement between the Germans and Mussolini and the partisans.[6] The various partisan groups, including the Communist Garibaldi Brigades, had been recognized by the Allied High Command and the Italian government in Rome, and placed under the authority of the National Council of the Resistance. The Italian government had appointed General Raffaele Cadorna, of the royal Italian Army – the son of the commander-in-chief during the First World War – to be President of the National Council of the Resistance, which was composed of representatives from the Communist and non-Communist partisan groups.

On 25 April Mussolini and Graziani met Cadorna and other members of the National Council of the Resistance in Cardinal Schuster's palace in Milan. Mussolini asked if the Resistance and the Allied commanders would guarantee his life and the lives of his ministers and their families if they surrendered. Cadorna told him that the British commander-in-chief, Field Marshal Sir Harold Alexander, had already announced that soldiers of Mussolini's Italian Social Republic would be treated as prisoners of war if they surrendered, but that anyone guilty of war crimes would be put on trial. Cadorna could promise Mussolini only that he would receive a fair trial.

Mussolini said that he could not agree to surrender without consulting his German allies. He was then told that the German General Wolff had already offered to surrender without informing Mussolini.

According to the statements of some of those who were present, Mussolini violently denounced the Germans for their treachery; but reports of disagreements between Mussolini and the Germans have often been exaggerated.

Mussolini told Schuster and Cadorna that he would have to consider Cadorna's proposals, and left the meeting, saying that he would return in an hour's time. After he had gone, some Communist and Socialist members of the Resistance Council arrived, and criticized Cadorna for having promised Mussolini that he would be handed over unharmed to the Allies. Mussolini did not return to Schuster's palace;[7] he decided to try to escape to Switzerland. Next morning the partisans entered Milan and took over control of the city.

Mussolini went to Como, and on 27 April, with Bombacci and other members of his government, he joined a group of two hundred German soldiers who were setting out in their trucks and trying to reach the Swiss frontier. Mussolini sat in the last truck, wearing the helmet of an airman in the German Luftwaffe as a disguise.

The convoy drove up the west side of Lake Como, but was stopped at Musso by a large band of partisans. The partisan commander said that he would allow the German soldiers to go on to Switzerland, but not any Italians who were with them. As the partisans searched the trucks to see if there were Italians there, they found Mussolini, and one of the partisans recognized him. There were shouts of 'We've got Mussolini!', and they took him and all the Italians to Dongo.[8]

Before leaving Como, Mussolini had written to Claretta Petacci, telling her that he was trying to reach Switzerland with the German convoy, and urging her to try to escape. But she insisted on following Mussolini, and persuaded her brother Marcello to drive her in his Alfa Romeo in pursuit of the German column with which Mussolini was travelling. Their sister Myriam and her new lover had succeeded in escaping to Spain. Marcello and Claretta were stopped by the partisans, who identified them, and took them to Dongo to join Mussolini and his collaborators who had been captured with him.

At Dongo they separated Mussolini from the other prisoners. Claretta refused to leave him, so they were both taken to Giulino di Mezzegra and held under guard in a farmhouse.[9] Bombacci, Marcello Petacci and all the other prisoners were shot beside the lake at Dongo. Bombacci's last words were 'Long live Mussolini! Long live Socialism!'[10] Other leading Fascists, including Farinacci, were captured by partisans in the neighbourhood, and immediately shot. Preziosi and his wife jumped out of a fifth-storey window to avoid being captured and handed over to the vengeance of the Jews.

There are conflicting stories about what happened to Mussolini in the last hours of his life. The official story is much the most likely. The Council of the Resistance decided that Mussolini should be summarily executed. When Togliatti in Rome heard that Mussolini had been captured by the partisans, he sent orders by radio to the Communist members of the Resistance Council not to allow Mussolini to fall alive into British or American hands; as soon as his identity was established, he was to be executed.[11] Togliatti's attitude is understandable; too many British and American politicians had praised Mussolini in the past for his zeal in fighting communism.

The Italian anti-Fascists did not trust the British and American authorities to punish Fascist criminals. Of all the Fascists accused of war crimes after 1945, the Allies executed only one – General Nicola Bellomo. He had ordered the shooting of a British prisoner of war who had tried to escape. Bellomo was executed, despite the fact that he had afterwards performed useful service fighting for the Allied cause;[12] but the death sentence on Kesselring, who had ordered the shooting of the 335 Italian hostages in the Ardeatine caves, was commuted.

For many years it was thought that the Communist leader on the Resistance Council, Luigi Longo, had given the order for the summary execution of Mussolini without consulting the President, General Cadorna; but now the order to execute Mussolini has been found, and it is signed by Cadorna.[13] It was usually possible for the Communists in 1945 to persuade Cadorna to do what they wished.

The Communist partisan commander, whose pseudonym was Colonel Valerio, was in charge of the execution. His real name was Walter Audisio; he afterwards became a Communist deputy in the Chamber of Deputies in Rome. On the afternoon of 28 April he went to the house where Mussolini and Claretta had spent the previous night, and took Mussolini to a crossroads a little way from the house. Again Claretta refused to leave him, so they took her with them. Colonel Valerio read out the death sentence of the Resistance Council, and he and his comrades shot Mussolini and Claretta. After Mussolini had been wounded, the tommy gun jammed, but they finished him off a moment later with another gun. Claretta was killed by the first shot. It was 4.30 p.m.[14]

Two other versions have recently been told. One is that Mussolini was killed by a British secret service agent, who according to one story was a British subject of Italian origin named Salvatore, and in the other story was Captain Malcolm Smith. Either Salvatore or Smith is supposed to have killed Mussolini, on the orders of the British government, in order to prevent him from revealing, when he was put on trial as a war criminal, that he had been carrying on a secret correspondence with Churchill throughout the war.[15] The story is not only uncorroborated, but utterly improbable. If the letters from Churchill had been so incriminating and discreditable to Churchill that the British government were prepared to kill Mussolini to prevent him from disclosing them, Churchill would never have written them in the first place, for obviously it would have been possible during the war for Mussolini to show Hitler, or to publish in the German and Italian newspapers, any letters that Churchill was writing to him.

The other story is more plausible: that when Colonel Valerio arrived at the farmhouse to execute Mussolini, he found that he had already been shot by the partisans who were holding him at Mezzegra. It is said that Mussolini and Claretta were shot at 8 a.m. that morning in the courtyard of the farm, and not at 4.30 p.m. at the crossroads. The story is confirmed by a witness, then a young girl and now an old woman, who lived at the farm and saw Mussolini and Claretta shot at 8 a.m. She promised not to tell anyone for fifty years, but has now told her story as the fifty years have passed. A few weeks before Mussolini was killed, eighteen members of the partisan group who captured him had been taken prisoner and shot by Mussolini's Fascists, and the partisans had announced that as a reprisal they would shoot twice as many Fascists or German soldiers when they captured them. They had therefore shot Mussolini as part of the reprisal, without realizing that he was a special case who should be treated differently. The weakness in this story is that the partisans had already shown that they realized that Mussolini was a special case when they separated him from the other Fascist prisoners at Dongo.

The continuation of this story is less plausible. When Colonel Valerio arrived at the farmhouse, and found that Mussolini had already been shot, he was annoyed. The Communists and the Resistance Council had decided that Mussolini's execution should be summary, but at least it should be done under the authority of the Resistance Council, not as an arbitrary murder by individual partisans. Valerio therefore put on an elaborate piece of play-acting. A partisan who looked like Mussolini and a girl who looked like Claretta were dressed up to act the parts, and a mock execution was enacted at the crossroads, with blank shots fired at 4.30 p.m.[16] At this point the story becomes ridiculous.

The bodies of Mussolini, Claretta and the members of his government, and the others who had been shot by the lakeside at Dongo, were taken to the great square, the Piazzale Loreto, near the Central Station in Milan. The place was chosen because a few months earlier some partisans had been executed there by the Fascists. The fourteen corpses were hung up by their feet on an iron fence in front of a petrol station, and a great crowd who filled the square swarmed around them, insulting them, kicking them, and spitting on them. Many of those who kicked and spat the most were elderly and middle-aged women, the mothers of young partisans who had been captured and shot by the Germans and by Mussolini's Fascist militia.[17] Mussolini's body was afterwards rescued and in due course was buried in the family mausoleum in the cemetery of San Cassiano in Predappio.

Rachele, Romano and Anna Maria were arrested in Como by the partisans, but were protected by the American Army, and interned for some months in an internment camp before being released.[18] Vittorio escaped into Switzerland. Mussolini's papers, including his correspondence and his diary, have disappeared. Before he tried to escape to Switzerland, he gave them to the Japanese ambassador, Hidaka, who also reached Switzerland and returned them to Vittorio; and Vittorio entrusted them to a Catholic priest with instructions not to hand them over to anyone except on Vittorio's authority. But the priest delivered them to someone who had forged a letter from Rachele asking the priest to give the documents to the bearer. Today Vittorio says that he thinks he knows who has the documents, but will not reveal his name, and will only say that it is not the British.[19] Whoever it is has been keeping them without publishing them for fifty years.

The greatest sadness for Rachele was that Claretta Petacci, and not she herself, was with Mussolini when he died; but she was sure that his last thoughts were of her, his lawful wife, and their children.[20] Vittorio looked at it differently from his mother; for him it was an unpardonable crime for the partisans to murder a beautiful young woman like Claretta.[21]

The official story of Mussolini's death is much the most probable, and unless further evidence turns up to refute it, we can assume that he was killed by Colonel Valerio, and the Communist partisans under his command, at the crossroads at Giulino di Mezzegra at 4.30 p.m. on Saturday, 28 April 1945. Nineteen years earlier, when Mori held a lengthy trial of the Mafia leaders in Sicily, Mussolini had written to him urging him to deal with the prisoners in a more rapid way, in a way more in keeping with the spirit of the times, that is to say in a more Fascist way.[22] Colonel Valerio and his partisans dealt with Mussolini at Giulino di Mezzegra in a very rapid way, in a way very much in keeping with the spirit of the times, in a very Fascist way. They shot him, as the Fascists had shot so many Communists on his orders during the last twenty-five years.

Many of Mussolini's forecasts about the future proved to be correct. The Second World War did lead to the domination of the world for many years by the two super-powers, the United States and the Soviet Union, and led to conflict between them, though that conflict was not fought with quite the savagery with which Mussolini and his comrade Hitler had fought Bolshevism between 1920 and 1945. Italy today faces many problems; but, as a leading Italian politician has said, Fascism and anti-Fascism have passed into history.[23] They could easily once again become a problem of current politics in any country in the world as long as political leaders find that they can win enthusiastic support by inciting nationalist and racial hatreds.

# Sources and References

### ABBREVIATIONS

| | |
|---|---|
| *D.B.F.P., 1st Ser.* | *Documents on British Foreign Policy, First Series* |
| *D.B.F.P., Ser. 1A* | *Documents on British Foreign Policy, Series 1A* |
| *D.B.F.P., 2nd Ser.* | *Documents on British Foreign Policy, Second Series* |
| *D.B.F.P., 3rd Ser.* | *Documents on British Foreign Policy, Third Series* |
| F.R.U.S. | *Foreign Relations of the United States* |
| O.O. | *Opera omnia di Benito Mussolini* |
| Pini-Susmel | Pini, G., and Susmel, D. *Mussolini, l'uomo e l'opera* |

### Chapter 1. The Red Romagna (pp. 1–8)

1. Gibbon, *History of the Decline and Fall of the Roman Empire*, i.215.
2. De Begnac, *Vita di Benito Mussolini*, i.102; Mussolini, *La mia vita* (*O.O.*, xxxiii.219).
3. De Begnac, *Vita di Mussolini*, i.87, 132; Rachele Mussolini, *My Life with Benito*, 11.
4. Hostetter, *The Italian Socialist Movement*, i.341.
5. Woodcock, *Anarchism*, 317–18; De Begnac, *Vita di Mussolini*, i.88.
6. Hostetter, i.348–50, 354.
7. Ibid., 360.
8. Pini-Susmel, i.17.
9. Hostetter, i.401, 407–8.
10. De Begnac, *Vita di Mussolini*, i.99–101, 141, 161, 163, 170.
11. Edvige Mussolini Mancini, *Mio fratello Benito*, 10, 12 (where Arnaldo's date of birth is wrongly given as 11 February); Mussolini, *Vita di Arnaldo* (*O.O.*, xxxiv.142); De Felice, *Mussolini il rivoluzionario*, 6n.; Pini–Susmel, i.17.

*Chapter 2. The Difficult Child*

1. De Begnac, *Vita di Mussolini*, i.100; Mussolini, *Vita di Arnaldo* (O.O., xxxiv.144).
2. Mack Smith, *Mussolini*, 3.
3. Pini-Susmel, i.33–34.
4. Sarfatti, *Life of Benito Mussolini*, 29.
5. Rachele Mussolini, 61; Edvige Mussolini Mancini, 164.
6. Mussolini, *My Autobiography*, 21.
7. Sarfatti, *Life of Mussolini*, 35–36; Sarfatti, *Dvx*, 20–21.
8. Sarfatti, *Life of Mussolini*, 31.
9. Edvige Mussolini Mancini, 13.
10. Mussolini, *La mia vita* (O.O., xxxiii.231–3); Ludwig, *Talks with Mussolini*, 196.
11. O.O., xxxiii.237–8.
12. Ibid., 238–9
13. Ibid., 242.
14. De Begnac, *Vita di Mussolini*, i.242, 245–6, 254; Mussolini, *La mia vita* (O.O., xxxiii.246).
15. De Begnac, *Vita di Mussolini*, i.261–2; Pini-Susmel, i.64.
16. Balabanoff, *My Life as a Rebel*, 79.
17. For the incident at the polling station and the proceedings against Alessandro Mussolini, see Mancini's report, 29 Oct. 1902 (De Begnac, *Vita di Mussolini*, i.332–45).

*Chapter 3. Switzerland*

1. O.O., xxxiii.247–8; Pini-Susmel, i.67–68; De Begnac, *Vita di Mussolini*, i.264, 269.
2. De Begnac, *Vita di Mussolini* i.269; Pini-Susmel, i.68; Ludwig, 44.
3. De Begnac, *Vita di Mussolini*, i.278–9; Pini-Susmel, i.94, 424.
4. Pini-Susmel, i.78; De Felice, *Mussolini il rivoluzionario*, 29; O.O., i.3–4, 9–22, 27–197.
5. O.O., i.31–34.
6. A.J.P. Taylor, *Englishmen and Others*, 135.
7. O.O., xxxiii.248; De Begnac, *Vita di Mussolini*, i.273.
8. De Begnac, *Vita di Mussolini*, i.273.
9. Pini-Susmel, i.75–76; O.O., xxxiii.250–1.
10. O.O., xxxiii.251, 253–4; Pini-Susmel, i.77, 81–82.
11. O.O., xxxiii.252–3; Pini-Susmel, i.79–81.
12. Pini-Susmel, i.419.

13. Balabanoff, *My Life as a Rebel*, 57–59; Balabanoff, *Erinnerungen und Erlebnisse*, 76–78.
14. Balabanoff, *My Life as a Rebel*, 16–18, 25–35.
15. Pini-Susmel, i.421, 426; Gregor, *Young Mussolini*, 35–36n.; Vittorio Mussolini on Video, *L'era fascista*, Part 12, 'Benito Mussolini, mio padre'.
16. Pini-Susmel, i.83; De Felice, *Mussolini il rivoluzionario*, 35.
17. Pini-Susmel, i.420; De Felice, *Mussolini il rivoluzionario*, 35n.; Rachele Mussolini, 27; Edvige Mussolini Mancini, 32; Ludwig, 150.
18. De Begnac, *Vita di Mussolini*, i.286.
19. O.O., xxxiii.254; Pini-Susmel, i.77–78, 83–84; De Felice, *Mussolini il rivoluzionario*, 35.
20. O.O., xxxiii.1–37; see Gregor, *Young Mussolini*, 39–41.
21. De Begnac, *Vita di Mussolini*, i.298.
22. Ibid., 284.
23. Pini-Susmel, i.88; Balabanoff, *My Life as a Rebel*, 58–59.
24. O.O., xxxiii..255–6; Pini-Susmel, i.84–86; De Begnac, *Vita di Mussolini*, i.289–91; De Felice, *Mussolini il rivoluzionario*, 36.
25. O.O., xxxiii.258; Pini-Susmel, i.95, 424; Preti, *Mussolini giovane*, 22.
26. De Begnac, *Vita di Mussolini*, i.281, 302.
27. O.O., xxxiii.253.
28. Pini-Susmel, i.96–97, 424.

## Chapter 4. The Trentino

1. De Felice, *Mussolini il rivoluzionario*, 48; Ludwig, 46.
2. O.O., xxxiii.262.
3. Pini-Susmel, i.103, 425; De Felice, *Mussolini il rivoluzionario*, 49n.
4. Pini-Susmel, i.104, 427; Preti, 25.
5. Rachele Mussolini, 15–18.
6. Edvige Mussolini Mancini, 159.
7. Rachele Mussolini, 10.
8. Ibid., 15.
9. De Felice, *Mussolini il rivoluzionario*, 56; Pini-Susmel, i.113–14; De Begnac, *Vita di Mussolini*, ii.92–93.
10. De Felice, *Mussolini il rivoluzionario*, 69; Pini-Susmel, i.121.
11. Pini-Susmel, i.125.
12. O.O., ii.69–71; see also ibid., 99; De Begnac, *Vita di Mussolini*, ii.301–4.
13. O.O., ii.99.
14. Pini-Susmel, i.136–8.
15. Ibid., 134–5.

16. De Begnac, *Vita di Mussolini*, ii.155.
17. O.O., ii.169–70.
18. De Felice, *Mussolini il rivoluzionario*, 73; Pini-Susmel, i.138–9.
19. Pini-Susmel, i.139.
20. De Begnac, *Vita di Mussolini*, ii.291–4, 316.
21. Ibid., ii.237, 319–21, 328–31, 335–6, 341–9, 352; De Felice, *Mussolini il rivoluzionario*, 74; Pini-Susmel, i.141–4.
22. O.O., xxxiii.39–141, especially pp. 46, 66–71, 118, 140, 143; Garibaldi, *Clelia*, passim.
23. Mussolini, *Il Trentino veduto da un socialista* (O.O., xxxiii.149–213).
24. Rachele Mussolini, 19.
25. Ibid., 20–21.
26. Ibid., 23.
27. Ibid., 24; Mussolini, *la mia vita* (O.O., xxxiii.268); Pini-Susmel, i.153, 167–8.
28. O.O., iii.5.
29. Ibid., 137.
30. Ibid., xxxv.11–15.
31. Ibid., iv.53.
32. Ludwig, 44.
33. Le Bon, *The Crowd*, 55, 57.
34. Gregor, *Young Mussolini*, 88; and see Sarfatti, *Life of Mussolini*, 289–90, 331.
35. Lenin, *Collected Works*, v.384, 400, 421, 426, 451–2, 464, 466, 475–6.
36. Lenin, *What the Friends of the People Are* (ibid., i.166)
37. Marx, *The Eighteenth Brumaire of Louis Bonaparte*, 23.

## Chapter 5. The Libyan War

1. *The Times*, 30 Aug., 1, 4, 6, 11, 12, 13, 14, 15, 19, 20, 21, 22 Sept. 1911.
2. O.O., xxxv.15.
3. *The Times*, 29, 30 Sept. 1911.
4. Gregor, *Young Mussolini*, 112, 115.
5. Ibid., 112.
6. Marx, *Capital*, i.728–30.
7. Gregor, *Young Mussolini*, 17, 118.
8. Sarfatti, *Life of Mussolini*, 172; De Begnac, *Vita di Mussolini*, iii.129.
9. De Felice, *Mussolini il rivoluzionario*, 105; Pini-Susmel, i.177.
10. *The Times*, 2, 3 Oct. 1911.
11. O.O., iv.75–76.

12. Ibid., 104.

13. Ibid.., xxxiii.268; Pini-Susmel, i.180–4.

14. O.O., xxxiii.215–69, especially pp. 238–9.

15. Ibid., 245.

16. Kapp, *Eleanor Marx*, i.26, 289.

17. O.O., xxxiii.269.

18. Sarfatti, *Life of Mussolini*, 176.

19. O.O., iv.113.

20. De Felice, *Mussolini il rivoluzionario*, 124–6.

21. Ibid., 127.

22. Ibid., 127–8.

## Chapter 6. Red Week

1. Rachele Mussolini, 27; Pini-Susmel, i.190; De Felice, *Mussolini il rivoluzionario*, 137.

2. O.O., xxxv.17–19.

3. Pini-Susmel, i.262.

4. Rafanelli, *Una donna e Mussolini*, 8–10.

5. Ibid., 51.

6. Balabanoff, *My Life as a Rebel*, 117, 123–5.

7. Ibid., 107–10.

8. De Felice, *Mussolini il rivoluzionario*, 188.

9. *Giovanni Huss il veredico* (O.O., xxxiii.271–327).

10. De Felice, *Mussolini il rivoluzionario*, 145; Pini-Susmel, i.220–1.

11. For 'Red Week', see Pini-Susmel, i.226–8; De Felice, *Mussolini il rivoluzionario*, 201–13; *The Times*, 11 June 1914.

12. De Felice, *Mussolini il rivoluzionario*, 204.

13. Mussolini, *My Autobiography*, 33.

14. O.O., vi.45.

## Chapter 7. The Break with Socialism

1. De Begnac, *Vita di Mussolini*, iii.279; O.O., vi.239–40.

2. O.O., vi.287–8.

3. Trotsky, *My Life*, 201.

4. Joll, *The Second International*, 163.

5. Ibid., 169.

6. Ibid., 176, 179.

7. Information from Anita Garibaldi.

8. Ludwig, 87.

9. O.O., vi.361–3.
10. Ibid., xxxv.29–34.
11. Rafanelli, 170, 172.
12. Ibid., 168.
13. Ibid., 173–8.
14. Ibid., 186–7.
15. Ibid., 188; Pini-Susmel, i.250.
16. Pini-Susmel, i.253–4.
17. De Felice, *Mussolini il rivoluzionario*, 263–4, 682–3.
18. Pini-Susmel, i.266–8.

## Chapter 8. The Interventionist

1. De Felice, *Mussolini il rivoluzionario*, 302.
2. Ibid., 273–87, 732; Edvige Mussolini Mancini, 50.
3. Rodd to Curzon, 8 Sept. 1919 (*D.B.F.P.*, *1st Ser.*, v.437–8).
4. *La guerra d'Italia*, passim.
5. O.O., xxxv.36–37.
6. O.O., vii.120–2.
7. Ibid., 180–2; *La guerra d'Italia*, 322.
8. *La guerra d'Italia*, 254.
9. O.O., xxxv.48–49.
10. Pini-Susmel, i.285.
11. *La guerra d'Italia*, 294–9.
12. O.O., xxxv.52.
13. *La guerra d'Italia*, 312, 324, 326.
14. O.O., xxxv.53–54.

## Chapter 9. Corporal Mussolini

1. Pini-Susmel, i.293, 296.
2. Hibbert, *Benito Mussolini*, 43n.
3. Mussolini, *Il mio diario di guerra* (O.O., xxxiv.3–113); Edvige Mussolini Mancini, 54–73.
4. Sarfatti, *Life of Mussolini*, 227; Sarfatti, *Dux*, 181.
5. O.O., xxxiv.41.
6. Pini-Susmel, i.303–4, 449; Police report on Mussolini (De Felice, *Mussolini il rivoluzionario*, 730–3).
7. O.O., xxxv.58–62.
8. Pini-Susmel, i.314–15; Mussolini to Edvige, 13 Aug. 1916 (Edvige Mussolini Mancini, 65).

9. Pini-Susmel, i.315, 449; Edvige Mussolini Mancini, 65; Rachele Mussolini, 29.
10. Pini-Susmel, i.315.
11. Ibid., 325; Mussolini, *Il mio diario di guerra* (O.O., xxxiv.111).
12. For Mussolini's experiences in hospital, see O.O., xxxiv.113; Pini-Susmel, i.324–7; Sarfatti, *Life of Mussolini*, 229–32; Rachele Mussolini, 33–34; Edvige Mussolini Mancini, 71–73; Ludwig, 49–50.
13. Pini-Susmel, i.325.
14. Ibid., 329.

## Chapter 10. *The Fascio di Combattimento*

1. Edvige Mussolini Mancini, 75.
2. O.O., ix.93–96; x.32, 267–9, 283–6, 339–41.
3. O.O., x.17, 32, 191–3, 252–4; De Felice, *Mussolini il rivoluzionario*, 276n., 349, 731.
4. O.O., x.305–6; see also O.O., xvi.134–6; Sarfatti, 243.
5. *Punch*, 20 June 1917.
6. O.O., xii.96–99.
7. De Felice, *Mussolini il rivoluzionario*, 362.
8. O.O., x.69–70.
9. Sarfatti, *Life of Mussolini*, 238;
10. Templewood, *Nine Troubled Years*, 154.
11. O.O., x.41–43.
12. Ibid., 111–13.
13. Ibid., 373.
14. Ibid., 63.
15. Ibid., 240–2.
16. Ibid., 400–1; Mussolini, *My Autobiography*, 59;
17. Ibid., 415–18; De Felice, *Mussolini il rivoluzionario*, 399.
18. O.O., x.228.
19. Ibid., 256.
20. De Felice, *Mussolini il rivoluzionario*, 391, 722–4.
21. O.O., x.363–5.
22. Ibid., 359.
23. O.O., xi.257.
24. Ibid., 454.
25. Arnold-Forster, *The Blockade*, 29–35.
26. Mussolini, *My Autobiography*, 66; and see Sarfatti, *Life of Mussolini*, 277.
27. De Felice, *Mussolini il rivoluzionario*, 506–8, 725–6; Pini-Susmel, i.389–92.

28. De Felice, *Mussolini il rivoluzionario*, 506–7; Sarfatti, *Life of Mussolini*, 265.
29. De Felice, *Mussolini il rivoluzionario*, 510.


*Chapter 11. The Bolshevik Menace*

1. Lyttelton, *The Seizure of Power*, 52; Pini-Susmel, ii.5; Sarfatti, *Life of Mussolini*, 268–9.
2. De Felice, *Mussolini il rivoluzionario*, 532, 559–62; Sarfatti, *Life of Mussolini*, 268–70; Rachele Mussolini, 36–37; O.O., xv.184.
3. Sarfatti, *Life of Mussolini*, 40–42, 273, 275; Mussolini to D'Annunzio, 18 Sept. 1919 (De Felice, *Mussolini il rivoluzionario*, 360–2, 559, 562).
4. O.O., xiv.101.
5. Rachele Mussolini, 38; Sarfatti, *Life of Mussolini*, 272.
6. De Felice, *Mussolini il rivoluzionario*, 573.
7. Ibid., 574–6; Sarfatti, *Life of Mussolini*, 273.
8. O.O., xv.28–29, 33–37, 64–65, 120–2.
9. Ibid., 108–9, 157; see also Lyttelton, 54.
10. De Felice, *Mussolini il fascista*, 35, 762–3.
11. Balabanoff, *My Life as a Rebel*, 243–4.
12. O.O., xv.187, 212.
13. Churchill, 'Zionism versus Bolshevism' (Churchill Archives, CHAR /8/ 36, pp. 92–93); Nesta Webster, *Secret Societies and Subversive Movements*, passim; Nesta Webster, *World Revolution: the Plot against Civilization*, passim.
14. Churchill Archives, CHAR 8/36, pp. 90–97.
15. O.O., xiii.168–70; Michaelis, *Mussolini and the Jews*, 12.
16. De Felice, *Storia degli ebrei italiani sotto il fascismo*, 6; Einaudi, 'Italy: Economic and Financial History' (in *Encyclopaedia Britannica*, xxx.572).
17. O.O., xv.269–71.
18. Ibid., 175–7.
19. O.O., xii.151–2.
20. *The Times*, 1 July 1920.
21. Ibid., 28 Aug. 1920.
22. Villari, 'Italy: Political History' (*Encyclopaedia Britannica*, xxx.563–4).
23. Balabanoff, *My Life as a Rebel*, 311–12.
24. Woodcock, *Anarchism*, 333.

## Chapter 12. *Castor Oil and Arson*

1. Segrè, *Italo Balbo*, 35.
2. Ibid., 38–39; Lyttelton, 61.
3. Segrè, 37.
4. Ibid., 34.
5. Ibid., 40; Lyttelton, 61.
6. Segrè, 39, 44; Lyttelton, 61, 452.
7. Segrè, 47, 53.
8. Ibid., 52–53, 56; Sarfatti, *Life of Mussolini*, 262.
9. H.L. Thomas's memorandum, 5 Feb. 1921 (PRO/FO 371/6166/ C2650).
10. O.O., xvi.140–2.
11. Ibid., 181–2; and see Sarfatti, *Life of Mussolini*, 37.
12. O.O., xvi.216–18.
13. Ibid., 214–15; and see Sarfatti, *Life of Mussolini*, 283.
14. O.O., xvi.225–8.
15. Ibid., 239–45.
16. Ibid., 248, 262, 286, 363, 374.
17. Ibid., 356–7.
18. Bruni, *Giuseppe Caradonna e la destra nazionale*, 51–52.
19. Ibid., 52–53.
20. O.O., xvi. 417–18.

## Chapter 13. *The Treaty of Pacification*

1. Segrè, 77.
2. Duggan, *Fascism and the Mafia*, 122–3; Balbo, *Diario 1922*, 74–82.
3. Segrè, 58.
4. Ibid., De Felice, *Mussolini il fascista*, i.35, 762–3.
5. Video, *L'Era fascista*, Part 2, 'Nasce il fascismo'.
6. O.O., xvi.227–8.
7. The 'Patto di pacificazione' (in De Felice, *Mussolini il fascista*, i.753–5).
8. O.O., xvii.84–86.
9. Farinacci, *Storia della rivoluzione fascista*, iii.141.
10. Ibid., iii.143, 147.
11. Segrè, 62–65.
12. Ibid., 68.
13. Ibid., 62.
14. O.O., xvii.124–6.

15. De Felice, *Mussolini il fascista*, i.756–63.
16. *The Times*, 15, 21, 28 Oct. 1921.
17. O.O., xvii.216–22; Segrè, 69.
18. O.O., xvii.289–300.
19. Bruni, 53.
20. De Felice, *Mussolini il fascista*, i.5.


### Chapter 14. *The General Strike*

1. O.O., xviii.69–72; Lyttelton, 75.
2. O.O., xvii. 204–5.
3. O.O., xviii.427.
4. O.O., xvii.390–2.
5. *The Times*, 11 Feb. 1922.
6. O.O., xvii.393.
7. O.O., xviii.256–7; Michaelis, 16–17; Ludwig, 159.
8. Segrè, 72.
9. Ibid., 81.
10. Ibid., 84–85; Duggan, 122–3.
11. Balbo, 102–4; Segrè, 86.
12. Balbo, 109–10; Segrè, 87.
13. Villari, 'Italy: Political History' (*Encyclopaedia Britannica*, xxx.565).
14. Ibid., De Felice, *Mussolini il fascista*, i.272–3.
15. Gibbs to Graham, 7 Aug. 1922 (PRO/FO 371/7659/C 11526); Villari (in *Encyclopaedia Britannica*, xxx.565–6); De Felice, *Mussolini il fascista*, i.273–4.
16. Gibbs to Graham, 7 Aug. 1922 (PRO/FO 371/7659/C 11526).
17. Segrè, 88–89; De Felice, *Mussolini il fascista*, i.274.
18. Graham to Curzon, 11 Aug. 1922 (PRO/FO 371/7659/C 11525).
19. Graham to Curzon, 22 Aug. 1922 (PRO/FO 371/7659/C 12148).


### Chapter 15. *The March on Rome*

1. De Felice, *Mussolini il fascista*, i.322–3.
2. Farinacci, iii.400–1.
3. Lyttelton, 84.
4. Farinacci, iii.402–3.
5. Segrè, 97.
6. Ibid., 100.
7. Ibid., 99–100.

8. Information from Professor Salvatore Spinello.
9. Farinacci, iii.422–5; Villari (in *Encylopaedia Britannica*, xxx.566).
10. Segrè, 103–4.
11. Ibid., 106.
12. Rachele Mussolini, 45.
13. Segrè, 108–9.
14. Farinacci, iii.428–9.
15. Lyttelton, 85.
16. Rachele Mussolini, 46.
17. Lyttelton, 89–90; Farinacci, iii.430–1.
18. Mack Smith, 63.
19. Farinacci, iii.430.
20. Rachele Mussolini, 45–46.
21. Lyttelton, 90–91; Segrè, 106.
22. Graham to Curzon, 29 Oct. 1922 (PRO/FO 371/7659/C 14797).
23. Segrè, 106–7; Lyttelton, 85.
24. Lyttelton, 92, 456; Segrè, 113.
25. Graham to Curzon, 28 Oct. 1922 (PRO/FO 371/7659/C 14816).
26. Lyttelton, 456.
27. Graham to Curzon, 31 Oct. 1922 (PRO/FO 371/7659/C 15130/366/22).
28. Rachele Mussolini, 46; Sarfatti, *Life of Mussolini*, 312–13; Pini-Susmel, ii.252.
29. Rachele Mussolini, 47; Sarfatti, *Life of Mussolini*, 314; Pini-Susmel, ii.252–3; Lyttleton, 95.
30. Pini-Susmel, ii.441.
31. Graham to Curzon, 30, 31 Oct. 1922 (PRO/FO 371/7659/C 14926, 15130/366/22); Sarfatti, *Life of Mussolini*, 316.
32. Ludwig, 97; Sarfatti, *Life of Mussolini*, 315.
33. Graham to Curzon, 31 Oct. 1922 (PRO/FO 371/7659/C 14983).

## Chapter 16. Prime Minister

1. Graham to Curzon, 2 Nov. 1922 (PRO/FO 371/7659/C 15149).
2. O.O., xix.3–4, 8–9, 11–12; *The Times*, 1 Nov. 1922.
3. O.O., xix.24–28.
4. Pini-Susmel, ii.274.
5. Ibid.; Sir E. Crowe's memorandum, 4 Dec. 1922 (*D.B.F.P.*, *1st Ser.*, xviii.362–5).
6. O.O., xix.40.
7. Ibid., 44–50.
8. Rachele Mussolini, 50.
9. *The Times*, 9, 11, 12 Dec. 1922; Pini-Susmel, ii.281.

10. *The Times*, 28, 30 Oct., 18 Nov. 1922.
11. Ibid., 13 Dec. 1922.
12. Sir E. Crowe's memorandum, 4 Dec. 1922 (*D.B.F.P.*, *1st Ser.*, xviii.362–5).
13. Graham to Curzon, 11, 12 Jan. 1923; Curzon to Graham, 18 Jan. 1923. See also Graham to Curzon, 31 Mar. 1923 (*D.B.F.P.*, *1st Ser.*, xxi.27, 27n., 183–4).
14. Graham to Curzon, 15 Jan. 1923; Lindsay's memorandum, 15 Jan. 1923; Crewe to Curzon, 15 Jan. 1923; Layton to Graham, 24 Jan. 1923 (*D.B.F.P.*, *1st Ser.*, xxi.29–32, 30n., 31–32n.).
15. Lyttelton, 104.
16. Graham to Curzon, 23 Mar. 1923 (PRO/FO 371/8897/C 5600); Bonomi, *From Socialism to Fascism*, p. ix.
17. Segrè. 127–8.
18. O.O., xix.195–6.
19. Lyttelton, 145.
20. Nicolson, *King George the Fifth*, 374.

## *Chapter 17. Corfu*

1. Bentinck to Curzon, 6 Aug. 1923 (*D.B.F.P.*, *1st Ser.*, xxiv.798).
2. Kennard to Curzon, 17 July 1923 (ibid., 770–1).
3. Information from Ambasciatore Marchese Rossi Longhi.
4. Bentinck to Curzon, 28 Aug. 1923; Kennard to Curzon, 31 Aug. 1923 (*D.B.F.P.*, *1st Ser.*, xxiv.939–40, 949–51; and see 936).
5. Kennard to Curzon, 30 Aug. 1923 (ibid., 943 and n.).
6. Graves to Bentinck, 2 Sept. 1923; Kennard to Curzon, 2 Sept. 1923; Foschini's terms, 31 Aug. 1923; Solari to Governor of Corfu, 31 Aug. 1923; Solari to Graves, 31 Aug. 1923; Bellini's proclamation, 31 Aug. 1923; Bentinck to Curzon, 4 Sept. 1923 (ibid., 963–8, 963n., 964n., 965n.).
7. Ibid., 954n.
8. Curzon's memorandum, 1 Sept. 1923 (ibid., 944n.).
9. Curzon's note, 6 Sept. 1923 (ibid., 980n.).
10. Curzon to Kennard, 3 Sept. 1923 (ibid., 971–3).
11. Cecil to Curzon, 3, 4 Sept. 1923; London to Curzon, 5, 6 Sept. 1923; Crewe to Curzon, 4 Sept. 1923; Kennard to Curzon, 4, 5 Sept. 1923; Bentinck to Curzon, 5, 6 Sept. 1923 (ibid., 972n., 974–85, 995–9).
12. Baldwin to Curzon, 5 Sept. 1923 (ibid., 972–3).
13. Churchill to Mrs Churchill, 5 Sept. 1923 (Spencer Churchill Papers, CSCT 2/16); Gilbert, *Winston S. Churchill*, comp. v.59–60).
14. Crewe to Curzon, 4 Sept. 1923 (*D.B.F.P.*, *1st Ser.*, xxiv.974).

15. Kennard to Curzon, 4 Sept. 1923 (ibid., 975).
16. Kennard to Curzon, 10.05 p.m., 4 Sept. 1923 (ibid., 977–8).
17. Kennard to Curzon, 6 Sept. 1923 (ibid., 995–6).
18. Bentinck to Curzon, 9 Sept. 1923; London to Curzon, 10 Sept. 1923 (ibid., 999, 1017).
19. Curzon to Cecil, 5 Sept. 1923 (ibid., 986–7).
20. *Morning Post*, 29 Dec. 1923.
21. Crewe to Curzon, 25 Sept. 1923 (*D.B.F.P.*, *1st Ser.*, xxiv.1065–6).
22. Cecil's memorandum, 14 Sept. 1923 (ibid., 1041–2n.).
23. Kennard to Curzon, 5 Sept. 1923 (ibid., 984).
24. Mosley, *My Life*, 117.
25. Treaty of Rome, 27 Jan. 1924 (*D.B.F.P.*, *1st Ser.*, xxv.282n.).
26. Pini-Susmel, ii.280.
27. Crewe's reports, 29 Jan., 4 Feb. 1924; Graham to MacDonald, 2, 5, 7, 15 Feb. 1924; MacDonald to Graham, 4 Feb. 1924; Hodgson to MacDonald, 14 Feb. 1924 (*D.B.F.P.*, *1st Ser.*, xxv.330–2, 335, 337–40, 342–3, 349, 351–3).
28. Lyttelton, 139–48, 463–4; De Felice, *Mussolini il fascista*, i.585.

## Chapter 18. Matteotti

1. Lyttelton, 141–8, 238, 464–5.
2. Del Giudice, *Cronistoria del processo Matteotti*, 14.
3. Pini-Susmel, ii.373; Lyttelton, 240.
4. De Felice, *Mussolini il fascista*, i.625–6.
5. Information from the On. Giancarlo Matteotti.
6. Lyttelton, 239; De Felice, *Mussolini il fascista*, i.619.
7. Lyttelton, 241; information from Mrs Parkin.
8. Del Giudice, 71; Pini-Susmel, ii.389.
9. Information from the On. Matteotti.
10. Pini-Susmel, ii.378.
11. De Felice, *Mussolini il fascista*, i.624.
12. Lyttelton, 248.
13. *The Times*, 21 June 1924; *Daily Mail*, 20 June 1924.
14. *The Times*, 10 June 1924.
15. Lyttelton, 248; Pini-Susmel, ii.382–3; Rachele Mussolini, 68.
16. Barmine, *Memoirs of a Soviet Diplomat*, 207–9.
17. Lyttelton, 241.
18. Ibid., 243.
19. Del Giudice, 8, 43; Pini-Susmel, ii.384.
20. De Felice, *Mussolini il fascista*, i.674; Pini-Susmel, ii.266; iii.26–27.
21. Lyttelton, 264.

22. O.O., xxi.235–41; Lyttelton, 265.
23. Villari (in *Encyclopaedia Britannica*, xxx.569).

### Chapter 19. Consolidating the Dictatorship

1. Rachele Mussolini, 55.
2. *The Times*, 27 June 1924.
3. Lyttelton, 243.
4. Ibid., 271.
5. Ibid., 484.
6. Rachele Mussolini, 62; Ludwig, 105, 156.
7. Rachele Mussolini, 60.
8. Ibid., 78.
9. Ibid., 60.
10. Ibid.
11. Lyttelton, 282. For Mussolini's attitude to the freemasons, see Sarfatti, *Life of Mussolini*, 177–8.
12. Lyttelton, 279, 291.
13. De Felice, *Mussolini il fascista*, i.790.
14. Graham to A. Chamberlain, 8 Nov. 1924 (*D.B.F.P.*, *1st Ser.*, xxv.432).
15. Hibbert, 99.
16. A. Chamberlain to Graham, 23, 24 Feb. 1925 (*D.B.F.P.*, *1st Ser.*, xxvii.101, 105).
17. See correspondence between A. Chamberlain, Graham, Crewe, Nicolson, Eyres, etc., 4 Feb.–29 Apr. 1925 (ibid., 61–68, 62n., 72–87, 74n., 92–94, 96, 103, 105–12, 107–8n., 116–18, 121, 125, 129, 129–30n., 161–3).
18. Petrie, *Life of Sir Austen Chamberlain*, ii.266.
19. Graham to A. Chamberlain, 14 Oct. 1925; Minutes of meetings at Locarno, 5–16 Oct. 1925 (*D.B.F.P.*, *1st Ser.*, xxvii.874, 1078–1175).

### Chapter 20. The Terrorists

1. Pini-Susmel, iii.31–32.
2. Ibid., iii.32.
3. Michaelis, 36–40.
4. Gaisford to A. Chamberlain, 6 Feb. 1926 (*D.B.F.P.*, *Ser. 1A*, i.404; O.O., xxii), 68–73.
5. Graham to A. Chamberlain, 10, 12 Feb. 1926 (*D.B.F.P.*, *Ser. 1A*, i.415–18, 430–2;) O.O., xxii.74–78.
6. Graham to A. Chamberlain, 28 July 1926 (*D.B.F.P.*, *Ser. 1A*, ii.194).

7. Petrie, ii.295–6.
8. Edwards, 'The Foreign Office and Fascism' (*Journal of Contemporary History*, v(ii).154–5).
9. Mrs Churchill to Churchill, 20, 25 Mar. 1926 (Spencer-Churchill Papers, CSCT 1/14); Gilbert, *Winston S. Churchill*, comp. v.675–6, 677n.).
10. Churchill to Mrs Churchill, 26, 28 Mar. 1926 (Spencer-Churchill Papers, CSCT 2/19); Mary Soames, *Clementine Churchill*, 212.
11. Hitler to Mussolini (no date) (in De Felice, *Mussolini il duce*, i.433–4). See also Michaelis, 22, 24.
12. Rachele Mussolini, 58.
13. Letti, *OVRA*, 26–28 (where 'Ashbourne' is wrongly printed 'Hasbourne').
14. Lyttelton, 312.
15. Graham to A. Chamberlain, 12 Mar. 1926 (PRO/FO 371/11397/C 3282).
16. Law of 3 Apr. 1926, Articles 1, 20, 21; Charter of Labour, Articles 1, 2, 19 (in Einzig, *Economic Foundations of Fascism*, 125, 129, 133, 143–4).
17. Graham to A. Chamberlain, 30 Nov. 1926 (PRO/FO 371/11397/C 12778).
18. Pini-Susmel, iii.63–64.
19. Petrie, ii.329–30.
20. Drummond to Simon, 13 Dec. 1934 (*D.B.F.P.*, *2nd Ser.*, xii.325n.).
21. Ibid., *Ser. 1A*, ii.925–6.
22. Pini-Susmel, iii.72–78.
23. Ibid., iii.78.
24. Rachele Mussolini, 58.
25. Pini-Susmel, iii.76; *New York Herald Tribune*, 1 Nov. 1926.
26. Letti, 39; Lyttelton, 296–7.
27. Pini-Susmel, ii.419.
28. Ibid., ii.418–21.

*Chapter 21. The Mafia*

1. O.O. xxii.261–3, 286–8, 290–1.
2. Edwards (in *Journal of Contemporary History*, v(ii).156).
3. Churchill's statement to the press, 20 Jan. 1927 (Churchill Archives, CHAR G/82B, 139, 143–4; Gilbert, *Winston S. Churchill*, comp. v.916n., *The Times*, 21 Jan. 1927).
4. Graham to A. Chamberlain, 21 Jan. 1927 (Gilbert, *Winston S. Churchill*, comp. v.916).

5. Pini-Susmel, iii.91.
6. Bosworth (in *Journal of Contemporary History*, v(ii).173).
7. Child's Foreword to Mussolini, *My Autobiography*, 5.
8. O.O., xxxiv.184.
9. Mussolini, *My Autobiography*, 203–6.
10. Ibid., 5–6.
11. Duggan, 17, 78, 85, 124–5, 128, 133, 136–7, 151, 211.
12. Ibid., 181; O.O., xxii.374–5.
13. Duggan, 227–32.
14. Ibid., 231.
15. Ibid., 230.
16. Ibid., 233.
17 Graham to A. Chamberlain, 1 Aug. 1928 (*D.B.F.P.*, Ser. 1A, v.233).
18. Duggan, 118, 250, 254–5, 257.

### Chapter 22. The Concordat

1. O.O., xxiii.256–8, 263, 365–6; Lyttelton, 351.
2. Salvemini, *Under the Axe of Fascism*, 280–2.
3. Ludwig, 115, 168.
4. O.O., xviii.206.
5. Lyttelton, 508; Sarfatti, *Life of Mussolini*, 70.
6. Rachele Mussolini, 52.
7. Ibid., 57.
8. Pini-Susmel, iii.61; Lyttelton, 419.
9. *Primo libro del fascista*, 62, 64, 70–71; Lyttelton, 408.
10. Lyttelton, 408–9, 509.
11. Pini-Susmel, iii.151–4.
12. Ibid., 154–5.
13. Ibid., 156; Lyttelton, 419.
14. Rachele Mussolini, 66–67.
15. Pini-Susmel, iii.157, 207; Lyttelton, 510; De Felice, *Mussolini il duce*, i.393–4.
16. O.O., xxiv.384.
17. Ibid., 43–90. See also Ludwig, 171.
18. Pini-Susmel, iii.168; Ludwig, 173.

### Chapter 23. The Fascist Regime

1. Lyttelton, 482.
2. Fiori, *Vita di Antonio Gramsci*, 254, 266, 270, 325–6, 333, 336.
3. Letti, 61–65, 77; Lyttelton, 298; De Felice, *Mussolini il duce*, i.99–100.
4. Zuccotti, *The Italians and the Holocaust*, 248–9.
5. Letti, 49–50.
6. Information from the On. Giancarlo Matteotti.
7. Pini-Susmel, iii.233. For the anti-Fascist activities of Giustizia e Libertà, the Alleanza nazionale per la libertà, and the Giovane Italia, see De Felice, *Mussolini il duce*, 119–22, 121n.
8. Lyttelton, 394–401; and see De Felice, ibid.
9. Michaelis, 49, 59, 61, 62n., 78; Zuccotti, 29–34.
10. *Camicia Rossa*, 15 Jan., 15 July, 12 Dec. 1930; Oct. 1931; Apr. 1932; Mar., May 1933; June–July, Aug. 1934; Feb. 1935; Michaelis, 29, 31, 62n.
11. *Art and Power*, 13–14, 19, 34, 39–41, 120–1, 123, 127–8, 131–3, 135, 137–9, 178–9, 181; Lyttelton, 382–9, 503–4.
12. Segrè, 274–5.
13. Lyttelton, 402–13, 420–1, 431, 508.
14. Ibid., 384, 412.
15. Ibid., 408.
16. Information from Mrs Parkin.
17. Mrs Parkin's school copybooks.
18. *Enciclopedico almanacco delle famiglie*, 1934. See also the gift for schoolchildren awarded by *La Rivista Filatelica d'Italia* (published by Mondatori), showing the route of the March on Rome.
19. Lyttelton, 503.
20. Mussolini, *Storia di un anno*, O.O., xxxiv.412; Pini-Susmel, iii.156.
21. Lyttelton, 411.
22. *The Times*, 16 May 1931; and see De Felice, *Mussolini il duce*, i.30n.
23. Ludwig, 211.
24. Information from Signor Fiorenzo Pangrazi.

### Chapter 24. The Duce at Work

1. Rachele Mussolini, 67.
2. Ibid., 69–70; information from Signor Romano Mussolini.
3. Rachele Mussolini, 62.
4. Ibid., 70; Michaelis, 33, 34n.

5. Rachele Mussolini, 70; Pini-Susmel, iii.190, 192–3.
6. Rachele Mussolini, 62.
7. Information from Signor Romano Mussolini.
8. Ludwig, 115–16.
9. Clare Sheridan, *To the Four Winds*, 201–2; Anita Leslie, *Cousin Clare*, 188–90.
10. Information from Anita Garibaldi.
11. Silone, *Pane e vino*, 228–9.
12. Video, *Balconi e Cannoni*, Parts 1 and 2. Ludwig, 187.
13. Mosley, 358, 360.
14. O.O., xxiii.122.
15. Ibid., xxv.148; Lyttelton, 432.
16. Stephan, *The Russian Fascists*, 183–4.
17. Ludwig, 11, 14.
18. Ibid., 56, 59–60, 63–65, 207–12, 219; Pini-Susmel, iii.209. For other plays written by Mussolini, see De Felice, *Mussolini il duce*, i.31n.; Sarfatti, *Life of Mussolini*, 275.
19. Ludwig, 74, 136, 193, 210.
20. *Art and Power*, 19, 21; Mussolini, *My Autobiography*, 256.
21. Segrè, 150–9.
22. Ibid., 197–8.
23. For Balbo's flights in 1928–9, see ibid., 193, 201–5.
24. Ibid., 206.
25. Ibid.
26. Ibid., 220–7, 237–55, 264.
27. Ibid., 249.

### Chapter 25. Depression and Disarmament

1. Rachele Mussolini, 73.
2. Graham to Chamberlain, 12 Mar. 1926 (PRO/FO 371/11397/C 3282); Salvemini, *Under the Axe of Fascism*, 131.
3. Salvemini, *Under the Axe of Fascism*, 120, 127, 144.
4. Pini-Susmel, iii.267.
5. Pini-Susmel, iii.272.
6. O.O., xxvi.10.
7. Ibid., 197–8.
8. Postgate, *How to make a Revolution*, 63–64.
9. Gilbert, *Winston S. Churchill*, v.456–7.
10. *Enciclopedia Italiana*, xiv. 847–51.
11. Avon, *Facing the Dictators*, 76.
12. Ibid., 29–30.

13. O.O., xxiii.116–23.
14. Ibid., xxv.141–4.
15. Simon's reports on his talks with Beneš and Titulescu, 25–26 Mar. 1933 (*D.B.F.P.*, *2nd Ser.*, v. 106–11).
16. Rachele Mussolini, 79.

### Chapter 26. Hitler

1. Simon to Rumbold, 8 May 1933 (*D.B.F.P.*, *2nd Ser.*, v.204).
2. Graham to Simon, 4 Mar. 1933 (ibid., 56–57).
3. Graham to Vansittart, 24 Mar. 1933 (ibid., 104–5). See also Graham to Simon, 3 Apr. 1933 (PRO/FO 371/16720/C3042); Michaelis, 58–59n.
4. Simon to Graham, 30 Apr. 1933 (*D.B.F.P.*, *2nd Ser.*, v.136–7).
5. Graham to Simon, 13 May 1933 (ibid., 238).
6. Graham to Vansittart, 15 July 1933 (ibid., 430).
7. Graham to Wellesley, 11 Oct. 1933 (ibid., 674–5).
8. Graham to Wellesley, 15 Oct. 1933 (ibid., 684–5).
9. Graham to Simon, 21 Oct. 1933 (ibid., 702).
10. Michaelis, 61, 67; Rintelen to Dollfuss, 2 Feb. 1934; Braunthal, *The Tragedy of Austria*, 204–5.
11. De Felice, *Mussolini il duce*, i.483.
12. Ibid., 487–8.
13. Ibid., 494–5; Pini-Susmel, iii.298–9.
14. Edvige Mussolini Mancini, 147; De Felice, *Mussolini il duce*, i.496; Rachele Mussolini, 81.
15. O.O., xxvi.263–4.
16. Rachele Mussolini, 81–82.
17. De Felice, *Mussolini il duce*, i.498, 499n; Murray to Simon, 11, 14, 17, 18, 23 Aug. 1934; Simon to Murray, 16 Aug. 1934; Simon to Campbell, 3 Sept. 1934 (*D.B.F.P.*, *2nd Ser.*, xi.14–15, 22–23, 25–26, 30, 40, 66).
18. De Felice, *Mussolini il duce*, i.517; Avon, 111–12.
19. Avon, 113.

### Chapter 27. Ethiopia

1. De Felice, *Mussolini il duce*, i.605.
2. *Enciclopedia Italiana*, xiv. 851.
3. Michaelis, 115.
4. Garratt, *Mussolini's Roman Empire*, 52–53.

5. Middlemas and Barnes, *Baldwin*, 792.
6. Tabouis, *Blackmail or War*, 77, 81.
7. Secret Franco-Italian Agreement, 4 Jan. 1935; Laval to Mussolini, 7 Jan. 1935 (De Felice, *Mussolini il duce*, i.530, 532).
8. Minute of 11 Apr. 1935 (*D.B.F.P.*, *2nd Ser.*, xii.876).
9. Middlemas and Barnes, 831.
10. O.O., xxvii. 72–74.
11. Avon, 237.
12. Drummond to Simon, 21 May 1935 (*D.B.F.P.*, *2nd Ser.*, xiv.277–81).
13. Avon, 206; Middlemas and Barnes, 795.
14. *Diaries of Cynthia Gladwyn*, 253.
15. Avon, 225.
16. Eden's memorandum (June 1935) (ibid., 221–5); Minutes of the Mussolini–Eden meeting, 25 June 1935 (*D.B.F.P.*, *2nd Ser.*, xxiv. 336–40).

## Chapter 28. Defying the World

1. Rachele Mussolini, 82.
2. O.O., xxviii.193–4; xxix.61–64.
3. Middlemas and Barnes, 853.
4. Templewood, 178.
5. Ibid., 164–5.
6. Rachele Mussolini, 83; Pini-Susmel, iii.327.
7. Pini-Susmel, iii.328.
8. Sagittarius, *Sagittarius rhyming*, 27.
9. Avon, 262.
10. Minutes of talks between Hoare and Laval, 10 Sept. 1935; Edmond to Hoare, 19 Sept. 1935 (*D.B.F.P.*, *2nd Ser.*, xiv.595–607, 647); Templewood, 163–9.
11. Leaper's minute, 14 Sept. 1935 (ibid., 625–6).
12. Memorandum (Sept. 1935) (ibid., 686–7); Templewood, 163; Pini-Susmel, iii.330.
13. Drummond to Hoare, 17 Sept. 1935 (*D.B.F.P.*, *2nd Ser.*, xiv.633). Avon, 262.
14. Guariglia, *Ricordi*, 263–4.
15. Hoare to Drummond, 23 Sept. 1935 (*D.B.F.P.*, *2nd Ser.*, xiv. 678–9).
16. Pini-Susmel, iii.331.
17. O.O., xxvii.158–60.
18. Pini-Susmel, iii.332.

Chapter 29. Victory

1. *Evening Standard*, 26 June 1936; Churchill's draft (Churchill Archives, CHAR 8/543).
2. Churchill to Hoare, 25 Aug. 1935 (*D.B.F.P.*, *2nd Ser.*, xiv.737).
3. Avon, 273.
4. Montgomery to Hoare, 16 Sept. 1935 (*D.B.F.P.*, *2nd Ser.*, xiv.631). See also De Felice, *Mussolini il duce*, i.62.
5. De Felice, *Mussolini il duce*, i.761.
6. Ibid., 624–5, 761; Pini-Susmel, iii.335.
7. Guariglia, 274–5; *L'Echo de Paris*, 9 Oct. 1935.
8. Information from Anita Garibaldi.
9. Guariglia, 286–7.
10. Ibid., 287–8.
11. Ibid., 288–9.
12. For the Hoare-Laval talks, their proposals, and the reaction to them, see Templewood, 179–91; Middlemas and Barnes, 883–99; Guariglia, 290–300; Avon, 298–311.
13. De Felice, *Mussolini il duce*, i.721–3.
14. Guariglia, 294, 297–8.
15. Pini-Susmel, iii.340; information from Linda Magagnoli and from Mrs Biancamaria Parkin.
16. Guariglia, 303.
17. *Daily Herald*, 25 Feb. 1936.
18. Avon, 293, 327; Hansard, 24 Feb. 1936.
19. Review of Gayle-Plummer, *Rising Wind*, in *Times Literary Supplement*, 3 Jan. 1997, p. 32.
20. Avon, 327; Hansard, 24 Feb. 1936.
21. Avon, 328.
22. Garrett, 99–101.
23. Ibid., 101.
24. Ibid., 101–2; Martelli, *Italy against the World*, 256.
25. Pini-Susmel, iii.343; *La Menzogna della Razza*, 164–7, 171–6.
26. Garratt, 102n.
27. *Art and Power*, 38.
28. Avon, 346.
29. Pini-Susmel, iii.326.
30. Guariglia, 304–5.
31. Middlemas and Barnes, 936; *Evening Standard*, 17 Apr. 1936 (Churchill Archives, CHAR 8/543).
32. Middlemas and Barnes, 930.
33. Guariglia, 309; Ziegler, *King Edward VIII*, 210–11, 271.

34. O.O., xxvii.259–60.
35. Ibid., 265–6.
36. Guariglia, 312–13.
37. Rachele Mussolini, 86–87.
38. Guariglia, 312.
39. O.O., xxvii.268–9.
40. Feiling, *Life of Neville Chamberlain*, 296; Avon, 380.
41. O.O., xxviii.26.


Chapter 30. The Spanish Civil War

1. Rachele Mussolini, 88–89.
2. Pini-Susmel, iii.354.
3. Michaelis, 93; Groussard, 'L'Allemagne de Hitler fut la seule nation à secourir l'Ethiopie' (in *Le Figaro*, 26 Mar. 1959); Avon, 292; Pini-Susmel, iii.337; Garratt, 63.
4. Pini-Susmel, iii.356; Michaelis, 136.
5. Guariglia, 191, 193, 205.
6. Thomas, *The Spanish Civil War*, 114.
7. Ibid., 286, 296–8.
8. Ibid., 298–9.
9. Avon, 401, 405.
10. Gilbert, *Winston S. Churchill*, v.781–6.
11. Thomas, 357; Avon, 432, 454; Pini-Susmel, iii.359.
12. Rachele Mussolini, 91.
13. Avon, 403.
14. Thomas, 796.
15. *Camicia Rossa*, Apr. 1937.
16. Michaelis, 131n.
17. Pini-Susmel, iii.360.
18. Salvemini, *Carlo and Nello Rosselli*, 65–67.
19. Thomas, 598.
20. Ibid., 416.
21. Rachele Mussolini, 91.
22. Vittorio Mussolini, *Vita con mio padre*, 79–80, 84–85.
23. Churchill, 'The Great Dictators' (in *News of the World*, 10 Oct. 1937) (Churchill Archives, CHAR 8/566); see also in 'Dictators on Dynamite' in *Colliers' Magazine*, 3 Sept. 1938 (Churchill Archives, CHAR 8/620, p. 7a).
24. Feiling, 335, 337; Templewood, 259; Avon, 559, 561, 573–4, 579.

Chapter 31. *The Racial Laws*

1. *La Mensogna della Razza*, 281.
2. Ibid., 291, 293–6; Michaelis, 115. See O.O., xxviii.263.
3. *La Mensogna della Razza*, 294, 297.
4. Ibid., 281–2.
5. Ibid., 277–8, 284–6.
6. Segrè, 346, 348.
7. Ibid., 307–10; Pini-Susmel, iii.376–8.
8. Segrè, 321; *La Mensogna della Razza*, 289 n.20.
9. *Art and Power*, 263, 281; Pini-Susmel, iii.394–6; Hibbert, 111.
10. O.O., xxviii.248–53, where the speech is given in Italian translation; Video, *Balconi e Cannoni*, Part 2. For Mussolini's other engagements in Germany, see O.O., xxviii.245–7; Knappe and Brusan, *Soldat*, 99; Zeitschell's memorandum, 24 May 1943; Mollier's report, 25 Aug. 1938 (Michaelis, 102–3, 159–78, 168–9n., 179).
11. Michaelis, 40, 54–55, 94, 102–3, 154–5, 158–60, 166, 191; *Ciano's Diary 1937–1938*, 40.
12. Michaelis, 138.
13. O.O., xxix.67–71.
14. Feiling, 350–1; Pini-Susmel, iii.406.
15. Michaelis, 146–7.
16. Ibid., 152–3; De Felice, *Storia degli ebrei italiani*, 541–2, 660–2.
17. *Ciano's Diary 1937–1938*, 136; Landra to Mussolini, 27 Sept. 1940 (in *La Mensogna della Razza*, 367–8).
18. *Ciano's Diary 1937–1938*, 149.
19. Ibid., 74; Rachele Mussolini, 60.
20. Pini-Susmel, iii.280.
21. Ibid., iii.298; iv.94, 182.
22. Ibid., iii.361–2; iv.58, 122.
23. Rachele Mussolini, 132.
24. Pini-Susmel, iv.122, 183.
25. Minutes of meeting of Council of Ministers, 1 Sept. 1938 (Michaelis, 169).
26. O.O., xxix.125–6, 146, 165. For the extent of German influence in the introduction of the racial laws in Italy, see Michaelis, 117–29.
27. Michaelis, 189.
28. Ibid., 171–2.
29. Ibid., 170–1.
30. Ibid., 173.
31. *Ciano's Diary 1937–1938*; 174.
32. Ibid., 137.

## Chapter 32. Munich

1. N. Chamberlain to his sister, 20 Mar. 1938; N. Chamberlain's diary, 20 Mar. 1938 (Feiling, 334, 348); Hoare to Halifax, 25 Mar. 1938 (Templewood, 289, 294–5, 297).
2. O.O. xxix.141–3.
3. Feiling, 368.
4. Domarus, *Hitler Reden und Proklamationen*, ii.1058.
5. Henderson to Halifax, 13 Sept. 1938 (*D.B.F.P.*, *3rd Ser.*, ii.306–7).
6. *Ciano's Diary 1937–1938*, 155.
7. Ibid., 156.
8. O.O., xxix.144–7.
9. Pini-Susmel, iii.423.
10. O.O., xxix.155–6.
11. Newton to Halifax, 21 Sept. 1938 (*D.B.F.P.*, *3rd Ser.*, ii.444–5).
12. O.O. xxix.156–60.
13. *Ciano's Diary 1937–1938*, 165; Perth to Halifax, 27, 28 Sept. 1938; Halifax to Perth, 28 Sept. 1938 (*D.B.F.P.*, *3rd Ser.*, ii.561, 587–91, 596–7, 600–3, 608).
14. For the Munich Conference, see Sir Horace Wilson's report, 1 Oct. 1938 (*D.B.F.P.*, *3rd Ser.*, ii.630–5).
15. O.O., xxix.167n.; see also *Ciano's Diary 1937–1938*, 168.
16. O.O., xxix.192.
17. *Ciano's Diary 1937–1938*, 191–4.
18. Perth to Halifax, 4 Oct. 1938; Halifax to Perth, 26 Oct. 1938 (*D.B.F.P.*, *3rd Ser.*, iii.322–3, 342; *Ciano's Diary 1937–1938*, 174; Michaelis, 192–3.
19. Churchill's article 'What does Mussolini want?', in typescript, published sub.tit. 'Counting the Cost of Italian Policies Abroad' in the *Daily Telegraph*, 30 Jan. 1939 (Churchill Archives, CHAR 8/645).
20. Rachele Mussolini, 99.
21. O.O., xxix.225, 225–6n.; xxxv.128–31; *D.B.F.P.*, *3rd Ser.*, iii.538–9.
22. N. Chamberlain's Diary, 15 Jan. 1939 (Feiling, 393).
23. O.O., xxix.228–9.

## Chapter 33. Non-Belligerency

1. Rachele Mussolini, 100.
2. Roosevelt to Mussolini, 7 Dec. 1938 (*F.R.U.S.*, 1938, i.858–60); Michaelis, 195–6, 213.

3. Ciano, *Diario*, i.30–31.
4. O.O., xxix.246–8.
5. Michaelis, 220–1.
6. Ciano, *Diario*, i.44–45.
7. O.O., xxix.252, 474–5.
8. Ciano, *Diario*, i.73.
9. O.O., xxix.261–2.
10. Feiling, 403.
11. Avon, 99.
12. Michaelis, 264.
13. Mussolini to Hitler, 25 Aug. 1939 (O.O., xxix.415–17).
14. Ciano, *Diario*, i.156–7; Michaelis, 271–3.
15. O.O., xxx.31.
16. Michaelis, 284.
17. Ibid., and 284n.
18. Ibid., 278n.
19. O.O., xxxv.140–2, 164–5.
20. Lord Lloyd, *The British Case*, 37–39.
21. Michaelis, 285; Minutes of Mussolini's talk with Ribbentrop, 10 Mar. 1940 (O.O., xxxv.143).
22. Mussolini to Hitler, 3 Jan. 1940 (O.O., xxix.424).
23. Ibid., 423–7.
24. Hitler to Mussolini, 6 Mar. 1940 (ibid., 427–31).
25. Minutes of Mussolini's talk with Ribbentrop, 10 Mar. 1940 (O.O., xxxv.143–53).
26. Ibid., 166–71.
27. Mussolini's memorandum, 31 Mar. 1940 (O.O., xxix.363–7).
28. Mussolini to Hitler, 11 Apr, 1940 (O.O., xxix.432–3); Pini-Susmel, iv.70.
29. German newsreel of May 1940.
30. Gilbert, *Winston S. Churchill*, vi.341.
31. Churchill to Mussolini, 16 May 1940 (Churchill, *The Second World War*, ii.107).
32. Mussolini to Churchill, 18 May 1940 (ibid., 107–8; O.O., xxix.444).
33. Gilbert, *Winston S. Churchill*, vi.411–13; Churchill, *The Second World War*, ii.108–11; Birkenhead, *Halifax*, 458 (from Halifax's diary, 27 May 1940).
34. Pini-Susmel, iv.75.
35. O.O., xxix.403–5; Video, *Balconi e Cannoni*, Part 1.

*Chapter 34. The War between Blood and Gold*

1. Victor Emmanuel III's Order of the day, 12 June 1940; Mussolini to Hitler, 12 June 1940 (O.O., xxx.161, 259); Churchill, *The Second World War*, ii.114; Pini-Susmel, iv.83.
2. Mussolini to Hitler, 26 June 1940 (O.O., xxx.162).
3. Mussolini's report, 19 June 1940; Mussolini to Hitler, 22 June 1940; Hitler to Mussolini, 22 June 1940 (O.O., xxx.2–5, 162); Deakin, *The Brutal Friendship*, 10–11.
4. Segrè. 3–4, 382–3, 392–400.
5. Ibid., 402, 405.
6. Pini-Susmel, iv.94, 183; information from Dr M. Smith and Dr W. Felton.
7. Churchill, *The Second World War*, ii.482.
8. Mussolini to Hitler, 19 Oct. 1940; Hitler to Mussolini, 5 Dec. 1940 (O.O., xxx.170–2, 179–80n.; xxxv.178–82).
9. Mussolini to Hitler, 19 Oct. 1940 (ibid., 170–2).
10. Mussolini to Hitler, 22 Nov. 1940 (ibid., 174–9).
11. Churchill, *The Second World War*, ii.481; information from Mr P. Pancrazi.
12. Minutes of Mussolini's talk with Hitler, 19 Jan., 25 Aug. 1941, and with Franco, 12 Feb. 1941 (O.O., xxxv.187–201).
13. For the Mussolini–Franco meeting, see ibid., 188–97.
14. Churchill, *The Second World War*, iii.54; O.O., xxx.56.
15. Rachele Mussolini, 107. For Mussolini's visit to the troops in Albania, see O.O., xxx.60–69.
16. Michaelis, 291–2.
17. Ibid., 304–5; Lamb, *War in Italy*, 37–38; information from Mrs Parkin.
18. Churchill, *The Second World War*, iii.72–80.
19. Ibid., 81.
20. Ibid., 196.
21. De Felice, *Mussolini il duce*, i.311–13; O.O., xxx.90–101.

*Chapter 35. Marching on Moscow*

1. Ludwig, 116.
2. Rachele Mussolini, 111.
3. Fest, *Hitler*, 642–3.
4. Rachele Mussolini, 111.
5. Mussolini to Hitler, 23 June 1941 (O.O., xxx.197–202).
6. Pini-Susmel, iv.132; Art and Power Exhibition, London (Oct.1995–Jan. 1996).

7. O.O., xxx.103–5.
8. Ibid., 113–14.
9. Mussolini, *Parlo con Bruno* (O.O., xxxiv.205–6); Rachele Mussolini, 109–10.
10. Mussolini, *Parlo con Bruno*; Mussolini, *Pensieri Pontini e Sardi* (O.O., xxxiv.193–269, 278).
11. Minutes of Mussolini's talk with Hitler, 25 Aug. 1941 (O.O., xxxv.197–201).
12. For Mussolini's visit to Rastenburg and the army in Russia, see Vittorio Mussolini, 126–32; Pini-Susmel, iv.140–2; O.O., xxx.113–18.
13. Rachele Mussolini, 111; Vittorio Mussolini, 154.
14. O.O., xxxii.277.
15. Hitler to Mussolini, 16 Feb. 1943 (*Hitler e Mussolini*, 128–32; Deakin, 185; O.O., xxxi.243n.); Ribbentrop to Kasche, 21 Apr. 1943 (Hory and Broszat, *Der Kroatische Ustascha-Staat*, 145); Roberts, *Tito, Mihailović and the Allies*, 105.
16. Mussolini to Hitler, 23 June 1941 (O.O.., xxx.201)
17. O.O., xxx.140–1n.
18. Rachele Mussolini, 112.
19. O.O., xxxi.12–21.
20. Ibid., 54–57.
21. Ibid., 89–93, 89n., 90n.; Churchill, *The Second World War*, iv.270–1; Gilbert, *Second World War*, 333–4.
22. Pini-Susmel, iv.180–1.
23. Churchill, *The Second World War*, iv.528–38; information from P. Pancrazi.
24. O.O., xxxi.134–45.
25. For Mussolini's illness, see Rachele Mussolini, 113–21.
26. O.O., xxxi.112–13.
27. Ibid., 118–33.
28. Ibid., 134–45.
29. Michaelis, 334 and n.
30. Ibid., 312; Lamb, 38.
31. Michaelis, 334.
32. Ibid., 307–8.

## Chapter 36. The Twenty-Fifth of July

1. Deakin, 264–6.
2. Mussolini's speech to the Grand Council, 24 July 1943; Mussolini, *Storia di un anno* (O.O., xxxiv.199–205, 320).
3. Duggan, 272–3.

4. Information from Salvatore Spinello.
5. Deakin, 242.
6. Pini-Susmel, iv.241–2; Mussolini, *Pansieri Pontini e Sardi* (O.O., xxxiv.296–8).
7. Ibid., 242; information from Mrs Parkin.
8. Rachele Mussolini, 126.
9. Pini-Susmel, iv.246–7.
10. For Grandi's resolution and the debate in the Grand Council, see Minutes of the 187th Meeting of the Grand Council, 24–25 July 1943; Mussolini, *Storia di un anno* (O.O. xxxi.199–205; xxxiv.345–53); Pini-Susmel, iv.247–54.
11. Pini-Susmel, iv.255.
12. O.O., xxxi.206–8.
13. Pini-Susmel, iv.256–8.
14. Rachele Mussolini, 130.
15. For Mussolini's talk with the King, and his arrest, see Mussolini, *Storia di un anno* (O.O., xxxiv.356–61, 367–71); Pini-Susmel, iv.260–3, 269, 275–8.
16. Pini-Susmel, iv.278.
17. Rachele Mussolini, 130–2.
18. Ibid., 132–6.
19. Michaelis, 342; Guariglia, 567, 571; Lamb, 206.
20. Mussolini, *Pensieri Pontini e Sardi* (O.O., xxxiv.294–5, 299).
21. Guariglia, 573–4, 585, 587–99, 601–5, 609, 615, 620, 622; *Hitler e Mussolini*, 190–7; Churchill, *The Second World War*, v.88–99.
22. Guariglia, 647; Mussolini, *Pensieri Pontini e Sardi* (O.O. xxxiv.282–3).
23. Mussolini, *Storia di un anno* (O.O., xxxiv.362–6).
24. Lamb, 99, 104–9, 125–9.
25. For Mussolini's escape, see Deakin, 543–7; Pini-Susmel, iv.315–20; Hibberd, 267–81.
26. Rachele Mussolini, 137–9.

### Chapter 37. The Italian Social Republic

1. Rachele Mussolini, 145.
2. O.O., xxxii.1–5.
3. Rachele Mussolini, 146–7.
4. O.O., xxxii.8–9; Deakin, 634; Pini-Susmel, iv.350.
5. Pini-Susmel, iv.362–4.
6. Mussolini, *Storia di un anno* (O.O., xxxiv.371).
7. Information from Romano Mussolini; Sarfatti, *Life of Mussolini*, 53.

8. Petacco, *Il comunista in camicia nera*, 3, 11, 70, 88, 105, 107, 110–11, 123, 153–6; Pini-Susmel, i.63; Bruni, 52; Lamb, 80.
9. De Felice, *Storia degli ebrei italiani*, 527–8.
10. Michaelis, 362, 367–9, 378.
11. Ibid., 392.
12. Ibid., 365.
13. Information from P. Pancrazi.
14. Michaelis, 334n.
15. Rachele Mussolini, 160.
16. Michaelis, 334n.
17. Information from P. Pancrazi.
18. Ibid.
19. Mussolini, articles of 21 Dec. 1943 and 7 Jan. 1944; *Storia di un anno* (O.O., xxxii.280–3, 289–92; xxxiv.311–19).
20. Deakin, 642–4; Lamb, 84.
21. Ciano to Churchill, 23 Dec. (1943, wrongly dated 1944), and the Foreign Office translation into English (in Churchill Archives, CHAR 20/192/11).
22. Minister in Berne to the Foreign Office, 8 Feb. 1944; Brendan Bracken to Churchill, 25 Jan. 1945; J. H. P. to Longford, 28 Jan. 1945 (Churchill Archives, CHAR 20/192/17, 24).
23. For the trial of Ciano and his co-defendants, see Deakin 635–40; Lamb, 82–94; Pini-Susmel, iv 385–7.
24. De Felice, *Mussolini il fascista*, i.624n.
25. Lamb, 84–85; Dolfin, *Con Mussolini nella tragedia*, 189, 195–7, 199–203; Rachele Mussolini, 153–4, 302; Edvige Mussolini Mancini, 215–17.
26. Mussolini to Edda Ciano, 13 Jan., 15 May, 10 July 1944 (O.O., xxxii.208–10); Pini-Susmel, iv.399, 406, 413, 426–7; Video, *L'era fascista*, Part 12.

### Chapter 38. Mussolini at Bay

1. Rachele Mussolini, 165–7.
2. Lamb, 104, 274.
3. See, for example, his secretary Dolfin; his wife Rachele; his sister Edvige; his son Vittorio; Mussolini's interviews with Ivanhoe Fossani, 20 Mar. 1945, and with Nicoletti on 18 April. 1945 (O.O., xxxii.168–82, 186–90).
4. Lamb, 275–7, 283–4.
5. Ibid., 64–68, 278.
6. Ibid., 57–59; Rachele Mussolini, 156; information from Mrs Parkin.

7. Rachele Mussolini, 156.
8. Lamb, 66–68.
9. Ibid., 124, 219, 291.
10. O.O., xxxii.112–16, 136.
11. Ibid., 61, 89–91.
12. Ibid., 56–64; Rahn, *Ruheloses Leben*, 257.
13. O.O., xxxii.347.
14. Ibid., 57.
15. Lamb, 215.
16. Rachele Mussolini, 156.
17. O.O., xxxii.343–5; see also ibid., 75–84.
18. Ibid., 369–72.
19. *La Menzogna della Razza*, 200–3.
20. O.O., xxxii.87–92.
21. Ibid., 348–9.
22. Pini-Susmel, iv.429–30; Fest, 708–10; Vittorio Mussolini, 214–15.
23. Pini-Susmel, iv.430.
24. Deakin, 709–13.
25. Pini-Susmel, iv.407.
26. Vittorio Mussolini, 105.
27. O.O., xxxii.390–1.
28. Dolfin, 255–6; Rachele Mussolini, 151; information from Romano Mussolini.
29. Information from Romano Mussolini.
30. Petacco, *Dear Benito, Caro Winston*, opp. p. 108.
31. Ibid., opp. p. 108, letter ii; Gilbert, *Winston S. Churchill*, vi.262.
32. Petacco, *Dear Benito, Caro Winston*, 45–59; Andriola, *Mussolini Churchill Carteggio segreto*, 195–205; Lombardo, 'Mussolini Churchill', in *Epoca*, 24 Sept. 1995.
33. Video, *L'era fascista*, Part 12.
34. Gilbert, *Winston S. Churchill*, viii.132–58; Lord Moran, *Winston Churchill*, 291–305.
35. Clare Sheridan, *To the Four Winds*, 330.
36. O.O., xxxii.112–16.
37. Ibid., 126–38.
38. Pini-Susmel, iv.454; Video, *Balconi e Cannoni*, Part 1; Lamb, 279–80.

*Chapter 39. Nemesis*

1. Lamb, 296–8.
2. Ibid., 299.
3. See pp. 187–8, supra; Churchill Archives, CHAR G/82B/143.

4. Vittorio Mussolini, 223.
5. O.O., xxxii.460–1; see also ibid., 227.
6. Lamb, 298.
7. For the talks between Mussolini and the Resistance leaders, see ibid., 299–301.
8. Pini-Susmel, iv.526–30.
9. Ibid., 509, 531, 534–5.
10. Ibid., 526; Petacco, *Il comunista in camicia nera*, 221–2.
11. Pini-Susmel, iv.536.
12. Lamb, 171.
13. Lampedi's report to the Italian Communist Party (1972), in *Unità*, 23 Jan. 1996.
14. Pini-Susmel, iv.537.
15. Farnell, 'Churchill "had Il Duce killed to save face"' (*Sunday Telegraph*, 10 Sept. 1995).
16. Pisano, *Gli ultimi cinque secondi di Mussolini*, passim; Phillips and Woods, 'British agents "ordered death of Il Duce"' (*Sunday Times*, 14 July 1996). See also De Felice, *Rosso e Nero*, 144–8.
17. Alatri, *Mussolini*, 94; Video, *L'era fascista*, Part 10; information from Mrs Parkin.
18. Rachele Mussolini, 179–84.
19. Vittorio Mussolini, on Video, *L'era fascista*, Part 12; see also Appendix by Crisolini, etc., in Edvige Mussolini Mancini, 229–33; De Felice, *Rosso e Nero*, 136–43.
20. Rachele Mussolini, 180.
21. Vittorio Mussolini, 228–9.
22. Duggan, 230.
23. The Onorevole Gianfranco Fini, speech to the Royal Institute of International Affairs in London, 15 Feb. 1995.

# Bibliography

MANUSCRIPT SOURCES

Churchill Archives, Churchill College, Cambridge.
Foreign Office Archives, Public Record Office, Kew.
Mrs Biancamaria Parkin's documents, Dulwich.

PRINTED SOURCES

ACERBO, G. *I fondamenti della dottrina fascista della razza* (Lecture in Florence, 27 Jan. 1940) (Rome, 1940).
*Agenda Enciclopedica Almanacco delle famiglie 1934* (Turin, 1934).
ALATRI, P. *Mussolini* (Rome, 1995).
ANDRIOLA, F. *Mussolini-Churchill carteggio segreto* (Casale Monferrato, 1996).
ARNOLD-FORSTER, W. *The Blockade 1914–1919* (Oxford, 1939).
*Art and Power: Europe under the Dictators 1930–45* (by D. Adeo, T. Benton, D. Elliott, I. B. White) (London, 1995).
Art and Power Exhibition: Europe under the Dictators (London, Oct. 1995–Jan. 1996).
ATHOLL, Duchess of. *Searchlight on Spain* (Harmondsworth, 1938).
*Atti Parlamentari: Camera dei Deputati* (Rome, 20 Dec. 1921).
AVON, Earl of. *The Eden Memoirs: Facing the Dictators* (London, 1962).
BALABANOFF, A. *Erinnerungen und Erlebnisse* (Berlin, 1927).
— *My Life as a Rebel* (London, 1938).
— *Ricordi di una socialista* (Rome, 1946).
BALBO, I. *Diario 1922* (Milan, 1932).
BARMINE, A. *Memoirs of a Soviet Diplomat* (London, 1938).
BASTIANINI, G. *Uomini, case, fatti: Memorie di un Ambasciatore* (Milan, 1959).

BIRKENHEAD, Lord. *Halifax: The Life of Lord Halifax* (London, 1965).

BONOMI, I. *From Socialism to Fascism* (London, 1924).

BOSWORTH, J. B. 'The British Press, the Conservatives, and Mussolini, 1920–34' (in *Journal of Contemporary History*, v(ii).163–82) (London, 1970).

BRAUNTHAL, J. *The Tragedy of Austria* (London, 1948).

BRUNI, P. *Giuseppe Caradonna e la Destra Nazionale* (Rome, 1996).

*Camicia Rossa* (ed. E. Garibaldi) (Rome, Apr.1931–Dec. 1943).

CARSTEN, F. L. *Eduard Bernstein 1850–1932* (Munich, 1993).

*Chronicle of the 20th Century* (London, 1988).

CHURCHILL, W. S. *The Second World War* (London, 1948–54).

CIANO, EDDA MUSSOLINI. *My Truth* (London, 1977).

CIANO, G. *Ciano's Diary 1937–1938* (London, 1952).

— *Diario*: vol. i, 1939–1940; ii. 1941–1943 (Rome, 1950).

*Daily Herald* (London, 1936).

*Daily Mail* (London, 1924–8).

*Daily Telegraph* (London, 1939).

DEAKIN, F. W. *The Brutal Friendship* (London, 1962).

DE BEGNAC, I. *Palazzo Venezia* (Rome, 1950).

— *Vita di Benito Mussolini* (Milan, 1936–40).

DE FELICE, R. *Mussolini*

— Part 1. *Mussolini il rivoluzionario 1883–1920*;

— Part 2. *Mussolini il fascista 1921–9*;

— Part 3. *Mussolini il duce 1929–39*;

— Part 4. *L'Italia in guerra 1940–3*;
   (Turin, 1965–86)

— *Rosso e Nero* (Milan, 1995).

— *Storia degli ebrei italiani sotto il fascismo* (Milan, 1977 edn.).

DE GRANI, A. J. 'Curzio Malaparte: The Illusion of the Fascist Revolution' (in *Journal of Contemporary History*, vii.77–89) (London, 1972).

DEL GIUDICE, M. *Cronistoria del processo Matteotti* (Rome, 1985).

*Documents on British Foreign Policy 1919–1939* (London, 1947–86) (referred to as 'D.B.F.P.').

DOLFIN, G. *Con Mussolini nella tragedia. Diario . . . 1943–1944* (Gazzanti, 1950 edn.).

DOMARUS, M. *Hitler Reden und Proklamationen 1932–1945* (Würzburg, 1962–3).

DUGGAN, C. *Fascism and the Mafia* (New Haven and London, 1989).

EDWARDS, P. G. 'The Foreign Office and Fascism 1924–1929' (in *Journal of Contemporary History*, v(ii).153–61) (London, 1970).

EINAUDI, L. 'Italy: Economic and Financial History' (in *Encyclopaedia Britannica*, 13th edn., xxx.572–8) (London and New York, 1926).

EINZIG, P. *The Economic Foundations of Fascism* (London, 1933).

*Evening Standard* (London, 1936–8).

FARINACCI, R. *Storia della rivoluzione fascista* (Cremona, 1937–9).

FEILING, K. *The Life of Neville Chamberlain* (London, 1946).

FEST, J. C. *Hitler* (London, 1974).

FIORI, G. *Vita di Antonio Gramsci* (Rome and Bari, 1966).

*Foreign Relations of the United States: Diplomatic Papers* (Washington, D.C., 1966–80) (referred to as 'F.R.U.S.').

GARIBALDI, G. *Clelia* (Milan, 1870).

GARRATT, G. T. *Mussolini's Roman Empire* (Harmondsworth, 1938).

GIBBON, E. *The History of the Decline and Fall of the Roman Empire* (London, 1887 edn.).

GILBERT, SIR M. *Second World War* (London, 1989).

— *Winston S. Churchill* (London, 1971–88).

GLADWYN, C. *The Diaries of Cynthia Gladwyn* (ed. M. Jebb) (London, 1995).

GRANDI, D. *Il mio paese: Ricordi autobiografici* (Bologna, 1985).

GREGOR, A. J. *Italian Fascism and Developmental Dictatorship* (Princeton, N. J., 1979).

— *Young Mussolini and the Intellectual Origins of Fascism* (Berkeley, Los Angeles and London, 1979).

GROUSSARD, S. 'L'Allemagne de Hitler fut la seule nation à secourir l'Ethiopie contre l'Italie' (in *Le Figaro*, 26 Mar. 1959).

GUARIGLIA, R. *Ricordi 1922–1946* (Naples, 1950).

Hansard: *Parliamentary Debates, Official Report* (London, 1938).

HIBBERT, C. *Benito Mussolini* (London, 1962).

HITLER, A. See Domarus.

*Hitler e Mussolini. Lettere e documenti* (Milan, 1946).

HORY, L., and BROSZAT, M. *Der Kroatische Ustascha-Staat 1941–1945* (Stuttgart, 1964).

HOSTETTER, R. *The Italian Socialist Movement* (Princeton, N.J., 1958).

INTERLANDI, T. *Contra Judaeus* (Rome and Milan, 1938).

— *I nostri amici inglesi* (Rome, 1935).

JOLL, J. *The Second International 1889–1914* (London, 1955).

KAPP, Y. *Eleanor Marx* (London, 1972–6).

KNAPPE, S., and BRUSAN, T. *Soldat* (London, 1993).

*La Guerra d'Italia 1915–1916* (Milan, 1916).

LAMB, R. *War in Italy 1943–1945* (London, 1993).

*La Menzogna della Razza* (ed. F. Bottino and F. Castellucci) (Bologna, 1994).

LAMMERS, D. 'Fascism, Communism, and the Foreign Office 1937–39' (in *Journal of Contemporary History*, vi(iii).66–86, London, 1971).

LE BON, G. *The Crowd* (London, 1947 edn.)

LENIN, V. I. *Collected Works* (Moscow, 1960).

LESLIE, ANITA. *Cousin Clare* (London, 1976).

LETTI, G. *OVRA, Fascismo, Antifascismo* (Rocca San Casciano, 1952).

LEWIS, L. *Echoes of Resistance* (Tunbridge Wells, 1985).

LLOYD, Lord. *The British Case* (London, 1939).

LOMBARDO, D.M. 'Mussolini Churchill' (in *Epoca*, 24 Sept. 1995).

LUDWIG, E. *Talks with Mussolini* (London, 1933).

LYTTELTON, A. *The Seizure of Power: Fascism in Italy 1919–1929* (London, 1973).

MACK SMITH, D. *Mussolini* (London, 1981).

MARTELLI, G. *Italy against the World* (London, 1937).

MARX, K. *Capital* (Moscow, 1965–6).

— *The Eighteenth Brumaire of Louis Bonaparte* (London, 1926).

MAZZANTINI, C. *In Search of a Glorious Death* (Manchester, 1992).

McCLURE, W.K. 'Italian Campaigns' (in *Encyclopaedia Britannica*, 13th edn., xxx.551–5) (London and New York, 1926).

MEGARO, G. *Man in the Making* (London, 1938).

MICHAELIS, M. *Mussolini and the Jews* (Oxford, 1978).

MIDDLEMAS, K., and BARNES, J. *Baldwin* (London, 1969).

MORAN, Lord. *Winston Churchill: The Struggle for Survival 1940–1965* (London, 1966).

*Morning Post* (London, 1923).

MOSLEY, SIR O. *My Life* (London, 1968).

MUNRO, L. S. *Through Fascism to World Power* (London, 1933).

MUSSOLINI, B. *Claudia Particella, l'amante del cardinale.* See *Opera omnia.*

— 'Fascismo: la dottrina' (in *Enciclopedia Italiana*, xiv.847–51). (Rome, 1932).

— *Giovanni Huss il veridico.* See *Opera omnia.*

— *Il mio diario di guerra.* See *Opera omnia.*

— *Il Trentino veduto da un socialista.* See *Opera omnia.*

— *La mia vita dal 29 luglio 1883 al 23 novembre 1911.* See *Opera omnia.*

— *My Autobiography*, with Foreword by Richard Washburn Child (London, 1928).

— *Opera omnia di Benito Mussolini* (Florence, 1951–62) (referred to as 'O.O.')

— *Parlo con Bruno.* See *Opera omnia.*

— *Pensieri Pontini e Sardi.* See *Opera omnia.*

— *Storia di un anno.* see *Opera omnia.*

— *Vita di Arnaldo.* See *Opera omnia.*

MUSSOLINI MANCINI, EDVIGE. *Mio fratello Benito* (dictated to Ricci Crisolini) (Florence, 1957).

MUSSOLINI, RACHELE. *My Life with Mussolini* (London, 1959).

MUSSOLINI, VITTORIO. *Vita con mio padre* (Milan, 1957).

— Video. See Video.

NANNI, T. *Bolscevismo e Fascismo alla luce della critica marxista, Benito Mussolini* (Bologna, 1924).

*New York Herald Tribune* (New York, 1926).

NICOLSON, H. *King George The Fifth* (London, 1952).

PETACCO, A. *Dear Benito, Caro Winston* (Milan, 1985).

— *Il comunista in camicia nera: Nicola Bombacci tra Lenin e Mussolini* (Milan, 1996).

PETRIE, SIR C. *The Life and Letters of the Right Hon. Sir Austen Chamberlain* (London, 1939–40).

PINI, G., and SUSMEL, D. *Mussolini, l'uomo e l'opera* (Florence, 1953–5) (referred to as 'Pini-Susmel').

PISANO, G. *Gli ultimi cinque secondi di Mussolini* (Milan, 1996).

POSTGATE, R. *How to make a Revolution* (London, 1934).

POZZI, H. *Black Hand over Europe* (London, 1935).

PRETI, L. *Mussolini giovane* (Milan, 1982).

*Punch* (London, 1917).

RAFANELLI, LEDA. *Una donna e Mussolini* (Milan, 1975).

RAHN, R. *Ruheloses Leben, Aufziehungen und Erinnerungen* (Düsseldorf, 1949).

ROBERTS, W. R. *Tito, Mihailović and the Allies 1941–1945* (New Brunswick, N.J., 1973).

ROCCA, G. *Cadorna* (Milan, 1985).

SAGITTARIUS. *Sagittarius rhyming* (London, 1940).

SALVEMINI, G. *Carlo and Nello Rosselli* (London, 1937).

— *Under the Axe of Fascism* (London, 1936).

SAN SEVERINO, BARON B. Q. DI. *Mussolini as revealed in his political speeches (November 1914–August 1923)* (London, 1923).

SARFATTI, M. *Dvx* (Milan, 1926).

— *The Life of Benito Mussolini* (London, 1925).

SEGRÈ, C. G. *Italo Balbo* (Berkeley, Ca., 1987).

SHERIDAN, CLARE. *To the Four Winds* (London, 1957).

SILONE, I. *Pane e vino* (London, 1937).

SOAMES, MARY. *Clementine Churchill* (London, 1979).

STEPHAN, J. J. *The Russian Fascists* (London, 1978).

TABOUIS, GENEVIÈVE. *Blackmail or War* (Harmondsworth, 1938).

TASSINARI, G. *Faschistische Wirtschaftslehre* (Rome, 1937).

TEMPLEWOOD, Viscount (Sir Samuel Hoare). *Nine Troubled Years* (London, 1954).

*The Times* (London, Aug. 1911–Feb. 1933).

*T.L.S. Times Literary Supplement* (London, 1997).

THOMAS, H. *The Spanish Civil War* (revised edn., Harmondsworth, 1965).

TROTSKY, L. *My Life* (London, 1930).

VANSITTART, Lord *The Mist Procession* (London, 1958).

Video: *Balconi e Cannoni: I Discorsi di Mussolini.* Parts 1 and 2.
Video: *L'Era fascista dalla nascita alla repubblica sociale*
— i. *L'Italia prefascista*
— ii. *Nasce il fascismo*
— iii. *Verso la dittatura*
— iv. *Conquiste e primati*
— v. *Ali italiane nel mondo*
— vi. *Gli anni del consenso*
— vii. *La gioventù italiana del littorio*
— viii. *La guerra d'Etiopia e di Spagna*
— ix. *L'Italia in guerra*
— x. *La repubblica sociale*
— xi. *Benito Mussolini, mio padre,* Parte 1.
— xii. *Benito Mussolini, mio padre,* Parte 2.
VILLARI, L. 'Italy: Political History' (in *Encyclopaedia Britannica,* 13th
  edn., xxx.558–71) (London and New York, 1926).
*Washington Post* (Washington D. C., 1926).
WEBSTER, NESTA. *Secret Societies and Subversive Movements* (London,
  1924).
— *The French Revolution: A Study in Democracy* (London, 1919).
— *World Revolution: The Plot against Civilization* (London, 1921).
WOODCOCK, G. *Anarchism* (Harmondsworth, 1963).
ZIEGLER, P. *King Edward VIII* (London, 1990).
ZUCCOTTI, S. *The Italians and the Holocaust* (London, 1987).

# Index

NOTE; Mussolini is abbreviated to M. throughout index.